Theory and Practice in Renaissance Textual Criticism

Theory and Practice in Renaissance Textual Criticism

Beatus Rhenanus Between
Conjecture and History

JOHN F. D'AMICO

UNIVERSITY OF CALIFORNIA PRESS
Berkeley   Los Angeles   London

University of California Press
Berkeley and Los Angeles, California

University of California Press, Ltd.
London, England

Copyright © 1988 by
The Regents of the University of California

LIBRARY OF CONGRESS
Library of Congress Cataloging-in-Publication Data

D'Amico, John F.
Theory and practice in Renaissance textual criticism : Beatus
Rhenanus between conjecture and history / John F. D'Amico.
        p.   cm.
        Bibliography: p.
        Includes index.
        ISBN 0-520-06199-3
    1. Classical literature—Criticism, Textual.   2. Rhenanus, Beatus,
1485–1547—Views on criticism.   3. Criticism, Textual—History—16th
century.   4. Transmission of texts.   5. Humanists.   6. History,
Ancient—Historiography.   7. Editing—History—16th century.
                            I. Title.
        PA47.D35 1988
        470'.92'4—dc19   88-1064
                                                                  CIP

Printed in the United States of America
1   2   3   4   5   6   7   8   9

In Memoriam Dilecti Patris Mei

Contents

Foreword

When John D'Amico dedicated this book to the memory of his father, he did not know that he himself would not live to see it appear. His death has deprived American historical scholarship of a distinctive and powerful voice, and has robbed John himself of the just reward for his many years of unremitting work. True, his learned articles and seminal book on the intellectual life of Renaissance Rome had taught many readers to prize his erudition, his energy, and his unassuming dedication to topics as important as they were unfashionable. His warmth and generosity had won him many friends in Europe and America alike. But this second book would have established him as one of the leading intellectual historians of his generation. Its excellence is also the measure of other books and studies John had already projected but would not complete, and of the further acclaim that awaited him.

In correcting the proofs of John's book, we have done our best to follow his intentions, as attested by the final typescript; only occasionally have we ventured to emend the facts or texts that he offered. We would like to thank John's editors at the University of California Press for their commitment and cooperation. We owe thanks also to Arthur Field, Lisa Jardine, and John Monfasani, all of whom shared in the reading of the proofs. It is a pleasure to have had such help in paying this last tribute to a scholar who, as Beatus Rhenanus said of one of his contemporaries, was *profecto dignus longiore vita multis de causis.*

Princeton, New Jersey   Anthony Grafton
15 March 1988   David Quint

Preface

One of the pleasures of completing a book is the opportunity it provides to thank friends and institutions for their support. This is especially so in this case since I came to write this study as a result of coincidences. While I have been dealing with Beatus Rhenanus for several years, my previous work had not centered on him as a textual critic; rather, his religious and historical views had been my primary interest. However, the reading of Jerry Bentley's book on the humanists as scriptural editors and Anthony Grafton's study of Joseph Scaliger posed in my mind a series of questions about textual criticism that I decided to try to answer by looking at Beatus as a textual critic. I found in his various editions of and annotations to classical and patristic writers much more on the nature of Renaissance textual criticism than I had expected. My original plan was to write a short article that would have concentrated on Beatus' editions of Tertullian, and so it might have remained had I not been given the time to devote all my energy to this research through a summer grant in 1985 from George Mason University and an Ethel Wattis Kimball Fellowship for the academic year 1985–1986 from the Stanford University Humanities Center. The American Philosophical Society made it possible for me to consult Beatus' own library in Sélestat. I also had the advantage of access to the Stanford University Library, The Folger Shakespeare Library, the Library of Congress, the libraries of the University of Pennsylvania, the University of California at Berkeley, the American Academy in Rome, and the Biblioteca Nazionale in Rome.

Several individuals have directly or indirectly aided me in this enterprise, and I wish to thank them personally. Discussions several years ago at the Villa I Tatti with Salvatore Camporeale, Elizabeth Cropper, Charles Dempsey and David Quint helped turn my attention to the types of questions I encountered in studying Beatus. Lewis Spitz offered both his friendship and good advice while I was at Stanford, and I value both highly. He and Jerry Bentley, Anthony Grafton, Lawrence Ryan, Erika Rummel, Edward Courtney, and Diana Robin also read the manuscript at various stages and the latter were especially generous in helping me turn Beatus' Latin into English; Caroline de Wald also kindly offered suggestions for translating. Judith Brown, Lawrence Bryant, Sabine MacCormack, Elizabeth Eisenstein, Michael Goodich, Stephen Ferruolo, Walter Jackson, Carl Landauer, Harriet Ritvo, Kevin Sharpe, the other fellows at the Stanford Humanities Center and the unsuspecting students in my Renaissance Intellectual History course patiently listened to me as I talked on and on about Beatus and textual criticism and asked some searching questions. Similarly, James Weiss and Zachary Schiffman discussed Beatus and related matters with me. Marvin Becker, Philip Berk, Donald Kelley, and Werner Gundersheimer remained supportive throughout my work. Bliss Carnochan, the Director of the Stanford Humanities Center, and Morton Sosna, the Associate Director, provided a congenial and stimulating atmosphere in which to work. My colleagues at George Mason University, Jack Censer, Prasenjit Duara, Marion Deshmuck, and Sheila ffolliott, also heard more than they probably wanted to hear about Beatus. M. H. Meyer and his fine staff at the Bibliothèque humaniste in Sélestat made my too-short stay there pleasant and productive. Professors Pierre Fraenkel and Peter Schaeffer kindly supplied me with offprints and materials on Beatus. The University of California Press has been exemplary in its treatment of me and this manuscript. Finally, Paul Grendler and Alfred Marion once again demonstrated their deep friendship and intellectual stamina by taking a critical part in my work from the very beginning; their criticisms helped me to keep working.

Friendship cannot make up for my own deficiencies, but I wrote this book in an atmosphere of much goodwill, and I hope that it will in some measure repay these many kindnesses.

Abbreviations

ARG	*Archiv für Reformationsgeschichte*
AABHS	*Annuaire de la Société des Amis de la Bibliothèque humaniste de Sélestat*
BHR	*Bibliothèque d'Humanisme et Renaissance*
Briefwechsel	*Briefwechsel des Beatus Rhenanus*, ed. Adalbert Horawitz and Karl Hartfelder. Leipzig: Teubner, 1886.
CTC	*Catalogus Translationum et Commentariorum: Mediaeval and Renaissance Latin Translations and Commentaries*, vols. 1–5, ed. F. Edward Cranz and Paul Oskar Kristeller. Washington, D.C.: Catholic University of America, 1960–1984.
Contemporaries	*Contemporaries of Erasmus: A Biographical Register of the Renaissance and Reformation*, ed. Peter G. Bietenholz and Thomas B. Deutscher, 3 vols. Toronto: University of Toronto, 1986–1987.
Correspondence	*Correspondence of Erasmus* in *Collected Works of Erasmus*. Toronto: University of Toronto Press, 1974–.
DBI	*Dizionario biografico degli italiani*, vols. 1–. Rome, 1960–.
EE	*Opus Epistolarum Des. Erasmi Roterodami*, ed. P. S. Allen et al., 12 vols. Oxford: University Press, 1906–1958.
IMU	*Italia medioevale e umanistica*
Index	*Index bibliographicus des Beatus Rhenanus* in *Briefwechsel*, pp. 592–624.
JWCI	*Journal of the Warburg and Courtauld Institutes*

Pauly-Wissowa *Paulys Realencyclopädie der classischen*
                  Altertumswissenschaft

PL   *Patrologiae cursus completus . . . series latina,* ed.
                J. P. Migne, 221 vols. Paris, 1844–1890.

RQ   *Renaissance Quarterly*

INTRODUCTION

Renaissance humanism's program of cultural reform through the recovery and study of classical antiquity required an intensive investigation of the corrupt state of ancient texts. In unearthing previously unknown works from monastic libraries and in giving well-known ones a new and more sophisticated reading, the humanists sought to reconstruct the actual words of the authors they considered fundamental. While, by the middle of the fifteenth century, they had developed many of the philological and historical concepts needed to support a new attitude toward ancient writings, the technical procedures needed to secure accuracy were still lacking. Humanists slowly articulated a relatively clear explanation of the sources of manuscript contamination and the means of correcting them. The development of these textual skills highlights one of the most important contributions that humanists made to modern scholarship and provides a better understanding of Renaissance historical thought.

A. E. Housman, noting the rarity of good textual critics and the individual nature of the endeavor, once wrote: "It has sometimes been said that textual criticism is the crown and summit of all scholarship. This is not evidently or necessarily true; but it is true that the qualities which make a critic, whether they are thus transcendent or no, are rare, and that a good critic is a much less common thing than for instance a good grammarian. . . . Textual criticism, like most other sciences, is an aristocratic affair, not communicable to all men, nor to most men."[1] In accord with these sentiments, the formulation and progress of Renaissance textual criticism, to a great extent, form the story of several individuals' advances over dominant attitudes. The inadequacies of available texts generally were recognized as major

1

stumbling blocks to a classical revival, and, during the late four-
teenth and fifteenth century, numerous scholars worked to restore ancient texts. Yet even with the increased textual activity
of the sixteenth century the value of any method proposed was
limited to the small number of scholars who were searching for
and comparing manuscripts in a rudimentarily systematic manner. An examination of some of the most accomplished of these
scholars can establish the lines of development and acceptance
of their procedures while offering an invaluable means for understanding how the humanists struggled to solve the problems
of corrupt manuscripts. Ultimately (and most important in a
historical context), Renaissance textual criticism ceases to be the
tabulation of correct emendations and conjectures an individual scholar made—although some humanists did in fact contribute substantially to the amelioration of ancient texts—and becomes instead an exposition of the intelligence, diligence, and
procedural care a critic brought to his work and the way it
affected his entire scholarly and literary production. The study
of textual criticism, therefore, has a central place in the intellectual history of the Renaissance. Remarkably, so fundamental an
element in humanist scholarship generally has been taken for
granted.

   This neglect of the history of Renaissance textual criticism
has been rectified partly by recent studies of the most important
figures. One beneficiary of this trend has been Lorenzo Valla;
several studies have shown his great textual sophistication.
Scholars have called Angelo Poliziano the best Renaissance textual critic, and he has received careful attention. The recovery
and study of his *Miscellaneorum centuria secunda* show how exacting his scholarship is and how much superior his technique is to
that of his contemporaries.[2] Lesser figures such as Flavio
Biondo, Domizio Calderini, Ermolao Barbaro, and Filippo
Beroaldo the Elder also have been reevaluated in recent scholarship. Outside of Italy, Desiderius Erasmus, Guillaume Budé,
Justus Lipsius, and Joseph Scaliger have received renewed interest. While this research has developed a greater appreciation of
the skills of Renaissance textual criticism,[3] the majority of German scholars of the first half of the sixteenth century still await

modern treatment. To a great extent, the dominating personality and intellect of Erasmus have cast a shadow over all of them.

Any account of Renaissance textual criticism should accord a prominent place to the German humanist Beatus Rhenanus (1485–1547). Three decades of close work with Parisian, Alsatian, and Swiss presses gave him an understanding of the mechanics of publishing and editing which complemented his great knowledge of antiquity. Several scholars, above all Erasmus, helped him early in his career to appreciate the problems of moving from manuscript to printed book. But, after his own editorial practices passed through several stages and false starts, he slowly devised his own critical attitude toward manuscripts, basing it on relatively clear principles of improvement and on the causes of manuscript corruption. Although there were limitations on his use of manuscripts, Beatus did display a sophisticated theory of manuscript consultation and conjecture in his mature work. From his first manuscript-based edition, the *Historia Romana* of Velleius Paterculus (1521), through his editions of and notes on Tertullian, Pliny, Tacitus, and Livy, Beatus' progress as critic was impressive. As a historian of ancient and medieval Germany, he has been justly praised for his originality. It has not been fully appreciated that his contribution to historical scholarship was dependent on and subsequent to his work as a textual critic. A careful consideration of his editions and annotations, which appeared over some thirty years, shows how Renaissance Germany's most famous editor and historian devised the most original textual critical technique of his day.

Textual criticism cannot be easily separated from editing in general and philology in particular, and in what follows the three interconnect. Yet there are several justifications for concentrating on Beatus' textual criticism. First, Beatus' progress as editor, philologist, and historian was interwoven with his mature textual critical method. Without an established means of dealing with textual problems, he could never have resolved certain historical and philological dilemmas. Further, Beatus' discussion of his manuscripts forms a distinct element in his scholarship. This feature is as prominent in his historical writings as in his editions of classical writers. His study of manuscripts, after some early false starts, reached maturity in his extensive annotations to Pliny in 1526; thereafter, he had the confidence to deal with such problems in a more secure and less prolix manner. The annotations to Pliny, therefore, constitute Beatus' clearest explanation of his textual criticism. They functioned as a type of textbook of the paleographical method of manuscript correction and were intended as a model for others. Generally, Beatus' textual method allowed him to produce classical and patristic editions of the highest quality. His contributions to the textual traditions of Tacitus, Tertullian, Pliny, Livy, and Velleius Paterculus are of fundamental importance. As the most accomplished critic of his day in Germany, and one of the most respected in Europe, he articulated a means of rescuing the actual words of ancient writers from corrupt transmissions.

Moreover, Beatus' textual criticism was closely connected to his view of history. Since textual criticism is essentially a historical enterprise, Beatus' deep knowledge of history affected his treatment of manuscripts as testimonies of the ancient heritage. The study of manuscripts also made clear the need to understand their corruptions in order to correct them. There was, therefore, a constant interaction between textual criticism and history. One way to understand the interrelationship is to examine the genesis of Beatus' textual criticism and its use in the writing of history.

A further advantage in studying Beatus' textual criticism is to reemphasize the fuller dimensions of German humanists' scholarship by placing it in context with Italian and French traditions. This is not to deny its ultimate dependence on Italian humanism, but rather, in admitting this, to see how German scholars incorporated and modified the Italian (as well as Erasmian) precedents. Studying Beatus and his scholarship further helps to maintain a proper balance in evaluating the influences on German humanism, modifying without rejecting the central positions attributable to Erasmus on the one hand and Luther on the other. An appreciation of German humanism becomes more complete and clearer through the study of such an accomplished figure as Beatus.

Modern attitudes and expectations toward printed versions of ancient literature (classical and patristic) differ markedly from those of the Renaissance scholars. For modern readers a classical text exists as a result of the critical apparatus constructed to account for it. We expect to find the *apparatus criticus* as a guarantor of the fidelity of the text to its manuscript sources. Renaissance readers were not prepared to find their texts so encumbered. While we are provided with the results of full collations of available manuscripts, Renaissance readers did not demand an editor to collate fully or to offer extensive proof of what he had done. Only occasionally did Renaissance editors feel the need to justify their emendations and conjectures through citations of manuscript authority and to offer examples to demonstrate the method they followed. Those who did so were helping to educate readers in a new attitude toward texts. Editors used *annotationes* and *castigationes* to show their textual skills and propagate their views.

In order to accomplish all this, the Renaissance editor often had to provide long, complicated notes. Beatus was especially conscious of the various roles an editor had to fulfill, and consequently his annotations are rich in methodological statements. He made clear to his readers the presuppositions and practical elements that underlay his work, and he tried to demonstrate them in detail, especially in his notes to Pliny, Tacitus, Livy, and Tertullian. Working with printed books and a few manuscripts, Beatus helped to put the textual traditions of these writers on a new, more secure foundation.

When describing and evaluating a Renaissance editor and textual critic, it is tempting to judge him by a modern Lachmannian methodology, expecting him to provide an exact nomenclature and hierarchical organization for all known manuscripts of an author.[4] There is the danger of Whiggery in evaluating a stage in any scientific or semiscientific enterprise. Obviously, we cannot hold Beatus or any other Renaissance critic to a standard that developed centuries later. Still, it is inevitable that the historian will refer to modern principles, sometimes unconsciously. Beatus was in some form an ancestor of Lachmann. Properly perceived, modern critical technique can be the basis for understanding the originality of Renaissance editing. Our modern ideas should help us to appreciate Beatus, not deprecate his accomplishments or those of his contemporaries.

It is not my intention to repeat the work of the editors of classical texts who have collated Beatus' emendations and conjectures with the manuscripts and other editions. Rather, my aim is to show how Beatus came to make his emendations and conjectures, the procedures he developed to justify them, and where he belonged in Renaissance intellectual history. From this perspective, his errors are as valid for the Renaissance historian as his correct divinations, and they are often more interesting. If one may paraphrase a modern scholar, we can learn as much from Beatus when he is in error as from others when they are correct.[5] Beatus, like all humanist critics, was involved in a task of historical reconstruction; this is what makes his textual work worthy of general attention.

Chapter 1 outlines Renaissance textual criticism's development before Beatus. It has two foci: first, the Italian humanists who initially defined the problem and offered various means of dealing with corrupt manuscripts; second, Erasmus. Northern European textual criticism was not dependent solely on Erasmus' work, but for Beatus the Dutch humanist was the fundamental influence. Chapter 2 places Beatus in the context of early sixteenth-century German humanism, especially the educational forces that shaped his development and his first faulty uses of manuscripts. Chapter 3 describes Beatus' textual critical method in detail by concentrating on his annotations to Pliny's *Naturalis historia;* it explains his rationale for his method and provides examples of it. Chapter 4 investigates further examples of Beatus' mature textual method. Chapters 5 and 6 move from textual criticism to history by demonstrating the textual critical basis for Beatus' historical scholarship. As a group, the chapters should establish the formative forces shaping Beatus' editing and his success at solving difficult textual problems.

My overall aims have been twofold. First, I have tried to present Beatus as a prime example of Renaissance textual criticism. His procedure, I believe, may be taken as a representation of the best ideas about texts and their recovery in the first half of the sixteenth century. Consequently, his thoughts about textual problems and editing should possess a broad interest. Second, I have emphasized the relationship between this aspect of Beatus' work and Renaissance historiography in Germany.

Both aims are undertaken from the point of view of Renaissance intellectual history rather than from the perspective of classical scholarship or of modern textual criticism. Questions that would interest students of the latter perspectives are ignored here; it is not that such questions are invalid or unimportant, but they can be treated better by scholars in those fields. My intention has been consistently to place Beatus and his textual criticism in his intellectual milieu, to stress the coincidence and interdependence of his textual and historical criticism, and to show what he actually did to his texts. Within these limits, I hope that scholars in other disciplines will find my narrative of some value. What follows is by no means the final word on Beatus (and I must emphasize the summary treatment of many topics). Yet it should provide a foundation from which to appreciate his position as one of the most accomplished scholars of the sixteenth century and thereby help in the reevaluation of the humanist contribution to Renaissance intellectual history.

1
TEXTUAL CRITICISM IN
THE RENAISSANCE

Since the revival of classical learning at the end of the four-teenth century, some humanists actively searched for manu-scripts of ancients texts.[1] Discoveries in the fifteenth century brought to light some of the most famous products of the an-cient world. The reputation of such a major figure as Poggio Bracciolini (1380–1459),[2] for example, who visited Northern European monastic libraries for classical treatises while attend-ing the Council of Constance (1415–1417), would have re-mained secure simply on the basis of his manuscript discoveries had he made no other scholarly or literary contributions. Once recovered, a text was copied and circulated among humanists, thereby beginning the long process of interpretation. At no stage in this undertaking was there much opportunity to con-trol the accuracy of the texts disseminated. Access to the newly discovered manuscript, which was often mutilated or difficult to read, was available to very few readers. Manuscripts were often lost after being transcribed, while copyists added their own defects and spread inaccurate readings.

Some form of textual renovation was implicit in the nature of humanism. Concern for language, which was the heart of hu-manist pedagogy, led to an emphasis on the word as the door to reality.[3] While few humanists developed this into a complete philosophy, it still remained the operating principle for all rheto-ricians and philologists. Meaning was connected to and depen-dent upon the integrity of the word, and the wrong word led to falsehood. In order properly to understand a text, one had to discover the actual words of the author; this usually meant ex-tracting them from the corrupt manuscripts. In theory, all ancient texts should be thoroughly studied and restored. Textual criticism, therefore, was a logical result of humanism, although its execution was not always equal to the ideal.

One obstacle to the development of a complete textual critical method was the humanist emphasis on eloquence. A writer's style first attracted the humanists, and they felt that they had so mastered the rules of Latin that they could second-guess an ancient author. Command of style resulted in an undervaluation of the need to deal critically with the surviving manuscripts of a writer. While it might be too simplistic to counterpose a literary to a philological attitude toward ancient texts, since the two went together in the best humanists' work, nevertheless, a devotion to literary values tended to impede a primary dependence on manuscript authority in reconstructing an ancient's work.

The invention and spread of printing made possible a broader diffusion of more stable and readable texts. As printing disseminated supposedly standardized texts, scholars felt more acutely the need for accurate versions.[4] The manuscript book had always been a unique entity; no two were the same. Each carried the marks (positive and negative) of its copyists' interests and skills. Each was tailored to its owners' needs and preferences. There was no standardization. Even chapter and book divisions were inconsistent. Rarely did medieval scholars appreciate the problem of corrupt manuscripts and the need for a textual critical approach. Variant versions were seldom compared.[5] Medieval universities tried to enforce some uniformity in manuscript production for teaching purposes, but this required rigid surveillance and was never fully successful or universally applied.[6] A reader of a printed text expected that everyone read the same words (which was not always true) and would be in a position to discuss them coherently. The entire nature of scholarship (and textual criticism in particular), however, was transformed by printing.

PRESUPPOSITIONS OF PRINTING

Printing's potential for advancing learning, and perhaps increasing one's income, attracted the humanists.[7] Scholars turned their attention to publishing and worked closely with printers to produce corrected and dependable texts. Such enthusiasm did not always promote accuracy. Printers, rushing to issue texts as quickly as possible, emphasized accuracy less than marketability. Editors, in turn, accepted such demands for speed and were anxious to supply readers with usable, if imperfect, versions of ancient works. Even had fidelity to the manuscripts been the basic criterion of early printing, there existed no means by which to achieve such a goal. Since printers adhered to no set body of editorial principles, the quality of texts varied greatly. Copies of the same edition might contain discrepancies, since changes were made even during printing. Often a new edition was little more than a reprint of a previous one that had itself been based on a single corrupt manuscript haphazardly or only partially corrected. The errors, poor guesses, or faulty readings of one edition passed easily into the commonly accepted version, the *vulgata.* (One of the objects of printers was to issue texts that would become the standard versions or *vulgata.*) Adding to such occasions for error were the hectic working conditions in printing houses. In an endeavor as unsystematized as Renaissance editing, individual talents meant more than the common principles espoused by the scholarly community.

In general, there were two basic means of correcting or emending texts in the Renaissance. The first was *emendatio ope codicum;* that is, a manuscript-based system of correction. Usually, it implied selective comparison of sections of one or more manuscripts or the printed versions of a text. It did not refer to any systematic collation of all manuscripts in their entirety.[8] The second was *emendatio ope ingenii* or *emendatio ope coniecturae,* the use of the editor's talents and knowledge through conjecture to propose better readings independent of manuscript authority. During the Renaissance conjecture meant guesswork; that is, a reading lacking manuscript or independent authority. It was something the editor divined, and *divinatio* was synonymous with *coniectura.* Simple improvement by any means was designated *emendatio* and might or might not encompass *coniectura.*[9] The manuscript-based and the guesswork methods competed with each other, with individuals favoring one procedure over another, although in the same edition both techniques could be at work. Nevertheless, *emendatio ope coniecturae* was the more common, and it was never displaced by its rival. The basic debate in textual criticism centered on the extent to which conjecture should be used and at what stage it should be employed.

Humanist editors and textual critics agreed that available manuscripts should form the basis for all corrections. While as a principle this was commendable, its significance depended on the details of its implementation. Fundamental questions had to be answered. Which manuscripts should be preferred and why? Did an archetype of a text actually exist? Are manuscripts' errors of any value in extracting the true reading? Should material obtained from collateral authors be preferred to material in manuscripts that were regarded as corrupt? Should the sense of a passage determine which words should be changed? Should the reader be informed of all the corrections an editor had made, only the most important, or none? What was the relationship between printed text and other manuscript versions? In most cases editors did not even conceive of such problems.

Deference to manuscripts often coincided with ignorance of their geneses or indifference to their use. Editors only vaguely understood the complex process of determining the relative authority of several manuscripts. Rather, all manuscripts permitted an editor to display his knowledge of Latin and Greek, his acquaintance with classical culture, and his own taste, ingenuity, and sensitivity to style. Even when an editor consulted one or more manuscripts, the resulting edition was not usually based on the collation of all known or available manuscripts. He lacked the means of judging what constituted recent interpolations or of evaluating an older or more correct reading among competitors. Emendation theory, therefore, argued for a combination of manuscript evidence and an editor's critical *ingenium*, with the latter dominant in practice.

The reasons for inconsistent attitudes toward manuscripts were several. Perhaps the fundamental one mirrored humanist attitudes toward the past and its recoverability. Renaissance critics were not engaged in a scientific enterprise but in creative (even romantic) archaeology. While manuscripts were artifacts that revealed the past, their corrupt state also concealed it. Editors felt required to make an imaginative leap beyond them in order to extract valid readings. This generalized sense of manuscripts' value for uncovering the past meant that they were not treated as unique entities with their own stories; a *codex* was *antiquus* or *vetus,* usually without more precise definition. Further explanations tended to be unhelpfully broad. The distinctions between *modernus* and *antiquus* clouded intermediate stages. *Codex antiquissimus* regularly designated a manuscript as opposed to a printed book.[10] Adding to this vagueness was a preference for more recently written, and hence more legible, manuscripts. The humanists' confidence in their control of Latin and Greek easily overcame the limits implicit in manuscripts. Often they simply ignored problematic readings. An editor felt no more constraint in emending faults in ancient texts than in recent ones. Nor did he feel any requirement to state when he was altering manuscript readings on his own authority. When selecting a contemporary work for reprinting, he might publish a previous, inferior version because of the ease and economy of typesetting rather than utilizing the newest version corrected by the author himself.[11]

Early printing shops' practices intensified the shortcomings of textual exploitation. The manuscript or a copy of it was usually corrected by the editor, who sent it to the printers with particular instructions written in the margins; the printers then set it with little review. Once the text was printed, the manuscript was often discarded (and then not infrequently lost) and not always used to check the published version. The printers were not always scrupulous in their work, and proofreading was often hasty. The reader received a text that, according to title pages or introductory letters, had been carefully collated and corrected and was more faithful to the author's intention than the original manuscript. He could do little more than take the editor at his word or try to find his own manuscript version; even for scholars this latter alternative was impractical, and even if successful it would not affect the texts already printed in defective form. Accuracy and standardization cannot be claimed as hallmarks of early printing.[12]

RENAISSANCE TEXTUAL CRITICISM BEFORE PRINTING

New attitudes favoring extensive manuscript consultation, accurate citation, and regular collation developed slowly, but even before printing some humanists had come to appreciate the problems in handling manuscript authority and had tried to develop the means to restore accurate readings. Petrarch's attention to manuscripts of ancient writers initiated the Renaissance textual critical tradition. He, in turn, revived ancient textual practices of manuscript consultation.[13] Since Petrarch never explained clearly his procedure, subsequent humanists had to depend on examples of his corrections found in his manuscripts.

There are indications of a critical sense developing in the work of the humanist chancellor of Florence, Coluccio Salutati (1331–1406). In his *De fato et fortuna* (2, 6) Salutati discussed the corrupt state of the manuscripts of Augustine's *De civitate Dei* and of Seneca's letters.[14] Salutati realized that scribes had introduced numerous errors into his manuscripts. Either through omissions, willful changes, or the addition in the text of marginal materials, scribes had altered ancient writings. Ignorant of the substance of what they were transcribing, scribes changed words thoughtlessly. Later readers introduced their own unfounded conjectures. Such corruptions were not a recent phenomenon; indeed, they had begun soon after the author had issued his text to the public. Salutati was as conscious of the defects in the transmission of contemporary writers, such as Dante and Petrarch, as in that of the ancient and patristic authors, and generally he preferred to depend on the older versions when they were available. This led Salutati to propose a solution to the problem of corrupt manuscripts. He advocated that manuscripts be collected in public libraries, where scholars could properly collate them. Salutati was especially sensitive to the dangers of excessive zeal in emending texts. Since Salutati corrected his own manuscripts carefully, he probably conceived of such a process as the best means of providing purer forms of authors' words and of assuring some control over the texts' dissemination.

Salutati's Florence included other humanists engaged in

manuscript studies. Among these perhaps the most exceptional, both in accomplishments and in personality, was Niccolò
Niccoli (1364–1437).[15] Niccoli spent his considerable patrimony
in acquiring ancient texts, which he consulted extensively. A
characteristic of his textual work was a careful scrutiny of the
individual letters that made up the words of questionable passages in an attempt to arrive at proper interpretations. He
treated his manuscripts conscientiously and changed them as
little as possible. Even when making a correction, he left the
rejected version visible so that another reader could consult it.
His careful correction of texts through comparison of manuscripts earned him praise in his own day and from modern
critics.[16] His method incorporated elements that would become
basic to Renaissance textual criticism.

Both Salutati and Niccoli had understood the threat facing
scholarship from corrupt manuscripts, but they and their contemporaries lacked a theory upon which to base systematic
corrections. Any advance in textual criticism would require the
development of a sophisticated historical attitude toward the
fluctuations in the Latin language that would allow a reader to
determine the idiom appropriate to a text. This important task
was formalized by Lorenzo Valla (1407–1457).[17] Valla understood that the Latin language had undergone numerous
changes over time, and he argued that a reader must be sensitive to this in order to judge what an ancient writer might have
written. Once this historicity of diction and style had been
established, a philological technique capable of criticizing a
text became possible. Valla took the lead first in his attack on
the linguistic and historical falsifications in his *Diatribe* against
the so-called Donation of Constantine and then, more pro-
grammatically, in his *Elegantiae*.[18] In the latter, a master textbook of Latin style, Valla showed himself aware of the vagaries
implicit in textual transmission; to deal with these he expressed the need to treat manuscripts critically and to compare
received readings with ancient usage. Valla demonstrated this
process most fully, by example, in his *Emendationes* to Livy and
his *Annotationes* to the Latin New Testament.

Valla made significant contributions to the study of Livy in
his *Emendationes* to the first six books of the *Ab urbe condita*.

These contain his fullest treatment of a major Roman historical source and had a rather peculiar genesis.[19] Valla issued them as part of an attack on his fellow humanist Bartolomeo Facio while both were resident at the court of the King of Naples. Facio and Antonio Panormita, the leader of the humanists in Naples, had tried their hand at emending the *Codex regius* of Livy, which had been given to the King of Naples, Alfonso the Magnanimous, by Cosimo de' Medici in 1444. As part of his polemic, Valla decided to prove his superiority over his enemies by correcting their Livian scholarship. In preparing his work, Valla had access not only to the *Codex regius* but also to the *Codex Agenensis* (British Museum, Harleian 2493), which included corrections made by Petrarch, and at least one other manuscript (Valencia, Cathedral Library, 173). Valla noted Petrarch's corrections as well as those of other Florentine humanists, thereby demonstrating his familarity with and ability to evaluate previous Renaissance textual criticism. Thus he located his work in the humanist tradition of Livian scholarship and showed his own grasp of the nature of textual emendation.

The *Emendationes* show their author's desire to indicate where his enemies had erred and to expound the correct manner of textual retrieval. In accomplishing these two tasks, Valla argued that his opponents had erred in trusting their control of Latin rhetoric rather than careful use of the manuscript in order to correct the text. Valla referred to his manuscript sources and the corruptions in them which had misled his opponents. He accused his antagonists of an excessive number of errors (*Taceo mille in locis vestrum in orthographia errorem*).[20] He noted how letters became confused and falsely seemed to form different words.[21] He emphasized the paleographical origins of error; he noted how corruptions resulted from unfamiliar handwritings and maintained that an analysis of these errors could yield correct readings. On the basis of his attention to the sources of corruptions, a number of passages he emended conjecturally have been accepted into the standard modern version.

Related to the textual observations in the *Emendationes* are Valla's translations of Greek writers, since they posed similar difficulties. At the request of Pope Nicholas V, Valla made Latin versions of Thucydides and Herodotus.[22] In order to arrive at a proper text, he had to correct the Greek manuscripts at his disposal. These translations have become valuable tools in reestablishing Greek readings, and Valla's conjectures have been accepted in several cases. Unfortunately, he never discussed in detail his emending procedure, so we cannot determine exactly how he went about his work as a translator.

Even more significant historically were Valla's notes on the New Testament.[23] These exist in two forms, the early *Collatio* (ca. 1442) and the fuller *Annotationes* (1450s). They testify to Valla's dissatisfaction with the corrupt Vulgate, which had influenced theological formulations. To correct Scripture Valla consulted Greek and Latin manuscripts, compared their readings, and specified which he felt was most appropriate. His treatment of the Greek text of the New Testament, however, was not a major undertaking, since he (as Erasmus would after him) concentrated on correcting the Latin Vulgate. Valla understood that similar pronunciation of words (since transcription was often done from read texts), homonyms, and assimilation (the adding of a word to one passage from another) could all produce error. He also appreciated the deliberate changes made by scribes in order to make passages sensible. By questioning translations unsupported by the Greek or inconsistent with other passages, Valla treated the sacred text as a historical document. Scripture was subject to the same laws of decay as any other literary artifact and was similarly recoverable by the same techniques of linguistic and textual explanations.

Valla did not articulate a complete theory of textual criticism. Still, the *Collatio* and *Annotationes* were major advances in the historicization of Scripture and all received texts, even though they pointed the way to a complete textual critical method rather than demonstrated how to devise such a system. Despite Valla's skill and reputation, his contemporaries did not follow his lead with much alacrity; the *Annotationes* were to remain without influence until Erasmus published them in 1505.

Unlike his fellow humanists, Valla developed a philosophical foundation for textual studies. In his *Elegantiae* and, more fundamentally, in his *Dialecticarum disputationum libri III*, Valla enunciated the principle that reality is found in the particular thing or word rather than through an idealized philosophy that posits abstract, universalized propositions explained in technical language.[24] Since truth can only be obtained from the careful scrutiny of the contours of the particular, a careful treatment of a text's constituent elements (paleographical, contextual, and grammatical) is the only way to arrive at a true reading. For Valla *res* and *verbum* went together and demanded particularized treatment. Truth results from establishing the words of a text as a historical product and not from discussions of ideal forms and logical propositions. Thus for Valla textual criticism, and historical thought generally, could uncover reality.

Despite this sophisticated view, Valla never used his treatment of Livy as part of a broader discussion of the ancient world; his only history, of King Ferdinand of Aragon, was rhetorical in nature.[25] But Valla had established principles that concurred with growing humanistic practices. Valla's close contemporary, Flavio Biondo (1392–1463), advanced Roman historiography by using ancient sources in his histories of ancient Rome and medieval Italy.[26] Although extensive information on Biondo's textual work is lacking, we do know that he corrected a manuscript of Ammianus Marcellinus, taken from the monastery of Fulda, which Niccoli and Poggio had also studied.[27] The readings that he proposed subsequently entered into his famous history, the *Roma instaurata*.[28]

One fundamental extension of the historicization of texts was the development of a nomenclature to describe different handwritings.[29] Characterization of hands was a basis for any paleographical system, although, as in most such matters, the humanists laid out certain general definitions without much consistent elaboration. They distinguished broadly between *litterae antiquae*, that is, Caroline minuscule (believed to be an ancient hand) and its humanist variants, and *litterae Gothicae* or *Longobardae* or *modernae*, the "corrupt" later hands. These categories paralleled the humanist view of the corruption and decline of the Roman language and culture; as the latter required revival, so did handwriting.[30] The humanists in fact were comparing various medieval hands rather than ancient and medieval ones. The terms of the taxonomy were not always clear, and the supporting ideology remained vague. Still, there was a growing sense of historical stages in the development of handwriting. The *litterae antiquae* could be seen in clearest fashion not only in epigraphical remains and in coins that were being collected but also in the capitals and uncials of some manuscripts. On the basis of their observations, the humanists spoke of the *litterae maiusculae* or *maiores,* uncial or ancient capitals either epigraphical or handwritten. These paleographical observations would help lay the foundations for an analysis of manuscript corruptions that had resulted from the inability of scribes to read different hands.

Humanist pedagogues, in overcoming textual problems for their teaching, helped to popularize an awareness of the need for textual criticism of ancient texts among their students. This is evident even early in the Quattrocento, as seen in the work of the Paduan master Gasparino Barzizza (1360–1431).[31] As part of his educational program, Barzizza had to establish reliable versions of the major school authors in order to comment on them. He searched out and collated, often with the help of his students, manuscripts of the authors he taught. While usually remaining true to his collated manuscripts, he resorted to conjecture when they failed him in some way. One indication of his interest in textual matters was his relative appreciation of the paleographical foundation of emendation. He understood the scribal origin of error and how to deal with it. While not an originator of a new method, Barzizza, like other teachers such as Guarino da Verona, helped to standardize the humanist emendation practice and passed it on to his students.

THE ADVENT OF PRINTING

Since Salutati, Niccoli, and Valla worked before the advent of printing, they did not struggle with the added problems that resulted from the printer's need to provide a large number of more-or-less correct and standardized texts. The Italian scholars who early collaborated with the Germans who brought the new art of printing to Italy, especially Rome, had to consider the new errors that arose in moving from manuscript to printed book and to justify to readers the superiority of their work over that of manuscripts or other printed versions. The availability of large numbers of texts that came from the presses, moreover, offered the basis for a more systematic treatment of ancient writers. Scholars soon realized the need to collate manuscripts with the *vulgata* to propose their own corrections and to criticize others. Printing offered the possibility of progress in textual criticism, though this was not immediate or automatic.

From the early years of printing, some humanists realized its dangers as well as its opportunities. This is evident in the work of the humanist diplomat, ecclesiastic, and classsical commentator, Niccolò Perotti (1429–1480).[32] In a letter to Francesco Guarnieri, Perotti offered his ideas on textual problems as part of a critique of the edition of Pliny the Elder's *Naturalis historia* in 1470 by Giovanni Andrea Bussi (1417–1475),[33] bishop of Aleria, an active collaborator of the German-Roman printers Sweynheym and Pannartz. Since Perotti himself was involved in editing Pliny, his primary concern was to criticize Bussi by providing contrasting rules for the proper handling of classical texts.[34] Perotti criticized scholar-editors who did not give proper attention to the available manuscripts of works they were publishing. He wanted editors to add nothing without the authority of manuscripts, other relevant writings of an author, analogous material from collateral writers, or from grammatical forms of another language. In the process of producing an improved text, the careful investigation of the manuscripts is the first step, but certainly not the last. Perotti understood, at least in a general way, the sources of manuscript corruption and the need to correct them through careful observation.[35] Unfortunately, when he came to apply his method to specific writers, he was not noticeably more scrupulous than Bussi. He did mention his manuscripts, but, like most Renaissance editors, he offered no precise identifications of them or specifics about their state. Despite Perotti's limitations as a textual critic, he realized that printing had introduced new problems, and he was willing to tackle them, even in an author as problematic as Pliny.

The individual Perotti criticized was not quite as indifferent to manuscripts as Perotti maintained. Bussi had his own method for dealing with manuscripts. For his 1468 Roman edition of the *opera* of Jerome,[36] he reported that he had used a number of corrupt manuscripts that he had emended as best he could. To his credit, Bussi acknowledged that subsequent scholars could improve upon his work. His procedure did not appreciably differ from that of his contemporaries, and his edition of Jerome became the base text for later editions.

While Perotti's attack on Bussi shows him as one of the first scholars to assess properly the meaning of the new art of printing, he was best known not as the editor of Pliny or as a critic of manuscripts but as a commentator on ancient writers. Above all, he produced one of the monuments of Renaissance classical learning, the *Cornucopia, sive commentarii linguae latinae.*[37] In form the *Cornucopia* is a grand commentary on the poet Martial, but in fact it consists of a series of detailed observations on the Latin language. It both demonstrated Perotti's erudition and provided a mine of information on classical vocabulary, history, and culture. Such commentaries as the *Cornucopia* offered an explanation of every word in the text, usually by reference to collateral ancient authorities.[38] Its concentration on the word was a reaction to the dialectical, metaphorical, and metaphysical tendencies of the medieval commentators and a practical application of the historical theories of men such as Valla. Such commentaries suited the needs of the teachers who used them to explain difficult passages to their students. It was a functional if not an original or very critically nuanced means of interpreting classical literature. In typical humanist fashion, such commentaries could become a polemical forum for competing literary schools, and a humanist often gave more attention to his commentary than to the text he was supposedly correcting.[39]

By the end of the fifteenth century, decades of work on classical authors produced noticeable progress in textual criticism. In addition to more frequent appeal to manuscripts, at least rhetorically, some humanists reformed their procedures accordingly. Rather than comment on every word in a text, some scholars began to select the most important or taxing problems to discuss. In replacing the *ad litteram* commentary, the annotation format allowed for more concentrated textual investigations. This change meant that annotators realized that certain sections of a text were more corrupt or unclear than others and required special attention. In addition to allowing for selective treatment, such notes also could be published separately and keyed to the *vulgata*. Like the word-for-word commentary, an annotation could serve as an arena for wide-ranging discussions. Collateral authorities—that is, other ancient authors who discussed similar topics or used the same literary style—were still more prominent than manuscript citations in the annotations, but these authorities were used with greater sophistication; this was especially true as Greek authors became more widely available.

The annotation format would become standard for commenting on a classical writer and for offering textual observations. In an annotation, a scholar could present variant readings and explain his preferences. Grammatical and etymological explanations could be easily summarized and examples employed. The annotation form continued to offer the scholar the opportunity to express his own opinion on a variety of textual, historical, and contemporary questions. As a result, it is in the annotations of Renaissance writers that a modern scholar can find the humanists expressing themselves most fully on textual matters.

The process of publishing and annotating Latin and Greek texts (the latter usually in Latin translation) in *editiones principes* occupied the humanists in the first generation of printing. Since editors did not follow exacting standards, a printed book contained numerous errors and faulty conjectures. Still, once the main body of the classical heritage had become available in standard, if defective, form as *vulgata* editions, advances in textual criticism could be made more easily. This became possible in the last decades of the fifteenth and the first quarter of the sixteenth century, a protean period in the development of Renaissance textual criticism.

POLIZIANO

Italian scholars pioneered the advances in textual scholarship in the later fifteenth century. Filippo Beroaldo the Elder (1453–1505), who had taught in France and exerted much influence as professor at the University of Bologna, produced annotations on such authors as Pliny and Apuleius, writers who were notorious for their difficult subject matter or style.[40] His interest was less in textual questions than in the philological, historical, and "mystical" contents of the text; nevertheless, he did provide a model for handling complex authors. His student, Giovanni Battista Pio

(1475?–1542?), followed his lead and wrote annotations on a variety of prose writers and poets.[41] He was especially fond of authors whose archaic vocabulary and complex syntax required him to exert his erudition to the fullest.

While Beroaldo and some of his contemporaries helped create new standards for editing and annotating, the best representatives of textual scholarship in Renaissance Italy were Ermolao Barbaro (1453–1493) and Angelo Poliziano (1454–1494). Barbaro used and raised to a high level the accepted procedures of textual criticism in his day, while Poliziano surpassed all by revolutionizing classical studies.

A Venetian nobleman and cleric, Barbaro was a scholar of great breadth whose interests encompassed philosophical, scientific, and literary matters.[42] Among these the most important for textual criticism was his set of *Castigationes* to Pliny's *Naturalis historia*, the large and corrupt text that had elicited Perotti's letter and was to have an important place in Beatus Rhenanus' career.[43] The history of Pliny's work is a complicated one; the narrative itself is often obscure because of discussion of unfamiliar topics in natural history. Textually, Pliny's enormous encyclopedia was among the most corrupt of major ancient texts. Its value as a scientific source, however, made it frequently read, if not always clearly understood. The *editio princeps* was issued at Venice in 1469 by the German printer Johannes da Spira or Speyer.[44] In the fifteenth century it was followed by fourteen further printings and by a series of commentaries by such humanists as Perotti, Beroaldo, and Marc'Antonio Coccio (Sabellicus, 1445–ca. 1506); Poliziano also proposed random emendations. All these scholars used manuscripts and offered their own conjectures. Into this complicated arena Barbaro hoped to bring order.

Barbaro made his editorial procedure clear to his readers. He followed a set method by placing in the text the words he felt were corrupt and then stating his own corrections in the notes.[45] While proclaiming the doctrine of *emendatio ope codicum*, he was not consistent in adhering to it. No clear identifications of his manuscripts appear in his notes, and the specific citations are few. References to manuscript readings were simply noted as *vetus lectio* or *antiqua lectio*. More common in Barbaro was his dependence on the consensus of authors, a technique that involved the search for analogies from Latin and Greek writers as a basis for conjecture. Indeed, Barbaro displayed a marked willingness to resort frequently to conjecture, which he preferred to collation and which he used at several levels. Often, his conjectures were simply corrections of passages offering little difficulty, changes of one letter or alternate spellings. Others were more complicated, since they required a major change in what he found in the *vulgata*. In the *Castigationes,* Barbaro usually followed one of three procedures.[46] Sometimes he proposed his own conjecture. At other times he offered a list of variants that more or less resembled each other but differed from the vulgate reading. Finally, he counterposed a parallel passage from another ancient author without further comment. For the most part, the *Castigationes* concentrate on textual questions, and Barbaro did not digress into tangential areas. Barbaro's work was greatly appreciated by his contemporaries, and he helped to put the study of Pliny on a firmer basis.[47]

Barbaro surpassed his contemporaries, with the exception of Angelo Poliziano (1454–1494),[48] as a textual critic and classical scholar. Poliziano displayed originality in his treatment of ancient authors, Greek and Latin. He devoted much time and effort to reading numerous manuscript versions of classical texts, taking careful notes and collating them. He scrupulously recorded his findings in his *Miscellanea,* two collections of textual observations that were meant to be the basis for more systematic treatments.

Poliziano's technique in observing specific elements in his manuscripts and recording them had no equal in his day.[49] Although he was not the first humanist to consult manuscripts systematically, only he offered a procedure for identifying their provenience, for dating them and determining their genealogy, for citing them in a clear and specific manner, and for describing them paleographically and codicologically. He appreciated the special value of even corrupt manuscript readings as vestiges of the author's actual words. He codified a definite hierarchy of authorities for correcting texts, something at which other humanists had only hinted. First in authority were the readings found in the old manuscripts themselves (*veterum auctoritas codicum*); second was the support that could be collected from other ancient writers (*testimonia scriptorum idoneorum*); and third was the sense of the text itself (*sensus*), which was a relatively nonarbitrary form of conjecture, since it was extracted from the text. Such a process offered the basis for placing textual criticism on a relatively objective footing.[50]

Poliziano realized that not all manuscripts were the same. He contrasted the readings found in *codices vetusti* or *antiquissimi* with those found in *codices recentiores, novi et vulgatissimi* as well as with those in printed books. Concordance among the readings of the old manuscripts he treated as the final proof (*de quo nihil est quod quisquam ambique pronuntiat, cum vetera omnia exemplaria in eo conspirent*).[51] When the oldest authorities disagreed among themselves, Poliziano resorted to context. Manuscript readings derived from collation were to be the beginning of correcting ancient authors. Poliziano's comparisons of manuscripts with themselves or printed texts demonstrate his great care. In collating the Bembo manuscript of Terence with the 1475 Venetian printed version, Poliziano carefully copied the errors as well as old corrections he found in the manuscript. He did so because he believed they contained the *rectae lectionis vestigia*.[52] Poliziano was more than just an accurate collator. He realized that manuscripts differed in age and reliability.[53] He identified an author's best manuscript and gave it special attention. He understood, for example, the unique value of the Bembo Terence and the close attention it merited. In attempting to reconstruct a true reading, he sought to explain the source of error either as the result of a scribe's carelessness or ignorance, or of changes introduced by emendators.[54] When he did conjecture in order to supply missing sections, he usually used special sigla to inform the reader of his own interventions.[55]

While committed to *emendatio ope codicum*, Poliziano accepted *emendatio ope coniecturae*, but only as a last resort. He specifically criticized his contemporaries, such as Beroaldo, for depending on their own conjectures even against the agreement of the old manuscript readings.[56] When offering a reading different from those of the manuscripts, Poliziano followed a paleographical analysis of what he found as the means of uncovering the *vera lectio.*[57] Thus conjecture was tied to the manuscript through a paleographical reconstruction. Despite the false readings caused by copyists, the *vera lectio* could be recovered from their errors. Certainly, Poliziano felt himself justified in proposing his own paleographically based conjectures where others had offered a variety of readings.[58] Significantly, he understood the similarities among several different manuscripts of the Pandects, Virgil, and Terence, which he had consulted and grouped according to their paleographical affinities.[59]

One characteristic of Poliziano's textual critical method, which became prominent in Beatus Rhenanus, was his desire to lead his readers through the process by which he arrived at his readings. Poliziano cited a questionable reading, then offered a manuscript version or selected a reading from various manuscripts or extracted from the manuscript a slightly different reading or, if all else failed, proposed his own conjecture. One useful example of the process is found in his rejection of the word *Stratocle* in Cicero's *De officiis,* I, 18, 62 (modern reading is *hinc noster Cocles*).[60] He investigated three manuscripts to correct this passage. One was his own, another of *media fere antiquitas* from Bologna, and the third was a much older one from the Medici library. He found in these three different forms: *Stratocle, Stercocles,* and *Stercodes.* In explaining these variations he noted that, for example, *c* and *l* could come together to form a *d.*[61] From these close investigations of the manuscripts he extracted the *vera et integra forte lectio.* As he explained, *Stercocles* was actually *noster Cocles,* or *hinc noster Cocles.* He subsequently found another manuscript from the library of Santa Croce *non veterem admodum sed omnino apud saeculum forte prius scriptum multisque locis emendatissimum,* which offered the reading *Coclites.* He then provided several examples to show how the words could have been pronounced to form one word and hence cause the misreading. Finally, he defended his version (which is found in modern editions) as supported by *antiquitatis auctoritas* rather than as *coniectura nostra.*[62]

Poliziano further realized that after careful investigation individual manuscripts could be grouped together and treated as a unit, and that from them the critic could arrive at the archetype of the text. He was unique in this, and it alone would place him in the forefront of Renaissance textual critics. Moreover, like

Barbaro, he appreciated the value of collateral Greek and Latin writers. His control of Greek was especially important in giving him the ability to sense when a Latin writer was paralleling a Greek form and thus offering a key to understanding Latin anomalies. In depending on the Greek origin of Latin usages, Poliziano was willing to propose an obvious Greekism even against the concurrence of the manuscripts, no doubt realizing the tendency of the scribe to mistake such a word.[63] Poliziano had arrived at a method that would lead to a more or less "scientific" treatment of ancient writings, one that avoided the arbitrariness of his predecessors and contemporaries and substituted a graduated system of authoritative alternatives.

Unfortunately, Poliziano's influence in his day was limited. Working usually alone and over time with different manuscripts, he could not broadcast his views widely, and he did not live long enough to prepare any edition of a classical author as a model for others. Further, he was offering a radically new method of textual analysis, and few were willing to follow his detailed, rather technical, and impersonal lead. Humanists were much more inclined to display their talents through conjecture than they were to follow a relatively objective system with little outlet for self advertisement. His tendency toward polemic also limited Poliziano's influence as well as earning him and his method enemies. The humanist Giorgio Merula criticized him for his attempts to reconstruct the words of the ancients.[64] Merula's attack on Poliziano, however, did not concentrate on the theory of manuscript consultation and textual criticism, but on particular readings that Merula, on the basis of his own sense of the Latin language, felt his rival had misconstrued. This dispute shows how most humanists concentrated on interpretative questions that would display individual skill rather than on discussions of the new and more objective elements in Poliziano's work. An even more forceful rejection of Poliziano's method is found in Baptista Mantuanus, the famous poet, who dismissed Poliziano's spelling of the name *Vergilius* simply because he had found it so written in ancient manuscripts.[65] For Mantuanus one manuscript reading without any special authority sufficed.

Despite such resistance, Poliziano did attract some followers.

The Florentine Pietro Crinito (ca. 1465–ca. 1507) included a series of textual observations on classical and more recent writers in his *De honesta disciplina*.[66] Crinito inherited some of Poliziano's critical attitudes, but he did not follow him in the systematic criticism of manuscripts. On occasion, he discussed manuscripts and their corruptions but in no organized fashion.[67] One promising student of Poliziano's method was Pietro Bembo (1470–1547).[68] He helped Poliziano collate the *codex Bembinus* of Terence and was himself sensitive to textual problems. Ultimately, Bembo preferred to devote his talents to literary composition and rule-making rather than textual analysis. Only in the next generation did Poliziano find his true successor in Piero Vettori (1499–1585).[69] Vettori employed Poliziano's attention to careful manuscript analysis in editing a wide variety of Latin and Greek authors. His editions made him a master of textual criticism and an influential propagator of Poliziano's ideals.

TEXTUAL CRITICISM IN NORTHERN EUROPE

While scholars such as Barbaro and Poliziano were making major advances in textual criticism, Northern European humanists lagged behind their Italian contemporaries.[70] In general, Northern humanists at the beginning of the sixteenth century had not incorporated in their work the Italians' concern for the establishment of accurate texts. In part this was attributable to the dominance of scholasticism in the Northern University system.[71] With its dependence on Aristotelian logic and metaphysics, scholasticism undervalued the humanists' literary and classical studies and ignored their concern for stylistic canons and search for exact linguistic reconstruction of texts. Logic and metaphysics, not philology, provided scholastics with the means of understanding a text. Thus Northern European pedagogy inhibited a commitment to textual study. In part, Germany's relative tardiness reflected the time needed to transfer the new textual methods from Italy. While Italian-based printing firms dominated the production of classical texts, printers in German lands usually concentrated on Latin and vernacular religious and medieval texts.[72] New techniques for correcting classical works came either from visiting Italian scholars or from students who had studied in Italy. Not surprisingly, Northern scholars manifested the same limitations as most of their Italian contemporaries in editing classical texts—a certain arbitrariness in conjecture and a cavalier attitude toward manuscripts.[73]

There were other reasons for this delay. Northern humanists were more concerned with certain fundamental pedagogical and moral questions relating to the compatibility of classical and Christian values than the Italians, who largely had solved these problems decades earlier. Simply put, the Northerners were more apt to deal with classical writers who satisfied their careful moral scrutiny than they were to restore corrupt manuscripts in order to provide critical texts of all ancient writers.[74] This attitude delayed the integration of the best Italian procedures with native talents. Indeed, this integration became a part of their humanist tradition only when encountered in a Northern European who was sensitive to Italian textual advances; that is, only when Erasmus was able to adapt Italian humanism to Northern needs and preferences.

Still, by the beginning of the sixteenth century the transfer was nearing completion and the stage was set for the broader acceptance of new attitudes. Thereafter, two approaches toward textual problems dominated Northern Europe, and the desire to reform society through education determined these. One approach interpreted textual matters as subordinate to moral ones; the other tended to regard these matters as preparatory to moral and literary concerns and ultimately complementary to them. The first was the pre-Erasmian tradition; the second, Erasmian.

The center of the Northern European intellectual tradition and of publishing and textual criticism was Paris. Its university housed several competing philosophical and pedagogical schools. It was there that Guillaume Budé (1467–1540)[75] would provide a great model for Renaissance philology and initiate French dominance in Hellenic studies. The careful scholarship of Budé and his successors, however, was to come in the 1520s and later. At the beginning of the sixteenth century, interest in humanism, editing, and textual problems centered on the person and work of Jacques Lefèvre d'Etaples.

Lefèvre (ca. 1460–1536) is an example of the moral concerns described above.[76] He is especially relevant, since Beatus Rhenanus studied with him and owed his first contacts with the press to him. Lefèvre had traveled in Italy and there personally encountered several of the most important Italian intellectuals. His interests encompassed a variety of new and traditional subjects. He followed Ermolao Barbaro in espousing a revived Aristotelianism based on direct translations from the Greek and free of scholastic commentaries. But he also advocated the Neo-Platonism of Marsilio Ficino and Giovanni Pico della Mirandola, which he felt was in accord with Christian doctrine. For authentic Christianity he looked to the Fathers of the Church, both Greek and Latin, as well as to mystical writers such as Pseudo-Dionysius the Areopagite, Ramón Lull, and Nicholas of Cusa. Through his teaching and forceful personality, he was the major force in spreading one approach of the *studia humanitatis* among his students at Paris.

Printing was the means by which Lefèvre popularized his ideals of moral and cultural rejuvenation through contact with the purified sources of Christian and ancient knowledge.[77] While he reprinted Italian editions of the Church Fathers,[78] he was responsible for a variety of *editiones principes,* especially of medieval mystics, which required solving textual problems. Certainly Lefèvre realized that traditions were corrupt,[79] but this did not lead him to concentrate on them. He and his associates occasionally mentioned the state of their manuscripts, but they did not expand on their procedures for emending them.[80] To a great extent, Lefèvre's problems were less severe than those of other humanists, since generally the medieval texts had not suffered as severely as classical ones in their transmission. The absence of the classics in his editorial output further indicates an indifference to the questions that motivated men like Poliziano and Barbaro.

Lefèvre was not insensitive to textual matters. He understood the need to consult the original Greek in order to correct Latin translations. Similarly, when presenting a Greek writer in Latin, such as Aristotle, he often printed alternate translations so that the reader could select the one that seemed most appropriate.[81] His students inherited and used these procedures. The major defect in his work was the limited extent to which he explained the intricacies of his treatment of a text. Lefèvre directed his energies toward interpreting the philosophical, religious, or mystical significance of a treatise. Lacking strong historical instincts, he did not reflect upon the causes of and remedies for manuscript corruptions.

As he grew older, Lefèvre turned increasingly to Scripture and helped lead Northern humanists in its study. Although Lefèvre would devote much time to this endeavor, he did not offer any major textual advances. In his *Quincuplex Psalterium* (1509),[82] for example, he mentioned several manuscripts that he had consulted, but he did not provide any details about them or use them in a critical manner. Rather, he continued to publish differing versions of the Latin translations side by side with his commentary. His real aim was to provide a mystical interpretation of Scripture and not to pioneer in textual criticism.

His limits as a scriptual and textual critic can be clearly seen in Lefèvre's edition and translation of the epistles of Paul.[83] The translation he provided did not reflect any consistent critical procedure. While he was aware of the philological complexities involved in scriptural scholarship and supplied much valuable material relating to them in his commentary, he did not follow his own lead throughout his edition. Theological considerations set the rules for him; he even altered the text in order to arrive at what he felt was doctrinally more acceptable. As a consequence, Lefèvre's scriptural work stands in sharp contrast to that of Desiderius Erasmus, Northern Europe's most accomplished textual critic at the beginning of the sixteenth century.

ERASMUS

Erasmus' intellectual program rejected the mystical and philosophical basis of Lefèvre's scriptural exegesis and, consequently, his textual work.[84] Erasmus' desire to reform society through the promotion of the *studia humanitatis* required the availability of reliable texts of important ancient writers. Further, he wished to avoid the excesses of interpretation that in his view had marred medieval exegesis. He struggled to remain as close to an author's words as possible. This attitude led to his enormous editorial output, including many of the major classical writers as well as substantial portions of the Fathers of the Church. Moreover, none of his contemporaries could claim equal familiarity with manuscripts. His peripatetic life permitted him to investigate libraries in several countries, and he used some of their manuscripts in preparing his editions.

An early indication of Erasmus' textual work is his edition of Cicero's *De officiis* (Paris, 1501); it was the first annotated classical work he published. In his introductory letter, he described his method and contrasted it with the standard humanistic commentaries. He criticized commentaries that covered all the words of a text rather than selecting the most important questions. He singled out the Roman humanist and orator Pietro Marsi (ca. 1430–1509) and his commentaries on Cicero's writings for comparison.[85]

> Instead of the commentaries by Pietro Marsi (how I wish these had been selective rather than exhaustive!), I have appended a large number of brief notes, my intention being that, like little stars, they should conveniently illuminate each obscure passage.... And I have worked equally hard at improving the text. I found a great many flaws, as one would expect in such a familiar work; one scribe will throw the order into confusion as he copies, while another will replace a word, which perhaps had eluded him, with an approximation. These flaws are of course not monstrosities, but still they are intolerable in such a great author. I have corrected all of them, partly by informed guesswork based on Cicero's style, so that at least I can promise the reader that no copy is closer to the original text than the present edition.[86]

Lacking any manuscript authority, Erasmus corrected the text by collating the printed versions and relying upon his own command of Latin style. As was true with most humanist editors, his claims of bringing the text closer to the original were highly rhetorical.

As he continued to work with corrupt texts and became more expert in handling them, Erasmus developed a more measured view of the editor's task. In his search for the true words of the author, Erasmus advocated a set procedure.[87] First, an editor must establish the corrected text; second, he must separate spurious from authentic works; and, finally, he must elucidate the problematic passages in the authentic texts. It is the first element in this hierarchy which presented the most immediate difficulties. Erasmus first selected either a single manuscript or a specific printed edition as the basis for his own work, and then he identified what he felt were the problematic passages and proceeded to correct them. Manuscripts were consulted but not thoroughly collated, and no real effort was made to establish their genealogy and interrelationships. Although he respected the value of manuscript authority, he did not propagate a method of using it systematically. While Erasmus was to remain an active editor throughout his life, it is appropriate for comparison to Beatus Rhenanus to concentrate on the editions he issued between 1515 and 1520 when both worked at the firm of Johannes Froben in Basel. In this way, one can evaluate what Beatus learned from the Dutch humanist.

The skill of Erasmus as an editor and his limits as a textual critic are most evident in his edition of the Greek New Testament, first entitled *Novum Instrumentum* and subsequently called *Novum Testamentum,* together with a new Latin translation and the annotations he appended to it.[88] In order to establish a reliable text upon which to base his new Latin version, Erasmus consulted and evaluated several manuscripts in order to correct the Vulgate. He received his first assistance in navigating Scripture's textual quagmire when he discovered Valla's *Annotationes* in 1504 in the Monastery of Parc; in 1505 he was the first to publish them. This discovery was a major event in Erasmus' scholarly development.[89] Valla showed Erasmus how to deal with questionable passages and how to arrive at more acceptable readings through procedures that were basically philological. Partly with Valla's assistance, Erasmus began the long process of writing his own annotations to the New Testament. But since Valla had consulted only a limited number of manuscripts, he could not provide Erasmus with a complete critical method. Erasmus had to develop a more effective technique on his own.

The *Novum Testamentum* was based on many years' work; unfortunately, Erasmus was not always careful about identifying the manuscripts he consulted and how he used them.[90] For the

Greek text, Erasmus made his printing corrections and emendations on one of the Greek manuscripts he consulted in Basel. Basel offered several good manuscripts of the New Testament, but we know that Erasmus did not consult them all; hence his collation was not as complete as it could have been and did not always reflect the best readings available. Indeed, he occasionally rejected superior manuscripts, since he lacked any theory for establishing a hierarchy among them. Erasmus must have realized the problem, since his later editions of the New Testament included new material drawn from additional manuscripts.

While Erasmus' criticism of his manuscripts benefited from Valla's work, he surpassed him in the quantity and quality of his *annotationes,* especially in matters of Greek.[91] In them Erasmus often included extended discussions of questionable points and the reasons for preferring one variant to another. One important source for the correction of Scripture was the writings of the Greek and Latin Fathers who occasionally provided readings superior to those found in the Greek manuscripts themselves. Erasmus realized that there were occasions when neither his manuscripts nor the Fathers could offer solutions, and in these cases he resorted to conjecture, with some success.[92] He was sensitive to the corruptions made by copyists; he realized that in some cases they had mistaken homonyms, while in others they corrupted their texts through assimilation—that is, they introduced a phrase from one passage into another. Further, he noted that some scribes purposely altered the text, either because they felt a passage was missing some phrase or needed some explanation, or because they wanted to make the text correspond to a particular theological viewpoint. In his treatment of such cases, Erasmus essayed the idea of the "principle of the harder reading" (*difficilior lectio*),[93] arguing that a scribe was more likely to corrupt a word or phrase into something familiar rather than into something unfamiliar. Hence the more difficult variants are the most likely to be correct.

In his treatment of ancient texts, Erasmus proved to be an astute and original critic. His faults, such as not describing his manuscripts clearly, are evident, but so are his accomplishments—the principle of the harder reading and the number of conjectures that have won approval or at least have not been completely rejected. Erasmus' contribution to biblical textual criticism in the *Novum Testamentum* was real; however, it was not his intention simply to advance Greek scriptural scholarship. His purpose was to establish a good and accurate Latin version of the New Testament.[94] Consequently, his criticism of the Greek text was ancillary; he engaged in emending it as an aid to the Latin translation. Textual criticism was not an end in itself and was not meant to consume his time or talents beyond a certain functional stage. But the New Testament was not the only text that received his critical scrutiny.

Among the classical writings Erasmus edited in Basel were the letters of Seneca, called *Lucubrationes*, which he issued in 1515.[95] For them, Erasmus consulted two manuscripts in England, one belonging to the library of the Archbishop of Canterbury and the other to King's College, Cambridge. He valued their corruptions, since they could offer the basis for uncovering true readings.

> These [manuscripts] were imperfect and even more full of error than the current copies. . . . One thing, however, helped me: they did not agree in error, as is bound to happen in printed texts set up from the same printers' copy; and thus, just as it sometimes happens that an experienced and attentive judge pieces together what really took place from the statements of many witnesses, none of whom is telling the truth, so I conjectured the true reading on the basis of their differing mistakes. Besides which, I tracked down many things as it were by scent, following the trail of actual letters and strokes of the pen. In some places I had to guess; although I did that sparingly, knowing that the surviving works of such great men are a sacred heritage, in which one should move not merely with caution but with proper reverence. . . . Not that I have failed to notice that many errors still remain; but they are of a kind that without the aid of ancient codices could hardly be removed by Seneca himself.[96]

Erasmus had devised a method for arriving at the lost readings locked in the faulty manuscripts. He accepted conjecture but only when employed carefully and sparingly. The manuscripts must be consulted first. In his 1517 edition of Suetonius' *Lives of the Caesars*, Erasmus prided himself on restoring a

Greek passage that had eluded all previous scholars. He was able to do so "by following the indications, such as they are, of a very ancient codex."[97] His method was fruitfully applied to the Church Fathers.

Jerome was Erasmus' favorite Latin stylist, and he worked on his letters for several years.[98] In his introduction to the 1516 edition, he discussed the difficulties he had encountered.[99] He traced the poor state of the text to incompetent scribes who did not understand the Greek and Hebrew words Jerome had written or had deliberately added to or subtracted from the text. He provided a clear explanation of his procedure and the sources of corruption.

> To begin with, the labor of comparing together so many volumes is very tedious. . . . Often I had to work with volumes which it was no easy business to read, the forms of the script being either obscured by decay and neglect, or half eaten away and mutilated by worm and beetle, or written in the fashion of Goths or Lombards, so that even to learn the letter-forms I had to go back to school; not to mention for the moment that the actual task of detecting, of smelling out as it were, anything that does not sound like a true and genuine reading requires a man in my opinion who is well informed, quick-witted, and alert. But on top of this, far the most difficult thing is either to conjecture from corruptions of different kinds what the author wrote, or to guess the original reading on the basis of such fragments and vestiges of the shapes of the script as may survive. . . . There are several reasons for this. One is that [Jerome's] actual style is far from ordinary. . . . As a result the farther his style is from the understanding of ordinary people, the more blunders it is defiled with. One man copies not what he reads but what he thinks he understands; another supposes everything he does not understand to be corrupt and changes the text as he thinks best, following no guide but his own imagination; a third detects perhaps that the text is corrupt, but while trying to emend it with an unambitious conjecture he introduces two mistakes in place of one, and while trying to cure a slight wound inflicts one that is incurable.[100]

Here Erasmus provided his readers with a concise statement of the problems facing a textual critic and the means available to solve them. In his notes to the letters, he applied his principles.

In collecting material for the edition of Jerome's letters, Erasmus consulted several manuscripts. Although he mentioned them, he did not provide much information about them. Indeed, what we know of his manuscripts must be surmised from other sources rather than his notes. The bases for the edition, in fact, were two printed editions, Rome, 1468, and Mainz, 1470. Thus, while Erasmus offered an eloquent defense of a textual method and a sound explanation of the sources of corruption, his own editorial practice does not give us a clear illustration of his principles.

Despite these limits, Erasmus in his *scholia* to the letters did provide certain general procedures that would influence Beatus Rhenanus. Although he did not specify which manuscripts provided his readings, Erasmus did cite various versions of a faulty passage. In such cases, he conjectured and tried to describe the source of error. He noted why and how confusion in the original caused transcription mistakes.[101] In general, these observations and explanations were the type Beatus would offer in his own notes as a means of explaining both the state of his text and the basis for any improvements.

The problems evident in the edition of Jerome's letters are also found in the 1519 edition of the *Opera* of the third-century bishop of Carthage, Cyprian.[102] Again, Erasmus was energetic in obtaining manuscripts. He wrote to Antonius Papinius, Abbot of the Benedictine Monastery of Gembloux, in order to obtain manuscripts of Cyprian's works.[103] The Abbot complied with his request.[104] Lefèvre supplied a manuscript from Paris.[105] Although Erasmus cited his manuscripts (those of Gembloux and the one from Paris) often, he relied to a great extent on three printed exemplars for his text.[106] Erasmus' edition also suffered from the speed with which it was prepared and issued; it took barely a year.

When Erasmus reissued the Cyprianic texts in 1530, he added a new treatise, *De duplici martyrio*. This work was spurious, written by Erasmus himself in response to the religious extremism of the Reformation but issued under Cyprian's name.[107] This was not the first time Erasmus had manufactured a pious forgery. In his *Novum Testamentum* he supplied the concluding Greek version of the Book of Revelations, which was missing in his manuscripts, by retranslating it from the Latin.[108] Obviously, Erasmus did not follow his own principle that an editor had the duty to identify and exclude spurious works. Even in such an advanced stage of his career, Erasmus could treat ancient writers in a markedly carefree manner.

There was one other area of his scholarship in which Erasmus showed his ability to deal with corrupt texts—his translations from the Greek.[109] In some cases Erasmus used manuscripts of the Greek text, while in others he depended on printed versions. In either case, his sources often contained so many errors that he had to correct them extensively and conjecture better readings. In so doing, he appreciably increased the accuracy of his Greek texts, and several of his conjectures are still accepted. In the case of Erasmus' translation of the *Tractatus tres* of Galen, Beatus Rhenanus seems even to have improved on Erasmus, adding his own corrections to the printed translations.[110]

There were limits to Erasmus' textual criticism, especially in the way he cited his manuscripts. Despite these, he did represent a new attitude toward textual problems among Northern European humanists, and his method was to replace that of Lefèvre. Erasmus had a clear understanding of the causes of manuscript corruption and the place of conjecture. He understood that a critic had at times to depart from the manuscripts and rely on his own knowledge and *ingenium,* but only when the manuscripts were compromised. Sometimes, a critic might have to depend more on his *ingenium* than manuscript authority, but ultimately he must decide the point at which this occurs, and second-guessing cannot take away from the degree of Erasmus' success.

In some ways Erasmus' approaches to textual criticism paralleled his suspicion of an extensive, in his view, allegorical interpretation of Scripture dominant in the Middle Ages and still favored by men such as Lefèvre. Attempts to interpret the text in various nonliteral senses went back to Origen, a Father whom Erasmus studied carefully and whose allegorical work he did not always accept.[111] While he employed allegory in his own work, Erasmus judged its excessive use a threat to the clear meaning of Scripture. His primary aim was to return as closely as possible to the very words of Revelation so that the truth would become clear. A text that was as reliable as possible had to be established before the truth could be expounded, and this required the removal of textual errors.

As will be seen in more detail below,[112] Erasmus did not develop a theory that incorporated textual criticism into a general view of the past. His practical attitude toward textual criticism and editing generally betrayed a limited historical orientation. Restored texts were good things because of the information they provide and the aid they offer for stylistic development. But to establish the past in its integrity, whether historically or through the restored ancient archetype, was not one of Erasmus' chief concerns. Textual criticism was a useful tool and not a distinct element of historical analysis. The text—even Sacred Scripture—had for Erasmus a certain autonomy distinct from its historical context.

Erasmus encountered great enthusiasm among the humanists in German lands, especially those in Alsace and Switzerland, whose attitudes toward religion and education mirrored his own.[113] The humanists associated with the University of Basel and Froben's printing house in particular became his close friends. These men printed manuscripts they found in German and Swiss libraries.[114] Erasmus was to show them how to perfect their exploitation of manuscripts and to make fundamental contributions to scholarship. In these humanists Erasmus found his most willing students, and among them the most loyal was Beatus Rhenanus.

2

THE NOVICE CRITIC

Beatus Rhenanus' early career as an editor and textual critic in general reflected his contacts with older, more famous scholars, above all Lefèvre d'Etaples and Erasmus. The young Beatus was strongly attracted to these forceful personalities, and his studious and sincere disposition readily responded to the dominating intellectual forces in his environment. There is a correlation between the major orientations of his early career and his associations with important contemporaries. He was not, however, simply a passive instrument of other men's wills, and as he matured he became progressively more independent in thought and action. In time, his close association with the printing press and his experiences as an editor gave him the confidence to follow his own interests and to trust his own instincts. This partial dependence and incipient independence account for his emergence rather slowly and only after some false starts as a sophisticated textual critic, philologist, and historian.

It is usual to divide Beatus' career into a series of phases—a philosophical-humanistic, a philological, and finally a theological one.[1] Although this division does recognize a dynamic element in Beatus' thought, it also misses some of the complexities within each phase. Perhaps a more useful sequence would be to posit three phases with different configurations—one that combined philosophy and pedagogy, another philology and theology, and a third philology and history—in which textual criticism was the basis for Beatus' other scholarly advances. The first stage covers Beatus' early years; the second from approximately 1515 to 1525, and the third the period from 1526, the year of the appearance of his annotations to Pliny, to his death. These were not clearly defined or fully distinct. Theology and church history, for example, early interested him and reflected his own religious views; while they remained central to his thought after 1525, they assumed a more scholarly form. The final period witnessed Beatus' most important editorial and historical productions. Still, this periodization has value, since it emphasizes the growth in Beatus' work and thought and their essentially scholarly nature.

The first period reflected Beatus' education. He grew up at a time when humanism in Germany and Northern Europe, which had been formed partly on Italian models and partly on indigenous religious traditions generally, was refashioning the educational and intellectual tenets of late medieval society.[2] Beatus responded enthusiastically to these new ideas and became their loyal advocate. While this first phase of his development highlights his dependence, it also demonstrates the fundamental basis for his later scholarship.

THE YOUNG HUMANIST

Born on 22 August 1485 in the small free imperial town of Sélestat (or Schlettstadt) in Alsace, Beatus remained throughout his life attached to the strong German patriotic sentiments that flourished in this border area.[3] His family had emigrated to Sélestat from nearby Rhinau by the middle of the fifteenth century and adopted the name Rinower in various spellings. It prospered in its new home.[4] Beatus' grandfather earned citizenship, and his father, Antonius, grew wealthy as a butcher and served in the city's government. His mother died while he was a child. Beatus lived in relative affluence, enjoying in his adult years inheritances from a rich uncle and his father. Consequently, he was able to devote much of his life to study.

As the sole survivor of three sons, Beatus could expect his father to provide for him in all ways. Antonius laid the intellectual foundations for Beatus' mature years by enrolling him in the humanistic school of Sélestat.[5] This school was the city's most famous institution, and it enjoyed renown throughout Rhineland Germany. It had been founded in 1441 by the cleric Louis Dringenberg (1410–1477).[6] Dringenberg first studied with the Brothers of the Common Life, who imbued in him the new, more personal piety that would become a hallmark of Northern European humanism; he subsequently received higher degrees from the University of Heidelberg. He established his school on the principles propagated by the Brethren—a deep religious commitment coupled with a strict pedagogical regimen. In the balance between letters and religion, the latter dominated. The curriculum Dringenberg provided for his school was conservative; it was basically a modification of the traditional medieval *trivium* and *quadrivium.* While the system was strongly influenced by scholastic abstractions and rules, Dringenberg introduced a broader, more direct contact with Latin literature. He even created a small library for his charges, although its contents were primarily religious. Its medieval character can also be seen in the lack of any instruction in Greek. Fundamentally, Dringenberg's attention centered on his students' spiritual formation rather than their literary sophistication. For him a text's value in teaching was determined by its moral tone and contents rather than its artistic or scholarly merit. Without proposing any radical pedagogical reforms, Dringenberg founded a school that appealed to the citizens of the Rhineland towns. His emphasis on character formation appealed to the civic officials and prominent burghers who wished their sons to be conscientious citizens.

After Dringenberg's death, the school passed under the direction of Krafft (or Crato) Hoffmann (1450–1501).[7] A layman who also had degrees from Heidelberg, Hoffmann was more influenced by and more committed to the new humanistic pedagogy than Dringenberg had been. While he continued his predecessor's semimedieval curriculum and his emphasis upon religious and moral development, he also introduced new classical and humanistic texts. He thus exposed his students to new ideas on language and history. His choice of ancient writers—Suetonius, Valerius Maximus, Virgil, even selections of Isocrates in Latin translation—guaranteed a morally upright education flavored with classical Latinity. Those ancient authors, above all the poets, whose topics were considered unfit for Christian youth were ignored. In addition to ancient writers, Hoffmann also employed Italian humanists' writings in his teaching. As Beatus so aptly noted of his teacher, "literas cum sanctis moribus docebat."[8]

Hoffmann's successor was Hieronymus Gebweiler (1472–1545).[9] He had studied at Basel and Paris and subscribed to the same ideals as his predecessors. Under his leadership, the humanistic elements in the curriculum increased, and he introduced new textbooks, including Lefèvre d'Etaples' philosophical primers, which reflected this orientation. It was under Gebweiler's direction that Beatus was introduced to many of the most important currents of Northern European humanism. Gebweiler had broad interests that included history (which he might have passed on to Beatus), and he became a prominent religious figure in Alsace during the early stages of the Reformation.

In this humanistic school the students came to appreciate the literary qualities of the ancients and the need to imitate the best of them, at least to a degree. As was true with German humanism generally at that stage of its development, a marked emphasis was given to late Latin writers and contemporary Italian humanistic pedagogical and literary texts. The common German humanistic idea of Latin eloquence was still far from the more exacting standard that Erasmus would champion. Yet eloquence was accepted as a proper accompaniment to good learning, since it could make every type of knowledge more attractive.

The Sélestat school resembled the important Italian humanistic schools of the fifteenth century, such as those of Guarino da Verona and Vittorino da Feltre. All these foundations functioned very much like English public or American preparatory schools. While not exclusively attended by the wealthy, the school allowed the sons of the well-to-do to receive the most modern education that emphasized the values of service and leadership; the combination reflected and validated the students' social positions. Further, since the social class of many of the students was basically the same, they fostered close ties of friendship that would guarantee the young men close relations with other prominent individuals who could assist them in their later careers. Beatus, for example, had schoolmates who became important in the religious and political affairs of Alsace and Germany in the first half of the sixteenth century and who shared his political and intellectual orientations. In the future these men would be able to aid Beatus in his civic duties and in his scholarly needs.

The instruction Beatus received in his school years (1498–1503) provided him with a sound basis for his later scholarship. Beatus was an excellent student and advanced quickly; his Latin instruction was especially good (there was only a little Greek taught at Sélestat even in Beatus' day). His later ability to conjecture successfully in difficult authors attests to the excellent linguistic foundations he acquired at school. His precociousness can be seen in his school notebooks and manuscripts, many of which survive. One, for example, contained Virgil's *Bucolics* and *Georgics* together with Ovid's *Fasti* 3–6 and book I of Martial, which he copied with a commentary when he was fourteen.[10] He readily accepted the mixture of eloquence and morality presented by his teachers. In later years he praised the Sélestat school and regretted what he felt was the decline of educational standards from those of his youth.[11]

School exposed Beatus to many elements of humanistic learning. In addition to his Latin instruction, he also received the rudiments of philosophy from Gebweiler. One important aspect of these school years was the beginning of his own book collection.[12] In time, his library was to be one of the best private scholarly collections of his day and a major research tool. Finally, the moral principles the school imbued in its students also played an influential, indeed, dominating role in his development. Like his schoolmasters, Beatus conceived of his education along strict moral and religious lines, and his learning as preparatory to a Christian life.

For his advanced training Beatus went to the University of Paris (1503–1508). His social and intellectual background are evident in this decision. Gebweiler had studied at Paris, and probably urged his best students to imitate him. Both Beatus and his father must have appreciated the contacts to be made in the great capital. Further, since Beatus did not intend to receive a professional degree, Paris offered the best opportunities for intellectual growth. Like the other accomplished students from Sélestat, Beatus sought wider horizons before returning to assume a prominent position in Alsatian life.

PARIS AND LEFÈVRE D'ETAPLES

When Beatus entered Paris on 9 May 1507, he found the university in the midst of major intellectual change and scholarly turmoil.[13] The medieval scholastic pedagogical and philosophical traditions—Scotist, Nominalist, and Thomist—competed with one another for dominance, just as the new humanistic learning was making allies among the younger faculty and students. Humanism had come to Paris partly as an import, the university having attracted several Italian humanists in the second half of the fifteenth century. These men brought their native land's literary and textual interests into an environment that had been devoted to scholastic dialectic and disputation. While Paris did not always have access to the best representatives of Italian humanism, those who did come to teach helped to establish the humanistic learning there. Moreover, the type of humanism that flourished in Paris closely resembled that of the Sélestat school. As a consequence, Beatus' experiences at Paris intensified his commitment to humanistic learning as an extension of religion and morality.

The university offered Beatus great intellectual stimulation. He continued his study of Greek and deepened his appreciation of Latin literature by attending the lectures of Italian humanists teaching at the university. Especially noteworthy was the poet Fausto Andrelini (1462–1518), some of whose writings Beatus would edit after leaving Paris.[14] The most important of his teachers, however, was Lefèvre d'Etaples. Lefèvre taught at the College of Cardinal Lemoine, where Beatus resided, and a deep mutual affection developed between master and disciple. Beatus entered Lefèvre's circle and became one of his trusted collaborators.[15]

Beatus responded positively to Lefèvre's program combining religious and philosophical values with an appreciation of literary standards, a union that complemented nicely what he had learned in Sélestat. In Beatus Lefèvre found a student who had a firm command of Latin and logic (the latter acquired by reading Lefèvre's writings in Sélestat) and who possessed a serious attitude toward his studies. Lefèvre increased Beatus' moral view of scholarship, and the young German esteemed his teacher as a major philosopher and a positive force in the restoration of good learning.

Above all, Lefèvre introduced his talented student to printing. Because of its university, Paris was a great center of European publishing. Lefèvre appreciated the value of the printing press in disseminating his scholarly and moral ideals, and he enlisted his best students to work with the press. Beatus first acted as an editor and proofreader for the Parisian printer, Henri Estienne.[16] Thus Lefèvre helped set the basic direction of Beatus' later career as an editor.

For Estienne, Beatus contributed to several publications associated with Lefèvre and his group. He composed a poem for the title page of the commentary on Lefèvre's *Artificialis introductio per modum Epitomatis in decem libros Ethicorum Aristotelis* by Lefèvre's close friend and another of Beatus' teachers, Josse Clichtove (1506/1507).[17] In 1505 Beatus contributed verses to Lefèvre's commentaries on Leonardo Bruni's humanistic translations of Aristotle's *Oeconomica* and *Politica*. Similarly, he supplied verses for Lefèvre's translation of John of Damascus' *Theologia*.[18] For Lefèvre's edition of Ramón Lull's *Contemplationes*, published in 1505 by the house of Jean Petit, Beatus again wrote an introductory poem.[19] These activities show Beatus' favor with Lefèvre and his printers. Beatus became acquainted with Josse Bade Ascensius, a close friend of Lefèvre and Erasmus and a publisher of humanistic and classical texts.[20]

While Beatus was able to learn at first hand about printing, it is unlikely that his work for Estienne and Petit fostered a critical attitude toward manuscripts. As noted above, Lefèvre and his circle had little interest in textual and philological matters. They concentrated on issuing reprints of moral and philosophical treatises and translations of Greek texts; it was not their intention to spend much time searching out and correcting old and unknown manuscripts. Even when they relied on manuscript versions for publication, they tended to select recent ones that were relatively easy to read and that presented fewer editorial difficulties than the copies of ancient writings. Still, Beatus' Parisian experiences dominated his intellectual concerns for a decade. As homage to his university days, Beatus concluded his

great history of Germany, the *Rerum Germanicarum libri tres*
(1531), with praise for Paris.[21]

Beatus returned to Alsace in Autumn 1507 with a master of
arts degree. He brought with him the ideals of Lefèvre's moral
and intellectual reform program and a belief in the importance
of printing for their successful propagation. He planned a trip
to Italy to further his education, but political upheavals south of
the Alps deterred him.[22] While he never visited Italy, Beatus
did find much to keep him intellectually occupied at home, and
he probably felt that he already had had contact with some of
the most important contemporary cultural innovators. He continued to correspond with his friends in Paris, and with new
ones in Germany, such as Johannes Reuchlin. Beatus settled in
Strasbourg where he participated in that city's *sodalitas litteraria,*
and he was also a member of a similar *sodalitas* of Sélestat,
founded by the humanist Jacob Wimpfeling, and of Basel.[23]
These *sodalitates* included a number of local scholars, littera-
teurs, and civic figures with shared humanistic interests. Beatus'
most important undertakings were again press-related. With
his Parisian publishing experience still fresh, he became associated with printers in Strasbourg, where he resided from 1507
till 1511. He first worked for the printer Johannes Gruninger,
for whom he prepared some verses of the popular Italian humanist poet Baptista Mantuanus.[24]

More significant was his association with the press of Matthias Schürer.[25] Schürer (1470–1519) had been Beatus' contemporary at school in Sélestat. Schürer founded his firm in 1508
and used it to disseminate humanist learning; he was also the
first in Alsace to print Greek texts. Beatus began his work for
Schürer by producing an edition of Fausto Andrelini's *Epistolae
proverbiales et morales.*[26] In this new publishing environment
Beatus continued to draw on his Parisian friends for inspiration. His editions of Trebizond's *Dialectica,* Andrelini's *Epistolae,*
and Baptista Mantuanus' *De fortuna Marchionis Mantuae* followed upon his receiving the Paris editions of these works.[27]
This was not to be a unilateral relationship, however. The Parisian edition of writings of Nemesius of Emesa (mistakenly attributed to Gregory of Nyssa) was a reprint of the one on which
Beatus collaborated.[28]

Beatus' post-Parisian printing program covered a variety of topics: Latin eloquence, Neo-Platonism, patristics, humanist pedagogy—areas that reflected Lefèvre's influence. Significant in these was the number of Italian humanist treatises. Northern humanism generally depended on Italian sources for grammatical, rhetorical, and philological models as well as for classical editions. There was a growing audience for these books, and publishers were anxious to supply it with a variety of new versions of Italian imprints.[29] Beatus naturally felt at home in this pursuit, since his teachers both at Sélestat and at Paris had used and praised the Italian humanistic blending of good Latin with current scholarship.

BASEL AND ERASMUS

In 1511 Beatus moved to Basel, and this initiated a new phase in his intellectual development.[30] He was drawn to that city originally by a desire to improve his command of Greek. Although he remained throughout his life a Latin scholar, indeed one of the best of his day,[31] Beatus studied Greek at Sélestat and at Paris under the direction of Georgius Hermonymus and François Tissard. It was at Paris that he purchased his first Greek text.[32] He mastered the language well enough to offer textual emendation to Greek passages in his later work. But his fullest study of Greek came in Basel, where he found a teacher in the Dominican patrologist and Hellenist, Johannes Cuno of Nuremberg (1463–1513).[33]

Like many other humanists of his generation, Cuno had gone to Italy to complete his education.[34] There he encountered some of the newest trends in humanistic thought. Cuno studied at the University of Padua (1503–1510), where he came under the influence of the growing Hellenic revival. He benefited from attending the lectures of excellent teachers, above all the Greek scholars John Gregoropoulos and Marcus Musurus and the Italian Hellenist Scipione Fortiguerra, called Carteromachos.[35] Musurus was the most prominent of these; he edited the major ancient Greek plays for Aldus Manutius and commanded a Europe-wide reputation. His students acquired a good command of the Greek classics and the technique of correcting

Greek texts and rendering them into appropriate Latin. Under Musurus' direction Cuno collected a series of Greek manuscripts, especially those containing the writings of the Fathers of the Church, who were to be his special interest. Cuno remained devoted to his teachers and had a high regard for their abilities.[36]

In Venice Cuno developed a close relationship with the Aldine press.[37] He was privy to Aldus Manutius' thoughts and reported that the Italian at one point contemplated moving his press to Germany. Cuno brought to Basel a spirit of careful scholarship and the zeal to propagate classical studies which had inspired Aldus to undertake the *editiones principes* of several Greek writers. Aldus propagated among his associates the desirability of providing readers with clear Greek or Latin texts rather than issuing detailed commentaries with much tangential information that deemphasized the words of the authors; the text, not lengthy digressive commentaries on it, was to be the editor's sole concern, and Cuno accepted this rule.

Cuno's influence accounts for a new element in Beatus' editing. In 1512 Beatus contributed to Cuno's edition of Nemesius of Emesa's *De natura hominis* (but misattributed to Gregory of Nyssa) in Latin.[38] Beatus received Cuno's corrected version of Burgundio of Pisa's Latin version. He added his own translation of two letters of Gregory of Nazianzus, from a Greek copy Cuno had taken from Musurus' collection,[39] and dedicated his introductory letter to Lefèvre.[40] While this undertaking offered Beatus only limited opportunity for textual criticism, since he concerned himself with stylistic and translation matters, Cuno helped him become aware of the problems in correcting Greek texts.[41] Also of importance to Beatus' development were the Greek manuscripts that Cuno left Beatus at his death.[42] Thus Cuno provided Beatus with the opportunity not only to advance his command of Greek but also to deal with some new editorial elements. While his influence on Beatus would be surpassed by that of Erasmus, Cuno was of value in his scholarly development.

The edition of these patristic writings was issued by the press of Johannes Froben in Basel, and that printing house was the other great attraction of Basel for Beatus. While there were to be disagreements with Froben which led to periods of estrangement, Beatus' association with Froben was fundamental to his career. By the time of Beatus' arrival in Basel in 1511, the press that had been founded by Johannes Amerbach and continued by Johannes Froben was among the most famous in Northern Europe for its patristic and humanistic editions.[43] The Fathers, above all the Latin Fathers, were to be among the prime interests of the press.[44] In order to accomplish his plan of issuing versions of the Latin Fathers, Amerbach and his successors solicited manuscripts from various monasteries, which they corrected for publication.[45]

One scholar prominent in Amerbach's program was the cleric, doctor of theology, and his former teacher, Johannes Heynlin of Steyn (de Lapide) (1430/33–1496).[46] Heynlin had studied in Paris, where he had begun his work for the press. He edited selected writings of Ambrose, Cassiodorus, Aristotle, and the German Benedictine, Johannes Trithemius. He was a careful critic, anxious to produce accurate texts. He used marginal notes to explain difficult passages and to offer some variant readings. His edition of Cassiodorus' *Expositio Psalmorum* provides an interesting example of the conservatism of editorial practice, since it formed the basis for all subsequent editions including the standard modern one.[47] Considering the long-term value of many of Amerbach's editions, it is regrettable that details of the editorial practices of his press are few.

Beatus easily fitted into the Amerbach-Froben printing establishment, since Amerbach's sons, Bruno and Basil, had been his schoolmates at Sélestat and Paris.[48] Moreover, the press depended on students, recent graduates, and professors from the University of Basel as advisers, editors, and proofreaders; this was a group close to Beatus in age and interests. Beatus' success at Froben's can be measured by the important duties he assumed there, even acting as a general editor and corrector for his own and other scholars' work and living for a time in Froben's house. Through this close editorial work, Beatus became increasingly aware of how errors could enter into printed books and the difficulties implicit in correcting manuscripts for publication. Despite the hectic nature of the printing shop, Beatus had great enthusiasm for his work and urged his friends to send any materials they had which the press could issue.[49]

Especially attractive to Beatus (as it was to be to Erasmus) was the firm's stated intention to issue editions of the Latin Fathers. Italian humanistic writings formed a notable element in Beatus' early editing. It is useful to consider these reprints in further detail in order to define the intellectual content of his early work. We may divide them somewhat arbitrarily into three categories.[50] The first consists of educational treatises, including, among others, the *De modo et ordine docendi ac discendi* (1514) by Battista Guarino (1453–1505), son of the famous educator, Guarino da Verona, George of Trebizond's *Dialectica,* and Theodore of Gaza's (1400–1478) *Grammaticae institutiones* in a translation by Erasmus (1516). The second category included literary and historical treatises. This larger group featured the works of some prominent Italian scholars: Pomponio Leto's (1428–1497) *Compendium historiae romanae;* Filippo Beroaldo the Elder's *De terrae motu et pestilentia cum annotamentis Galeni;* Mantuanus' *De fortuna Francisci Marchionis Mantuae;* and Andrea Alciati's (1492–1550) annotations to Tacitus (1519). The smaller texts within this subdivision were poems and orations. As a unit, they were all meant to demonstrate especially the place of eloquence in humanist education.

The final group centered on moral philosophy and theology. Among these works were Andrelini's *Epistolae* and *De virtutibus cum moralibus tum intellectualibus* (1508); Gianfrancesco Pico della Mirandola's (1469–1533) *Hymni heroici tres;* and Paolo Cortesi's (1465–1510) *In Sententias,* a humanist reworking of Peter Lombard's theological primer *Liber Sententiarum* (which Bade also issued in the same year). Beatus considered them models for the blending of Latin eloquence with philosophy and theology. In most cases Beatus simply reproduced previously printed treatises, limiting his contributions to new introductions (in which he took every opportunity to praise his old university professors and their accomplishments) and stylistic improvements. Their derivative nature limited the opportunity they offered for textual criticism.

With the exception of Alciati's annotations on Tacitus, Beatus drew from the Italians more moral and pedagogical lessons than philological or historical ones. Still, he was familiar with some of the best Italian editors and philologists through his growing library.[51] It included Filippo Beroaldo the Elder's commentaries on Apuleius' *Golden Ass* and Pliny, and Barbaro's *Castigationes* on Pliny and Pomponius Mela. More significantly, Beatus owned and used Poliziano's *opera*, especially his *Miscellanea*. Beatus had to rely on such texts for his information on Italian scholarship. Unlike Erasmus, who had visited Italy and had found an early guide in Lorenzo Valla, Beatus depended on no single Italian model but combined his own experiences, Northern European scholarship, and readings in Italian philology to develop as a textual critic.

Basel and Froben's press further contributed to Beatus' textual skills by allowing him to meet and associate with like-minded scholars. At Froben's Beatus encountered other young graduates who shared his devotion to classical and early Christian studies. Above all, Beatus met Desiderius Erasmus upon the former's arrival in Basel in 1515 to work on Froben's edition of the *opera* of Jerome.[52] The relationship between the two men was to be very close and one that both cherished. Erasmus dedicated his commentary on Psalm I, *Beatus vir* and his *Epistolae ad diversos* to Beatus and was supportive of his scholarship.[53] Beatus had a keen interest in Erasmus' writings and acted as an advocate of his friend's interests with Froben. He helped to correct Erasmus' publications and solicited more for the press. He even clashed with Froben and his partner Wolfgang Lachner in order to secure proper treatment for Erasmus.[54] Beatus' advocacy of Erasmus' writings was part of his general struggle to keep Froben dedicated to scholarly enterprises and prevent him from issuing collections of texts and engaging in fast money-making activities that, in Beatus' opinion, had come to dominate the output of the press.

Although Erasmus called him his alter ego, and Beatus was to write the first serious biography of his friend,[56] there were important differences between them. Above all, there were their divergent attitudes toward history, a matter that will be investigated later. But when they first met, Erasmus' obvious brilliance and fame exerted a great attraction on Beatus. As he grew closer to Erasmus, Beatus began to move away from the ideas and interests that had characterized his apprenticeship with Lefèvre. The Dutch scholar had little patience for Lefèvre's mystical-philosophical theology and published a different set of authors. More important Erasmus and Lefèvre publicly and acrimoniously clashed over the interpretation of Scripture.[57] Simply put, Erasmus moved Beatus toward a new concentration on textual criticism and away from Lefèvre's mystical philosophy.[58] Despite his great importance to Beatus, Erasmus was not solely responsible for what Beatus was to become. There were limits to what Erasmus could teach his younger friend, and it is necessary when assessing their intellectual affinities not to lose sight of their differences in the face of the obvious similarities and Beatus' devotion to Erasmus.

From the beginning of their association, Erasmus led Beatus into new and more complex textual questions. Beatus observed his friend's editorial technique at first hand by assisting in his publishing ventures. As mentioned earlier,[59] Erasmus' attitude toward his texts was practical: textual problems had to be solved in order to produce a clean text with which to instruct the public; above all, corrected texts were to provide a trustworthy basis for educational and moral reform. To Erasmus the chief tasks of an editor were to correct the text, to separate authentic from apocryphal works, and to explain difficult passages. In his editing Erasmus worked from a base text, usually printed, which he corrected with the assistance of available manuscripts. In many ways Erasmus' genius lay in his ability to conjecture brilliantly.

Beatus first observed Erasmus at work while assisting in the edition of Seneca's *Lucubrationes,* a collection of the Roman's letters and other writings (1515).[60] Beatus and his colleagues at the press had the responsibility of overseeing its printing and proofreading. In fact, they did much more. They made substantive contributions on their own and corrected the text when they felt there were obvious errors even though they lacked manuscript authority. Erasmus' Seneca became one of Beatus' first attempts at textual criticism of a classical author, and it had some significance in his editorial career.

In a letter to Erasmus written during the printing of the *Lucubrationes,* Beatus called to his friend's attention the poor state of certain passages and the corrections he had made to them. He explained that "On the spur of the moment, when that sheet [which contained the errors] had already begun to be printed, I emended it like this; whether I was as clever as I was brave, I do not know."[61] He cited some of his changes:

> I have done [i.e., emended] in many places, restoring, for instance, 'dementissime' for 'clementisse', 'peierat' for 'perierat', 'detestabili via' for 'de stabili via', 'vota' for 'nota', and much else of the same sort.

For the most part Beatus' emendations were minor, but he felt uncomfortable in making them, as he admitted:

> But I do not like always relying on my own judgment, especially ex tempore, and under pressure from men who cannot stand delay. If only we had an ancient copy, there is nothing I should enjoy more than to emend this text in the places that are still left uncorrected, for by so doing I should be of use to scholars and advance your reputation, although you do say in your preface that you have removed most of the mistakes but not all.[62]

In another letter to Erasmus, where he discussed the printing of Seneca, Beatus regretted the poor work of the proofreader and expressed his own attitude toward such work:

> I could wish the copy were clearer and the reader a little more careful. But he does not detect all the mistakes, nor am I the man, if he sometimes does detect them, to set them all to rights, both because my knowledge is so very limited and because to be over-clever in someone else's book has something foolish about it.[63]

The laudable conservative attitude evident in these sentiments would characterize the rest of Beatus' career.

Despite the care Beatus took in making his changes, Erasmus complained of poor proofreading. He had provided the press with a rather complicated manuscript that caused the correctors a great deal of trouble. The vagueness of Erasmus' instructions and the amount of work he left to the printers to do, however, partly exculpates Froben's staff. Wilhelm Nesen, whose work Erasmus faulted, was so confused by the lack of specific instructions that he did not know which of Erasmus' marginal notes should be included in the body of the text.[64]

The principles Erasmus proclaimed in his edition of Seneca naturally influenced Beatus.[65] Still, he lacked the immediate opportunity to put them into practice. In 1515 Beatus published Seneca's *Ludus de morte Claudii* or *Apocolocyntosis,* and Synesius Cyrenensis' *De laudibus calvitii* (which were issued together with Erasmus' *Moriae encomium*). In the case of the *Apocolocyntosis* Beatus worked from the defective 1513 *editio princeps* produced by the Professor of Rhetoric at the University of Rome, C. Sylvanus Germanicus.[66] The Roman edition was extremely poor, since it was based on one defective manuscript that lacked the Greek phrases Seneca had inserted. Germanicus' attempts at supplying these deficiencies were unsuccessful, and there was much for later editors to do. In order to explain the numerous ancient allusions in the text, Beatus produced a series of scholia. Lacking any manuscript authority, he resorted to conjecture; this was especially the case with missing Greek quotations for which the 1513 edition provided no help.[67] Five years later, in his edition of Velleius Paterculus, Beatus mentioned criticisms that others had made of his scholia. There were those, he said, who faulted his rashness in restoring some passages and questioned his understanding of them. Beatus defended himself, on the one hand, by recalling the poor state of the text, which had made his task difficult, and on the other, by noting that conjectures were always necessary in interpreting poetry. Rhetorically he asked, "And is it not a great thing to have part of a precious thing if it is not possible to have the whole?"[68] This was not the last time Beatus would have to defend his textual procedures against critics.

Erasmus' editions of Jerome's letters, the New Testament, and the *opera* of Cyprian of Carthage also served as useful models for Beatus, especially the first, since he acted as one of its proofreaders.[69] In 1520 Beatus aided Erasmus in trying to obtain a Parisian manuscript for his edition of Cyprian of Carthage's *opera*.[70] Because of Erasmus' vague method of citing his manuscripts, Beatus could have extracted only generalized ideas about manuscript consultation from these editions. What he certainly did learn from Erasmus was the need to correct texts by recourse to manuscripts and the importance of making his material accessible to the reader. For example, Erasmus supplied annotations, a life of the author, and other important supporting materials to his edition of Cyprian to make the text more useful, and Beatus incorporated these elements in his own editions. Thus Erasmus proved to be of real if limited value to Beatus in the development of a critical use of manuscripts. Consequently, it is proper to date Beatus' career as a textual critic from his encounter with Erasmus. In following him, Beatus rejected the procedure he had learned from Lefèvre and advanced on the principles Cuno had represented.

THE *EDITIO PRINCEPS* OF VELLEIUS PATERCULUS

A new element evident in Beatus' work at this period was history. Erasmus did not offer him much of a model for historical scholarship; indeed, Erasmus and Beatus had very different attitudes toward history, a topic which will be discussed later.[71] However, Erasmus did edit a series of ancient biographies that had a historical dimension: these included Quintus Curtius Rufus' *History of Alexander the Great* (1517) in cooperation with Beatus, and the *Scriptores Historiae Augustae,* together with Suetonius' *Lives of the Caesars,* in 1518.[72] Further, Beatus' teacher Gebweiler composed a chronicle of Strasbourg.[73] Beatus' associates in Paris, while not historians, did study French history and issued some historical texts.[74] Before 1519 he had engaged in some minor historical work. He wrote a biography of the popular preacher Geiler von Kaiserberg,[75] contributed to an edition of material relating to Emperor Henry IV,[76] and edited Pomponio Leto's *Opera,* which discussed Roman antiquities. In his dedicatory letter to Leto's *Opera* (1510), addressed to the historian Dietrich Gresemund, he discussed antiquities and ancient monuments and his own investigation of ancient ruins.[77] Occasional references in his correspondence show his interest in historical topics. For example, a 1510 letter to Reuchlin mentions the *Itinerarium* of Antoninus, which Beatus would use in his mature historical compositions.[78] There was a strong patriotic quality to Alsatian humanism which manifested itself in writing history.[79] Beatus knew this tradition, although he never manifested the narrow chauvinism that informed some of these histories. Chance also played a part in Beatus' growing concentration on history. He fortuitously discovered important manuscripts. Still, had he not been inclined to follow their lead and had not history interested him deeply, he never would have devoted the bulk of the remainder of his life to it. Significantly, once he began to work closely with texts, Beatus' historical sensitivities became more marked.

The first proof of Beatus' development as a historian is his short commentary, or *Commentariolus,* on Tacitus' *Germania.*[80] As a proud German, he naturally valued this unique description of the early Germans.[81] The *Commentariolus* demonstrated Beatus' understanding of historical change. Unlike his fellow German humanist historians, Beatus appreciated the disjunctions between ancient, medieval, and modern Germany. Few scholars had handled historical change so securely and knowingly or had realized so well the differences among the several stages of German history. Unfortunately, Beatus issued his edition without new manuscript sources; he relied on the 1515 Roman printing of Tacitus edited by Filippo Beroaldo the Younger.[82]

Since Beatus' aim in the *Commentariolus* was to dispel the confusion resulting from the different names given to the German tribes and their changing residences, he had to give careful consideration to the names as they appear in their ancient and modern forms and if and why they might have been corrupted. In so doing, he enunciated a view of conjectural textual analysis based on historical premises. The reader, he argued, must understand "at what time [a text] was written, by whom and about what, then compare the new texts with the older or vice versa, always keeping in mind the changes which have taken place. If you follow this our admonition, you will feel a great advantage in these histories."[83] Such sound principles without manuscript support meant that Beatus conjectured on what he felt were scribal errors.[84]

Beatus drew on a variety of historical sources. Among contemporaries he cited the Italian jurist Andrea Alciati, whose annotations on Tacitus Beatus published in 1519,[85] and, unfortunately, the history of Berosus, which had been fabricated by the Italian Dominican Annius of Viterbo but which was generally accepted then as genuine.[86] Among the ancients, he quoted Pliny, Pomponius Mela, Solinus, Ptolemy and Velleius Paterculus.[87] In addition to these, Beatus also relied on his knowledge of German etymology to explain names and terms.[88] This treatment shows that Beatus had not yet come to a full appreciation of Tacitus. For example, he referred to Tacitus' *Historiae* for the conflated texts of the *Annales* and *Historiae;* later he would be the first to employ the name *Annales*.[89]

One of the most arresting elements in the *Commentariolus* is Beatus' use of the term *media aetas*.[90] Some scholars assign to Beatus a priority in the use of the term *medieval* to designate a modern periodization scheme. Close inspection shows that Beatus used the term somewhat inconsistently. While he understood the differences between writers of various historical periods, he did not make clear distinctions between the writers within these periods. Late ancient and late medieval writers could fall into the same temporal division, thus providing an overbroad chronology. Nevertheless, the use of the term does have some interest for Beatus' textual work, since it establishes his realization of the temporal differences as a key to correctly identifying ancient references. Its use, even with its divergences from modern usage, confirms the sense of historical disjunction in Beatus' thought, which is necessary for any fruitful textual work.

Beatus' performance in the *Commentariolus* highlights his beginnings as a careful philologist and historian. Further, it shows him to be superior to his predecessors in cutting through centuries of terminological confusion and arriving at a more accurate understanding of Tacitus' narrative. The *Germania* commentary was a worthy prologue to his major historical enterprises, his annotations on Tacitus in 1533 and 1544, and his great history of Germany, the *Res Germanicae*.[91]

Beatus' first independent opportunity to treat a historical text came in 1515 when by chance he discovered in the Benedictine Monastery of Murbach the unique copy of Velleius Paterculus' *Historia Romana,* a name he gave to the titleless manuscript. In early 1521 the *editio princeps* of Velleius Paterculus appeared.[92] Velleius' treatise was a compendium of early Roman history and an account of contemporary events to the reign of Tiberius.[93] Since only part of the full text has survived, it is impossible to determine the author's general plan. Velleius was a soldier (who was especially familiar with events in Germany) and bureaucrat who turned to history as an avocation. His ability to condense material did not always produce a clear narrative, but since he was a devotee of accuracy, his history has real merit for its biographical information and his attention to literature and the arts. Especially appealing to Beatus was the extensive treatment of German events that Velleius knew at first hand. While lacking the literary or analytical qualities of a Livy or a Tacitus, Velleius still holds a place in classical historiography because of the paucity of surviving material relevant to his period. To a sixteenth-century humanist this previously all but unknown historian of a crucial time in Roman and German history was a spectacular find.

The *Historia Romana* was Beatus' first venture dependent solely on a manuscript source, and it shows his limitations clearly. He had to work from a fragmentary and erasure-filled manuscript, probably of the eleventh century, which had no beginning and was greatly mutilated. As Beatus noted in his introduction, the manuscript was *prodigiose corruptum*, "so that everything had to be restored through human talent."[94] Granting the poor state of the manuscript, Beatus followed a faulty editorial procedure. Instead of working directly from the manuscript, he corrected a transcription done by an unnamed friend who due to the speed of his work (*properanter ac infeliciter ab amico quodam descriptum*) produced an even more corrupt copy. Beatus had delayed issuing his edition for three years in the hope that he could obtain a copy that he believed Giorgio Merula had discovered (he came to reject this opinion, properly). Finally, "a most learned man" (perhaps Erasmus) urged him to publish what he had. To aid the reader, he added a biography of Velleius that, he admitted, was mostly hypothetical,[95] and a title. The poor condition of the manuscript concerned him greatly, and he censured those who had allowed ancient authors to become so corrupt. Still, improvement was always possible as long as manuscripts, even corrupt ones, could be restored through learning and judgment.[96] Beatus complimented those few learned Benedictines who once had been active in preserving writers such as Velleius but regretted that, later, other monks had turned against the ancient writers and prevented their study.[97]

Beatus did not personally supervise the printing of Velleius, since he was at Sélestat due to a resurgence of plague at Basel and perhaps also because of his father's poor health (he died on 15 November 1520).[98] He sent his corrected copy together with the original to the printers and instructed them to consult the original as well as his copy. The printers did not follow his instructions but simply set the faulty copy. Beatus became aware of this only in the middle of the printing process when his scribe and familiar, Albert Burer, called it to his attention.[99] Burer acted as the man on the scene in Basel for his employer while Beatus was away. In order to improve the text, Burer collated the Murbach manuscript with the printed version and appended a series of corrections to the *editio princeps*.[100]

In his emendations Burer provided variant readings from the manuscript. But he also conjectured what he felt were better readings, in part by reference to other historical sources, in part by drawing on his knowledge of Latin, and in part by analyzing corruptions. He noted marginal readings and scribal errors.[101] Perhaps most interesting among his comments were his discussions of the paleographical qualities of the old manuscript.

> Indeed, those who have read through copies of ancient authors, will have read often—not always and everywhere—*t* for *d*, and again *d* for *t*, so that *haut* for *haud*, *aput* for *apud*, and *at* for *ad*, and many things of this type. They are acquainted likewise with many copies of the ancients written without majuscule letters, without punctuation, and further without spaces at all between the phrases.[102]

A further specification about the paleographical aspect of the manuscript also helps to date it. Burer noted that *a* was written as *cc* and that this is found *in quibusdam aliis veterum codicibus*. This would indicate that the manuscript was written in a form of Caroline minuscule.[103] Burer's observations may be taken as an indication of the growing sensitivity to paleographical characteristics in Froben's shop by Beatus and his associates.

Alerted by Burer, Beatus tried to improve his work by adding marginal notes even during printing. In these he explained specific historical points that remained unclear in the text. To indicate possible alternate manuscript readings, he used an *alias* before the proposed word; his own conjectures were made clear through the use of *forte* or such phrases as *forte legendum est* and *puto legendum esse*. In explaining difficult passages he informed his readers when there were lacunae,[104] and when the scribe's ignorance resulted in error.[105] In a concluding letter addressed to the reader, Beatus despaired of further emendation without new manuscript support. He reiterated his complaint about the poor state of the Murbach codex and the time he had spent on it, a theme that was to be repeated in his work on Tertullian.[106] The Velleius edition showed that he had some distance to go before he could be considered an accomplished textual critic.[107]

Despite Burer's and Beatus' attentions, the printed Velleius remained in a confused state. One problem is the differences among various copies of the *editio princeps* that contain Burer's emendations, divergences resulting from the stop-press procedure.[108] They show that Beatus normalized certain readings at one stage of the printing but later changed them. These alterations and the uncertainty of finding them in any specific exemplar make it "difficult to obtain a clear and systematic picture of Rhenanus' editorial practice."[109] It also shows that Beatus did not have a clear procedure for improving his edition. He continued to make emendations in his own copy of Velleius but he never used his later critical talents to produce a new, more accurate edition, probably because no new manuscript evidence became available.[110]

At the same time that he was working on his edition of Velleius, Beatus was also preparing two sets of historical-rhetorical treatises for Froben. His pedagogical interests and Froben's needs for marketable material account for the publication of a series of rhetorical treatises, the *Rhetores latini minores*, derived from a manuscript in the library of Speyer.[111] These minor pieces, which included works of Rutilius Lupus, Aquila Romanus, Sulpitius Victor, Fortunatianus Atilius, and Augustine, had been popular in the Middle Ages and received much attention from humanists, including Petrarch. Although of limited importance in Beatus' overall production, it is a further example of his growing concentration on manuscripts.

The second collection consisted of seventeen ancient and modern panegyrics, including Pliny on Trajan, Ermolao Barbaro on the Emperors Frederick III and Maximilian, and Erasmus on the Duke of Burgundy.[112] In a dedicatory letter to Lucas Bathodius, a local cleric,[113] Beatus stated that he had to follow his own judgment in preparing the texts, since he lacked any old manuscripts to compare to the versions he had. In the text Beatus cited his conjectures with such phrases as *alias* and *legendum ut puto*. For the panegyrics in honor of the Emperor Constantine and his successors, Beatus provided historical information and short introductions to several of them to assist the reader.[114]

THE *EDITIO PRINCEPS* OF TERTULLIAN

On 11 March 1521, Beatus wrote to George Spalatin, the adviser to the Elector Frederich of Saxony and one of Martin Luther's early supporters, discussing the edition of Velleius Paterculus that he had dedicated to the Elector. Beatus took the opportunity to comment favorably on Luther and to review recent military events. He added a postscript about his most recent undertaking.

> I am now publishing the *opera* of Tertullian, nay rather the faulty [version of Tertullian's writings]. For certain books are so remarkably corrupt, that hardly one sentence remains. But still it ought to be continued since I began it. I neither hunt nor reach out for glory [in doing this]. I merely wish to be of use [to others].[115]

This modest attitude was as typical of Beatus as were his complaints about the state of his manuscripts. In both cases the statements were true.

The *editio princeps* of Tertullian's *opera* was the most significant product of Beatus' early editorial career.[116] The Church Fathers had been special favorites of his Sélestat teachers, Lefèvre, Cuno, and Erasmus; the Amerbach and Froben press had taken the Latin Fathers as its special task. It was logical that Beatus should become involved in the Renaissance revival of patristics. The humanists found in the Fathers a Christian paral-

lel to their interest in pagan antiquity and a valuable support
for their advocacy of rhetorical education over scholastic pedagogy.[117] Froben seems to have been proud of the work and gave
it a fine artistic presentation complete with woodcuts by Hans
Holbein the Younger.[118]

Tertullian had a peculiar *fortuna* since the second century.[119]
While he was the first Latin Christian theologian, he departed
from the Roman Church on several issues. Essentially an ex-
treme moralist, his unforgiving disposition toward sin and the
sinner led him to join the rigorist heretical Montanist sect.[120]
His association with this movement helped make all his work
suspect to the orthodox. While read throughout the early Middle Ages, his vehement denunciation of philosophy and secular
knowledge caused the scholastics to avoid him. He appealed to
the humanists because of the rhetorical strain in his theology
and the valuable information on the early Church he supplied.
Since only Tertullian's *Apologeticus* had been published before
1521 (the *editio princeps* was Venice 1483), Beatus' edition was a
major event in patristic studies.

The circulation of Tertullian's writings in the Middle Ages is
a complicated matter.[121] Six collections of his treatises with differing selections were made in attempts to produce an orthodox *corpus*. Of these six versions the most important is the so-
called *Corpus Cluniacense,* which was probably gathered in the
mid-sixth century in Spain and included over twenty treatises.
All the manuscripts Beatus used were related to the Cluny collection. Beatus, therefore, had at his disposal a large body of
Tertullian's writings, in versions, unfortunately, which were not
the best representatives of their family.

In his prefatory letter, dedicated to Erasmus' friend, the Hungarian bishop and patron of humanistic learning, Stanislaus
Turzo of Olmutz (dated 1 July 1521),[122] Beatus explained the
rationale for his edition. He compared his rescuing of Tertullian through the comparison of manuscripts to rendering unknown Greek writers into Latin and improving existing translations as a contribution to the cultural advances *in hoc vere aureo
renascentium Literarum secolo.* He began his study of Tertullian in
1520, when Jacob Zimmerman, dean of Colmar, permitted him
to study a "certain old codex" of some of the African Father's

writings which had formerly belonged to the monastic library of Payerne or Peterlingen, hence called the *Paterniacensis.* (It passed into Beatus' own library in Sélestat, where it remains as Ms. 88.) The manuscript, probably of the late twelfth or early thirteenth century, is written in late Caroline minuscule.[123] Subsequently, through another friend, Thomas Rupp, Beatus obtained a second Tertullian manuscript in two volumes from the Benedictine monastery of Hirsau in Wurtemberg. (The manuscript is lost.)

The arduous task of editing these defective manuscripts was compounded by the limited availability of the printing presses (two were used to print the *opera*). Beatus' original intention had been to print the Payerne text complemented by readings from the Hirsau manuscript where they overlapped, but he had to abandon this plan because of their corrupt state; a careful comparison had to be undertaken of those texts they had in common (they shared nine treatises).[124] Wishing not to tamper with a religious work, Beatus maintained in the text those corrupt passages he could not correct so that the reader could judge them.[125] He regretted that lack of time prevented his consultation of other and better manuscripts that existed in the monasteries of Gorze and Fulda and in Rome.[126]

While these procedures improved on those employed in Velleius, problems still remained. Though Beatus identified his manuscripts and gave the reader some idea of their condition, he did not delay publication to consult other manuscripts even though he knew they existed. Fortune, as he noted, was responsible for his work on Tertullian, but he did not greatly assist her. This reluctance to wait is especially unfortunate, since the Hirsau and Payerne manuscripts did not contain all the same texts; together they account for only twenty-three of Tertullian's treatises, including one pseudo-Tertullian work.[127] On the positive side, they did represent different branches of the same textual tradition. Beatus merely reproduced the 1515 Aldine edition of the previously printed *Apologeticus,* which was not included in either manuscript.

A recent study by M. Pierre Petitmengin comparing the surviving Payerne manuscript with the *editio princeps* provides a valuable commentary on Beatus' treatment of his manuscript sources at this formative stage of his career.[128] In addition to adding much information about the text, the article throws further light on the printing procedures of Froben's shop during Beatus' tenure there.

M. Petitmengin has shown that Beatus marked his manuscript in various ways as a means of instructing the typesetters. Within the manuscript itself he standardized orthography and punctuation. In the margins he indicated, by circling words and phrases, those that were to be set as marginal notes, while he marked as insertions those phrases that were to be incorporated into the text as emendations or corrections. Words that were to be set as capitals were underlined or rewritten in capitals. Sideheadings in capitals meant to highlight specific sections were spelled out in the margins of the manuscript at the points where they were to be incorporated into the printed version. (These notes are not always legible due to cropping of the manuscript.) The manuscript so marked, curiously, does not correspond in all particulars to the printed text. Additions and subtractions in the notes and emendations show that Beatus was the corrector for the book as it came off the presses. In arranging the treatises, Beatus reordered what he found in the manuscript. All the changes that Beatus made on his manuscript make it difficult to follow his procedures with certainty and may have caused problems for the typesetter.

Beatus displayed his textual improvements in several ways.[129] As noted above, obvious errors were corrected in the manuscript and silently printed. For the nine treatises where the Payerne and Hirsau manuscripts overlapped, Beatus based his text on the Payerne and emended it from the Hirsau text (he did not justify this preference for one manuscript). The two manuscripts had variant readings in part because the Hirsau scribe had tried to correct the text grammatically. Where the readings differed, Beatus noted them occasionally in the margin with *alias*. He announced his own conjectures with *forte*, although he was not consistent in this practice. In some cases Beatus added entire phrases in his manuscript which must have come from the Hirsau text, but he gave no indication of their provenance in his sidenotes. Obviously, he felt no need to defend or mention them because he must have believed they were what Tertullian had actually written. Additional marginal notes were included during printing to indicate, in more detail, problematic passages. Beatus sent off to the printers a manuscript that was still in need of additional editing.

At several places Beatus specifically discussed variant readings while noting his conjectures.[130] Marginal annotations that Beatus found in the manuscripts were occasionally printed as marginalia.[131] When proposing his own readings, Beatus at times explained why and how the base text had been corrupted, usually making his own judgments clear.[132] He blamed ignorant scribes for introducing so many errors that only better manuscripts could correct them.[133] While stressing his care in trying to solve textual problems and limiting his own comments so as not to overburden the reader, Beatus insisted on the inferior quality of his manuscripts and his own hard work.[134]

One point should be stressed in analyzing Beatus' treatment of Tertullian. He indicated some realization of the principle of the harder reading in his corrections. At one point he corrected the reading *debito* to *devito,* from a common to a less common word, by arguing that the scribes often confused *b* and *v*.[135] Beatus did not give any further explanation, but it is certainly important that he did not decide to follow the simplest solution to his problem, but searched for a deeper and more revealing one. In his later career Beatus was to continue this procedure and emend his texts from more obvious to more difficult readings.

Special difficulties in the *De corona militis* and the *Ad martyres* required the only annotations in the *editio princeps*.[136] Unlike the marginal notes to the other treatises (except the *Apologeticus*), the annotations to the *De corona militis* cover a variety of topics (those to the *Ad martyres* are rather meager). Several have textual observations. At one point he lamented: "In an author so uncommonly corrupt what do you do except conjecture [*divinans*] if there is time."[137] One reason for such corruptions was the *inscitia librarii*.[138] Particularly important in these annotations were the discussions of theological topics, especially the sacraments of baptism and the Eucharist. Beatus argued that the descriptions of early Christian ceremonies to be found in this treatise justified the annotations, since they could assist students of Christian antiquity, a subject that Beatus felt had been slighted by his contemporaries with their emphasis on pagan antiquity.[139] Collateral manuscript and patristic authorities were invoked to explain early medieval practices and contrast them with those of the early Church.[140] There was a polemical side to some of these annotations, since Beatus argued the decline of the Church from its ancient purity.[141] The annotations also permitted references to general characteristics of Tertullian's writings and discussions of his difficult Latin style.[142] These notes, together with introductions to each book (*argumenta*), an investigation of doctrinal problems in Tertullian's theology (*Admonitio ad lectorem de quibusdam Tertulliani dogmatibus*), a collection of *Definitiones ecclesiasticorum dogmatum* that discussed errors in Tertullian's theology,[143] a short *errata*, and a special index prepared by the Franciscan Conrad Pellican show this to be the most elaborate and sophisticated of Beatus' early editions.[144] While Beatus did make conjectures that were not clearly identified as such, his procedure was basically conservative, since he based his corrections primarily on the manuscripts available to him.

The editions of Velleius Paterculus and Tertullian highlight an important aspect of Renaissance textual work: the availability of important manuscripts.[145] In the case of the *Historia Romana*, Beatus had been searching in a monastic library for interesting texts and chanced upon it. At other times he received information about texts from Froben or from friends who acted as intermediaries. Beatus was especially fortunate in having near him some major monastic, cathedral, and university manuscript collections. He consulted the collection of Greek manuscripts that had belonged to Cardinal John of Ragusa and then belonged to the University of Basel. He thus took advantage of the excellent resources in the Rhineland. When he could not consult a collection personally, he relied on his friends' assistance. He trusted their work, sometimes improperly, as in the case of the *quidam amicus* who transcribed Velleius Paterculus for him.

BEATUS AND THE REFORMATION

One factor that influenced Beatus' treatment of Tertullian was his commitment to the Reformation.[146] From the beginning of the Lutheran movement till about 1523, when growing sectarian violence alienated him, Beatus was a more-or-less active advocate of Luther's anti-Roman and pro-German religious sentiments. Beatus at first saw in the reformer a fulfillment of Erasmus' dream of a renewed Christian society and a welcome critic of the excesses of the late medieval Church. His correspondence shows that Beatus was aware of the elements in Luther's theology from the outset of the Reformation. This information was provided by his friends, among whom were Ulrich Zwingli and his fellow citizen of Sélestat and future reformer Martin Bucer.[147] Beatus found Luther's writings critical of the Roman Church so appealing that he even advocated their publication by Alsatian printers.[148] His commitment to the Reform coincided nicely with his work on Tertullian.

Beatus found in Tertullian a thinker whom he considered valuable in the humanists' campaign to revive Christian morality and to criticize scholastic theology.[149] In 1521 Beatus expressed his rejection of scholasticism and his support for Reformed ideas with some vehemence. His discussion of confessional practices, which he included in his *Admonitio,* drew on the work of Johannes Oecolampadius (1482–1531), Hebrew scholar and fellow Froben employee, who made radical criticisms of the medieval Church.[150] Beatus' discussion was considered heretical enough to be condemned by the Catholic polemist and enemy of Erasmus, Jacobus Latomus, just as later some of his annotations to Tertullian were censured by the Spanish Inquisition.[151]

One of the prominent elements in Beatus' explanatory material was his history of Christian theology.[152] While this text will be discussed in detail later, here it should be noted that in it Beatus gave historical depth to Erasmus' critique of scholasticism. He sharply contrasted the simple teaching of the Church Fathers and the convoluted theology of the scholastics with their dependence on Aristotelian dialectics. A similar attitude informed Beatus' introductory letter to the *editio princeps* of Marsilius of Padua's *Defensor pacis,* also of 1521.[153] The *Defensor* was perhaps the most wide-ranging medieval attack on the papacy. Its rejection of papal authority and its exaltation of secular over ecclesiastical power made it an especially powerful piece of propaganda in the hands of the reformers. Writing under the pen name "Licentiatus Evangelicus," Beatus criticized the un-Christlike deeds of the medieval popes. He was especially anxious to point out scholasticism's negative influence on the Christian Church.

The Reformation's effect on Beatus' work as an editor is a complex matter; it intensified certain elements that had been prominent through his close association with Erasmus. For all his support of the Reformation, it did not redirect his development as a textual critic. While it made more apparent the need to return to the true words of Scripture, as Erasmus had taught, and intensified his interest in the historical development of the Church, the Reformation did not lead Beatus into scriptural studies. The essential patristic orientation of his theological thought was an Erasmian legacy and one that informed the rest of his life. As a textual critic Beatus was neither Catholic nor Protestant, rather he was first an Erasmian and then his own man.

Beatus' concern with the Reformation and its effects on the state of the Church was closely allied to his study of Church history. He was anxious to uncover new materials on early Christian practices, and corresponded with like-minded friends about patristic manuscripts.[154] In 1523 he published a collection of Greek patristic histories in Latin translation, the *Autores historiae ecclesiasticae*.[155] It included Rufinus' *Historia ecclesiastica* and his translation of Eusebius, Epiphanius Scholasticus' translation of Theodoret Cyrensis, Sozomenos and Socrates of Constantinople in an abbreviated form by Cassiodorus, known as the *Historia tripartita*, and a selection of Greek letters and synodal decrees in both Greek and Latin. In his dedicatory letter to Stanislaus Turzo, Beatus lamented the religious controversies of his day and explained the problems of dealing with deficient Latin translations.[156] First, he lamented that he had not had the opportunity to compare the Latin version with the original Greek and correct errors that occurred in the translation. Finding both manuscript and printed versions deficient, Beatus consulted other translations to determine, for example, Rufinus' method. He soon realized that Rufinus' translations were really paraphrases.[157] Further investigations showed other problems in the Latin versions he had. Cassiodorus' translation of the *Historia tripartita*, added to give the printed volume bulk, was stylistically poor. A Greek manuscript of Theodoret that once belonged to Cardinal John of Ragusa provided the texts of synodal decrees that are quoted in the text.

Within the body of the *Autores* Beatus followed the same procedure he had with Tertullian. He corrected punctuation and orthography and added the appropriate Greek words and texts he extracted from Ragusa's collection. He indicated alternate readings with *forte* and *alias*. Discussions of historical and theological topics in his marginal notes reflect Reformers' criticisms of scholasticism and the contemporary Church. He called attention to faulty translations and complained of poor readings caused by careless copyists.[158] A variety of collateral patristic and post-patristic sources were employed to explain difficult passages.[159] Froben republished the text in 1528, 1535, 1539, and 1544, and Beatus improved it by increasing and expanding his emendations and adding new materials in Greek and Latin.[160]

When later considering these early editions, Beatus felt that he had devoted much hard work to them and that his emendatory procedures had been sound.[161] He argued that he had taken a middle path in correcting and annotating his texts by avoiding the excessive number of notes that other editors used to increase their fame; rather, he hoped that his notes would be a real aid to his readers. He was sensitive to the defects of his early work and continued to fault the poor manuscripts for the remaining problems. There were limitations in Beatus' early editorial and textual work, but he continued to develop and did not repudiate his early, if faulty, scholarly endeavors.

Beatus worked under pressure in these early years. He had the responsibility of overseeing not only his own work but that of the Froben press generally. He produced editions that the press felt were desired by the public. But he was not a passive operative. He believed that the press should be used to advance the best literature and scholarship, and he fought for these principles. His devotion to high scholarly ideals inevitably clashed with the business attitude that dominated all Renaissance printing establishments, and this contributed to his becoming a scholarly recluse. This advocacy of scholarly publishing, as well as his support for the Reformation, gave a sense of urgency to much of his work which could not have provided the time for careful attention to textual details. Yet even increased time to edit would probably have improved only marginally his early, immature efforts. In these years Beatus commanded neither the knowledge nor the technique vital to issuing first-class editions. Nor did he know exactly how to inform his readers about his procedures or to elicit from them the type of agreement he sought and felt necessary. Beatus was beginning to understand the need to accomplish all these aims in the Tertullian edition, and in many ways it shows his real accomplishments. He was prepared to make a major advance in his work, and he had at hand the means by which to propagate an improved textual critical method.

3
A NEW TEXTUAL
CRITICAL METHOD

The political and social disorientations caused by the Reformation affected Beatus in several ways. At first, he had promoted the new religion in Sélestat, even donating copies of Lutheran writings to the city government so that they would be available to the reading public. Later, the political excesses of Luther's followers and the violence of the Peasants' War led him to abandon his pro-Reform stance and instilled in him a more moderate attitude toward the old Church.[1] The Erasmus-Luther controversy over the question of free will in 1524 further confirmed this reorientation. Like other humanists, Beatus was forced to choose which side to follow or, perhaps more accurately, which to avoid. While these events absorbed some of his time and energies, they had only short-term effects on his scholarly activities. The political and religious crises probably did intensify his intention to devote his last years more fully to his classical and historical scholarship.

Beatus' negative reaction to the Reformation was followed by his withdrawal from Basel and his permanent residence in Sélestat from 1528. Familial responsibilities probably made his return advisable. His desire to engage more fully in his own scholarly pursuits also made residence in Sélestat attractive. Life in Froben's shop had grown less pleasant for him. Beatus had been an integral part of Froben's establishment, but bitterness had developed over a quarrel with Froben and his partner, Conrad Wattenschnee, concerning financial recompense for his services as editor and corrector. After the dispute was finally settled, Beatus continued his association with Froben on a more limited basis.[2] Even without this encounter, his work's demands and his disagreements with Froben over the nature of the output of the press proved annoying. Events outside Froben's shop also had their effects. Basel was becoming a more difficult place to reside as Lutherans clashed with Catholics. The final break coincided with the attack on Beatus' orthodoxy by Jacobus Latomus. From 1525 Beatus followed once again an essentially Erasmian position; he distanced himself from the Reformation while still remaining critical of many of the Roman Church's teachings and practices.

THE *ANNOTATIONES* TO PLINY

Beatus' final departure from Basel followed the publication of one of the fundamental texts in his career, the *Annotationes* to Pliny's *Naturalis historia* (1526).[3] At no previous point had he so seriously confronted the nature of manuscript evidence, the sources of corruption, and a method for emendation. Although he annotated only sections of the preface and of books VII, VIII, X and XIV, Beatus produced 432 annotations (the bulk of which concern the *Praefatio*), some of great length. There had been only an implicit method of manuscript comparison and of rationalized conjecture in the Tertullian edition and little attempt to explain his method of correcting the text. Beatus had simply noted some characteristics in the form and content of his manuscripts and his own corrections without providing many details that would have permitted his readers to learn the technique of textual criticism he considered proper. In the Pliny annotations Beatus realized the value of informing his audience of his procedures so that they could appreciate his work and apply his method. Indeed, in many ways the annotations constitute a detailed and relatively systematic pedagogical manual for students. While his treatment of specific problems naturally resulted from the way they occurred in Pliny, his polemical and discursive observations were meant to help reform the standards of textual criticism and implant a new, improved method for rescuing ancient writings. His abundant examples of textual solutions would enable scholars to learn, judge, and apply his ideas.

His treatment of Pliny opened a distinct phase in Beatus'

scholarship by presenting him with a new set of textual problems. Since he produced the *editiones principes* of Velleius Paterculus and Tertullian, he did not have to assess and comment on previous editors' work. Pliny, in contrast, had received such extensive study that Beatus had to consider not only manuscript and printed materials but also other scholars' conjectures and explanations. In response to these new challenges, Beatus expressed a more mature textual criticism.

The *Naturalis historia* was one of the most important and complicated of extant classical writings.[4] Essentially an encyclopedia in thirty-seven books, it covers all aspects of natural history in the broadest sense. Full of digressions, the text provided a large body of valuable information as well as much myth and error on every subject from architecture to zoology. No other surviving ancient work was quite like it in bulk and breadth, and it proved to be an indispensable repository of ancient knowledge throughout the Middle Ages. Its popularity increased in the Renaissance when humanists expended much hard work in correcting and explaining its contents.

The abundant occurrences of unusual names and creatures together with quotations from Greek caused medieval scribes to introduce many errors in transmission. Indeed, one could write a history of humanistic exegesis and textual criticism from the editions of and commentaries on Pliny. Some of the best-known names in Italian Renaissance letters (Perotti, Platina, Barbaro, Beroaldo, Poliziano, Giorgio Valla) poured their talents into improving the text in whole or in part. Perotti's criticisms of Bussi's editorial technique were occasioned by the latter's edition of Pliny. Fascination with Pliny led to humanist battles over the meaning and accuracy of the ancients. The humanist Niccolò Leoniceno in 1492 conducted a learned debate with Pandolfo Collenuccio (a writer Beatus edited) in which he accused Pliny of introducing errors into his own text.[5]

The masterpiece of Italian Plinian scholarship was Ermolao Barbaro's *Castigationes Plinianae* (first version 1492 and expanded version 1493).[6] As was true with his contemporaries, Barbaro understood the problems in Pliny to be fundamentally textual. He realized that it was necessary to reestablish the text carefully before advancing any interpretation. Barbaro's work

became the starting point for all subsequent commentators and
was incorporated into other scholars' editions. Of lesser importance, but still enjoying some popularity, were the *Emendationes
seu annotationes in Plinium* by the Italian humanist Marco Antonio Coccio, called Sabellicus (1436–1506).[7] After Sabellicus'
work, the lead in Plinian scholarship passed to non-Italians.

The first Northerner to publish noteworthy material on the
Naturalis historia was the French scholar, Nicolas Bérault (Beral-
dus, ca. 1470–1545).[8] In 1516 Bérault issued a series of notes
on Pliny by other humanists. Among these were notes by the
French humanists Guillaume Budé (1468–1540) and Christophe de Longueil (Longolius, 1488–1522).[9] Neither had separately published on Pliny, so their inclusion in Bérault's compendium made them significant sources for other scholars. Beatus
knew this edition and extracted from it his knowledge of Budé's
and Longueil's comments on Pliny.

In 1525, at Froben's suggestion, Erasmus published the *Naturalis historia* with notes from earlier commentaries and some
new readings and dedicated it to Bishop Stanislaus Turzo. In
his introductory letter, Erasmus praised the work of his predecessors,[10] and provided a summary of his procedure.

> . . . so that the more detestable is the presumption of the cor-
> ruptors, the more reverently must all learned men, each to the best
> of his ability, apply his hand at correcting the work. Certainly it is
> unreasonable to venture nothing here when for so many this ven-
> ture has yielded successful results. It is presumption to introduce a
> new reading and discard the old one on the basis of any frivolous
> conjecture. But it is true respect to note separately that which has
> been discovered thanks to some probable arguments, and to assist
> learned men in further researches. Would that all great men in
> literature should come together in this magnificent work, in such a
> way that each put at the use of the others what he finds, until we
> possess an authentic Pliny. It is not a small recompense which is
> offered; one restored passage will win for a scholar an honorable
> remembrance among the learned. Such is the splendor of the name
> Pliny, such are the success and the utility of this work.[11]

Erasmus stated that he had corrected the text "ex vetustissimo
quodam codice, sed, ut fere sunt, depravatissime scripto,"[12]

probably the same manuscript from the monastery of Murbach which Beatus also employed in his annotations. Beatus treated Erasmus' edition as his copy-text.

Beatus was knowledgeable and appreciative of his predecessors' efforts. In a short introduction to the notes on the *Praefatio* of the *Naturalis historia,* he conceded that while many scholars had produced a large body of material on Pliny, new insights were still possible.[13] In the *Annotationes* Beatus reserved his most extensive comments for Barbaro's *Castigationes.* He greatly respected Barbaro and praised his learning in a variety of fields and his success in improving Pliny's text.[14] While he had left much for other scholars to do, Barbaro did provide a yardstick by which Beatus could measure his own work. So great was Beatus' admiration for Barbaro that he criticized him only reluctantly and in measured terms. He even tried to explain Barbaro's mistakes. Unfortunately, Barbaro's misreadings led to further deformations, since in emending a passage he usually changed the wording to agree with his correction. False corrections thereby generated further corruptions.[15]

For all his respect for his predecessors, Beatus understood that fundamental differences separated their textual critical procedures. Beatus faulted Barbaro for his excessive willingness to resort to conjecture by relying on parallels from other writers rather than on manuscript authority.[16] This preference for nonmanuscript evidence caused Barbaro to accept an approximation of Pliny's thought as a substitute for his exact words.

> And here I am forced to dissent from Ermolao Barbaro, not because he gives a reading alien to the thought of Pliny, but because Pliny wrote something quite different. Moreover, it is worth something to restore not only the sense of the author but also the very words he used.[17]

Beatus' and Barbaro's understanding of the means of restoring a text differed. While both accepted variant results of textual improvement as valid, for Beatus textual criticism sought not simply to recover the thoughts of the ancients but also to restore their very words; for him nothing else was acceptable or just to the ancients.

In addition to Barbaro's *Castigationes,* Beatus specifically discussed Longueil and Budé. In Beatus' opinion Longueil's learning and eloquence had led him to depend too much on his knowledge of Latin style and his own abilities in offering conjectures. Beatus labeled Longueil's method *fallax.*[18] Budé was a more accomplished classical scholar than Longueil, and Beatus was more familiar with his work through the close epistolary contact the French scholar had with Erasmus.[19] Budé's textual method, in Beatus' judgment, was superior to Longueil's because he had consulted manuscripts and had proposed corrections cautiously.[20] His careful methodology had allowed Budé to improve the text. Beatus admitted that he would have been saved much labor had he known of Budé's work earlier. Beatus believed that Budé had benefited from superior manuscript readings, and he noted when his own reconstruction of a reading concurred with the Budé manuscript's version. Further, Beatus knew Budé's other writings, especially his important treatise *De asse,* which he cited.[21]

The approach Beatus brought to Pliny was one he would maintain throughout his career. Since his discussion of his method in the *Annotationes* was meant to be programmatic, it is useful to look at some specific examples of his practice as well as his principles. Beatus briefly described his procedure in his introductory letter to the Polish nobleman and Erasmus' friend, Johannes a Lasco.[22] In Beatus' judgment Pliny's *Historia* was a prime example of the harm done to ancient writings as a result of corrupt manuscripts. Since the task of recovering such damaged material was a difficult but essential one, whoever struggles with corrupt manuscripts merits praise.[23] In his own case, Beatus had carefully consulted a manuscript from the monastery of Murbach, which Johannes Froben had brought to his attention. Murbach, located near Basel, had also provided Beatus with the exemplar of Velleius Paterculus (both manuscripts are now lost).[24] The availability of a new source led Beatus to discuss the need to collate manuscripts with printed texts.

In Beatus' opinion, previous commentators on Pliny had relied on their own abilities to emend the text without giving proper attention to manuscripts. The consultation and comparison of manuscripts constitute the safest means of arriving at an author's very words.

> And so it is true that he who wishes to be praised for restoring the monuments of authors must appeal to manuscript books, especially old ones. For this I say is the most dependable method of hunting out a sound reading from among the faults and of rescuing the genuine text from the ruins of the old exemplars—to gather gold from dung, that is. As a matter of fact, conjectures chosen from *ingenium* [that is, educated guesses] rather than from the surviving manuscripts are mostly false.[25]

This procedure, Beatus continued, has been confirmed through his own experience in dealing with the Murbach manuscript.

The entire tradition of the *Naturalis historia* had been corrupted by the editors' and commentators' tendency to rely on their own talents. Beatus lamented that previous scholars had been so bold as to insert into the text their own wrong conjectures. Consequently, such errors produced a defective version that hid Pliny's actual words. To remedy this situation, Beatus recommended that the corrupt passages in Pliny be published as found, their defects be made clear, and the editors' conjectures be added separately. Silent editorial additions made a later editor's task all the more difficult since it further removed the text from the original author's words. To avoid the possibility of confusing the reader, Beatus decided to publish his own annotations separately.[26]

In the body of his notes Beatus provided information about his manuscript and his printed sources, especially Bérault's edition, as well as details on his own evaluation of the readings he found, his thought process, and the general nature of manuscript emendation. He contrasted the readings in printed texts with those in his manuscript, noting specific examples of agreement and divergence, and indicating which he felt should be accepted. Beatus cited his manuscript by a variety of terms: *codex manu scriptus, volumen manu scriptum, antiquus codex, vetus volumen, vetus exemplar, manuscriptum quod apud me est, vetus codex manu scriptus, exemplar manu scriptum,* and *exemplar vetustum,* as well as *Codex Murbacensis.* Such a diversity of references characterized all his work and makes it difficult to determine when

and how Beatus used his manuscripts. He contrasted his manuscript readings with those *in vulgatis codicibus* or in the *exemplaria
typis excusa.*

The lack of any precise nomenclature for description results
in an especially perplexing but fundamental problem in understanding what Beatus wished to accomplish. He used the terms
vetus lectio, antiqua lectio, sincera lectio, germana lectio, and *vera lectio*
when describing various readings.[27] *Vetus lectio* and *antiqua lectio*
are synonymous. Neither necessarily refers to the readings
found in the vulgata, although they might.[28] This use varied with
common humanistic practice, such as in Poliziano and Barbaro,
where *vetus lectio* referred to manuscript readings.[29] Nor do
Beatus' terms necessarily mean the author's own words. Rather,
they signify the text that had been written down, basically the
archetype, before it was subjected to the vagaries of transmission. The author's words need not have been accurately transcribed in the archetype, hence they are not the same, although
usually they were. Since the *vetus lectio* was the closest thing to the
author's words, it was properly the object of Beatus' critical
method. As such, it is a hypothetical construction, something
Beatus believed had existed and was capable of restoration.

The *vetus lectio* must be distinguished from the *vulgata lectio,*
that is, the reading to be found in the published books. As
Beatus explained, the extent to which the *vetus lectio* is to be
followed depends on the extent to which it has been corrupted,
but it is to be preferred to the more recent printed versions.

> Certainly I see what is read in the printed texts [*in vulgatis
> aeditionibus*], I see also what the manuscript book contains. Nor do I
> depart willingly from the reading of the old book [i.e., his manu-
> script], in so far as possible, since it is clear how the presumptions of
> the learned has falsified our Pliny. Really, I think the common
> reading [*vulgata lectio*] ought to be judiciously corrected, if circum-
> stances allow, from what we call the old [reading, *vetus*], rather than
> the other way round—that the old [*vetus*] be corrected by the more
> modern [reading, *recentior*].[30]

Thus Beatus gave priority to the *vetus lectio,* even when corrupt,
since it offered the means by which the very words of Pliny
would be recovered.

Sincera lectio, germana lectio and *vera lectio*, as well as a variety of similar phrases,[31] denote the very words of the author. Beatus believed that ancient authors knew what they wanted to say and wrote it; it was transmitted through the archetype, and from that point errors began to enter the tradition. Thus Beatus could reject what the manuscript had, as well as the *vetus lectio*, in order to arrive at the *germana lectio*. The *germana lectio* was a construction that basically existed in Beatus' mind. It sprang from his belief that such a text actually had existed and that he had the means of recovering it. Unless the true words of Pliny had once existed, and unless there is a relationship between what was read in his manuscript or could be extracted from it and those words, then his whole system of textual recovery was merely another subjective enterprise with no claims to truth. Given these two fundamental propositions, Beatus could approach his text with great confidence and with an almost missionary zeal.

The lack of a defined and standardized textual critical vocabulary makes the full contours of Beatus' thought unclear. He seems to express in his statements about the types of readings clear temporal divisions, old versus more recent. But these are general statements, and there is no way in which one could define them in detail. His procedure was clear—to contrast the older, because it was more faithful to the original, to newer copies, which were less so—but he had not devised a means of expressing their comparative age.

Since an ancient text is something sacred, Beatus argued that any change must be done carefully and scrupulously and as a consequence of much hard work. Such a procedure contrasts with the conjectures based on an editor's pride and self-confidence. A dependence on one's own talents rather than a manuscript causes great damage. Consequently, unwarranted conjectures elicited forceful comment from him:

> See how holy it is to correct books and how reverently and cautiously it ought to be done. Perhaps in other things speed is worthy of praise, but in this matter nothing is more harmful. It would be fitting for sincere men in these and similar places frankly to admit that either the phrase is corrupt or that its meaning is not clear

[rather than to offer their own corrections without proper support]. Yet we are such that we want to seem to know everything and to be ignorant of nothing. Meanwhile we impose upon dull readers and stupid listeners, confident in this one thing, that the world lacks judgment and sometimes esteems unlearned things with exaggerated zeal.[32]

Care and humility in Beatus' opinion must characterize the editor's task. Further, he must be constantly searching (*curiosus*) for hints in the manuscript which would reveal the *vetus lectio*.[33]

Conjecture is, therefore, a last resort: "Conjecture is necessary when there is no aid from another source."[34] These other sources included collateral texts and the writings of near contemporaries. But corrupt manuscripts could offer much if they were properly treated, since their errors often conceal a true reading. Beatus compared these readings with precious metals mixed with the refuse of gold and silver shops.[35] Thus an editor must comb the remains of old but corrupt manuscripts, for without them conjecture is often false. Beatus argued that, on many occasions, hard work and careful analysis had unearthed correct readings from the defective manuscript and printed texts. He lamented that some had put more time into corrupting the text than he had in correcting it.[36] His solutions in many instances do show an improvement over previous readings. But it had taken him some time to realize the superiority of manuscript to printed text.[37] Thus a manuscript and all its elements must be thoroughly scrutinized before any conjecture should be undertaken. Every element written down (or erased), even if fragmentary, can yield a complete thought, if properly handled.

Beatus explained his method through numerous specific examples, since he realized that theory in such an undertaking as textual criticism must flow from practice. In a few instances he did offer general observations. He noted, for example, that *r* is often confused with *s*, *q* with *c*, and *b* with *v*, probably alluding to the similarities in these letters in pre-Caroline manuscripts, although he made no clear reference to the type of hand.[38] Seemingly also alluding to pre-Caroline minuscule, he explained that ancient manuscripts often have *a* written in a manner resembling the Greek α, which led copyists to mistake it for *u*.[39] Spacing between letters, which was common in old books, also deceived scribes.[40] Beatus further claimed that interpolated texts represent the misguided erudition of learned men.[41] Most interesting, he claimed that scribes commonly changed rare and unknown words into common ones (*Nam merae ineptiae sunt librariorum, raras et incognitas voces in consuetas et sibi notas temere mutantium.*)[42] This would seem again to be an allusion to the principle of the harder reading. Unfortunately, he did not expand on this point. Beatus did not call special attention to such rules; the reader simply saw them in practice.

One important characteristic of Beautus' treatment of his manuscript was what we may call his paleographical method. While neither he nor his contemporaries had a modern understanding of the principles of paleography, the persistence of his resort to paleographical characteristics and themes makes it acceptable to speak of his paleographical method of textual recovery. Beatus explained that:

> —it is not enough to take the meaning of Pliny or any other author from some source or other, unless you inspect the very letters in the old manuscripts, the very tittles themselves and nearly their every individual stroke diligently and repeatedly, especially if you are attempting to restore the true reading of an author you have set out to correct and what it was this author himself actually imparted.[43]

Here is a clear statement of this paleographical method of recovering an author's actual words.

Beatus believed deeply in this method. He argued that error often resulted from confusion over how words were written and that only careful investigation of what was written could uncover the true reading. Such scrutiny of the manuscript could elicit a reader's confidence more than any other method, in Beatus' view;[44] he even admitted to having been led astray by the paleographical peculiarities of his manuscript.[45] This paleographical method underlay Beatus' insistence on the comparison of manuscripts.[46] At several points he specifically defended such manuscript-based conjectures against those scholars who depended on their own talents alone. He noted that such men spent little time on their texts and considered it puerile to consult manuscripts. They did not appreciate the long, involved, and often frustrating labor involved, or the difficult choices that had to be made to produce useful texts rather than monuments to their editors' pride.[47] Although Beatus did not articulate the full dimensions of his paleographical method, his constant resort to it did constitute a touchstone of all his editing.

This paleographical awareness helps to account for Beatus' long and involved discussions when assessing corruptions introduced by unlearned and careless copyists and monks. Here again he offered some general propositions. Sometimes, he noted, the copyists simply misread their models by failing to identify a given letter.[48] Sometimes they misunderstood conventions in the manuscript they were copying.[49] At other times they decided a word was incorrect because they did not know it.[50] Further, *pro libidine sua*, a scribe changed a passage when trying to repair a lacuna,[51] or inverted both letters and words.[52] Monks added a unique source of corruptions by substituting familiar liturgical or biblical quotations for similar-sounding phrases.[53] Such an alteration, in turn, required additional modifications in a sentence. The change of several words (as represented by differences between the versions available to him) in order to make sense of a conjecture was a mark of a problematic passage for Beatus. He seems to have felt that the most probable solution to a dilemma was the one that required only one change; hence, he believed that his conjectures were successful when they could stand with what he found. This argument coincided with his preference for simpler readings.[54] Again, as with so many other elements in his work, Beatus did not expand on this principle.

Thus, either through carelessness or false knowledge, copyists introduced a wide range of errors that the textual critic must investigate. Beatus was especially critical of the scribe of his own manuscript, whom he called *indoctus* and *supinus*.[55] Beatus made some attempt to understand the psychology of the copying process and categorize the commonest errors.[56] Again, his approach was not to list these abstractly but to offer examples within individual annotations. While this reconstruction of scribal practices was not sympathetic, it does testify to Beatus' sincere intention to understand the whole process of corruption.

The learned also have contributed significantly to the depreda-
tion of ancient authors. These self-styled *docti* are content if they
leave no obvious problems in the texts they correct.[57] In Beatus'
judgment their errors were less excusable than those of the ignorant scribes: *alius paulo doctior et idcirco magis damnosus*.[58] He dated
their work from the beginning of the Renaissance in Italy, approximately a hundred years earlier, when interest in Pliny was
reborn.[59] Learned men and *professores,* basing themselves on
scribal mistakes, decided that they knew what Pliny wanted to say
and rashly, and wrongly, changed the text. Their faulty conjectures, often first placed in margins or given in lectures and later
taken into the text itself, were accepted by other readers, who
ascribed them to famous scholars. The result of this was a cumula-
tive debasement of the text.[60] Thus there was a compounding of
error in the whole process of transmission; error built upon
error through pride and self-confidence.

The mistakes and arrogance of the learned formed one of
Beatus' regular themes. The *indiligens diligentia* of the learned
produced poor texts corrected through conjecture rather than
manuscript consultation.[61] They refused to devote the time
required to perform their task properly.[62] Indeed, this emphasis on hard work was characteristic of Beatus' rhetoric as well
as his own practice. It carried almost a moral imperative and
was presented as fundamental to improving texts.[63] In some
ways, the attention of the learned to the manuscripts was regrettable. When these men found different readings in the
margins, they took the opportunity to pervert the text further,
for "the conjectures of everyone were assiduously but without
judgment swept into the text. "And thus were the ancient authors first corrected, that is to say corrupted. No one wanted
to put work into it, and hanging over the work for a long time
was shameful. So, therefore, no matter what came into someone's head, it got smeared into the books."[64] Since the printed
editions contain the errors of these presumptuous men, editors must turn to old manuscripts.[65] In Beatus' estimation ancient writers were in as much danger from the *docti* as from
ignorant scribes.[66]

Beatus conceived of his work as part of a militant campaign
to identify the errors of the scribes and the learned and to

demonstrate the proper technique of restoring the classical writ-ers.[67] But Beatus did not wish simply to ridicule scholars for misinterpreting texts or refusing to expend the needed hard work. His message was more positive—to show forcefully the correctness of his method. He offered his annotations as exam-ples of what could be accomplished by the consultation of manu-scripts, and he hoped that his example would move others to see the validity of his approach.[68] Beatus fully realized the diffi-culty of the enterprise and compared the editor to an Oedi-pus.[69] Despite these difficulties, the editor had what amounted to, in Beatus' view, a moral duty to uncover the very words of an ancient author through hard work and conscientious treatment of his sources.

The carelessness characteristic of medieval scribes and learned conjecturers, lamented Beatus, continues in the work of printers: "O scribes, copyists and the unlearned—most as-suredly a plague for good writers! If only today the same could not be said about certain printers!"[70] The poor proce-dures of contemporary typesetters paralleled the defects of medieval copyists. The medium had changed but not the atti-tudes. Where obvious questionable passages were present, Beatus complained that too often asterisks did not mark the place to alert the reader.[71] The speed with which typesetters did their work allowed for the introduction of new errors.[72] Although he appreciated that printing could prevent some errors,[73] these criticisms formed part of Beatus' dissatisfaction with the quality of printed books available in his day.

BEATUS AND BABARO'S PLINY

The hundreds of annotations Beatus wrote for the *Naturalis histo-ria* show him proposing a careful methodology and maintaining a consciousness of its limits. He treated his manuscript with great respect but did not prefer it in all cases to the *vulgata*. Rather, he scrupulously weighed the evidence before making a decision.[74] Although he maintained that he offered his conjectures only after long consideration, he was certainly aware of the greater probability of some conjectures.[75] His textual critical method with its emphasis on paleographical investigation in fact enabled him to see through numerous corrupt and mangled passages in order to arrive at logical versions or at least better alternatives to those he found in the *vulgata*.[76] There were, of course, still many cases of wrong conjectures. For example, he was not appreciably more successful than his contemporaries in reconstructing missing Greek passages.[77] Perhaps perversely, his errors are more interesting and informative than his correct conjectures. Often they show him discussing his proffered readings more fully, no doubt because even after his emendation they were so problematic that he felt greater detail was necessary.

Though Beatus sought to remain close to manuscript evidence, he occasionally had to see what was not there. This is the case in his treatment of the passage, *Ex illis nos velim intelligi, pingique conditoribus*, from Pliny's *Praefatio* 26. (The modern reading is *ex illis nos velim intelligi pingendi fingendique conditoribus*.) After rejecting others' emendations, Beatus explained that his manuscript had an erasure after *pingi*, indicating a lacuna.[78] This led him first to argue that *pictoribus* was originally written with spaces between the letters (*p i c toribus*) and this caused the scribe to supply the phrase *pingique conditoribus*, in part because the painter Apelles is mentioned later in the passage. But since Beatus believed that the ancients were exact in their speech (like other Renaissance humanists, he seems to have accepted the general reliability of ancient writers, although he did fault Latin and Greek writers for not understanding German words), a further reference to the sculptor Polyclitus moved him to reject his first conjecture. He then investigated with care, as he explained, the mutilated remains of the manuscript's reading and, after much labor, extracted Pliny's words. His new version argued that Pliny had written *pingi ειχονων autoribus,* and that the omega was misread by the scribe as *co*. The scribe joined *co* with *autoribus* to produce *conditoribus* while ειχον was elided with *pingi* to form *pingique*. Based on other passages in Pliny, Beatus concluded that painters and sculptors (actually engravers) could be referred to as *autores* but not *conditores*. Although Beatus' conjecture is not supported by subsequent manuscript evidence, he quite correctly identified a puzzling passage and proposed a plausible solution.

The longest and most intricate of Beatus' annotations incorporated a strong statement of his method and an extended example of its full operation. Since it also revolved around a corrupt passage in Pliny's *Praefatio,* the reader could early become familiar with Beatus' procedure. In discussing Greek and Latin book titles and the greater seriousness of the latter, Pliny wrote, according to the vulgate version: Nostri crassiores antiquitatum exemplorum artiumque quam facetissimi lucubrationum ut qui ait, Bibaculus eram, et vocabar Pantominus, asserit. Varro in Satyris suis sustulit et Flexibula. (The modern version is *Nostri graviores Antiquitatum, Exemplorum Artiumque, facetissimi Lucubrationum, puto quia Bibaculus erat et vocabatur. paulo minus adserit Varro in satiris suis Sesculixe et Flextabula.* The translation reads: "Our authors being more serious use the titles *Antiquities, Instances and Systems,* the wittiest, *Tails by Lamplight,* I suppose because the author was a toper—indeed Tippler was his name. Varro makes a rather smaller claim in his Satires *A Ulysses-and-a-half* and *Folding-tablet.*")[79]

First, Beatus specifically discussed and contrasted Barbaro's procedure with his own. Before considering Beatus' comments, it is necessary to summarize Barbaro's annotation, a rather long one for him.[80] Barbaro began by noting that his manuscript's *vetus lectio* differed from the *vulgata,* reading *puto* for *dico,* and *paulo nimis* for *pantominus.* From these differences he extracted a slightly different reading: *Nostri crassiores Antiquitatum, Exemplorum, Artium, quam facetissimi lucubrationum, ut qui ait Bibaculus, eram et vocabar; paulo minus asserit Varro in Satyris suis Sesculixem et Flexibula.* He found support for *Sesculixe* and *Flexibula* in the ancient writer Nonius Marcellus (in what was essentially Barbaro's rejection of an incorrect conjecture by Perotti) and in references to the first-century poet M. Furius Bibaculus he cited Quintillian, Suetonius, Macrobius and Caesar.[81]

In Barbaro's opinion the opening phrase was nonsensical, and he argued that it actually consisted of a series of specific titles. He corroborated this claim by references to Pliny, Varro, Verrius Flaccius in Festus' compendium, Valerius Maximus, and the known title of Bibaculus' work.[82] He explained the forms *Sesculixe* and *Flexibula* by appeal to analogies, and was willing to accept the word *pantominus.* Barbaro proposed a different reading, one that made Bibaculus the speaker in the text (*Puto qui ait, Bibaculus eram et vocabar, paulo nimis asserit*) and had an ironic sense.

Barbaro's procedure was to explain what he felt was defective in the original and correct it by reference to his manuscript (*vetus lectio*) and the allusions in the text. He did not propose only one acceptable reading but several that could properly suit the genuine parts of the text. The different readings were sometimes close to the vulgate readings. He appealed to collateral writers to establish the titles of works and the meaning of unusual vocabulary. He correctly identified these titles and the Varro reference, although he did not discuss in detail the phrase associated with Bibaculus. As a result, Babaro left the section only partly improved.

Beatus began his explanation by admitting that the passage under consideration was an especially corrupt one in which there are almost as many errors as words (. . . *in quo ferme tot sunt mendae, quot verba*).[83] The problem, however, was not the number of poor readings, even though great, but the errors that contain a certain element of truth. Beatus praised Barbaro for his learning and diligent efforts to restore classical texts[84] and his enormous knowledge,[85] but also he faulted him for his luxuriant style and search for new vocabulary (a sentiment with which Erasmus would have agreed).[86] In Beatus' judgment, Barbaro's *Castigationes* to Pliny are especially worthy of their author's talents. Beatus compared Barbaro's work on Pliny to the labors of Hercules. Even if he had not solved all the difficulties in Pliny, the learned world would still have owed him a debt. Despite the civic duties his position in Venice required of him, Barbaro dedicated his time to literary studies, especially of the most difficult and corrupt writers.[87]

The Murbach manuscript offered a reading that Beatus judged faulty (*Nostri grossioris antiquitatum exemplorum artiumque facetissimi lucubrationem puto quia ut Baculus erat et vocabatur paulominus. Asserit Varro in satyri sui sustulit et flexiabula*), although it is somewhat closer to the accepted modern reading than the vulgate. The need to consult the manuscript produced one of Beatus' clearest defenses of the use of manuscripts.

Let them go and let them say that they merit no praise who restore something from ancient codices, seeing how perfectly preserved those codices are and how beautifully corrected they are. I do not know how glorious it may be; I have experienced the fact that it is laborious to divine an old and genuine reading from corrupted copies. I would seem to the *studiosi* to be reproaching the source of my benefaction if I enumerated here how many times I inspected the manuscript and how many times I took it up and put it down even while working on something else how long I kept my mind's eye on this old document.[88]

Thus he claimed that his conjectures would be based on arduous and regular consultation of the manuscript.

Beatus felt that the mention of the poet Bibaculus was especially vexing, and that it had not been understood by previous commentators, including Barbaro. He offered his own interpretation of the text: *Nostri crassiores Antiquitatum, Exemplorum, Artiumque facetissimi, Lucubrationum puto, qui Antii civis erat et vocabatur P. Val. primus asserit. Varro in satyris suis sustulit et Flexibula.*[89] ("Our more serious authors use the titles *Antiquities, Instances,* and *Systems,* and the wittiest, I think, *Talk by Lamplight,* the first who did so was a citizen of Antias and was called P. Valerius. Varro in his satires took up *Folding-Tablet.*") He explained by paraphrase that Pliny here contrasted the Greeks with the Latins, the latter of whom as witty men contrived humorous titles such as antiquities and *exempla* and *artes.* Further, he argued that the title *Lucubratio* was first used by P. Valerius, that is, Valerius Antias, one of the "younger Annalists," a contemporary of Livy. Valerius wrote a history of Rome from its origins until the period of Sulla in 75. It was published about 75 B.C. and bore the name *Annales, Historia,* or *Historiae.* His work survives only in references by other classical writers, above all Livy, who depended on him as a source for battle numbers. In general, he was held in rather low repute as a historian. Beatus obviously extracted his identification from Velleius Paterculus (2.9.6) and Livy. In order to justify the use of the city name (Antias) to refer to Valerius, Beatus cited the same usage with Erasmus Roterodamus and Poliziano.[90]

Since Beatus' own reading differed from that of the vulgate and the manuscripts, he felt required to explain his choice at length; he did so without the benefit of a paleographical vocabulary. Therefore, he gave a long and detailed reconstruction of the source of the corrupt text. Because of the explicit explanatory aims Beatus undertook in it, the passage is worth quoting in full.

> Now we shall point out, in so far as one may proceed by guesswork, what misled the scribes, so that they contaminated this place so foully; let no one think that our correction is a dream, but let him see what moved me to read one thing rather than another. First, *QuiantIi* was written with the syllables together, and the rather unlearned scribe changed it into *quia ut,* and the majuscule letter *I* along with the next small one [i.e., *i*] he represented as *b,* which are not very different in script if you are not paying attention. What I am now saying can be shown better in letters drawn with the stroke of a pen than in letters printed by printing presses. Nevertheless, it suffices for grasping something of this point. Then by accident *ciuis* was written so that the first stroke of the letter *u* gave the appearance of the letter *l,* and *i* together with the other stroke, i.e., the second one, seemed to become a *u.* But in place of the first letters of that word, *c* and *i*—because they were joined below and because the *c* lacked its curve on the top—*u* again was substituted so that finally it became *ulus.* Now the two letters *Ii* standing alone displayed the appearance of the element *b.* *Ulus* was not satisfactory since it signified nothing. What was done? The scribe simply decided to compose from these letters and syllables a different word. Nor was this a better decision than if he could make *baculum* from *b* with *ulum* with the sole addition of *a* and *c.*[91]

Beatus continued to show the same process at work for the corruption of the name P. Valerius.[92] The reading *Bibaculus,* however, was not the scribe's fault alone. Rather, learned correctors, displeased with the reading, invented their own and altered the rest of the sentence to fit their conjecture, hence *baculum* was transformed into *Bibaculus* to form a name.[93]

To emphasize his method's value, Beatus specifically set it off from Barbaro's.

> I do not doubt that many will laugh at this diligence of mine as if it were a kind of superstitious anxiety because I am so involved in explaining the minute elements of letters so carefully. But what

would you do? Do I see this business as such that whoever wants to do it properly, is compelled to become a schoolboy again for the occasion? Nor was there any reason, as much as I can judge, that Ermolao [Barbaro] restored certain things less happily, than because he preferred to resort sometimes to the clues of authors rather than to work longer on the remains of old manuscripts. In this way from Aristotle, Aelian, Theophrastus and similar authors he sometimes restored the sense rather more accurately than the words, although it does seem to me that the meaning is not sufficiently restored except when the words have been properly corrected. Indeed, in my judgment plain emendation, provided that it be successful, is much more productive than a wordy discussion fortified with countless pieces too little on the topic. And this is my magic art for restoring so many splendid passages in this author. . . . Sometimes I explained my conjectures a little more fully not for the purpose of ostentation but so that I might instruct and encourage others to do the same.[94]

Beatus believed that through his method a critic could uncover true readings despite the poor state of his sources. He realized that he had not solved all the problems but believed that he offered a way for others to improve on his work. These annotations, therefore, stand as the central element in Beatus' work. They contained the fundamental ideas that would sustain all his editorial work.[95]

IN DEFENSE OF THE *ANNOTATIONES*

Various reactions greeted Beatus' *Annotationes*. Andrea Alciati in 1528 praised them.[96] Alciati respected Beatus' learning and diligence and urged him to expand his work to all of the *Naturalis historia*,[97] even though he doubted some of Beatus' emendations and proposed his own version in one case.[98] On the other hand, the French scholar Stephanus Aquaeus (Etienne de l'Aigue) attacked Beatus and his annotations in his own 1530 commentary on Pliny. To these criticisms Beatus responded in a letter appended to his *Rerum Germanicarum libri tres* of 1531.[99] A review of one of the several disputed passages will allow a comparison of Beatus' method with that of a contemporary.

A difficult problem arose at chapter 53 (79) of book VIII (8.

214). While discussing the varieties of wild and domestic animals, Pliny lists goats, the chamois, and the ibex. This last he describes as follows: "there are ibices, an animal of marvelous speed, although its head is burdened with enormous horns resembling the sheaths of swords, towards which it sways itself as though whirled with a sort of catapult, chiefly when on rocks and seeking to leap from one crag to another, and by means of the recoil leaps out more nimbly to the point to which it wants to get" (. . . *sunt ibices pernicitatis mirandae, quamquam onerato capite vastis cornibus gladiorum ceu vaginis, in haec se librat, ut tormento aliquo rotatus, in petras potissimum, e monte aliquo in alium transilire quaerens, atque recussu pernicius quo libuit exultat*). The *vulgata* differs at several points from the modern version both in individual words and in the number in the verbs.[100]

Beatus began his long annotation by noting that no one has understood this passage correctly.[101] He doubted the *vulgata*'s reading *gladiorumque vaginis* (and [as] the sheaths of swords), even though his own manuscript gave the same reading. Despite this coincidence, he believed that the problem with the entire passage stemmed from these words. Longueil's conjecture of *in haec se librat* to *in his se librant*, so that the phrase refers to the *vaginae gladiorum*, was inferior to his manuscript's version, *in haec se librat*, which for Beatus was the *germana lectio*. Beatus found the idea of animals with *vaginae gladiorum* unacceptable, and, reluctantly departing from the manuscript, proposed *lateque vagis* (wandering afar). In Beatus' opinion, the scribe had added the *g* and changed *t* to *d* since he did not like *glate*, and then provided the genitive plural and *ni*, thus corrupting the entire passage. Beatus continued his conjecture by arguing that the scribe had changed the original *ibix in haec se rotat* by altering *ibix* to *ivix* and thence to *inis* which he attached to *vagis* to produce *vaginis;* thus *vaginis* was originally *vagis ibix*. Now *lateque vaginis* did not sound right to the scribe, in Beatus' reconstruction, so he altered the *lateque* to *gladiorumque* to make sense. Beatus' emendation now reads: "There are *ibices* of great speed, although with heads burdened with great horns and wandering afar. The *ibix* balances himself on it as whirled by some catapult when he seeks to jump from one rock to another and by means of the recoil leaps out more nimbly to the point at which he wants to go" (*Sunt ibices pernicitatis mirandae, quanquam onerato capite vastis cornibus lateque vagis. Ibix in haec se librat, ut tormento aliquo rotatus in petras, potissimum e monte aliquo in alium transilire quaerens atque recussu pernicius quo libuit exultat*). Beatus believed that the passage was now *clarissima*.

Aquaeus belittled Beatus for not understanding Pliny's use of metaphor,[102] and countered that the manuscripts supported the *vulgata lectio*. Aquaeus seemed especially disturbed that Beatus had slighted Longueil. Beatus, in his turn, defended himself by admitting that he and all editors somehow err in trying to restore ancient authors.[103] He rejected Aquaeus' claim for a metaphorical reading by arguing that if Pliny had wanted to produce a metaphor he would have gone about it in a different manner. He remained convinced that he had conjectured correctly.

For his part, Beatus had his own criticisms to issue against Aquaeus in addition to what he felt was the ill will behind the attacks. While Aquaeus made much of resorting to his manuscript, Beatus complained that he more likely depended on collateral ancient authority for his emendation than on manuscript evidence.[104] Further, Aquaeus avoided dealing with many of the most difficult sections of Pliny, which required hard work. Basically, Beatus felt that Aquaeus had broken a certain decorum that should accompany textual work, since he believed that the whole process of correcting corrupt texts was so difficult and so uncertain that those who undertook the task should help rather than attack each other. Goodwill was as important as good technique and hard work if the ancient writers were to be recovered.[105]

This exchange demonstrates once again certain fundamental elements in Beatus' textual work. First, while his conjectures could be quite involved—indeed, many of these annotations are very long and complicated—they were not produced arbitrarily. As he noted, other scholars had had trouble with the above-cited passage, so he was not alone or unjustified in selecting it for emendation. In specifying what he felt to be errors, Beatus carefully explained their origins by showing how words were misread or miscopied as well as how marginal readings were incorporated into the body of the text. His reconstructions did originate with the manuscript readings rather than simply depend on the vulgate version. But style also played an important part in his work, as it did for his contemporaries. While Beatus misconstrued the problem relating to *gladiorum vaginae,* he properly noted its difficulty. While Beatus proclaimed a relatively conservative attitude toward emendation, he did not always carry his own principles into practice.

Aquaeus, who could be as prolix as Beatus, offered a better reading in this case but a less thorough explanation. Most important, he did not discuss Beatus' paleographical method or offer a rebuttal to it. His arguments were based on style or occasional citations of manuscript authority. But Aquaeus gave no reason why the reader should have accepted his reading over that offered by his opponent. Beatus had tried to explain his procedure with great care; Aquaeus made no equivalent effort, while his polemical attitude only clouded his criticisms.

Beatus twice returned to the *Naturalis historia.* The first occasion was in the *Res Germanicae* of 1531. Beatus cited Pliny at several points in this treatise; the most important of these was at the beginning of the third book, which deals with the peoples and cities of ancient Germany.[106] Beatus discussed the treatment of the ancient Germans from book IV (4. 98–99) of the *Naturalis historia.* This passage was misunderstood both because of ignorance of German by scholars and because of the poor manuscripts, which in turn permitted him to conjecture. Wildly inaccurate statements about the German tribes had been made. Thus some have made Vandals out of the Wends and Germans out of the Slavs. Such errors, noted Beatus, result not from lack of work or desire to do good but from a lack of judgment.[107] Similarly, scribes *etymologiam vocabuli ignorantes* have mistaken *Ingevones* for *Vigones* because *lapsus in veteribus scripturis creber est.*[108] After demonstrating a series of such mistakes, Beatus concluded by calling attention once again to the difficulty he had in dealing with the text of Pliny and by faulting those who refused to follow his principles: "Further, it is easy to see how much work it is to correct Pliny and how necessary it is, so that they serve letters worst who not only laugh at those who do this but also satirize them with invectives."[109]

In 1537 Beatus printed the annotations on book IX of the

Naturalis historia by the Venetian naturalist Francesco Massara.[110] In his introductory letter, Beatus praised Massara for bringing to his commentary first-hand experiences from his extensive travels in the Near East and restated his own editorial principles. He contrasted Massara's procedure of following manuscripts with other scholars' more casual use of them. He stressed the vital importance of collating manuscripts in order to produce a proper text. A knowledge of languages is a useful and splendid thing in understanding an ancient writer, but it does not replace the consultation of manuscripts.[111] Beatus' willingness to sponsor another man's treatment of Pliny indicates his scholarly commitment to support all valid attempts to serve ancient literature.

THE *ANNOTATIONES* AS A TEXTBOOK

To what extent then can Beatus' textual criticism be considered a method and what judgment can be made of its value and his use of it in the *Annotationes* to Pliny? Beatus believed his textual investigations constituted a method; moreover, he also seems to have felt that it was something new. He expressed the elements of his procedure many times and presented it as a complete construct, teachable and exploitable by others. It was meant to be an orderly means of exploiting defective manuscripts. That his procedure was faulty and incomplete, and that he was not always faithful to it in practice, might be an anachronistic criticism, although a real one. Certainly, there were personal and external limits to his methodology, and honesty requires that these be explained.

Although Beatus understood that the older manuscripts were preferable to the newer ones, he really had no means of presenting this as a methodological factor, since he lacked the technique to determine which manuscripts were in fact older and more valuable. Nor did he offer a means of devising a hierarchy based on assessing the actual readings extracted from them. For example, he stated but did not explain why Budé's manuscript had superior readings. Essentially, he lacked a large enough number of manuscripts of any one author on which to base such an analysis. Still, he argued that manuscripts were to be the foundation for textual criticism, although printed versions and other scholars' conjectures were to be employed as supplements. Only selected problematic passages were to be treated, their choice being determined by the problems other scholars experienced, by suspicious style or sense, and by a divergence with the *textus receptus*. Such passages were not identified by collation of manuscript and printed text, but rather the two were compared only when the critic had independently decided which texts were faulty.[112]

Codicological, paleographical, and contextual investigations must be used on questionable readings. If these techniques cannot provide good alternatives, conjecture is justified. But conjecture for Beatus is not a purely subjective endeavor. Since the *lectio sincera* was real and could be recaptured through the proper method and hard work, the objective quality of textual criticism was affirmed. Beatus' method was meant to have this same objectivity, since it could be applied to any writer by any critic with success, although he admitted that judgment was a variable.[113]

Above, Beatus' presentation of this method in the *Annotationes* has been labeled a textbook treatment. It is proper to ask how valid this categorization is and what place it holds in the development of Renaissance textual criticism. In order to answer these questions, or at least to offer some basis for assessment, it will be necessary to state exactly what Beatus was attempting in the *Annotationes* and then to compare his work with what is considered the first Renaissance textual critical primer, by the Italian humanist Francesco Robortello.

The *Annotationes* formed a textbook in the same manner in which his textual criticism was a method, because they were consciously meant to teach and to provide the essential elements needed by others to follow his lead. That Beatus did not call them a textbook should not take away from the obvious pedagogical intent of the repetition of principles. Further, like any good textbook writer, Beatus provided abundant examples of what is fundamentally a practical enterprise. Indeed, the examples, with their careful explanation of the sources of errors and the means of correcting them, are among the most important statements of Renaissance textual criticism that we have. The emphasis on the

Praefatio, which accounts for the largest section of the *Annotationes,* also suggests their exemplary quality. Beatus realized that a method was needed to bring uniformity and precision to textual criticism. He tried to supply the basis for a reevaluation of the entire process and a means of limiting the damage done to ancient writers by offering the *Annotationes* as a guide and a manual of practical demonstration.

In its individual elements Beatus' method can be seen in other writers, most obviously Erasmus. But probably only Poliziano had stated so explicitly a unified process of textual reconstruction, something with an objective quality to it and which other critics could employ successfully. With their conceptualization of problems and possibilities, their fundamentals and their examples, Beatus' *Annotationes* betray a remarkable sophistication. In summarizing contemporary principles, in extracting their most important elements and in generalizing their use through examples, Beatus was advancing scholarship.

One of Beatus' most admirable qualities was his receptivity to other men's efforts. Although he was proud of his work on Pliny, he had no illusions about the definitive nature of his conjectures. Rather, he urged other scholars to search out new manuscripts, consider them carefully, and not place excessive confidence in his or Barbaro's or anyone else's corrections. One's own eyes and experiences should be preferred to those of others. The task of producing a faithful text of Pliny, or any other ancient author, would continue as long as there were manuscripts that required careful collation.[114]

> I offer the reading of one German exemplar, another might offer the reading of an Italian manuscript, or a Spanish one, another a French and another a British, and I promise that there will be a time not far off when Pliny will be restored to his pristine state. Nothing can be done from simple conjectures, no matter how ingenious you are, ancient manuscripts are necessary. And so libraries are to be searched.[115]

Beatus did not make it clear at what point this process would have an end, that is, when it would be obvious that the very words of the author have been recovered. It would seem that when all manuscripts have been collated, the truth would be finally at hand.

Underlying this call for the investigation of all manuscripts was an appreciation of the uniformity of manuscript error.

> And manuscript books, as I have noted elsewhere, usually do not differ very much, for the faults of some book accidentally corrupted are transmitted down to us through written books as offspring.[116]

This view of the uniformity of errors in manuscripts of all countries means that the proper means of correcting them, of restoring the *vera lectio,* would be universally valid. Unfortunately, there was a lack of evidence on which to expand this principle. The rather small number of manuscripts representing different traditions available was an impediment to Beatus developing an idea of independent manuscript traditions.[117] This optimistic belief in establishing the *lectio sincera* was an index of the naivete of Renaissance textual criticism, and indeed of its entire attitude about the recovery of the past.

For all his care, there were excesses in Beatus' procedure. After reading through his conjectures, comparing them with the *vulgata* and the modern readings, one is left with the impression that his desire to propagate his method and establish its validity occasionally won over his better judgment. His concern to explain and leave memorable rules and ideas could be excessive. Certainly paleographical ingenuity could be as dangerous to restoring an author as stylistical or analogical conjectures. Despite these criticisms and for all its tentativeness, the care and wide-ranging expertise Beatus brought to Pliny remain impressive.

A constructive comparison with Beatus' *Annotationes* is Poliziano's procedure in correcting Pliny. Poliziano dealt with selected problems in Pliny in the *Miscellaneorum centuria prima,*[118] which Beatus possessed, and in the *Miscellaneorum centuria secunda,*[119] which was unknown in the Renaissance outside Poliziano's immediate circle. Poliziano had several manuscripts at his disposal: one from the Medici library, two from the library of San Marco, and one he had used in Naples. The Medici manuscript he described as *vetustissimum exemplar.* He compared his manuscripts to other versions of Pliny that were full of scribal errors.[120] Poliziano appealed to his manuscripts for readings that he either accepted or used as a basis for paleographical scrutiny. In general, his procedure was superior to Beatus', in part because he had access to more manuscripts.

The similarity between Poliziano's and Beatus' procedures can be established by reference to one passage that both men emended. This example is valuable because Poliziano's annotation is from the *Miscellaneorum centuria secunda,* which Beatus did not know. In *Praefatio* 18, the printed version read: *Quod dum ista, ut ait M. Varro, mussitamus* (Modern reading *dum ista* [*ut ait Varro*] *muginamur,* "while we were dallying [as Varro says] with these trifles").[121] Both Poliziano and Beatus realized that the *vulgata* was corrupt, and they found in their respective manuscripts the alternate reading *musinamur.* Both rejected this and turned to Festus, where they found the word *muginari.*[122] In addition to Festus, Beatus consulted Nonius Marcellus, another source of unusual Latin vocabulary.[123] On the basis of what they found in these ancient writers, both arrived at the same reading.

If Beatus was not as accomplished as Poliziano in all details, he nevertheless employed a parallel procedure. In his generation no scholar was as advanced as Beatus in his treatment of the ancients. More telling, as will be seen immediately, there were few of his successors who could surpass him in both the method he followed and the success he had in restoring corrupt passages.

BEATUS AND FRANCESCO ROBORTELLO

Beatus' *Annotationes* provide an invaluable insight into the procedures of Renaissance textual criticism. He demonstrated his ability to organize his own observations and principles and those of the most famous Renaissance editors and to form them into a consistent whole. He understood the need to teach others not simply any method, but *the* method. He felt that he had demonstrated his method's superiority to those of the competition. In order to provide a clear focus for Beatus' *Annotationes* as a milestone in Renaissance textual criticism, it is best to compare them to the first textbook of textual criticism.

Francesco Robortello (1516–1567) published his *De arte sive ratione corrigendi antiquorum libros disputatio* in 1557.[124] It represented his own experiences as an editor and annotator of classical texts. The *Disputatio* was an introduction to two books of annotations on Latin and Greek writers (*Variorum locorum in antiquis scriptoribus, tum Graecis, tum Latinis, annotationes*). These short commentaries were in part critical assessments of other scholars' work. Sharp-tongued and combative, Robortello clashed with several prominent scholars of his day, above all the editor and historian Carlo Sigonio.[125] The disputatious attitude that infected these annotations formed a notable aspect of the *Disputatio*, but it also included serious if unoriginal considerations of textual problems and an attempt to express standard opinion. The *Disputatio* was basically descriptive, and, as such, it provides a useful control for assessing Beatus' work.

Writing some thirty years after the appearance of the *Annotationes*, Robortello reiterated many of Beatus' themes: the importance of correcting ancient texts, the poor state of available editions, the errors introduced by scribes and the lamentable emendations of so-called correctors. Robortello considered himself the first to offer a systematic treatment of textual criticism, and, after some false modesty, he described his topic in some detail.[126] He divided the emendation of ancient writings into the traditional *emendatio ope codicum* and *ope coniecturae* (*Et quoniam corrupta auctorum loca emendantur aut coniectura, aut ex veterum librorum, qui manuscripti sunt, aut impressi, scriptione*).[127] In explaining the former, he provided an analysis of handwriting, above all Longobard script—that is, basically all medieval hands.[128] Robortello understood the corrupting effects of misreading ancient forms of letters. Conjecture is necessary when there are no new texts to assist the editor or when available texts are corrupted. At that point the editor must rely on *iudicium magnum* but still stay close to his manuscripts.[129] In describing the manner by which one could confirm emendations, Robortello maintained that accurate conjectures are supported by ancient manuscripts in three ways: by *notione antiquitatis, notione scriptionis antiquae,* and *notione locutionum et verborum antiquorum*, that is, knowledge of ancient history, handwriting, and style.[130] But if there are no ancient authorities and conjecture has been used, then correct readings can be supported by using eight additional means of analysis, in other words, eight means of determining the cause of error and how to rectify it: *additio, ablatio, transpositio, extensio, contractio, distinctio, copulatio, mutatio.* These represented various common transcription errors. This is really a verbose way of saying what other critics had said more simply.[131] In order to demonstrate these, he offered abundant examples from Greek and Latin writers.[132]

Robortello concluded his treatise with a call for *fides* among critics, reliance on manuscripts to emend texts. He offered a pedigree for this method, praising those men who had followed it and, therefore, warranted trust. Leading the group was Poliziano. Next came the Italians Giovanni Piero Valeriano, and Robortello's contemporaries Pier Vettori and Girolamo Ferrari.[133] Outside of Italy he cited Henricus Glareanus and Joachim Camerarius, *qui librorum auctoritate manuscriptorum nituntur.*[134] Robortello bestowed special praise on Beatus: "man of great learning, made use of a not dissimilar means [of manuscript consultation], who in taking errors from the works of Livy, Tacitus and Velleius and so many others, rendered a great service to all good men."[135]

The *Disputatio* mixed principle and example with several digressions on such topics as the materials used by the ancients for writing,[136] as well as persistent polemics against the author's enemies. As a textbook, it has the advantage of bringing together statements on several important themes. But Robortello did not advance textual criticism very far, certainly not beyond Beatus. Indeed, if force of example be taken as a fundamental pedagogical device, then the *Disputatio* is no marked improvement on Beatus' *Annotationes,* although it did have the advantage of dealing with Greek examples. Usually Robortello gave an example (occasionally two) to explain the source of corruption and its correction, and for the most part these are brief. At least at a rhetorical level Robortello, like Beatus, admitted the contingency of his own conjectures, although his claims are vitiated by his fiercely polemical style. In practice Robortello is not an outstanding guide. The generalized nature of his discussions, together with his polemical asides and the lack of any citation of specific manuscripts, render his work in a period before the existence of auxiliary sciences of limited use for teaching the reader the actual method of exploiting manuscripts. The long, careful, and particularized examples Beatus employed are lacking in Robortello (although they are more evident in the *Annotationes* that follow the *Disputatio*). Obviously Beatus' treatment of one manuscript for one text was both an advantage and a limitation, but since teaching and explanation were central to both men, Robortello did not find the means of improving on Beatus, at least not in his textbook. The Italian often seemed primarily interested in justifying his own conjectures and damning his opponents. His attitude was closer to that of Aquaeus than of Beatus. Moreover, since Robortello, a man not inclined to generosity, knew Beatus' work well and praised him in terms worthy of Poliziano, he must have owed much to the German's example. In summary, Beatus can claim a preeminence in understanding the need to propose a detailed explanation of a manuscript-based textual critical method.

THE SECOND EDITION OF TERTULLIAN

In one of his *Annotationes*, Beatus praised King Francis I's confessor, the Dominican Guillaume Petit (died 1536),[137] for collecting manuscripts of the Church Fathers and sponsoring their publication. Beatus offered him as a model for such activities.[138] Beatus followed his own exhortation in 1528 when the second edition of Tertullian appeared.[139] In his introductory letter to the reader,[140] Beatus emphasized the difficulties of his task and his extensive labors. With some authors, he explained, the sense is relatively simple, but with Tertullian one must have recourse to manuscripts in order to establish what he wrote. Beatus described the origin of the second edition and the trying circumstances surrounding it.[141] He had had no intention of dealing with Tertullian again unless he could obtain new manuscripts. He had waited eagerly for the manuscript from Gorze and one of the *De spectaculis*, but in vain. Nevertheless, Froben pressured Beatus to prepare a second edition because of the demand and the threat that rival editions would appear. The project went slowly because of dislocations resulting from the plague and Beatus' general indifference to the whole enterprise. Indeed, it was only when printing was well underway that Beatus became excited about his work. Even without any new manuscript authority, he had corrected many corrupt places and had made sense out of abstruse passages. (Beatus' copy of the *editio princeps* contains occasional additions and corrections in the margins, although they are not the numerous changes that appear in the second edition.) Obviously, he felt that he could see before him the success of his method. Working in the tumult of the printing shop with booksellers looking over their shoulders, Beatus and the other correctors did their work.

Beatus realized that some might question the extent of his conjectures in this new edition, and he admitted that there is no greater threat to an author than hasty change, as he had come to understand through his work on Pliny. Granting this danger, he argued that it is better to explain a hundred conjectures than to change wrongly a single syllable of a writer's work; such a system might offer less in the way of glory to the editor, but it was certainly the safest. As was true for all his work, Beatus wanted to make clear to the reader his conjectures and not hide them in the text as other editors had done. His careful treatment of Tertullian's treatises resulted in new sets of annotations for several treatises and expanded the sidenotes throughout.

In an introductory passage to the annotations for the *Adversus Hermogenem*, Beatus restated his method.[142] The poor state of the manuscripts, due to copious scribal errors and the difficult language, had made the work of restoration very difficult. In order to restore the text, he had to rely on his own judgment in conjecturing since he lacked any better manuscripts. He retained the earlier readings so that others might provide better solutions and added his conjectures in the annotations. He would have preferred to place them in the text's margins, but their length required greater space. In maintaining the older readings in the text, Beatus again echoed his basic attitude toward ancient texts: *Nam magna religione tractanda sunt veterum scripta.*

For the second edition Beatus had hoped to add new treatises. His primary goal was to issue the *De spectaculis.* He was frustrated in this because the lawyer Ulrich Fabritius of Koblenz had had the manuscript and had planned to issue it in his own name. Unfortunately, Fabritius had recently died and the present location of the manuscript was unknown. (By the end of his life Beatus had obtained a copy of the *De spectaculis* from a new manuscript, but he did not have time to publish it.)[143] Beatus had also planned to publish the pseudo-Tertullian poem *De Sodoma,* which Johannes Sichardus had discovered in the monastery of Lorsch.[144] The manuscript's extremely poor state prevented this.

In the introduction to the annotations to *Adversus Valentinanos,* Beatus noted that Tertullian's erudition and rhetorical training often rendered his style obscure. For this particular book Beatus had used a near-contemporary collateral source to Tertullian, the Greek writer Irenaeus (in Erasmus' 1523 edition).[145] Both Irenaeus and Tertullian discussed the same heretical doctrines, and Tertullian depended on his Greek predecessor for much information. He admitted that he had not solved all the problems and, recalling Pliny, urged other scholars to go to their libraries to consult other versions of Tertullian. He regretted that he had not seen the Gorze manuscript (political unrest had prevented consultation of the better manuscript at Fulda) and his inability to offer the *De spectaculis.* Despite these omissions and the limited availability of the press, Beatus felt that his efforts would benefit others.[146] The annotations show Beatus' diligence in devising new conjectures and in bringing his historical and theological learning to bear on confused passages.

Great effort was expended in making this new edition more valuable to the reader. While sidenotes with alternate readings remained or were expanded, it was the series of annotations that marked a major advance in Beatus' treatment of Tertullian. Beatus provided new conjectures and rethought earlier ones in his search for the *ipsissima Tertulliani lectio.*[147] A good example of his work is a difficult passage from *De corona militis* (I.5): *Nec dubito quosdam scripturas emigrare* (modern reading: *Nec dubito quosdam (secundum) scripturas emigrare.*)[148] In 1521 Beatus had proposed in the margin the reading *Forte iuxta scripturas* (which parallels the modern rendition of the passage).[149] In 1528 Beatus kept the reading *quosdam scripturas* in the text but marked it with an asterisk and advised the reader to turn to the *Annotationes*. In the annotation Beatus offered a long explanation of the passage.

He explained that he first had proposed *iuxta scripturas*, since *scripturas* cannot *emigrare*.[150] Next he thought that *hypocritas* would fit, but then felt that a better reading was *scraptas* (Beatus actually wrote *scarptas*, which is incorrect), since it agrees with female references in the treatise. To justify this conjecture he invoked the authority of M. Verrius Flaccus' *De verborum significatu* in Sextus Pompeius Festus' epitome, where it means fleeing women. However, since the *codex Festi* was defective and the reference was awkward, he sought further support in a citation to Plautus in Nonius Marcellus' collection of ancient Latin vocabulary, the *Compendiosa doctrina de proprietate sermonum*.[151] This conjecture is reinforced, he felt, by the sense of the passage, which argues that to die for Christ is a *virilis res*, while to flee shows cowardice, as well as by other passages in Tertullian. Beatus believed that Tertullian was the type of individual who investigated all the ancient writers and would have known this unusual word. So uncommon is the word that Beatus believed the ignorant scribe simply changed it to *scripturas*. As plausible as this reconstruction was, Beatus actually preferred to read *hypocritas*, as he explained, *propter sensum*. Building on the principle that scribes change hard words into easy ones, he doubted *hypocritas* because it is a common word and the scribe would not have been inclined to change it. Since the Hirsau manuscript also has *scripturas*, Beatus left it in the text so that the reader could decide.

This last observation led Beatus to call the reader's attention to the effort expended in correcting this defective passage and what a worthy endeavor it is to correct ancient writers.[152] Yet he felt all his hard work had been in vain. He now offered a different reading, *Nec dubito quosdam in cryptas emigrare*. He explained that in Rome those fleeing persecution took refuge in the catacombs. The Roman Christians' adherence to the evangelical injunction to flee persecution rather than calmly face death for Christ Beatus read as a slighting reference to the Romans because of doctrinal quarrels between Tertullian and the Roman Church (*De corona militis* is one of the treatises Tertullian wrote under the influence of Montanism). *Cryptas,* he continued, is a Greek word that the Latins had accepted. Beatus concluded by warning the reader about making textual alterations, since the change of one syllable in the text has necessitated this complex solution.

The fullest indication of Beatus' continued efforts to improve his earlier work is his treatment of *De pallio,* one of the most difficult shorter works in the Latin language.[153] Beatus' willingness to treat in detail such a taxing treatise testifies to his confidence in his talents and textual method. In 1521 Beatus admitted that the Hirsau manuscript was very corrupt, so much so that almost every sentence required emendation. But he had decided not to list every change in the margin. He advised that the manuscripts of Tertullian's writings in Rome, Fulda, and Gorze should be consulted.[154] In the 1528 edition Beatus decided to print side by side both the corrupt 1521 text and a heavily altered version based on his own conjectures, with the heading *Idem contextus, locis aliquot per coniecturas mutatis.* He felt that since the text was so corrupt and the language so affected, the parallel placement was advisable so that the reader could easily judge for himself. Beatus defended his conjectures since he believed that they made this difficult text more intelligible.[155]

The scores of major and minor changes in this short treatise represent one of Beatus' most systematic conjectural undertakings. In the first edition Beatus had transcribed the Hirsau text with certain obvious corrections, and we may assume that the printed text more or less accurately represented the manuscript. If so, we can agree that the manuscript was very corrupt. Its punctuation, spelling, and capitalization were erratic, while unusual words were often mangled. The new edition tried to correct these defects by reworking extended sections.

One example (III, 6) should suffice to demonstrate the extent of Beatus' corrections and the degree of his success. In order to allow ease of comparison, the 1521 version will be given first, followed by those of 1528 and 1539 editions (the last benefited from readings derived from the Gorze manuscript), and then the standard modern version. (The text in translation reads: "Nor do I speak of the sheep of Miletus, and Selge,[156] and Altinum, or of those for which Terentum or Baetica is famous, with nature for their dyer: but [I speak of the fact] that shanks afford you clothing, and the grassy parts of flax, losing their greenness, turn white by working. Nor was it enough to plant and sow your tunic unless it had likewise fallen to your lot to fish for raiment.")[157] The italics indicate changes in the versions.

1521

... nec de *ovilibus* dico Milesiis et Selgicis et Altinis, aut *quista rentium,* vel Betica *cluet* natura colorante. Sed *quoniam* et arbusta vestiunt, *de* lini herbida, post *virorem* lavacro nivescunt. Nec *si ut* satis tunicam pangere, et serere ni etiam piscari vestitum contigisset.

1528

... Nec de *ovilibus* dico Milesiis et Selgicis et Altinis, aut *quis Tarentum* vel Betica *cluit,* natura colorante: sed *iam* et arbusta vestiunt, *de* lini herbida: post *virorem,* lavacro nivescunt. Nec *fuit* satis tunicam pangere, et serere, ni etiam piscari vestitum contigisset.

1539

... nec de *ovilibus* dico Milesiis et Selgicis et Altinis, aud *quis Tarentum,* vel Betica *cluet,* natura colorante. Sed *quoniam* et arbusta vestiunt, *et* lini herbida post *virorem* lavacro nivescunt: nec *fuit* satis tunicam pangere et serere, ni etiam piscari vestitum contigisset.

Modern Version

... Nec de *ovibus* dico Milesiis et Selgicis et Altinis, aut *quis Tarentum* vel Betica *cluet* natura colorante, sed *quoniam* et arbusta vestiunt, *et* lini herbida post *virorum* lavacro nivescunt. Nec *fuit* satis tunicam pangere et serere, ni etiam piscari vestitum contigisset. . . .

The 1528 changes in part follow a clear analysis of the origins of corruption. *Quista rentium* is obviously corrupt and the separation of *quis* is evident. *Tarentium* is then easily altered into *Tarentum* as demanded by the proper noun *Betica,* which follows. *Cluet* to *cluit* is again a simple enough alteration on the basis of grammar, turning the present into a perfect, although Beatus later rejected this. The change of *quoniam* to *iam* probably reflects Beatus' unwillingness to accept the abbreviation as he found it, and probably a belief that the scribe simply added the first syllable on his own. The reading of *si ut* into *fuit* was again paleographically easy and demanded by sense. Other changes in the treatise required Beatus to conjecture the proper form for names and rearrange syllables. As a group Beatus' conjectures are half supported by the modern version.

The extensive conjectures that Beatus made to the *De pallio* have been judged severely by some modern editors.[158] There is much merit in these censures. Beatus did arbitrarily emend readings that he would restore in 1539 on the authority of the Gorze manuscript. Nevertheless, we should give him the benefit of the doubt, since the Hirsau manuscript was corrupt, and since he was trying to make sense of a difficult treatise. In such a situation arbitrariness might have been the only solution. In some cases Beatus offered readings that were not only improvements over those of the Hirsau manuscript but were confirmed by the later collation with the Gorze version; more than two dozen of them are to be found in modern editions. These conjectures, Beatus felt, were in accord with his method's general principles. Further, the extent to which he went to make his own conjectures clear is admirable as well as rather exceptional for the Renaissance.

It may be surmised that Beatus really did not find the solution he attempted in the *De pallio* a satisfactory one, since he never did it again. Indeed, to an extent, it was a regressive step, a return to the earlier period of humanist textual criticism when various readings were given side by side. Henceforth, Beatus would place in the annotations whatever he felt was necessary to explain or correct a text and leave in the text the *vulgata* version. In the second edition of Tertullian these parallel texts do provide a further glimpse into Beatus' thought processes.

An important change evident in the second edition (and which would become even more significant in the third) is an increased attention to the peculiarities of Tertullian's Latinity. In 1521 Beatus merely had noted how Tertullian's difficult Latin posed numerous dilemmas in interpretation.[159] In the second edition, he treated Tertullian's language more fully and added a section of *annotationes* devoted to illustrating its peculiarities.[160] One of Beatus' aims was to document instances of how Tertullian altered standard Latin. He admitted that, at first, he had not grasped the uniqueness of Tertullian's language, and consequently had been apt to blame scribes for inventing strange words. Later he came to realize that such an unusual vocabulary represented Tertullian's African origins.[161] African Latinity, the Renaissance designation for the style of second-century Latin writers from North Africa, especially Apuleius of Madaura, was noted for its difficult, often archaic vocabulary and convoluted syntax.[162] Only gradually did Beatus come to appreciate the idiosyncrasies of Tertullian's language as the key to understanding and reediting his writings.

Beatus did more than simply cite unusual words and constructions. His examination of Tertullian's language led him to explain the grammatical basis for its peculiarities. Tertullian, for example, changed declensions[163] and occasionally the cases of words.[164] Less evident was an understanding of the Greek basis for much of Tertullian's vocabulary, although this would become a prominent element in the 1539 edition.[165] Beatus continued to make explicit his conjectures and the need for the reader to judge his reconstructions.[166] In analyzing Tertullian's Latin style, Beatus sought to provide the reader with linguistic and syntactical tools for appreciating Tertullian's complex idiom.[167]

CONCLUDING EVALUATION

The expanded annotations show how anxious Beatus was to improve his work on Tertullian. Despite increased intervention into the text, he kept his attention on the text and its sundry problems. Even without new manuscript assistance, Beatus felt that he had learned enough to conjecture extensively without betraying Tertullian's meaning. In a sense Beatus was becoming bolder in treating an ancient writer as he was becoming more conservative in his call for reliance on manuscript authority.

It is important to offer some overall evaluation of Beatus' method and to establish where it belonged within the general movement of textual criticism in the Renaissance. Certainly the Pliny annotations and second Tertullian edition are mixed bags. While calling for fidelity to manuscript authority, Beatus at several points conjectured in a manner that was not substantially different from that of men such as Barbaro and Longueil, whom he condemned. He could be as arbitrary as others in deciding to ignore a manuscript reading. Generally, he used manuscripts as bases for his own conjectures, but not as the final authority. Ultimately, *iudicium* and *ingenium* outweighed the manuscripts too often.

This having been said, is there any justification for calling Beatus' method in some way new? There is when we consider carefully what he wished to accomplish and what he was working against. There were no theoretical or even practical handbooks for the textual critic; Beatus and his contemporaries developed their methods by actually correcting texts. Beatus understood the need to systematize this enterprise so that there would be some uniformity in the textual criticism and so that the true words of authors might be established. In composing his annotations, Beatus was moved as much by a moral as by a scholarly attitude. He wanted to teach the way it should be done and lead others. Conceptually, therefore, Beatus did have a new method, even if it bore strong resemblances to the methods of Erasmus and Poliziano and had definite limits in practice.

In appreciating the need to explain procedure so that all textual criticism would be brought into an established norm, Beatus was moving toward a broader view of his work. In calling for close attention to the manuscript (whatever his actual doings), he was establishing a principle that was good for all authors. In explaining how he did it, he provided the type of practical demonstration vital to eliciting the concurrence of others, a procedure that also explains some of his polemical statements. Further, in applying his method to Tertullian, Beatus associated the Church Fathers with the pagan classical authors as worthy of the same close textual attention. The system that could bring forth the true words of Pliny could also be used in the reconstruction of the Christian past and its teachings.

Both the Pliny annotations and the second Tertullian edition were important in Beatus' development, but they mark only a phase, albeit an important one, in his development. The 1530s and 1540s were to witness Beatus' most constructive editorial, and above all, historical productions. As he matured, his textual criticism became an effective tool both in clarifying ancient writers and in permitting him to move independently and with great expertise into historical criticism.

4
THE MATURE CRITIC

The *Annotationes* to Pliny and the second edition of Tertullian stand as major scholarly accomplishments. Whatever the problems that remained in Beatus' editorial products, they could not cancel out his real successes in articulating and propagating, if not always following, a consistent textual critical method. In the 1530s Beatus consolidated and employed his new skills to establish himself as one of the great editors of the Renaissance. In these years he also emerged as the finest German historian of his day. This last achievement depended upon his close study of manuscripts and the historical problems they presented.

In part Beatus accomplished so much in the 1530s because of his secure economic status and a lifestyle that removed him from most contemporary political and religious controversies, leaving him free to devote his time and energies to scholarship. In Sélestat he became a semirecluse.[1] He spent most of his time in his house with his excellent library, reading and annotating classical and early medieval historians. He seldom even dined with his friends, preferring the company of his books. He eschewed political and religious controversy, having received from the Emperor a dispensation from civic duties at the same time that he had been ennobled in 1523.[2] His scholarly seclusion was broken by a few trips to search for unknown manuscripts in nearby monasteries, and once he attended an imperial diet.

SENECA AND PROCOPIUS

The limitations of Beatus' activities extended to the press. His disagreements with Froben and his partners over money and the publication program had altered their relationship, and Beatus never again committed his energies to one publisher. More and more, he devoted his time to his own enterprises. There was a major exception to this: Erasmus. Beatus continued to help in the printing of Erasmian works. After Erasmus' death, Beatus supervised his friend's editions of Origen and John Chrysostom and wrote his biography for the *Opera* issued by Froben in 1536.[3] Beatus remained a faithful advocate of his friend's religious and moral ideals and maintained an Erasmian distaste for political and religious controversies. Yet in his scholarly work, both textual and historical, Beatus was striking out on his own, and his production of the 1530s and 1540s shows him emerging as a scholar of great influence throughout Europe.

Beatus' growing confidence in his method and his ability to apply it led him to reedit in 1529 Seneca's *Apocolocyntosis* or *Ludus de morte Claudii Caesaris.*[4] The generally popular 1515 edition dissatisfied Beatus. Numerous annotations in his own copy indicate his continued desire to improve it. Added to this was Beatus' participation in Erasmus' reedition of Seneca's writings, which had appeared in 1528; Beatus even assisted his friend in trying to obtain new manuscripts for it. The printing of the *Apocolocyntosis* was begun without any new manuscript evidence and only with Beatus' own conjectures based on his grasp of Latin style and philology. Despite this, Beatus remained faithful to the principle of *emendatio ope codicum,* and when he obtained a new manuscript he immediately began integrating its readings into his text even in the midst of printing.[5] This new manuscript, the *Codex Wissenburgensis,* came from the Monastery of Saints Peter and Paul of Wissembourg; it was lost after the printing was completed.

Since the codex contained traces of Greek, Beatus initiated a new attempt at emendation.[6] One of the phrases that he could read cited Homer, and he consulted that poet in the hope of discovering lost readings. Many passages still eluded him, so he offered his own conjectures in a series of *annotatiunculae.* The limited time available, due to the advanced state of the printing, required that they be brief. In these notes Beatus continued to explain his method and to criticize the *docti* who corrupted texts through faulty conjectures.[7] A conspicuous element in his treatment is the reconstruction of the Greek text from lacunae and garbled Latin phrases. He was especially successful in restoring the Homeric citations.[8] Old problems remained. References to the manuscript and his collation remain vague. It is often impossible to determine from his notes exactly when he was citing the manuscript directly; his emendations based on the *Codex Wissenburgensis* were confused with his own conjectures and were not treated as distinct elements.[9]

In a sense the time spent on Seneca was tangential to Beatus' major enterprises. Throughout the 1530s he made great progress as a historian and historical editor. In 1531 he issued in one volume a series of late ancient historians: included were Latin translations of Procopius' accounts of the Gothic, Persian, and Vandalic wars—in translations by Cristoforo Persona and Raffaele Maffei of Volterra—and their continuation by Agathias; Jordanes' *Liber de origine Gothorum;* Sidonius Apollonaris' letter on Theodosius; the *editio princeps* of the Greek text of Procopius' *On Buildings,* and Leonardo Bruni's *De bello contra Gothos.*[10] The book was printed by the Basel press of Johannes Herwagen and was based on a manuscript belonging to the humanist Conrad Peutinger.[11] This undertaking allowed Beatus to consider carefully some of the most important sources for early medieval history; the knowledge he acquired from them would be indispensable to his own work on German history. Beatus showed himself capable of evaluating the information he obtained from these sources and even of proposing his own ideas about such matters as the origins of the Goths. It did not offer much of an opportunity to investigate textual problems, since the translations appeared without the addition of annotations or explicit emendations. Beatus seemed content in accepting what was at hand.

THE *CASTIGATIONES* TO TACITUS

Also in 1531, Beatus' *Rerum Germanicarum libri tres* appeared.[12] This was a milestone in the study of Germany's past. Indeed, scholars have judged it the first solid treatment of German history. It helped to place the investigation of German ancient and medieval history on a new and more secure footing. As a history, it was greatly dependent upon Beatus' textual critical advances, since it included extensive criticisms of the most important ancient and medieval historical sources. Ancient historians were more systematically treated in Beatus' *Castigationes* to Tacitus' *opera* of 1533 and in his *Annotationes* to several books of Livy's *Ab urbe condita* of 1535.

Beatus' treatment of Tacitus represents one of his most sustained and successful editorial enterprises. Perhaps more than any other of his works, his *Castigationes* have been responsible for the high position he holds in the history of classical studies.[13] It is important to put his treatment of Tacitus into some broader context, both because of the importance of the texts themselves and because of Beatus' great influence on subsequent editors.

The recovery of Tacitus' *opera* constitutes a prominent subdivision in the history of the reception of ancient writers as well as in the history of political thought.[14] While not completely unknown in the Middle Ages, Tacitus was generally either ignored or improperly identified. During the Middle Ages the tradition of Tacitus' writings became confused, and the *Annales* and the *Historiae* were conflated into one treatise. Reflecting this medieval inheritance, the manuscript history is problematic and several elements in its transmission remain obscure. As was true with many ancient writers, it was only in the Renaissance that Tacitus reclaimed the attention he merited.

The sole source for *Annales* I–VI (although books V and VI were conflated in the Renaissance until separated by Ferretti in 1541) is the so-called Mediceus I, a ninth-century manuscript probably written at the Monastery of Fulda but housed at the Monastery of Corvey, whence in 1508 it was brought to Italy.[15] Pope Leo X purchased it and gave it to the humanist Filippo Beroaldo the Younger (1477–1518) to publish. Beatus had a fair amount of information about this manuscript from printed sources. He knew that it had been brought to Italy by a certain "quaestor," or papal representative, and that the pope had paid five hundred ducats for it.[16] Beroaldo published the *editio princeps* in 1515. Andreas Alciati provided a series of notes to accompany its republication in 1516. Beatus reissued Alciati's notes in his 1519 edition and used them in his own *Commentariolus* on the *Germania*.

The rest of the major works, *Annales* XI–XVI and the *Historiae,* had a more complicated history. The oldest surviving manuscript version is Ms. Laurentianus 68.2 (called Mediceus II), a manuscript in Beneventan script of the eleventh century from Monte Cassino.[17] It became known through Boccaccio and passed through the collection of Niccolò Niccoli to the library of San Marco in Florence. However, the *editio princeps,* which appeared at Venice in 1470, issued by Johannes de Spira, was based on a manuscript that is now lost. It also included the *Germania* and *Dialogus* and was reprinted several times in the fifteenth century. One of these was issued by Franciscus Puteolanus (del Pozzo) who added the text of the *Agricola;* this edition became the *vulgata.*[18] All the surviving texts were issued as a group by Beroaldo. Froben printed them as a unit in 1519 and with Beatus' *Castigationes* in 1533 and 1544.

In his prefatory letter to the reader, Beroaldo complained of the poor state of his manuscript and Tacitus' difficult language and offered a small number of annotations on problematic passages.[19] Since he was the first to correct books I–VI, most accepted conjectures belong to him. Alciati's notes explained various historical and geographical questions, but did not incorporate any new manuscript readings.[20]

In 1519 Beatus simply offered an improved reprint of Beroaldo's text together with his important *Commentariolus;* he lacked any new manuscript material. This commentary has had a peculiar history.[21] Froben first printed it anonymously together with the *Germania* in May 1519. In August an edition of the *opera* together with Alciati's and Beatus' notes appeared, again anonymously. The notes were completely reworked for the 1533 edition and then expanded once again for the 1544 edition. However, the authorship of the original 1519 notes remained generally unknown; when they were printed in the collection of Renaissance treatises on German history, the *Schardius Redivivus,* in 1673, they were attributed to the Swiss humanist historian Henricus Glareanus, who had worked at Froben's.[22]

In the 1519 edition the *Annales* and *Historiae* were simply reprinted. In 1533 Beatus offered a new series of emendations and conjectures based on a new manuscript source. This was a fifteenth-century Italian manuscript, the *Codex Budensis* (or *Codex Budensis Rhenani* or *Yalensis I*, as it is alternately called).[23] Beatus received this manuscript as a gift from his friend Jacob Spiegel in 1518.[24] Spiegel (ca. 1483–1547), a nephew of Wimpfeling, had been Beatus' classmate in Sélestat and was a correspondent of Erasmus; he took a law degree at the University of Basel and subsequently served as an imperial councillor and secretary; he shared Beatus' literary interests and produced his own commentaries on humanist writers.[25]

Oddly, although Beatus had this manuscript in 1518, he did not use it for the 1519 edition. Perhaps he then lacked the time to deal with the manuscript properly. Possibly the *Germania* alone interested him and not the other sections of Tacitus that the *Budensis* covered. Or perhaps Froben wanted just a quick reprinting and not a thorough reworking. The simplest explanation is that Beatus was still not sufficiently clear in his own mind about approaching the manuscript; nor was he prepared to delay publication until he had consulted all available materials. He did not yet appreciate the ideal of *emendatio ope codicum*. He followed the lax standards of his day by printing what was most convenient. Considering his faulty technique at that time, it was arguably best that he did not try to integrate the manuscript readings into his commentary. Whatever the reasons for the delay, in time the *Budensis* would assume an important place in Beatus' editing. The manuscript that Spiegel presented to Beatus has had in its turn a rather complicated history.

The *Budensis* formerly had belonged to the King of Hungary, Matthias Corvinus (1458–1490).[26] Like all other manuscripts of Tacitus, it is truncated, containing only books XI–XXI, that is, six books of the *Annales* and five of the *Histories*. The manuscript is in humanist script and probably was written in Northern Italy between 1450 and 1470. It is uncertain how or when the manuscript came to Hungary. It had been housed at Buda in the royal library together with another important Tacitus manuscript, the *Budensis 9*.[27] The library suffered some neglect after the king's death, and there was some alienation. Spiegel probably obtained the Tacitus manuscript when he visited Buda with the Emperor Maximilian I in 1514. After its use in 1533, the history of the manuscript becomes unclear. Apparently it was out of Beatus' hands by 1534, perhaps as the result of political events.[28] Whatever its travels, the manuscript must have remained near Basel, since it next appeared in the collection of the Rhenish military officer J.-P. Dorsner. The classical scholar J. J. Oberlin used it for his edition of Tacitus in 1801. The manuscript then passed into the hands of Samuel Teleki, Lord Chancellor of Transylvania, who acquired it at Strasbourg in 1805. It seems again to have disappeared, since it was not used by any later nineteenth-century editor of Tacitus. In 1935 it was given to the Yale University Library, where it is presently housed.

Since the *Budensis* is a deluxe, commercial manuscript and not a scholar's copy, there was little editorial care taken for its accuracy. The scribe who produced it had been careless and produced a very corrupt text. There are many erasures and several lacunae (at XI, 21, 5; XV, 20, 21; XIX, 47, 20; XX, 17, 22). In addition, there are a number of marginal corrections, done by no fewer than five different hands, including variant readings taken from printed versions. Textually, it is related to Mediceus I.[29] It has several interpolations and inversions and a number of variant readings that are unique to it. All of these peculiarities made Beatus' work difficult but also offered him an excellent opportunity to utilize his skills.

This second set of *Castigationes* constituted a marked improvement over the *Commentariolus* of 1519. The 1533 version was not final; in 1544 Beatus issued a greatly expanded version. While it breaks the chronological sequence that has been followed thus far in this study, it is best to treat the 1533 and 1544 *Castigationes* together, merely pointing out where Beatus expanded his notes rather than treating them as two separate enterprises. The method employed was the same in both editions; only the thoroughness of the explanations changed.

Beatus provided an overview of his work in two introductory letters, one addressed to Bernhard of Cles, Archbishop of Trent and subsequently a cardinal, and a second *ad lectorem*. The archbishop was a humanist patron, and Erasmus had dedicated his edition of Irenaeus to him.[30] In his letter to the archbishop Beatus simply emphasized that in restoring an author, one must first carefully examine the manuscripts and then introduce one's own judgment.[31]

A fuller discussion of the method of restoration is found in the letter *ad lectorem.*[32] Beatus compared the *vulgata aeditio cum exemplari manuscripto sed recentiori,* that is, the *Budensis.* Although Beatus realized that it was of recent origin, he still did not reject it as a basis for textual emendation. He argued that errors in texts cannot be uncovered without careful comparison of various elements of a writer.[33] Beatus offered two examples of his procedure by analyzing individual phrases in other writers: one was drawn from Livy and another from Cicero's *De senectute,* where the poet Naevius is quoted.[34] While the Livy example is dependent on a manuscript, the Ciceronian emendation is conjectural. For Beatus, ancient writers remained corrupted because of the *stulta persuasio,* which keeps men from extending the labor required to restore them carefully. He again restated his method.

> Moreover let no one think that I am so avid for changing [texts] that either I have added or have removed anything short of the authority of the manuscript book. Nor as often as it happens that there appears "I wrote," "I corrected," "I restored," should anyone suspect that this was done just from my own talent. For when I changed something following my judgment—which I did only in the case of manifest errors—I bring this to the reader's attention in my *Castigationes.*[35]

As to what constituted "manifest error," that is obviously where a scholar's *iudicium* had to be trusted—although again Beatus would expect such changes to be announced. In any case, Beatus again justified the hard work entailed in his method by calling attention to the good it does for literature and its students.

THE METHOD OF THE *CASTIGATIONES*

In his *Castigationes* Beatus made certain fundamental contributions to the history of the Tacitean texts. Throughout the Middle Ages, the *Annales* and the *Historiae* were joined together as one work without any clear name. Beatus was the first to insist

on the name *Annales*.[36] Since the *Budensis,* as all other manuscripts of Tacitus, lacked a title, the manuscript offered no assistance on this matter. Still, Beatus believed that *Annales* was fitting and defended his choice.[37] He noted that other scholars
had offered various names: Puteolanus suggested *Actionum diur-
nalium historiae Augustae* and Beroaldo *Ab excessu divi Augusti
historiarum libri,* although he did not know what the Corvey
manuscript actually read. Various ancient authors (including
Flavius Vopiscus and Jordanes) were also cited.[38] Unfortunately, a further reference to Tertullian's *Apologeticus* 16, which
mentions book five of Tacitus' *Historia,* which he did cite, did
not lead Beatus to propose the existence of a second work.[39]
The fact that none of the surviving manuscripts contained a
title led him to suspect that all the manuscripts were defective
and that much of the text was missing.[40] As was true for all
ancient writers, and despite the particularly high regard in
which he was held in antiquity, not all of Tacitus' works had
survived the devastations of the German invasions or the hostil-
ity of some early Christians. That part of Tacitus' *opera* that had
been preserved, Beatus conceded, was due to the work of the
monks. Those monks who valued learning and who had seen to
the preservation of Tacitus after the decline of the Empire were
to be commended for their contributions to scholarship. Such
were the monks at the Benedictine Monastery of Corvey.[41] This
evaluation of monastic contributions to the transmission of classical knowledge was rather more positive than Beatus' usual
harsh criticisms of monks as scribes and historians.

For all of Beatus' ingenuity in establishing a proper name for
Tacitus' *Annales,* there were limits to his skill. He only vaguely
realized that the ancient references to *historiae* and *annales*
might refer to different books, and hence he did not think that
he was dealing with two distinct works. The solution to this
problem escaped all until Justus Lipsius some thirty years later
reasserted their separate identities.[42]

When Beatus compared his manuscript with the printed text,
he used the *editio princeps* of books I–VI, although he knew and
cited other editions. For the sections covered in the *Budensis,*
manuscript authority was primary. Beatus departed from it only
when there were obvious errors that he could silently correct or

note in his annotations.[43] Different terms were used to describe the manuscript, including *exemplar regium, codex regius, codex Budensis, exemplar Budense, volumen Budense,* and *volumen Matthiae Corvini.* Manuscript-based corrections, as Beatus noted, were introduced by such phrases as *sic scripsi, castigavi,* and *reposui.* At several points in the *De Germania* Beatus mentioned an *aeditio* or *codex vetus,* which he had received as a gift from his friend Hieronymus Artolf.[44] Artolf (d. 1541),[45] a teacher at Basel and an associate at Froben's press, had helped Beatus collate the *De Germania* in 1519. This *aeditio vetus* was a copy of a printed text, identified variously as the Roman edition of Beroaldo and the Nuremberg 1473 edition. Beatus found it useful because of certain *annotatiunculae* it contained.[46]

One element of some prominence in the 1533 *Castigationes* was Beatus' growing sensitivity to Tacitus' Latinity. While he realized the special qualities of Tacitus' style and how it differed from the purer, Ciceronian language of Livy, he nevertheless felt that the former had written well of important matters. He discussed the peculiarity of Tacitus' Latinity in the *Thesaurus constitutionum locutionumque et vocum Tacito solemnium.*[47] While basically a catalogue of unusual elements in Tacitus' language and comparative examples, it offered some manuscript readings. Tacitus' unfamiliar vocabulary required the consultation of other writers, especially Livy. The *Thesaurus* underwent some changes from 1533 to 1544 which show a modification of Beatus' attitude toward scribes' work as he became more knowledgeable about later ancient Latinity. Overall, these alterations demonstrate his growing control of classical philology and his increased sophistication as an editor, as well as his view of the dynamic elements in the history of the Latin language.[48]

The *Castigationes* contain justifications for Beatus' conjectures similar to those found in Tertullian and Pliny. He criticized the other printed versions when he felt that they had made unjustified changes,[49] although he also respected his predecessors' contributions.[50] He rejected both manuscript and printed versions when he felt it was necessary.[51] His conjectures, he emphasized, were essentially based on what was found in the manuscript.[52] Beatus called attention to the tentativeness of his conjectures and advised his readers when a conjecture was simply his *in-*

ventio and could properly be rejected.[53] Such statements show both his continued sensitivity to the limits of all conjectures and his realization of their utility.

> Since this is mere conjecture taken from the traces of a corrupt manuscript, we do not put those [guesses] forward here so that anyone should automatically daub his book with them but in order that no one should think that I have dodged the labor of research.[54]

Beatus argued that his conjectures should be neither credulously accepted nor arrogantly dismissed, since they were based on hard work, careful thought, and the manuscript.

While the *Castigationes* included many of Beatus' conjectures, they did not include them all. He incorporated in the text certain changes without specifying them as conjectures: yet another example of the gap between his principles and their execution. Thanks to the careful comparison of Beatus' edition with the great edition of Justus Lipsius of 1574 by José Ruysschaert and a recent study devoted to Beatus' Latin manuscripts by Pierre Petitmengin, we have a clearer idea of the type and number of unacknowledged alterations Beatus made in the text itself and those manuscript readings he ignored.[55] While many of these changes indicate Beatus' great talent as a critic and have become standard, they also show that he did not follow his own rule of making clear to the readers all the emendations he made in his text. His terminology remained problematic, since it did not highlight the distinction between manuscript readings and his own conjectures. Since he did not offer explanations for all his changes, we cannot follow him in detail. Still, if we give him the benefit of the doubt, we may suppose that he felt that the changes were obvious and required no specific defense. What is also telling in his favor is that many of them are from the first five (i.e., modern six) books of the *Annales,* for which he had no independent manuscript support. Beatus probably felt that he was allowed greater latitude, since he had no external assistance.[56]

An example from book one of the *Annales* illustrates Beatus' talents in pure conjecture. At I,13,14, the *editio princeps* reads *Quousque patieris Caesar, non adesse aput te rei publicae?*[57] which

Beatus believed to be erroneous. In emending the text, he did not simply make the obvious but incorrect change of *aput* to *apud,* since *aput* is a proper spelling, but he conjectured the word *caput* without the *te* following. His reading (*Quousque patieris Caesar, non adesse caput rei publicae?*) is to be found in the modern editions. Other scholars have since tried to improve upon Beatus' conjecture but without success. The *te* has been given particularly close attention (expanded to *tandem* usually), but the alternatives do not make the sentence any clearer. Even without a manuscript for support, Beatus was able to improve the text in such a way as to avoid unnecessary additions or changes, following his rules of simplicity and of close adherence to what was in the text.

As was his custom, Beatus duly noted the poor state of the manuscript, its marginal annotations—which included various conjectures and misplaced phrases[58]—and its numerous erasures.[59] Peculiarities of Tacitus' style were explained, often by reference to the *Thesaurus.* Two elements Beatus emphasized were Tacitus' love of brevity[60] and his use of Greek constructions.[61] This growing acquaintance with Tactitus' (as well as Tertullian's) Latinity and his care in categorizing its special elements were distinct advantages when he conjectured.

In general, the notes do not contain extensive discussions; Beatus simply offered his conjectures, cited the manuscript readings, or listed possible alternatives. When they are lengthy, it is usually the result of historical detail and citations to collateral sources. Unlike the Pliny *annotationes,* they were not meant primarily to teach, and the occasional discussions of scribal errors or the *docti*'s false corrections are not extensive. When they do occur, they follow the general form used in the Pliny notes; for example, they mention scribal confusion of *u* and *y.*[62] References to more detailed discussion of Tacitus' language in the *Thesaurus* account for their brevity.[63]

A significant characteristic of the *Castigationes* is the use of historical arguments to support conjectures. Beatus' deep knowledge of the German and Roman history informs the *Castigationes.* The security with which Beatus handled history allowed him to exploit his evidence in several ways. When correcting the phrase *Eosdem agros Ansibarii occupavere* (*Annales,* XIII, 55, 1,

modern reading *Eosdem agros Ampsivarii occupavere*), Beatus cited
Ammianus Marcellinus' *Res Gestae,* XX, 10, 1–2, where he read
Ansuarii. Beatus argued that error resulted when *b* was misread
for *v.* Since the passage explained that the Chauci had expelled
the Ampsivarii from their home, Beatus took the opportunity to
note that the Franks had stemmed from the Chauci and that the
ancients used the term *Frank* to designate several different tribes
in the same manner as the name Suevi.[64] Whether depending on
collateral authority or drawing support from historical events,
Beatus never tired of indicating the hard work required.[65]

The 1544 edition varied from that of 1533 primarily in the
increased number and length of several of the *Castigationes.* In
some cases the old notes incorporated new information; in a
few cases material from the earlier edition was excised. As a
general rule the later annotations attest to Beatus' increased
knowledge of classical history and of Tacitus' Latin style. This
reworked version was a major advance in Tacitean studies, and
Justus Lipsius used it in his edition and commentary on Tacitus.
Lipsius mentioned Beatus at several points, usually to correct
him, but occasionally to praise him for his ingenuity.[66] The
praise was appropriate, since Lipsius took over several of
Beatus' conjectures as his own. As a result, they have passed
under Lipsius' name until modern scholarship has reclaimed
them for their rightful author.

Ironically, the expanded version of the *Castigationes* at first
actually harmed Beatus' reputation as an editor. Some scholars
undervalued his skill because they did not realize that the 1544
notes were built on those of 1533.[67] They believed that Beatus'
correct conjectures in 1544 simply incorporated without ac-
knowledgment those from the 1534 Aldine edition. In fact, the
Aldine readings appeared after Beatus' work and depended on
his emendations. Consequently, in his own day Beatus' work
was not fully appreciated; this misunderstanding may have
even led some to question Beatus' integrity.

Beatus' contribution to the text of the *Historiae* and *Annales*
was major and alone would place him among the great Renaissance editors.[68] It is not inappropriate to quote the most recent
editor and commentator on the *Annales* in order to establish
Beatus' place in the textual tradition of Tacitus. Praising Beatus

as "a scholar of the highest ability and foremost amongst the Latinists of his generation," F. R. D. Goodyear continues:

> Rhenanus' success may in part be measured by the ready absorp-
> tion of his conjectures and his observations into the common stock
> of material upon which his successors worked. But the conjectures
> at least may conveniently be separated out and assessed. They are
> naturally far fewer than Beroaldus', but they are not few, and they
> show the activity of an exceptionally penetrating and disciplined
> intellect. Indeed, I go further: if quality of emendations were the
> only criterion of scholarly excellence, Rhenanus might vie with
> Pichena and Nipperdey for the second place amongst Tacitean
> scholars. His conjectures are not often, one must admit, brilliant
> and exciting, but they possess the more valuable quality of often
> being right. In his patient attention to grammar and idiom, and his
> concern with logic and precision, Rhenanus might well be com-
> pared wtih Madvig.[69]

Such praise, after more than four hundred years of emendation, by a modern scholar intimately familiar with the text testifies to the centrality of Beatus' contribution.

Great as his service to Tacitus' major works was, Beatus also improved the texts of the minor writings. For these he had no new manuscript support and had to depend on his own knowl-edge and skill. When correcting the *Agricola,* he lamented that he had no new manuscripts to assist his work.[70] He doubted that Tacitus actually wrote the *De oratoribus dialogus,* although he admitted that whoever wrote it was learned.[71] Again, several of his conjectures have been accepted as the *vulgata* readings.

The Tacitean text that was closest to Beatus' interests and the one over which he worked more extensively than the others was the *Germania.* We have already noted the complicated history of his annotations to this work. These *Castigationes* show Beatus at his best and demonstrate his development as a historian. In gen-eral the 1519 *Commentariolus* was really not a set of textual emen-dations but rather a series of notes on specific names and places mentioned in the text. Thus it was very much an historico-geographical commentary. The *Castigationes* were properly tex-tual emendations meant to improve the state of the text. They were, naturally, informed with Beatus' broad historical knowledge, but that knowledge served an essentially textual critical function. In a few cases Beatus referred to his earlier work for fuller explanations of names.[72] Beatus' strong historical sense is evident throughout the *Castigationes,* such as in his implicit rejection of the false Berosus by not mentioning his name, although in 1519 he had cited him as a source. Further, the 1519 *Commentariolus* discussed in some detail several contemporary historians' opinions, while the later annotations rely much more on primary sources.[73] Beatus' aim in both versions was essentially the same, to explain the references to the German tribes and places mentioned in the *Germania.* What is different is the degree of his sophistication. As with the *Annales* and *Historiae,* Beatus' conjectures have undergone a reevaluation. One modern scholar, in noting that some fifty of his readings have been accepted, argued "that no single editor has ever rendered service to the *Germania* comparable with that of Rhenanus."[74]

The textual improvements that Beatus proposed in the *Castigationes* were not limited to Tacitus. In order to emend the text of in that author, Beatus also had occasion to correct collateral authors, especially historians. At *Germania,* 28.2, he conjectured an improved reading for Germanic names mentioned by Paul the Deacon in his *Historia Langobardorum.*[75] Toward the end of the *Germania,* 46. 3, the historian of the Goths, Jordanes, a *mendosus scriptor,* received the same treatment when Beatus corrected a reading found *in vulgatis aeditionibus.*[76]

The *Castigationes* to the *Germania* contain several interesting digressions on contemporary problems. In general, such notices were lacking in the notes to the *Annales* and the *Historiae;* one exception is a passing reference to Henry VIII of England.[77] In the *Germania* Beatus expressed himself on the troubles of his day in indirect ways. His patriotism led him to praise the virile spirit and the simplicity of the early Germans.[78] His knowledge of the German past caused occasional digressions.[79] He noted that other peoples can prosper under foreign skies but not the Germans.[80] He lamented the evils that afflicted modern Germany and complained of the moral failings of contemporary priests.[81] Beatus sharply contrasted Tacitus' picture of the morally upright ancient Germans with contemporary

Germany, which was being torn asunder by reform-minded zealots. The *Germania* was, therefore, not only an ancient monument in need of correcting but also an opportunity for Beatus to highlight contemporary national afflictions.

One final point should be made before passing from Tacitus.[82] In order to establish more fully where Beatus' work fitted into Renaissance textual criticism, it is useful to compare him to Justus Lipsius, who as mentioned above appropriated parts of Beatus' work. Lipsius published his edition of Tacitus almost fifty years after Beatus issued the first version of the *Castigationes*. The great *sospitator Taciti*, as Lipsius was known, made major contributions to the Tacitean text, but he did not display a textual method much superior to the German's. Lipsius used Beatus' edition for his *vulgata* text, but for his notes he used the edition of Domenico Ferretti of 1542. In citing from his various sources, Lipsius did not make it clear when he was borrowing conjectures from other scholars, citing from a manuscript, or proposing his own conjectures. Indeed, he was decidedly ungenerous toward the scholars he consulted for alternate readings or for hints as to better readings. He simply took over their work and then frequently criticized them. Lipsius used more manuscripts with greater sophistication than Beatus, but his methodology was no major improvement. In comparison with Lipsius (as with Robortello), Beatus emerges as as careful a scholar and generally more generous in his attitudes toward others. Given the decades that separated these men, Beatus' talents are the more exceptional.

The *Castigationes* to Tacitus marked a major phase in Beatus' development and were a monument to his talents. They represented a movement away from the explicit pedagogical concerns evident in the *Annotationes* to Pliny and toward a simpler, more direct means of citation and presentation of conjectures. He had reached a stage in his textual critical development in which he felt confident in most cases simply to call attention to his procedure and present its results for his readers' judgment. His willingness to undertake one of the most difficult of Latin writers testifies to his realization of Tacitus' importance and to his own serious intentions as a historian, while successful conjectures prove his broad knowledge of ancient history and philology and his keen critical sense.

THE *ANNOTATIONES* TO LIVY

One of the techniques Beatus employed to explain Tacitus was systematic comparison with Livy. Thus the 1533 *Castigationes* were closely related to the 1535 *Annotationes* to Livy's *Ab urbe condita*. In fact, in the *Castigationes* Beatus had already provided a series of improved readings of Livy based on his use of the manuscript he would employ in the *Annotationes*.[83] There was almost an inevitability to this, both as a continuation of Beatus' editorial work and as a fundamental element in his growing control of ancient history. Since Beatus considered and criticized previous editors of Livy, some background should prove valuable.

Humanist fascination with Livy began with Petrarch, who corrected the text while at Avignon.[84] He glossed the first and third Decades and made a fundamental contribution to improving the text in circulation. Florentine humanists in the first half of the fifteenth century were also active in correcting Livy. Their work passed to Naples in 1444 when Cosimo de' Medici presented a copy of Livy to King Alfonso, called the *Codex Regius*, which Antonio Panormita, Bartolomeo, Facio and Lorenzo Valla glossed.[85] In his *Emendationes in T. Livium* (covering books XXI–XXVI), Valla proved his superiority to his colleagues. These notes were a tour de force of textual skill and manuscript analysis. All the paleographical and linguistic knowledge that Valla commanded went into them.

In 1469 the *editio princeps* appeared in Rome. Edited by Giovanni Andrea Bussi, it contained the First, Third, and Fourth Decades (save for book XXXIII).[86] In his introductory letter to Pope Paul II and the papal nephew Cardinal Marco Barbo, Bussi recounted the humanist history of Livy, citing Petrarch's interventions in the text. He did not mention Valla or the manner of his own corrections. The text had been studied in the school of the great Vittorino da Feltre (Bussi's own teacher). Giovanni Andrea Campano reprinted the text soon after. He also discussed scribal errors and tried to give some idea of how they had deformed the text.[87] He noted how the copyists changed what they did not understand and could not read and then emended according to their own judgment. Campano hoped that the new art of printing would limit the number of such errors.

Bussi and Campano offered their "corrected" versions without notes or commentary. Marcantonio Sabellico, in his 1491 Venetian edition, provided a series of notes.[88] Like Campano, Sabellico had great hopes for printing.[89] His notes were valued and reissued by later Livy editors, Alexander Mutianus (Milan, 1495, 1505) and Josse Bade (Paris, 1511).[90] Bade initiated the Northern European publishing career of Livy. After him, Nicholas Carbach found and published in 1519 at Mainz a manuscript that allowed him to restore the missing section of book XL. This edition included prefatory letters by Ulrich von Hutten and Erasmus.[91] In his own introductory letter Carbach noted that the manuscript he found in Mainz was written in *Langobardis characteribus,* a general term for early medieval script.[92]

Between 1518 and 1521 the Aldine press issued an important version of Livy edited by Franciscus Asulanus (Francesco Toresano), which brought together all the new materials available.[93] In 1525 Jacobus Sobius produced an edition at Cologne.[94] Eucherius Cervicornus published his version in 1528,[95] and another Paris edition appeared in 1529.[96] In 1531 Froben issued an improved version that included the texts of books XLI–XLV, from a fifth-century manuscript at the Monastery of Lorsch, edited by Simon Grynaeus.[97] In a prefatory letter Erasmus described the manuscript as of admirable age but written in such a way that the letters were difficult to distinguish and that much care was needed in editing it.[98] Thus, by the time Beatus came to deal with Livy, he had a rich textual history to absorb.

Beatus based his notes on two manuscripts. The first was the *Codex Vormaciensis,* also called the *Codex Borbetomagensis.*[99] Beatus obtained this defective manuscript in 1529 from Reinhard von Rupper (Riepur), Dean of the Cathedral of Worms, through his friend Michael Westermann.[100] It provided the basis for the annotations from I, 20, 2 to VI, 28, 7. The second fragmentary manuscript came from the Chapter Library of Speyer. It contained books 26 to 40, with book 33 and part of 40 missing. Beatus used it to annotate the last section of book 26 to the end of the Third Decade at book 30.[101] Beatus called this manuscript a *vetustissimus codex* and described how the scribe had misplaced sections of the text, which required him to restore them in their proper place (book XXVI, 41, 18 to 43, 8). Both manuscripts were destroyed after printing, although a surviving page from the Speyer manuscript dates it to the eleventh century. The Speyer manuscript also was used by Sigismund Gelen to annotate the remaining sections.

Beatus collaborated in annotating Livy with Sigismund Gelen (Gelenius, 1497–1554).[102] Gelen also worked for Froben and he edited several of the same authors as Beatus, including Tertullian, Pliny, Velleius Paterculus, and Livy. Gelen's editorial range was impressive, covering a variety of Greek and Latin, ancient and patristic writers. Coming approximately a decade after Beatus, he benefited from the traditions established by Erasmus and Beatus at Froben's press and from the greater availability of manuscripts. In general, Gelen's textual method was the same as Beatus'; their strong and weak points were basically the same.

The similarity of their editorial approaches no doubt reflected Gelen's absorption of Beatus' methodology. For all the advantages he had in observing Beatus, Gelen did not really go beyond him. Certainly in the Livy edition his notes are indistinguishable in detail from Beatus'. He provided his readers with information on the state of his manuscripts,[103] complained of the errors introduced by the copyist[104] and the arrogance of the *docti*.[105] He was devoted to the same paleographical assessment of errors and criticized his contemporaries for their ignorance in reading old hands.[106] Insofar as Gelen was a student of Beatus, we may see the latter's method as having a normative character in the Froben circle.

The respect Gelen displayed for Beatus extended to following his conjectures to authors he was himself editing. This is seen in the example from Ammianus Marcellinus, which will be discussed later.[107] Beatus seems also to have held his friend in high regard, at least high enough to collaborate with him. Despite this, Gelen did not escape Beatus' critical eye. Beatus complained that Gelen had not given sufficient consideration to the manuscripts of Pliny in his corrections to the *Naturalis historia.* Both he and Erasmus regretted Gelen's tendency to tamper with the texts he proofread.[108]

In his introductory letter to Franz Delf, Gelen praised Beatus as a *vir acerrimi iudicii* who diligently searched for and found manuscripts of Livy in the libraries of cathedral chapters and monasteries.[109] His discoveries provided the basis for rescuing the *antiqua lectio* of Livy from darkness. To deal with the problems in the manuscripts and the discrepancies between manuscript and printed versions, Beatus made an accurate collation and corrected a good part of Livy's history so that the *sincera lectio* has been restored.[110] In assessing his own contribution, Gelen agreed with Beatus that the *recepta lectio* was contaminated, but that since it had been accepted for a thousand years it still offered a better base text than the new versions coming from printers. While Gelen admitted that he was not the first to have inspected the old manuscripts of Livy, he did maintain that many did not read old volumes with care. Like Beatus, he believed that his contributions could provide a clear picture of the problematic passages in the Speyer manuscript.

Beatus' annotations are rich in manuscript citations, conjectures, and philological and historical information. Gelen's account shows that Beatus had remained desirous of obtaining new manuscripts. The Monastery of Speyer especially attracted him.[111] In trying to arrive at sensible readings, Beatus consulted three printed editions of Livy, the Rome 1469 edition, the Aldine edition of 1520 edited by Franciscus Asulanus (which he collated with his manuscripts), and the Cologne 1525 edition of Jacobus Sobius. Beatus found these editions faulty and criticized them as well as printing in general.[112] He remained dedicated to proposing corrections *ad fidem vetusti codicis* and proclaimed that he followed the authority of his manuscripts wherever possible.[113]

The limitations of Beatus' method are also evident.[114] He referred indiscriminately to *antiquior lectio, syncera lectio, germana lectio, vetus lectio,* and *pristina lectio* as well as *archetypus* to designate his own reconstructions of the text. He even used two different terms for the manuscript in a single annotation.

While often citing manuscript readings with a variety of phrases (*ex veteri libro, ex antiquo volumine*, etc.) and setting off his own improvements (*emendavimus* and *addidimus*), he did not always distinguish the readings he extracted from the manuscript and his own conjectures. As was his custom, obvious errors were silently corrected in the manuscript. Nor did Beatus indicate cases when his manuscript and the Aldine exemplar differed but he preferred the Aldine reading.

One of the most disconcerting elements in Beatus' mode of citation occurs at the beginning of the sixth book when he quoted a reading, ". . . *in altero exemplari quod nobis ex Vuormacia communicavit D. Reinhardus a Rietpur primarii templi Decanus* . . . ," and then shortly after, ". . . *mox in altero exemplari manu scripto.*" These raise the question whether Beatus had a second Worms manuscript from which he extracted new readings.[115] Despite the seemingly explicit references to such a second manuscript, here Beatus is simply indistinct in his language. Lack of specificity has been seen in all his manuscript citations, and there is no reason to think that he has suddenly changed. Indeed, the similarity of expression when describing this other manuscript and the manner in which he originally identified the Worms manuscript make it certain that he was referring to one manuscript rather than two. Still, his language has raised a problem that has caused some concern over his citations.

More than he had in his earlier editions, Beatus betrayed a sharpness of tone in his notes. This is first evident in his discussion of scribal errors. The same themes that were prominent in the Pliny annotations are repeated here. He noted that it was the *mos librariorum* to change *u* to *b* and *b* to *u*.[116] One copyist he accused of changing a phrase *pro libidine sua*.[117] Another could not distinguish majuscule letters in an old manuscript and hence invented his own reading.[118] A single change of a word or of even a letter had distorted a passage's meaning.[119] At one point he remarked with obvious annoyance, "It is tedious to tell what deceived the scribe. Let us go quickly to other things."[120] He no doubt felt that through Pliny, Tertullian, Tacitus and now Livy, he had made this point often and forcefully enough.

Beatus' tone became even more censorious when he turned to the conjectures of scholars. He complained that it was easier to correct the mistakes of the scribes than the "corrections" of the learned.[121] Twice Beatus referred to learned conjecturors as "asini," once as "castigator infelix"; he remarked of one contaminated passage that "priscum verbum foede depravavit temeraria castigatoris manus."[122] One scribe erased a word he found in the text and introduced his own misreading.[123] At the beginning of book XXVIII, Beatus doubted the reading *Quum transitu Hasdrubalis quantum in Italia declinaverat belli,* which was found in all the printed texts.[124] He objected to *declinaverat* and proposed *inundaverat,* which he felt was more fitting. Since he believed there was an error, he sarcastically expressed a wish to hear the *professores* explain the passage. He suggested that the error had entered the text either through Petrarch or Vittorino da Feltre, who in turn influenced Valla. Another possible source of contamination was a monk who might have added *transitum* as a reminiscence of the Christian liturgy. Notwithstanding Beatus' conjecture, the accepted modern text supports the *vulgata* and vindicates Petrarch or Vittorino, if either was indeed responsible for the emendation.

Corruptions in the text in no way inhibited the *professores* in expounding their own versions of events and thereby compounding error. In glossing a passage in book II, 30, 1, Beatus commented,

> I am amazed how the professors get out of this when they discuss Livy in the public classrooms. And there is hardly another author read more widely in the schools. What did that Achilles of professors, Filippo Beroaldo,[125] allege who so often publicly and privately lectured on the Decades of Livy at Bologna?[126]

Thus even the greatest of the university lecturers fell into the habit of defending the impossible. As in many cases, Beatus' emendation of the text is partly sustained by modern evidence.

Beatus' bitterest complaints concerned the critics who simply put down on a page whatever comes into their minds without reference to manuscripts, and who are followed by the equally credulous readers.

> But no one wants to work. Whatever first comes into the mind, that we support. Then, unless solecism is manifest, they all follow a read-

ing of this type. Thus Beroaldo reads it, they say, so Sabellico, so Battista Pio. And who doubts it further? Indeed, these were learned and famous men, but who preferred to interpret all things rather than to understand them. They trusted in their own talents, they trusted in their learning. Nor did they think it necessary to consult manuscripts. Rather, they rarely did. In fact, they were content with the authority and the good name which they had created for themselves with everybody, so that *ipse dixit* was now pretty well sufficient. But it is another matter to correct the books of the ancient authors. For not only learning is necessary but also steadfast study, labor and diligence and above all sharp judgment.[127]

In exasperation with such men and their misplaced sense of authority, Beatus lamented, "O negligentiam nostram ingentem qui non dignamur veteres codices inspicere!"[128]

This theme led Beatus to question not only the diligence of editors but even their honesty, and to fault them for an inclination to lead readers astray. When discussing a passage in book XXVIII, 8, 11, referring to Philip of Macedon's movement from Corinth into Italy, he correctly expressed doubts, since a change of locations such as is suggested in the text was much too broad for the narrative.

It would seem to me obvious that someone wanted to deceive the readers. But it is amazing that this was not perceived by anyone up to this time. It is necessary here to say frankly what is the truest thing—that the *studiosi* confide too much in certain printing shops, as in Italy that of Asulanus, as if everything that comes from these were most carefully corrected. Those ought to be believed to the extent that we test the matter first with judgment and collation. Meanwhile the *studiosi* often pay the penalty they deserve for their credulity.[129]

Since he has not followed such an intellectually lax method, Beatus could say, "Trust me reader here for I will not deceive you," and "O misere tractatum Livium!"[130]

In justifying the confidence he expected, Beatus explained the state of his manuscripts and the reasons for his conjectures. He noted when there were recent additions written in it,[131] where marginal notes were present,[132] where there were erasures,[133] and where there were lacunae.[134] He cited readings from printed books that were marked with asterisks,[135] or when he felt a reading should have been so marked.[136] He also explained when his manuscript and the vulgate did not agree,[137] and when he was using conjectures.[138] He defended these latter by proclaiming that he did not offer them out of a sense of novelty and that he did not hide anything from the reader.[139]

Paleographical investigation remained fundamental to any discovery of the *vera lectio*. Although not as common as in the Pliny notes, Beatus did on occasion offer some details of a paleographical nature. In book I, Beatus doubted the reading *Itaque Pontinae manubiae* (I, 57, 7, modern reading: *Itaque Pometinae manubiae*) and explained:

> Although the old volume contains *Pomptinae*, I think nevertheless it ought to read *Pometinae manubiae*. Now the old exemplars almost one thousand years ago were written in majuscule letters. Now *E* majuscule is not dissimilar to *P*. Therefore, *POMETINAE* easily is turned into *POMPTINAE*.[140]

While again lacking specificity, Beatus would seem here to be referring to the use of uncial in old manuscripts, again indicating a growing sense of historical periodization of manuscripts.

In correcting Livy Beatus occasionally departed from the manuscript. Style then became an important element in determining what Livy had actually written. Indeed, ignorance of Livy's style had caused error in Beatus' view. He understood, for example, that Livy used archaic words.[141] Consideration of Livy's Latinity led Beatus to offer broader stylistic observations and exploit further manuscript evidence. He noted that Livy often used *qui* for *quis,* a usage characteristic of Tertullian and Cicero.[142] This stylistic peculiarity generated errors in all printed editions of Cicero's *De senectute* (21). Editors read *qui sibi, quibus ipsi debeant,* where they should have read *qui sibi, cui ipsi debeant.* Beatus had established this true reading from consultation of a manuscript he had found in the Church of Saint John in Sélestat. In addition to style, Beatus tried to explain problematic passages by appeal to historical context.[143]

Beatus believed that the truly learned would accept his views while the ignorant and stupid would not.[144] His method, in his view, was basically conservative and one that good judgment must acknowledge.[145] He proclaimed that all *studiosi* owed him gratitude for his exposing false readings in printed texts.[146] Ultimately, Beatus found his work its own justification:

> And I would gladly yield to the admonishment of anyone with better ideas not only in these Livian *castigationes* but in those of Pliny and other authors. Nay rather I will thank them in addition. For I desire literature to be supported.[147]

Like Erasmus, Beatus saw in the correcting of ancient writers a moral activity that was a vital element in reforming society.

The call for the collation of manuscripts, hard work, and critical judgment represented an ideal and is not necessarily always an accurate mirror of Beatus' procedure. Occasionally in the annotations to Livy he indicated that the availability of a new manuscript did not lead him to collate it fully with the printed version, but rather that he went to the manuscript to solve problems in particular passages. Thus he selected those passages for correction not from systematic collation but from sense and literary preference—in short, from his *iudicium*. In correcting the phrase *stramento intecta, omnibus velut de industria alimentis ignis* (XXVII, 3, 3), Beatus explained, "Since this phrase displeased me because of *omnibus* in the ablative, I inspected the old exemplar and found there written not *omnibus* but *omne*."[148] Later in the same book (XXVII, 25, 3), the problematic phrase *aliis sententiis notantibus praefectum* received similar treatment. Beatus disliked the vulgate reading and went to the Speyer manuscript, where he found written *aliis socii notantibus;* from this reading he conjectured that Livy had actually meant *aliis ocii notantibus praefectum*.[149] Beatus noted that the erroneous reading was mixed with the *germana lectio*.

> Who would think that there is any defect in these words? Nevertheless, here is a monstrous error. When I first read this passage, the word *sententiis* did not satisfy me, though it might have been put in the ablative, for *per sententias*. But why was a plural word necessary? I examined the Speyer manuscript and found there written *aliis socii notantibus*.

Further support for these comes from a reference in the annotations to Pliny. In commenting on a passage in book X at the end of his *Annotationes,* Beatus noted that "this place . . . is among the first which I began to restore."[150] Beatus obviously did not work from the beginning of the text he was restoring but selected problematic passages for treatment while reading. Such instances show that Beatus turned to his manuscript on specific occasions when he felt that the printed text was faulty; he did not make a collation of manuscript and printed text. In this Beatus followed a general Renaissance editorial practice.

More than in his other editorial endeavors, Beatus provided a scholarly pedigree for his work on Livy. He emphasized that the *volumen Vormaciense* was a copy of the *exemplar* corrected by Dexter Flavianus Nicomachus and Victorianus Nicomachus, the fourth-century Roman editors of Livy who provided posterity with the base text.[151] At one point he cited an annotation in the margin of the manuscript, which he ascribed to the Nichomachi or another old authority, and then argued that a scribe had integrated it into the text.[152] Through information in the Aldine edition, Beatus learned about more recent treatments of Livy by Petrarch, Vittorino da Feltre, Sabellicus, Bussi, Thaddeus Ugolettus, and Gian Battista Pio.[153] As already mentioned, Beatus believed that Petrarch and other Italians had been responsible for contaminating the text through their conjectures. He found that they had been too quick to conjecture from the sense of a passage. Valla, however, received special praise.[154] But although his *Emendationes* on Livy were available in two editions (Paris 1528 and Lyons 1532), Beatus did not discuss them in any detail, since he received his information on them indirectly, through other scholars.

It is regrettable that Beatus did not give greater consideration to Valla. Still, it is useful to compare Beatus to his erudite predecessor even if only briefly.[155] Both men followed essentially the same procedures. They concentrated on the text and usually did not wander from it. They used historical arguments both for explaining the text and for broadening the reader's knowledge. Finally, both depended on a paleographical method of carefully investigating words and letter forms. They usually informed their readers whenever they conjectured. Both men treated their texts with integrity and tried to follow a method that avoided what they perceived as the excesses of their contemporaries.

Scholarly treatment of Beatus' Livy annotations and references to the lost Speyer manuscript offer yet another instructive example of the changing reputation of Renaissance editing.[156] In the seventeenth and eighteenth centuries many scholars treated Beatus as an undependable witness of the Speyer readings. The availability of more manuscripts from different traditions led some to doubt that Beatus had accurately reflected his manuscript sources when offering emendations. Indeed, some considered him a liar. It was only in the nineteenth century, when fairly complete manuscript comparisons could be undertaken, that the validity of Beatus' textual method and his truthfulness were established. Since then, Beatus has taken his place among the major editors of Livy, and Renaissance textual criticism to a degree has been vindicated.

THE THIRD EDITION OF TERTULLIAN

Beatus followed Livy with a third edition of Tertullian in 1539.[157] He had not given so much of his own time to any other Christian writer, nor had he had so many manuscripts with which to correct an author. Although this new edition partly resulted from Beatus' growing knowledge of ancient Church history and his changing religious ideas, its immediate justification was the availability of a manuscript from the monastery of Gorze. He used this new authority extensively but in an indirect manner. Beatus had the manuscript collated with his printed edition by a monk at Gorze, Hubertus Custineus, with assistance from Dominicus Florentinus and Claudius Cantiuncula (Claude Chansonette).[158] Chansonette, a jurist from Basel, humanist, commentator on Erasmus' Greek New Testament, and manuscript collector, seems to have been the key figure. Froben had originally contacted him on this matter in May 1527 in preparation for the second edition of Tertullian. Chansonette seems to have performed his task carefully, comparing the manuscript and printed text and noting different readings. Nevertheless, the collation either was not ready in time for the second edition or difficulties with the text, perhaps the number of Greek words, prevented its use. Whatever the reason, it was not until the third edition that its readings were integrated into the *opera*. In accepting this collation Beatus could not control the work of his friends and he could not be certain that his own method had been employed in it. He put his confidence in work that could have been poorly executed. Nevertheless, he felt that he could judge it even without seeing the manuscript.[159]

This new material provided Beatus with the opportunity to expand his annotations and to revise the earlier text. Its exploitation was limited at first, since Beatus had not realized the number of Greek phrases Tertullian used. In preparing the new edition he was not in Basel, so Gelen had the task of overseeing the printing.[160] In other ways Beatus improved on the text. He added a section explaining the *Proverbia* that Tertullian used and cited additional proverbs, especially Greek ones, in the notes.[161] He knew that Tertullian had depended on Greek writers for much of his information, especially about the heretical writers, and cited a variety of Greek writers, most frequently Irenaeus. Tertullian's preference for Greek grammar especially interested Beatus. He noted the use of the elliptical Greek construction of ἔχω with the genitive, which Tertullian translated into *habeo* and the genitive.[162] Similarly, Tertullian used *habere* with the force of *posse* and *debere* in imitation of Greek.[163]

Beatus understood that Tertullian was not simply dependent on Greek forms for his usages. His growing appreciation of Tertullian's *elegantia Africana*[164] made him sensitive to the peculiar qualities of Tertullian's style. Beatus correctly noted the relationship of Tertullian's Latinity to that of Apuleius in their preferences for archaic vocabulary, vulgar idioms, and Greek forms.[165] Tertullian was a *novator vocabulorum,* and his original use of language required careful and expert study. Hence he turned *tessera,* a shortened form of a Greek word meaning a small square block or token, into *contesseratio.*[166] This example, in turn, gave Beatus an opportunity to discuss ancient Christian customs. This appreciation of Tertullian as a master of language caused Beatus to judge his style *solennis mos loquendi.*[167] Beatus' control of the elements that constituted Tertullian's language made him better able to exploit his new manuscript source.

Beatus used the collation made from the Gorze manuscript extensively to correct the text and mentioned it explicitly in several forms: *ex collatione Gorziensis, ex castigatiunculis Gorziensis codicis ad nos missae, ex indice ad nos missae collationis, ex Gorziensibus adnotamentis* and *ex annotatiunculis Gorziensibus.*[168] Despite such references, Beatus did not note every change he had made in the text, continuing a practice used in his earlier editions. The annotations consequently show only part of his debt to the Gorze readings. Even though Beatus had this collation before him, he did not follow it consistently; at times he favored readings from his other manuscripts, but his selections were rather arbitrary insofar as we can judge. When citing Gorze readings, he sometimes invoked the collation while at other times he referred to the *Gorziense exemplar* and cited readings *ex Gorziensi* as if he had consulted it himself. Even at this advanced stage of his career, Beatus' terminology could be confusing.

With three manuscripts available to him, Beatus gave a much fuller account of alternate readings and his conjectures.[169] When the three contained different versions of the same text, he cited their various readings.[170] Conjecture occasionally remained necessary *contra fidem exemplarium.*[171] In departing from the manuscripts and proposing his own readings, Beatus explained, "I know that one ought to handle the monuments of ancient writers scrupulously and ought not to change lightly or on the spot what one does not understand, and this is my custom."[172] Nevertheless, he changed what he felt required correction. Beatus expressed his satisfaction when the Gorze manuscript confirmed an earlier conjecture.[173] Paleography remained a basis for correcting error.[174] Collateral authors, especially Iraeneus and Cyprian of Carthage, also provided a means of solving some dilemmas.[175] At one point he invoked Erasmus' annotations to Jerome.[176]

When Beatus relied on his own conjectural abilities, he again showed himself a knowledgeable corrector. In a passage from the second book of *Ad uxorem*, 2, 4, Beatus emended the reading *Christus cecinit* to *Apostolus cecinit.*[177] He defended his change on the basis of what he suspected was a misreading of an abbreviation and the sense of the sentence. His reconstruction has been accepted as one of the most likely solutions for a problematic passage.

For all his conjectural skills, Beatus consistently looked to his manuscript. The availability of the Gorze collation permitted the addition of new sets of annotations. Since neither the Hirsau nor the Payerne manuscripts contained the *Apologeticus,* Beatus had simply reprinted an earlier version in 1521 and 1528 with only a few conjectural changes in the sidenotes. But in 1539, with the Gorze readings at hand, Beatus provided the *Apologeticus* with its own set of notes. As Beatus noted, no treatise of Tertullian benefited as much from the availability of a new manuscript as the *Apologeticus.*[178]

While Beatus often cited manuscript readings, the defects that are observable in his earlier editions remain. He depended on others for the collation, which he did not check personally. Nor did he provide any system by which to exclude readings or to favor the readings of one manuscript over those of another. General preference was given to the Gorze manuscript, but this was not justified by its superiority. Beatus' irregular methods of citing both his conjectures and the manuscript readings themselves make it impossible for later editors to reconstruct his lost codices.[179]

One set of treatises in the *opera omnia* presented special textual and interpretative problems. These were the antiheretical treatises, especially the five books *Adversus Marcionem,* the *De praescriptione adversus haereticos,* and the *Adversus Valentinianos.* As a group they dealt with questions that were generally little known in the Renaissance. Beatus gave his fullest consideration to the *Adversus Valentinianos;* indeed, it received the longest set of annotations.[180] Beatus was fortunate in having Erasmus' edition of Irenaeus to assist him, since Tertullian relied heavily on Irenaeus. Beatus took every opportunity to compare the two in order to offer clearer readings and exact explanations. The difficulty of the terms used by the heretical sects led Beatus to republish from the 1528 edition a list of Greek terms with Latin translations and a schematic diagram depicting the Valentinian cosmos.[181]

One example from the *Adversus Valentinianos* will demonstrate how Beatus brought all the elements of his technique into play when he rightly questioned the reading *Accipe alia ingenia circurianiana* (XXXVII, 1).[182] While he found justification for it in both Irenaeus and his manuscripts, he nevertheless felt that it did not belong in context. He proposed instead the word *lyncuriana,* which meant a gem or carbuncle. His reasoning was that since the *perspicacitas ingenii* was the sentence's theme, the comparison to the hard gem seemed sensible. He cited Pliny (8, 137) for the meaning of *lyncuriana.* Lynceus was one of the Argonauts and was noted for his clear vision. Beatus concluded by noting that his conjecture changed no other element in the sentence, an important criterion for him.

While for the most part the 1539 annotations were new, some simply repeated earlier ones, others were augmented with new information, and a few cases were radically rewritten to argue a different point. In an annotation to the *Adversus Valentinianos* (XIV, 4), Beatus read in 1521 *Quia nullum catuli laureolum fuerit exercitata,* which he properly judged corrupt. (The modern version reads *quia nullum Catulli Laureolum fuerit exercitata,* "because she [Achamotha] had not practiced herself in the part of Catullus' Laureolus. . . .")[183] Beatus argued that Tertullian had actually written *Quia millum catuli aureolum fuerit exercitata.* Taking the passage as ironic, Beatus felt Tertullian compared the Gnostic subdeity Acthamotha to a dog or cur (*catulus*) with a golden collar (*millum*).[184] He cited Festus for the meaning of *millum* and realized that Tertullian had used a Graecism.[185] He offered his version to the reader to assess, but admitted that he would have preferred *quis millum catulilla urceolum fuerit exercitata* because he believed that the passage alluded to teaching curs to jump over a pot of water.

Erudition led Beatus greatly astray in this case. The phrase was indeed faulty, but the ultimate solution was much simpler, as he realized in the third edition.[186] He now knew that the allusion was to a play by the playwright Catullus called *Laureolus,* staged in A.D. 41.[187] In the play a criminal was actually crucified on stage (although whether he died at that performance or a subsequent one is uncertain). Martial (*Spect.* 7), Juvenal (VIII), Suetonius (*Cal.* 57), and Josephus (*An. Jud.* XIX) mentioned it and its gruesome denouement, and Beatus cited them all as well as several other ancient authorities. Beatus must have found the correct reading in the Gorze collation, since he had a different lemma in 1539 (*Quia nullum Catulli Laureolum fuerit exercitata*). In any case, he had corrected his error. He was as worthy as Tertullian of the designation *omnis antiquitatis peritissimus*.

The difficulty of Tertullian's style and the relative obscurity of much of the history of the early Church required much space for explanations of the historical background of Tertullian's treatises.[188] Unlike his earlier classical editions, in which contemporary events were only occasionally mentioned, Beatus now discussed modern religious and theological developments. He altered several notes that had reflected Reformed ideas. The social upheavals caused by the Reformation led him to emphasize peace and harmony among Christians and to be more sympathetic to the papacy and its claims to doctrinal supervision. Overall, these changes show a growing conservatism that paralleled Erasmus' desire for some form of theological compromise.[189]

Tertullian's complex Latinity and subject matter, together with the poor state of the manuscripts, made a good edition a Herculean effort. Beatus struggled with these texts for almost twenty years and showed himself capable of using new methods to produce a dependable collection of Tertullian's treatises. If his procedure was still imperfect, the resulting editions were important contributions to Renaissance patrology. But Beatus was still not satisfied with what he had accomplished in this third edition. Soon after, he obtained another manuscript of Tertullian's writings. This one originated from Malmesbury in England and was sent to him by John Leland via the Portuguese humanist Damiao de Gois.[190] Although Beatus collated the manuscript, he never had the opportunity to use it to produce an improved edition. It was only after his death that Gelen incorporated material from this manuscript in issuing a new edition that appeared in 1550.[191]

One of Beatus' major accomplishments in the third edition of Tertullian was to base his treatment of the texts on a solid command of early Church history. He could do so because he had emerged in the 1530s as the most accomplished historian of the German Renaissance. His treatment of historical topics was to a great extent closely related to the textual problems he encountered in correcting Tertullian and the ancient historians. In order to understand Beatus' true stature as a scholar and textual critic, it is necessary to relate his editorial work closely to his historical understanding. When this is done, Beatus' eminence is further affirmed.

5

FROM TEXT TO CONTEXT I
Beatus Rhenanus and
Ecclesiastical History

Beatus' textual criticism and historical scholarship were closely allied. Ultimately textual criticism is a historical enterprise; it requires the critic to understand the process of manuscript corruption that occurs over time and posit the previous existence of an accurate text that can be reconstructed. Moreover, knowledge of ancient and medieval civilization must undergird any textual improvements. Much of Beatus' success as a textual critic flowed from his fundamental historical instincts, and his textual criticism enhanced this historical sense. There was a clear growth in Beatus' sophistication in handling his sources and discussing their textual problems. His annotations to ancient historians and his rediscovery of Velleius Paterculus have established him as a great Renaissance historical commentator; the erudition and keen judgment Beatus brought to his authors were of such a high order that his contributions remain of value.

The most impressive of Beatus' historical accomplishments was his discussion of the German past, the *Rerum Germanicarum libri tres*. This history of early Germany surpassed all earlier accounts by going beyond the moral-stylistic canons of earlier German Renaissance historiography and by avoiding the pitfalls of Reformation ideology; it was the finest product of historical scholarship in the German Renaissance. Save only in bulk, it was the German equivalent to Flavio Biondo's monumental histories of the late Roman Empire and the Middle Ages. It also helped fulfill the longstanding German humanist dream of a *Germania illustrata*.[1]

Beatus merits a study devoted solely to him as a historian. Within the context of his textual criticism there is abundant justification for a limited investigation of his historical work. As has been indicated, Beatus' historical and textual critical methods formed a unit. Regrettably, Beatus never gave expression to a philosophy of history or a detailed account of the place of history within the context of the *studia humanitatis.* His historical thought must be examined by showing how he wrote history and what techniques he brought to this endeavor. The limits of Beatus the historian were more those imposed by the faulty material available than any fundamental defects in his abilities.

ERASMUS AND BEATUS ON HISTORY

History also provides the key to a more balanced assessment of Beatus' relationship with Erasmus, since it was the point at which Beatus emerged as a complete scholarly personality distinct from his Dutch colleague. Beatus always confessed his debt to Erasmus and remained an Erasmian in his moral and religious ideals. In the latter part of his life, when he had withdrawn from Basel and devoted his energies to his own scholarly interests, Beatus continued to contribute to Erasmian projects. Despite this loyalty and deep affection, the two men actually had been growing further apart since the late 1520s. This can be documented from Erasmus' correspondence. In a letter to the Italian humanist Benedetto Giovio (1525), Erasmus expressed his indifference to the study of antiquities, which, he noted, interested Beatus.[2] A year later, he commented that Beatus had published "some little notes" on Pliny, a phrase that, considering the size of the annotations, could only be ironic and perhaps a little patronizing.[3] Finally, the correspondence between the two men ceased in 1529 although their names continued to be mentioned in their letters to others.[4] Despite these signs of distance, there never was any breach between the two; they always remained friends.

The reasons for this growing distance were fundamental. Elements in Beatus' scholarship disturbed Erasmus. To an extent Beatus represented both the fulfillment of Erasmian humanism and a major reshaping of it. In his basic religious and moral attitudes Beatus subscribed to Erasmian ideals. His advocacy of classical studies, his criticisms of scholasticism, the papacy, and late medieval religious practices were all in line with Erasmian values. His break with the Reformation reflected Erasmus' own actions and was influenced by them. Nevertheless, Beatus' textual and historical activities contrasted with Erasmus' and made him an early spokesman of a more thoroughgoing academic approach to scholarship than Erasmus'. Beatus championed only particular elements in the Erasmian tradition.

As noted above,[5] Erasmus considered textual criticism a practical activity. The object of textual criticism was the relatively accurate but readable product and not an involved conjectural structure. Erasmus' linguistic and moral theories did not mandate a highly articulated textual critical method. He wanted his contemporaries to master the Latin language by reading good moral writers. Moderns studied the best ancient Latin in order to have the most effective means of expression. Since the study of an ancient's style taught one to write better and thereby be understood more fully, there was little need to locate the ancients precisely in history. A general realization that Cicero's Latinity was fixed as a standard in the later Roman period or that the style of a writer such as Apuleius represented a time of change or, for some, of decline sufficed for Erasmus' needs. Detailed knowledge of an ancient writer's historical circumstances could not make a man a better stylist or more moral. Rather, too much time spent on the study of an ancient language and its practitioners could pose a danger by fostering a one-sided dependence on one stylist at the expense of other, perhaps morally superior ones. The object of Erasmian pedagogy was to write good Latin, not to make one a devotee of ancient Rome.[6]

The same reservation would apply to Beatus' paleographical method. While similar to Erasmus' practice, Beatus' devotion to explaining his system in detail contrasted with Erasmus' own short and often unclear explanations. Erasmus' interest in textual matters was not identical with Beatus' search for the *ipsissima lectio* as a historical reconstruction. The amount of time, precision, and extensive knowledge Beatus' method required could detract from the Erasmian advocacy of cultural and moral renewal. Erasmus' pedagogical and religious aims did not demand the type of time and effort Beatus lavished on his texts. Only Scripture was worthy of such treatment in Erasmus' estimation, and his own textual work was ultimately directed toward the interpretation of Scripture. Erasmus subsumed history to his own theological concerns, and he cultivated historical knowledge related to his scriptural studies. Beatus, however, never dealt with the text of Scripture.

Perhaps the best means of assessing Erasmus' expectation from his study of the past and a good gauge of the reasons for his reservations about Beatus' mature textual and historical scholarship is his treatise the *Ciceronianus* (1528).[7] This attack on the humanist cult of strict imitation of Cicero was also a defense of an eclectic and generalized historical view of the Latin language. To Erasmus it was foolish to try to capture the very words of Cicero and to be bound by that writer's idiom. For him this Ciceronianism with its limited perspective and emphasis on minor linguistic details represented a new scholasticism that could harm the moral teachings of the ancients. Ciceronian Latin was a historical product, but one without any special standardizing claims for Erasmus. Any attempt to canonize a style of a past period as *the* model in Erasmus' view was nonsensical. There was no such thing as the perfect style and no period that could claim absolute superiority: one read Cicero as one of several models in order to develop one's own literary style. Erasmus advocated an eclectic style that drew on all the ancients and was meant to reflect an individual's own talents and interests. Further, he felt that Ciceronian Latin reflected the needs and ideals of Cicero's day and not those of sixteenth-century Christian society. Pagan speech could not be completely incorporated into a Christian environment. This implied a definite limit to the quest to understand the ancient world that had produced a noble but non-Christian idiom. Historical fascination with it was subordinated to moral imperatives. Adding to this circumscribed historical sense was Erasmus' belief in the contemporaneity of the Latin language.[8] He maintained that Latin was still very much alive and growing and not simply a historical construct that had to be recaptured. He did not cultivate the sense of anachronism that was necessary for establishing any form of thorough historicism.

It must be emphasized that Erasmus was not hostile to history or indifferent to it. Indeed, he appreciated it and advocated its study. Nevertheless, he displayed a more general historical sense than did Beatus. Erasmus' approach to history was primarily literary, although in time a religious interest replaced it. Erasmus turned to history for anecdotes and moral *exempla* rather than as a source of specific knowledge.[9] This is evident in Erasmus' editing. History did not represent a major element in his publishing program, but it was certainly a part of it. Although he was an admirer of Tacitus and Livy, Erasmus edited no grand thematic writer. Rather, he turned to ancient biographies, especially the *Scriptores Historiae Augustae* and Suetonius. His own historical works were biographies, such as those of Jerome and some contemporaries.[10] For Erasmus history held no independent position. Like the ancient rhetoricians, such as Quintilian, he subsumed history into general literary and moral categories and did not treat it as a unique intellectual form with claims to close attention and long study. Still, Erasmus remained, at least to a degree, supportive of Beatus' work and even tried to obtain an Italian manuscript of Livy for him.[11]

Erasmus' moral-stylistic rather than historical basis for the selection of authors worthy of intensive study extended to Church history and ecclesiastical writers. Both Erasmus and Beatus discussed liturgical questions, especially the mass and confession, but Erasmus offered little historical detail. His interest was essentially to purge contemporary religious practices of what he considered scholastic additions. Obviously this meant that he had some sense of the historical changes in church practices, but he did not carry this awareness into an analysis of the particulars.[12] In dealing with the same questions, Beatus tried to show the historical development of the changes in practice, to give precise details, and to cite the relevant authorities.[13]

Ambiguity is also evident in Erasmus' attitude toward Tertullian, although there were extenuating circumstances in his case.[14] Since he was a Church Father, Erasmus naturally was inclined to favor him. He included him among the Fathers whose theology contrasted with the excesses of the scholastic theologians. But there were limits to Erasmus' acceptance of Tertullian's theology. In Erasmus' estimation Tertullian, like Origen, had a tendency to force scriptural interpretations. Tertullian's adherence to the Montanist heresy, his willingness to break the unity of the Church, his morbid concern for chastity, and his unforgiving nature all offended Erasmus. No doubt he would have preferred that Beatus devote some of his time to other, less controversial Fathers. Moreover, three different editions, each one with more textual, philological, and historical detail, certainly did not correspond to Erasmus' less exacting treatment of the Fathers. Erasmus the theologian used the Fathers as guides to interpret Scripture, the object of all patristic editing in his view, and a process that was not primarily dependent on historical reconstruction. Only Scripture in Erasmus' view was worthy of such careful scrutiny and constant editorial attention.

For Beatus, Tertullian offered information on the early history of the Church, which he used to develop his own theological opinions. The knowledge he extracted from Tertullian allowed him to construct, at least in outline, a historical view of the Church that supported his rejection of elements in the medieval Church as well as his ultimate rejection of the Reformation. Both Erasmus' and Beatus' acceptance of the Christian tradition led them to remain within the Roman Church, but Beatus' view of that tradition was much more solidly based in history, and more dynamic, than Erasmus'. Consequently, when we look into Beatus' treatment of theological topics we find him engaged in a detailed historical reconstruction.

RENAISSANCE ECCLESIASTICAL HISTORY

It would be inaccurate to label Beatus a Church historian, since he never gave extended attention to general institutional or doctrinal developments. He discussed specific topics in Church history as they arose in the works he edited, especially his annotations to Tertullian, the marginal notes to the *Autores ecclesiasticae historiae,* and scatterered references in the *Res Germanicae.*

While of a high quality, they concern us most when they are natural outgrowths of Beatus' textual and philological work. They demonstrate the same historical consciousness that underlay his textual criticism. As was true with his discussions of secular ancient and medieval topics, there was a definite growth in the sophistication of his exposition of ecclesiastical history. There was a major difference between his ecclesiastical and his secular history; his presentation of the Church's past overlapped with and received an impetus from the controversies surrounding the Reformation and thus always had a polemical quality to it. The Erasmian origins of his religious thought further intensified this tendency.

Ecclesiastical history did not hold an independent place in Renaissance historiography.[15] There certainly was a medieval ecclesiastical historical tradition, but it was of a very limited variety. A monastic chronicle was only partly historical, while scholastic theology was indifferent to the study of the past. Biographical collections of secular and ecclesiastical dignitaries offered no overview. Some seemingly historical works were really prophetic or millenarian in intent. The major early Church historians, Eusebius and his continuators, had no true medieval successors, save perhaps for Bede the Venerable. Consequently the Renaissance humanists lacked a recent tradition of acceptable models from which to develop an ecclesiastical history. The classical writers so dear to them provided no model for the treatment of the Church. The histories of Flavio Biondo, for example, simply discussed church history as part of his general theme of the decline of the Roman Empire. In the Renaissance, therefore, ecclesiastical history was basically inseparable from and subordinate to secular history, and when humanists did treat theological questions they simply referred to ancient Church historians or the Fathers in a general manner. The break with secular historiography would come in the Reformation and Counter-Reformation.

There was a significant exception to this general picture—the histories connected with the papacy.[16] In form they followed the medieval biographical tradition of the *Liber pontificalis*. The humanists who were resident at the papal Curia consequently wrote biographies of individual popes. The humanist Bartolomeo

Platina (1421–1481)[17] did offer a broader vision, since he related the lives of all the successors of Peter to his own time. Within this biographical theme, there was little room for broader institutional developments; a pope's reign tended to be only a small aspect of larger trends. Despite his access to the papal library, where he was librarian, Platina lacked the imagination needed to break any new ground.[18]

One major impediment to any history of the Church was the availability of sources. Certainly there were numerous monastic chronicles, but they offered only incidental material about events outside their own monasteries. To the humanists the history of monasteries seemed parochial. Without doubt the major advance in ecclesiastical history resulted from the humanists' interest in the Church Fathers and their translation and publication of a large body of ancient Church literature.[19] Ancient ecclesiastical writers such as Eusebius became accessible to readers. Patristic theologians, especially Jerome, also offered much information about the early life of the Church, especially about the heresies, most of which were known only from their opponents' writings. Whatever the genre, the humanists had made available a large body of historical information that could be molded into a broader view.

As an ecclesiastical historian Beatus both benefited from and contributed to the humanist patristic Renaissance. By the end of the 1520s editions of a variety of Church Fathers, Greek and Latin, were available either in the original language or in Latin translations. Among these were Ambrose, the Apostolic Fathers (Ignatius, Clement of Rome, Barnabas, Polycarp, Hermes), Dionysius the Areopagite, Arnobius Gallus, Athanasius, Augustine, Basil the Great, Cyprian, Cyril of Alexandria, Cyril of Jerusalem, Ephraim of Syria, Eucherius of Lyon, Eusebius, Fulgentius Ruspensis, Gregory the Great, Gregory Nazianzus, Gregory of Nyssa, Hesychius of Jerusalem, Hilary of Poitiers, Irenaeus, Jerome, John Chrysostom, John of Damascus, Lactantius, Leo the Great, Nilus, Origen, and Prudentius.[20] Froben's press printed several of these. We have already seen that Beatus went beyond the theological interests of most humanistic patrologists by publishing a selection of the early Church historians.

Beatus took advantage of this material and used it to treat

selected topics in the history of early Christianity. As mentioned earlier, his approach to church history related to Erasmian criticisms of the contemporary Church. Still, he knew Church history well and had such a solid control of ancient secular developments that few were in as good a position as he to explain complex ecclesiastical topics. That he did not turn to ecclesiastical history as a central enterprise partly reflected the controversial matters that sparked his interest, and partly the dominance of German history in his work. Nevertheless, Beatus found in the early history of the Church support for his theological views and a means of explaining contemporary religious practices. His broadest treatment of ecclesiastical history came in his *annotationes* and *argumenta* to Tertullian, and therefore was closely connected to his textual work.

ECCLESIASTICAL HISTORY AS ANTISCHOLASTIC POLEMIC

Beatus' search for a historical basis for his religious views can be followed in his treatment of a series of controversial topics highlighted by Erasmus and the Reformers—the deleterious effects of scholasticism on Christian theology, the differences between the ancient and contemporary sacrament of penance, early baptismal practices, and the development of the liturgy of the mass. Beatus, anxious to find historical justifications for accepting or rejecting the medieval Church's teachings on all these matters, provided capsule histories of his themes. These, in turn, led him to investigate other relevant sources, including ancient secular historians and medieval theological and legal treatises. Again, Beatus' citation of such a variety of sources contrasts with Erasmus, for whom a broad sense of the decline of the Church sufficed to establish the need for amelioration. Beatus, contrariwise, sought to be historically exact and relatively complete.

Beatus' discussions of religious topics reflected problems that arose in his editing. Their historical aspect grew over time; this is best seen in the great increase in the historical information supplied in his different sets of annotations to Tertullian. Since Beatus' historical work was closely tied to textual questions, there is a specificity to much of his scholarship which was demanded by the immediate context. The labor this required helps to explain why he published only one lengthy historical tract in his lifetime.

Illustrative of Beatus' attention to Church history was his explanation of the development of Christian theology, which prefaced the editions of Tertullian. Concentrating on the decadence of scholasticism, his summary of leading theological themes provides an essentially humanistic interpretation of the causes of the decline of Christian thought. It offered not only a justification for refurbishing Tertullian's reputation but also a defense for humanistic religious and theological concepts. It is worth quoting in full. (The sections in italics were added in 1539.)

> Formerly among the patriarchs and prophets, who were accustomed to revere the most secret mysteries of the Divinity rather than express them, the name of God was ineffable; and Christ himself, our Savior, and the Apostles entrusted to us the secret of the most holy Trinity in a very few words. But after the temerity of the heretics began to examine all subjects with great curiosity and to speak about everything, even calling into dispute the highest mysteries of the faith which more rightly one should adore rather than investigate, those first theologians, Tertullian, Origen, Cyprian, Jerome, Augustine, and the others of those times, were forced, although unwillingly, to dispute about divine matters, which they did reverently and modestly as their writings show. Jerome says that John the Evangelist when forced to refute the Hebronites soberly explained the divine birth of Christ. Then about the year of Salvation 1140 at Paris there were many who patched together summaries from the ancient theologians, like Peter Lombard, Peter Abelard and John Blethus. The summary of Lombard, who at that time taught at the University of Paris, began to be taken up by the scholastics. The theology of Abelard, as he entitled his book, was censured for error by certain ones, although still it was not written inelegantly, for recently it was found complete in a certain library. Blethus was later than these two. After the collection of Lombard, who later was made bishop of Paris, was accepted [as a textbook], they first began to take the title of doctor who studied it thoroughly and lectured on it to others, *who acquired the right of teaching. Now in the older books of the University of Paris which contain the constitutions of the school, they are called bachelors, a word deduced from bacillus or so it seems, as there was the handing down of*

the wand, as a certain sign of the license to teach, by which they were distinguished from outsiders in imitation of antiquity, if not of the Romans, certainly either of the Franks in Gaul or of the Goths and the Lombards in Italy. But, I am speaking of promotion, at the same time in Bologna they say that this happened in law after the establishment of the Rhapsody of Decrees by Gratian. Soon since the number of doctors were increasing, laws of promotion and of the number of years [of study] were established, and it was ratified that those discussing divine matters not only should follow the accepted statements of the school but should use the vocabulary and formulas of speech developed in that school, regarding which they should examine the opinions of certain old and new writers and not accuse them of heresy if they disagreed. *Moreover, this was done not without reason, namely for preserving the unity of teaching.* These are the terms used in discussing the Trinity: essence, persons, suppositions, notions, common and personal relations, constitutive relations of persons, the principles of generation, spiration and distinction, the relations of origin, circumincession, signs of nature and order, and from the nature of the thing and of the origin and many others of this type. And such is the beginning of the reign of theologians. Moreover, who can say that the ancients spoke as these speak, who divert all the philosophy of Aristotle, unlearnedly changed, into their theology.[21]

With the exception of the passages in italics, this history prefaced all three editions of Tertullian.

Beatus began his history with an Erasmian theme that Tertullian had prefigured—that adoration and reverence were the proper Christian attitudes toward the divine mysteries and that *impia curiositas* had a destructive effect on religion. Theology resulted from heretical attacks that dated to the time of John the Evangelist, as St. Jerome had shown.[22] In refuting heresy, the early Fathers maintained a reverent and modest stance toward matters that the heretics, and later scholastics, improperly tried to explain.

In Beatus' narrative there is an abrupt transition from the time of Augustine to the twelfth century. He did not discuss the thinkers between these two periods because he felt that there was a basic uniformity between patristic and early medieval theology which reflected a freedom from Aristotelian dialectics. He was aware of the Carolingian synodial decrees and theologians and cited them with approval, often from manuscripts.[23] Beatus certainly did not consider these medieval theologians equal to the Fathers, but he did posit a continuous tradition originating with the Fathers and stretching to the twelfth century. In accepting the Carolingian writers, Beatus agreed with Erasmus. Erasmus had edited one medieval treatise in his career, the Carolingian theologian Haymo's commentary on the Psalter and six songs from the Old Testament (1533).[24] The two humanists realized affinities between themselves and the Carolingians, in their rhetorical theologies and in their interests in ancient and patristic literature.[25]

Beatus underlined the nature of the major shift that took place in the twelfth century, *circa salutis annum MCXL*—the creation of a complete academic theology, namely, Scholasticism. This systematization was all-inclusive, and the accepted textbooks greatly influenced the process. Peter Abelard's *Theologia,* which was *non scripta ineleganter,* was unacceptable, while Peter Lombard's turgid compilation became the standard. Beatus could judge the value of Abelard's work because it had recently been discovered.[26] In connecting the Lombard's collection with the *Decretum,* he underscored the abandonment of original texts for summaries and commentaries, a theme that occupied Erasmus in his attacks on Scholasticism. Tertullian was one of the casualties of this revolution in theological method. The development of academic forms around such compilations resulted eventually in ossification. The growth of an academic establishment was the outward manifestation of a hermetic theology by which theologians stood apart (*ab alienis distinguerentur*) by their academic status. In 1539 Beatus expanded his discussion of academic insignia; the references to the Franks and Lombards reflected his study of medieval history and his concern for correct attributions.[27]

This whole academic structure enforced uniformity in terminology. The beginning of the rule of theologians consisted in devising and standardizing a new vocabulary. An ever more subtle and complex terminology sprang from and guaranteed theological systematization, thereby making it a progressively professional activity; one that excluded groups such as the humanists, who lacked theological degrees and shunned technical vocabulary. This structure, glorying in its own subtlety, imposed numerous *regulae* upon its participants. Tertullian's simple description of the Trinity in Beatus' view was clearer and more exact than the more complicated terminology the later theologians developed, but Scholasticism proved victorious.

This last theme recurs in the *Definitiones dogmatum ecclesiasticorum*, a series of statements correcting Tertullian's theology. Beatus consulted them in a transcription of a manuscript from the cathedral library of Strasbourg, which his friend Lucas Bathodius had made for him.[28] Since Tertullian lived close to apostolic times, *anno post Christum CL et ante,* he could not be guided by subsequent orthodox doctrinal statements. What he read in Bathodius' copy led Beatus to search in his own library for similar statements, and in these he discovered that the Strasbourg manuscript was to an extent a collection of Augustinian and conciliar excerpts that had been attributed to a variety of writers. In reading the manuscript's section on penance, Beatus found that it differed from the printed versions, which contained phrases reflecting later theological doctrines.[29] This divergence led him to insist once again, but this time in a specifically theological context, that whenever there are doubts, it is necessary to consult *exemplaria vetusta*. In contrast to scholastic rule-making and its implicit falsifications stand the simplicity and greater honesty of earlier times, which are extractable through textual criticism.[30]

A proper assessment of Beatus' attitudes toward Peter Lombard's *Liber sententiarum* and Gratian's *Decretum* is not simple. The short history of theology did not place on Peter full responsibility for initiating the process of theological decay. Beatus did not completely reject the *Sententiae*. He found value in it even though it was written inelegantly. In his short biography of Erasmus in 1540, he compared Peter Lombard to John of Damascus as a theological systematizer.[31] The Lombard sought to reduce the confusion that resulted from the variety of opinions by judicious selection. Beatus stated his regret that the Lombard's "method is looked for in vain in the commentaries of modern authors." Seemingly, Peter Lombard's compendium marked a period of transition between a patristic-based theology and the dialectical excesses of the Scholastics. It prepared the way for the Scholastics but in some manner was distinct from them.

It is interesting to speculate whether Beatus thought that the acceptance of Peter Abelard's *Theologia* as a school text might have changed the history of medieval Christian theology. Since it was written more eloquently than the *Sententiae,* it might have bred different progeny. Abelard was acquainted with classical authors and cited them, obviously an appealing point to the humanists.[32] In his openness to ancient rhetoric, Abelard would have marked a continuation of the patristic theology rather than a thorough acceptance of Aristotelian dialectics as the Scholastics did. If Beatus did consider Peter a link between ancient and Renaissance theological thought, then his displacement marked a missed opportunity in Christian thought.

In 1511 Beatus had been involved in an edition of Gratian.[33] While it is unclear whether Beatus actually took a hand in editing the work (unlike his friend Sebastian Brant, who had issued the *Decretum* for Amerbach and Froben in 1500, he lacked legal training, although he did have an interest in legal questions),[34] he was sufficiently familiar with it to criticize the text in the Tertullian edition. Despite the errors he found in the *Decretum,* at least in his early career, Beatus looked upon it as worth preserving, since it incorporated passages from the Fathers and the early synods.

The fullest discussion of Gratian occurred in the annotations to the *De corona militis.*[35] This is interesting on several grounds: the use of a comparative textual method to criticize Gratian, the appeal to manuscript sources, and the treatment of a central question in Christian theology—unwritten tradition. Beatus began his discussion by noting that he had found in a copy of Burchard of Worms' *Decreta* a passage from Basil the Great which concurred with Tertullian's teaching on ecclesiastical tradition. He compared the passage in Burchard (book III, chap. cxxvi) with one in Gratian (I. dist. xi) and found important differences.[36] Since the manuscripts of the *Decretum* were corrupt, he tried to reestablish the *syncera lectio.* The corruptions in the Gratian further led Beatus to cite a letter of Gregory the Great to Bishop Leandrus and another of Rabanus Maurus to Regenbaldus[37] in order to establish the continuity of ecclesiastical tradition. Thus a textual disagreement required the consultation of relevant materials in order to establish proper Church custom.[38]

THE HISTORY OF PENANCE

Beatus' investigation of the development of the sacrament of penance presents a more elaborate historical picture.[39] Whether and how to forgive sins committed after the initial cleansing of baptism was a formative question for the early Church. Its solution helped to determine the power of Church officials, above all the bishops. The ecclesiological significance of penance meant as much to sixteenth-century as to second-century Christians. Thus, through an investigation of the historical roots of penance, Beatus treated a topic of immediate interest to his contemporaries. In Tertullian, Beatus had access to an important spokesman of Christian penitential practices and an ideal source for any historical reconstruction. This was so, Beatus believed, because Tertullian had sought knowledge from the earliest period.[40] Especially important was the definition of the relationship between the ancient rite of exomologesis, or public penance, and the private or auricular confession of the Middle Ages.

Early Christians disagreed about whether sinners could be readmitted to the Church after baptism. Some felt that certain sins were so severe that the Church could never permit an adulterer, a fornicator, a murderer, or an idolater to return to the fold. On this problem Tertullian offered two different answers. In his Catholic period he maintained that, through a special rite of fasting and submission, the offender could be received once, but only once, more into the congregation. In his later Montanist phase he proposed a different view. While Montanism preached the continued validity of prophesies, Tertullian emphasized the sect's rigoristic morality. Accordingly, he restricted the Church's ability to forgive grave sins. He wrote his treatise *De poenitentia* while a Catholic, and Beatus used his *argumentum* and annotations as well as the *Admonitio* to provide historical details. A close study of his discussion has the further advantage of providing a clear example of the types of changes Beatus made in his annotations.

In the discussion of penance in the first edition of the *Admonitio*,[41] Beatus did not use the Greek term *exomologesis* (although it did appear in the *argumentum* to the *De poenitentia*). Exomologesis was the early Church's public rite of penance, and Beatus asserted a relationship between this early practice and private confession.[42] As will be seen below, Beatus came to favor the term through his reading of Erasmus. In the *Admonitio*, Beatus defended the propriety and antiquity of the public penance that Tertullian described and its priority over private (*secreta*) penance through confession to a priest; he never denied that penance was an ancient Christian rite. While the contemporary Church used private rather than public penance, a common bond united both. Beatus marshaled a body of authorities to substantiate the antiquity of penance, especially Augustine's sermon 351, called *de medicina poenitentiae*.[43] Beatus argued that public exposure to excommunication motivated sinners to undergo the public humiliation of exomologesis, a custom that was maintained in his own time during episcopal visitations. Beatus' exposition of the antiquity of exomologesis showed that the modern Church differed from the ancient one. Private confession, while not condemned, was shown not to be of great antiquity.

Relatedly, Beatus attacked contemporary confessional manuals that applied the Scholastic theological categories to confessional practices. By the end of the Middle Ages, they had come under severe criticism for endangering the penitents' consciences by their excessive emphasis on the circumstances, frequency, and severity of sins. Beatus cited his friend and fellow Froben collaborator, Johannes Oecolampadius (1482–1531), who rejected confessional practices in his *Paradoxon, Quod non sit onerosa Christianis confessio* of 1521.[44] Oecolampadius had a strong interest in patristic literature, and Beatus praised him for investigating *veterum theologorum monumenta*. Beatus argued that in denying that private confession to a priest had been an ancient Christian tradition, Oecolampadius was seeking to help his troubled fellow Christians.[45]

In his own treatment of penance Beatus modified his views over time. In the first version of the *argumentum* to the *De poenitentia*, Beatus was very much in sympathy with Oecolampadius' ideas. He indicated what he felt were the defects in private confession in line with what Oecolampadius had written, but he did not deny that private confession had stemmed from the rites of public penance used by the ancient Christians. When he revised this section in 1539, he showed himself much more positive toward private confession. In all versions, however, he invoked patristic and early medieval authorities in order to establish what the Church's practices had been. Especially important was the attention given to the Penitential Canons, which were in effect until the seventh century and which were succeeded by the Penitential Books of the Carolingians.[47] Isidore of Seville, Bede, Theodulphus of Orleans, Betanus, Rabanus, and the Byzantine Suidas were consulted to provide further information on penance.[48] Beatus laid some stress on the testimony of Ambrose and a Pseudo-Chrysostom text to argue for the priority of confession to God over that to a priest.[49]

To highlight what he felt were the errors of contemporary confessional practice, Beatus contrasted the confessional theology of Thomas Aquinas and Duns Scotus with that of Johannes Geiler von Kaylersberg (1445–1510), whose biography Beatus had written.[50] Although Geiler's views were mentioned in 1521, the discussion was greatly expanded in 1539. Beatus was critical of the tendency toward morbidity and overscrupulosity that contemporary confessional manuals engendered; this reflected the Scholastic tendency to codify and to invent useless distinctions.[51] To counter such abuses he invoked Erasmus, who echoed Tertullian's attitude toward penance.[52]

In the third edition of Tertullian Beatus invoked Erasmus' *Exomologesis sive modus confitendi* (1524).[53] Erasmus found in private confession a rite that he accepted on the basis of the authority of the Church rather than historical precedent. While he could discover no justification for its institution by Christ, he did feel that it had definite advantages. Like Beatus, he doubted its antiquity and was equally sensitive to its abuses. He attributed most of the fault surrounding private confession to bad priests, hypocrisy, and overscrupulosity.[54] While Beatus and Erasmus basically agreed, they differed in their concern with explaining the historical background of penance. Where Erasmus' moral concern was satisfied with broad historical generalizations, Beatus supplied a historical analysis of the development of pen-

ance, citing several ancient and medieval writers in order to show
the reasons for change. Citation of Carolingian theologians was
an important indication of Beatus' historical understanding of
the development of Christian theology.

Beatus brought to his discussion of penance a desire to avoid
controversy, partly because Catholic theologians had specifically criticized his support for Oecolampadius' views, and partly
because he was more inclined in 1539 to accept Rome as a
guarantor of peace than he had been in 1521. In the later
editions of Tertullian, Beatus even excised the references to
Oecolampadius, who had become a major Reformer, in an effort to separate himself from a radical critique of confession.
For all the problems of confessional practice, Beatus appealed
to a council to solve them in the face of the politico-ecclesiastical
upheavals that afflicted his time.[55]

This treatment of penance was dynamic; it reflected Beatus'
growing knowledge of patristic and early medieval writers as
well as changes in his theological and religious positions. In the
third edition he expanded his discussion of his sources and
used them in a comparative manner. Church councils, secular
historians, legal texts, and medieval theologians as well as the
Church Fathers were all enlisted in the service of historical
explanation. Given the polemical origins of his discussion, it is
an index of Beatus' maturity that by 1539 the historical context
of his discussion of penance was markedly more prominent.

Just as penance was a source of controversy in the Reformation, so were baptism, the origins of the mass, and the Eucharist. On these topics the Reformers invoked the Church Fathers
to demonstrate the decline of Christian purity. Tertullian was
an extremely important spokesman on baptismal and eucharistic practices, especially in his treatise *De corona militis*.[56] In part
he aimed to defend unwritten tradition as the source for valid
Christian practices. He therefore described the ceremonies surrounding baptism and the eucharist as proper even if Scripture
did not mandate them. Tertullian's appeal to actual practice
made a historical treatment of his statements imperative.

Beatus, from the beginning of his study of Tertullian, valued
the *De corona militis*. In the *editio princeps* he supplied it with one
of the two sets of annotations, and by far the most extensive.

These annotations grew in size in subsequent editions. In them Beatus explained Tertullian's arguments and outlined differing ecclesiastical practices. He expressed pleasure in doing so, since he was casting light on some of the more obscure customs of the early Church.[57] The first topic discussed in detail is baptism. Beatus probably developed his later thoughts on baptismal practices against the teachings of the Anabaptists. As was true with his contemporaries, he considered the Anabaptists a major threat to civil and religious peace; they were the only reformed religious group Beatus specifically criticized. Accordingly, his revisions gave special emphasis to infant baptism.[58]

Beatus used his exposition of baptismal practices both to show what the ancient custom had been and how it had changed over time, an analysis that became progressively more marked and nuanced, especially in its demonstration of historical change. He explained that the early Church had baptized adults because of the large number of pagans who were converting daily to Christianity. The Church had discarded this practice, as was shown by Carolingian laws which required infants to be baptized at specific times of the year and which outlawed all other baptisms save in the threat of death. The specific texts Beatus mentioned were those collected by the ninth-century abbot of St. Wandrille, Ansegisus. Beatus consulted copies of this compilation in the library of St. Foy in Sélestat, in the cathedral library in Strasbourg, and a copy in his own library.[59] To the Carolingian tradition of infant baptism, Beatus remarked that exceptions were made for the Danes, Norsemen, Slavs, and similar people who were then embracing Christianity because of the wars among the Germans and the civil unrest caused by the Huns, Avars, and Hungarians.[60] Beatus used the ritual books called the *Agenda* to add details on the baptismal ceremonies. These ceremonies, he noted, were altered *non sine causa*.[61]

One of the most significant elements in this treatment of baptism was the expression of a historically relativistic view of Church ceremonies. Beatus understood that dynamic political and social conditions required changes in the ecclesiastical practices and that these had occurred since the beginning of the Church. Further, he accepted divergences in Church customs as natural reflections of valid national differences: "And the

East has its customs. . . . and the West has its. For ceremonies vary according to the differences of the churches and regions."[62] But granted such diversity, Beatus still felt the need for some control, and he stated that the authority of the Church should be accepted and all opportunity for dissent avoided.[63] To demonstrate the diversity in baptismal customs, Beatus invoked Gregory Nazianzenus, Jerome, the fourth-century bishop of Nola and poet, Pontius Paulinus, and the eleventh-century bishop of Worms, Burchard.[64] Thus baptismal customs had changed according to geography and need.

Even more vexing in Reformation Europe were the problems of the meaning of the Mass and the nature of the Eucharist, and again Beatus approached these matters in a historically relativistic manner. Beatus expanded his early treatments of the development of the liturgy of the mass and the eucharist dramatically in 1539. He went beyond the discussion found in the *annotationes* to the *De corona militis* and produced a separate historical dissertation on the mass. Thus, at the end of his life, and at a time when there was much discussion on the nature of the mass among Catholic and Reformed theologians, Beatus created a thorough historical evaluation of a pressing ecclesiastical question. Even before the Reformation some Alsatian humanists had proposed liturgical reforms.[65] Their call for a more popularly appealing liturgy was greatly intensified in the early years of the Reformation, when the Reformers sought to make the mass agree more with what they considered the ancient Christian practices. This desire led naturally to the investigation of the Fathers for information on the early Church's liturgical activities. Several Reformers issued their own liturgical plans. Tertullian was to be a very important source in these discussions and could be invoked in various ways.

In his discussion Beatus first emphasized that the Eucharist was known to the ancient Church and that the early Christians had celebrated the *agape*, or Christian love feast. Thus, unlike contemporary opinion that the eucharist was a good act, he argued that the early Christians had understood it in a more dynamic fashion as doing good.[66] He then passed to describing the changing elements in the mass. He admitted that modern practices differed from the ceremony that Tertullian knew.[67]

This elicited from Beatus a desire for the restoration of the earlier, simpler procedure.[68] To indicate further the changes that had occurred, Beatus presented information supplied by his friends. Paul Volz, a learned Benedictine abbot, brought to Beatus' attention evidence that showed that earlier laymen had had access to the cup during the mass.[69] Further, the Carthusian Conrad Pellikan, who had prepared the index for the first edition of Tertullian, had recently found certain old constitutions describing the same practice.[70] Finally, sometime after the appearance of the *editio princeps*, Beatus had seen at Mainz six tubes (*fistulae*) that had been used for dispensing wine at mass.[71] Similarly the pope shares the cup with deacons and subdeacons. Thus ancient custom included communion under both species for the laity and Beatus urged his readers to investigate these early Christian practices.

In his treatise Tertullian described how the early Christians came together before daybreak to partake of the eucharistic feast. Beatus admitted that while this practice was not instituted by Christ or his Apostles, it certainly originated with their successors.[72] In a long section added in 1539, Beatus cited Church canons governing medieval Eucharistic practices.[73] Once again he established the differences between the ancient, medieval, and contemporary churches and called attention to misinterpretations that poor texts, specifically those of Gratian, caused.[74] Beatus concluded that he had exposed these historical changes for those interested in Christian antiquity. But he also hoped that they would lead men to see in the papacy a guarantor of peace in the Church.[75]

Beatus did not systematize his discussion of the mass until 1540, when he contributed an introductory letter to the Latin translation of John Chrysostom's *Missa*.[76] To a great extent this treatment was an extension of that found in the Tertullian annotations. It employed the same sources, either consulted directly or indirectly through collections and other scholars' writings. In it Beatus made several references to manuscript sources that he had corrected, including Tertullian.[77] In explaining the office of the *archicapellanus*, he complained of the joining of Greek and Latin words to form a new one, and then described the duties of the office by citing an *exemplum literarum Ludovici regis* and *alterum*

Othonis I.[78] Further identification of these documents has been unsuccessful. In discussing a passage in Sulpicius Severus' *Life of Saint Martin*, he offered a conjectural emendation, changing the word *amphibalon* to *amphimallon*, meaning a wool garment. His reading is still accepted.[79] This history confirms that Beatus had been a diligent student of the Christian liturgical practices and worthy of the title historian of liturgy, which Prof. Pierre Fraenkel has given him.[80] So informative and useful was this short work that the Protestant theologian-historian-polemicist, Flaccius Illyricus, used it in his own history of the mass and published it twice.[81]

Beatus composed this letter at a time when there was much debate over liturgical practices in an attempt to arrive at some agreement among moderate Catholics and Reformers, a group that included many of Beatus' friends, including Martin Bucer.[82] Consensus had become very important to the Erasmians as a means of settling Protestant-Catholic disputes. Indicative of this desire for a peaceful solution to religious controversy, by the 1540s Beatus had come to accept a new view of the peace-keeping place of the papacy in disputed matters. Indeed, one of the major results of his study of Church history was a more positive assessment of the papacy. This did not mean that he had forgotten his earlier critical comments or that he was willing to grant the papacy any absolute primacy, but rather that he now concluded that the cause of peace took priority. In 1521 Beatus read Tertullian in a decidedly antipapal manner,[83] but in 1539 he presented a more sympathetic appraisal of the Roman pontiffs' value. He was especially anxious to show that the papacy could advance religious concord in a period of constant civil and ecclesiastical conflicts.[84]

HISTORY AND THE HERESIES

A close consideration of the relationship between theology and history is also evident in the individual annotations to Tertullian's antiheretical writings, above all the *Adversus Valentinianos* and the *Adversus Marcionem*.[85] The controversies surrounding the Reformation increased interest in the heretical movements of the early Church. Yet there was generally only a passing knowledge of these early groups in the sixteenth century and only a little in the way of solid historical fact, apart from what was to be found in a writer such as Eusebius. These heretical movements were basically known from the writings of their orthodox opponents, who did not give their enemies' views a clear exposition. Fortunately for Beatus, recent publications, including Erasmus' important editions of Cyprian of Carthage, Tertullian's successor as North Africa's great Latin theologian, and Irenaeus' *Adversus Haereses,* allowed him to form a relatively clear picture of these sects. Irenaeus combated the same groups as Tertullian, and the African writer relied on him for much of his information, and provided Beatus with essential material.[86] The complexity of heretical doctrine and Tertullian's reliance on Greek terminology to explain it made these annotations prime examples of Beatus' philological and historical skills. The general unfamiliarity of most of the material to his readers further required extended discussions.

A short summary of key theological ideas of Valentinianism will help to make the following examples from the *Adversus Valentinianos* clearer. Valentinianism was a Gnostic sect.[87] Valentinianus, a second-century Egyptian, taught that the heavenly world, called the Pleroma, consists of a variety of worlds or aeons. These aeons, usually a sexual pair, had names that partly reflected idealized concepts—Silence, Man, Church—and were arranged in tetrads. Two tetrads were especially emphasized, and they, in turn, formed the Ogdoad. Generally, however, there was a preference in the system for triads. This extended to men, who were divided into pneumatics, who lived a true spiritual life and would go to heaven; the choics, who were mired in matter; and an intermediate group called the psychics, who would enjoy some lower form of salvation; included in this last group were the non-Valentinian Christians. The world exists as a result of error or ignorance. This is so because the last aeon, Sophia, in seeking to know God better, had partly fallen outside the Pleroma. It was from Sophia's ignorance of God that the world came into being. A pair of aeons, Christ and the Holy Spirit, are "brought forth" by Nous to give form to what

Sophia has left behind when she returned to the Pleroma—that is, her purpose to know God. Further, the world has its own purpose, which is called Achamoth.

The complexity of the system led to confusion. The depiction of ideas, such as ignorance, as individual beings allowed the opponents of Valentinianism to ridicule it. Tertullian was a master of sarcasm and irony, and his discussion of the Valentinian theories made the editor's task very difficult. Beatus had to determine when Tertullian was being ironic and when he was offering a clear explanation. In order to help him deal with the heretical system and evaluate Tertullian's presentation, Beatus relied to a great extent on Irenaeus. The close relationship between Irenaeus and Tertullian led Beatus to assess Tertullian's close word-for-word dependence on his Greek source.[88] Beatus tried to help his reader follow Tertullian's Greek-based terminology describing the Valentinian subdeities by providing a table listing them in Greek and Latin.[89] Explanations about the other heretical sects active in the early Church and their ideas also had to be provided to clarify Tertullian's statements.[90] In characterizing Gnosticism, Beatus not only related its use of female priests but also its veneration of pictures and other artistic representations of Christ. He specifically reported that the Gnostics venerated a portrait of Christ supposedly owned by Pilate. Beatus continued by comparing this to icons that were used in the East, as indicated by one recently brought to Germany by Raymond Fugger and given to Otmar Luscinius, a popular Franciscan preacher at Basel who joined the Reformation.[91]

In his annotations Beatus supplied the information necessary to clarify the complexities in Valentinianism. He listed chief figures in the sect and noted how they differed.[92] It is hardly surprising that the interpretations and nomenclature of the aeons would cause problems. Beatus read in his manuscripts *Bythios et Mixis et Hedione* (VIII, 2).[93] He knew from Irenaeus that the aeons were arranged in sexual pairs, and that the scribe ignorant of this must have erred in his transcription. After providing examples of several of these pairs, he proposed that the names *Ageratos, Henonis,* and *Autophyes* were somehow lost in the manuscripts. The modern edition of the *Adversus Valentinianos* adds the names *Ageratos et Henosis, Autophyes.* This conjectural emendation is attributed by modern editors to the late–sixteenth-century editor Jacobus Pamelius, who published Beatus' annotations with the censures of the Spanish Inquisition as appendices to his own edition of Tertullian. It would seem, however, to have originated with Beatus.[94]

A valuable example of an annotation that moves from specific textual and philological to broader historical questions centers on the explanation of Greek forms used in the *Adversus Valentinianos*.[95] The note begins with a discussion of Tertullian's use of Greek and then turns to the need to adapt language to audience. He maintained that since Tertullian was forced to rely on Greek writers for his theological ideas, it was natural for him to have copied Greek. In Tertullian's day, according to Jerome, there was available in Latin among Christian writings only the Old and New Testaments and writings of Victor, the thirteenth bishop of Rome, and of Apollonius.[96] To emphasize the point, Beatus listed over thirty early Christian Greek writers to place against the two Latins. Some of these were no doubt translated into Latin, Beatus continued, but Tertullian would have read them in the original, since he would have preferred to drink *ex fontibus* rather than *ex lacunis*. Included among the translated authors was Irenaeus, who occasionally is mentioned among the Latin writers although he wrote in Greek. Greek was also the first language of the Roman bishops, so they required interpreters in order to communicate with their Latin flock. This last observation led to a historical analogy. St. Bernard, when preaching the crusade before the Emperor Conrad and the German princes, required a translator, just as the Anglo-Saxon missionaries did when converting the north Germans.

This annotation contains several interrelated points. First, Beatus identified a difficulty in Tertullian's style, which resulted from his dependence on Greek. Since there were specific historical reasons for this, Beatus generalized on the case of Tertullian to make a statement on the linguistic state of the early Church, and, by comparison, the superiority of the Greek theologians in the early Church. The list of Greek writers prior to Tertullian provides a useful catalogue of important early theologians and highlights the deficiency of the Latin Church and the central importance of Tertullian's work. Finally, Beatus demonstrated

that the Church almost from its beginning had experienced differences in language, and this continued through the Middle
Ages. The annotation, thus, is a short essay on the linguistic
history and problems of the Church.

Beatus found abundant material on the Valentinians and the
Marcionists in Tertullian's treatises. He had a different problem in trying to understand Tertullian's own heretical views.
Montanism emphasized the continued validity of prophesy in
the Church, but Tertullian was concerned only with its rigorist
moral attitudes.[97] Such views led to his condemnation by the
Roman Church. The Montanists were no better known to
Beatus' contemporaries than the other heretical groups, and
there is a certain tentativeness in his treatment of them. This is
evident in his annotations explaining the term *psychici*. Beatus
understood the Gnostic contrast between the pneumatics, the
choics, and a third middle group, the *psychici*.[98] He found the
same terminology in Tertullian's Montanist writings, although
in the corrupted form *physici* as well as the proper *psychici*, the
former in the *De monogamia* and the latter in the *Adversus
Praxeam*.[99] In discussing them, Beatus related that Tertullian, in
his zeal for chastity, abstinence, and martyrdom, accepted the
new doctrine and broke from the Church. He understood that
physici and *psychici* referred to those who were inclined to natural or animal things. Although he read *physici* in his manuscript,
he admitted that it might be *psychici*, and appealed to St. Paul's
language in Corinthians for support.[100] The term, in whatever
form, was the name the Montanists gave to the orthodox, who
would not fully enjoy heaven. Beatus did not regularize the
terms in the text, in keeping with his principles of informing his
readers of any change, but his annotations explain his awareness of Tertullian's meaning and the import of his terminology.

One problem that continues to perplex scholars of Tertullian
is an exact chronology of his writings. When trying to establish
the dates of Tertullian's activities, Beatus had to rely on hints
given by the author. Such was the basis of his approximate
dating of the *De pallio* and of Tertullian's conversion.[101] Drawing on a reference to the tripartite imperial power Tertullian
made in chapter 2, Beatus proposed the reigns of Septimus
Severus, Clodius Albinus, and Pescennius Niger in 193. He

cited Spartianus from the *Scriptores Historiae Augustae* in support.[102] His reconstruction remains one of the two possible dates accepted by modern scholars.[103]

SECULAR SOURCES OF ECCLESIASTICAL HISTORY

Since Beatus never offered a systematic exposition of ecclesiastical history, we cannot detail his thoughts on a variety of issues. Generally, the necessity of explaining particular questions dictated the construction of his annotations. Special topics, often those that allowed him to make connections with contemporary German practices and problems, received broader coverage. In the marginal notes to the *Autores ecclesiasticae historiae*, Beatus described the development of Christian temples,[104] which led to a discussion of Alsatian ecclesiastical practices and another on early Christian schools in Alexandria, which incorporated modern examples.[105]

Treatment of the early history of the Church required references to the secular history of the late Empire, and Beatus' annotations show his familiarity with the major sources of late ancient history. He naturally cited various Roman and early medieval evidence. One that interested him was the *Notitia Dignitatum*,[106] which is essentially a list of the various civil and military officials of the later Roman Empire. Written about 430, it provided a convenient source on late Roman administration. Beatus knew the *Notitia* from a Speyer manuscript, which contained several other useful texts, including the *Itinerarium provinciarum Antonini Augusti* (parts of which Beatus had obtained as early as 1512).[107] He cited the *Notitia* in several ways, including *Scotus in libro de insignibus magistratuum ad Theodosium Augustum*, which betrayed a belief that the text had originated in Ireland. Gelen published it in 1552 from the Speyer manuscript.[108] Related to this was the *Codex Theodosianus*, which, while published in 1528 by Sichardus, Beatus used in manuscript.[109] Ansegisus' collection of Frankish laws[110] and a letter of Theodoric the Ostrogoth to Abundantius also probably were known to him in manuscript.[111] As befitted a historian of Germany, he enjoyed explaining a reference to the Germanic wars of Marcus Aurelius when they were mentioned in the *Ad Scapulam*, by citing from Julius Capitolinus in the *Scriptores Historiae Augustae*.[112] Similarly, he explained the origin of the name Strasbourg and attacked contemporary Italian humanists who criticized German customs or who, in his opinion, did not give proper consideration to German history.[113]

On occasion Beatus proposed major changes in his treatment of historical topics. This is evident in *Ad uxorem* I, 4, 7, at the words *Non Gallicos vultus, nec Germanicos baiulos*.[114] (Modern reading is *non Gallicos mulos, nec Germanicos baiulos*.) In 1528 he began by complaining of the time he had spent on this phrase. At first he had thought *mulos* was the proper reading rather than *vultus*, but because of the mention of the *baiuli* (porters), Beatus thought that some office or minister was meant, and that he was dealing with an obscure word that the scribe had misread. He proposed *Nec Gallicos acoluthos, nec Germanicos baiulos*,[115] explaining that this referred to a Byzantine dignitary. He then noted that in ancient times the Roman matrons traveled in sedan chairs carried by Germans.[116] Beatus concluded his annotation with a reference to German attacks on Rome.[117] In 1539 Beatus followed a new procedure and broke the annotation into two separate sections. Since he continued to keep *Non Gallicos vultus* and *nec Germanicos baiulos* in the text, we may assume that the Gorze manuscript did not offer any new reading; at least none is cited. His note for *Non Gallicos vultus* explains the reference *propter candorem*, especially if the Gauls are compared with the Greeks, Syrians, Spaniards and present-day Italians. Jerome, Lactantius and Ammianus Marcellinus are called on to support this interpretation.[118] The note *Nec Germanicos baiulos* provides a short discussion of ancient Roman modes of travel. He concluded by again referring to Germans in Rome acting as papal attendants.[119]

In order to correct what he decided was a corrupt reading, Beatus called upon his knowledge of Roman and medieval history. While at first he conjectured a reading that has come to be standard, he changed his mind in order to maintain continuity with what he felt was the meaning of the sentence. Seemingly with added manuscript support for the original version he had found, Beatus turned his attention to explaining it. Nevertheless, he still took advantage of the annotation to comment on ancient customs and cite appropriate authorities. In the final reference to Rome, Beatus reiterated an alliance between the papacy and the German people.[120]

SUMMARY

As a group these annotations represent a serious consideration of Christian history. What is also significant is that they flowed from Beatus' treatment of Tertullian's treatises. Textual criticism of so difficult a Church Father necessitated more than simple grammatical adjustments. Even these were not easily accomplished, since Tertullian's use of Greek constructions made the restoration of his Latin a complicated matter. Beatus was able to diagnose properly Tertullian's Latin style with its preference for obscure vocabulary, neologisms, and foreign forms. But this linguistic understanding was only the beginning of the process of explanation. Beatus also had to bring to his annotations broad historical knowledge.

In treating the ceremonies and traditions of the early Church, Beatus undertook subjects that required him to comment on controversial matters in his own time as well as in Tertullian's. Thus erudition was closely allied to contemporary considerations. Beatus remained basically careful and even-handed in his discussions of these topics. What Beatus desired was to explain the origins of changes in ecclesiastical ceremonies, but not to offer a prescriptive solution to the controversies of his day. History had shown him that things change and that there was a natural quality to these changes. Disagreements over such alterations could only lead to the breakdown of religious peace, as had happened in the Reformation. Beatus' historical explanations were meant to be a basis for religious consensus and peace. In this endeavor, he had come, for historical as well as religious reasons, to accept the conciliating power of the Roman pontiff. His acceptance of the papacy was essentially a consequence of historical factors: diversity was both natural and desirable, but only to a point. When controversy threatened to make diversity a basis for divergence, then the value of a papal authority was clear. As with Erasmus, the alternatives to papal power seemed dangerous in Beatus' eyes.

The inspiration for Beatus' ecclesiastical history was ultimately Erasmian, but Beatus found a means of expressing these ideas more fully through history. He gave the development of ceremonies and doctrines the type of historical dimension at which Erasmus had hinted but which he had not developed in any detail. Beatus understood the need to look back in order to determine what was proper in his day. Ecclesiastical history was, quite simply, a matter of immediate importance to Beatus and his generation. In coming to it with his great critical skill, Beatus was able to advance knowledge of the early history of the Church without providing the occasion for further religious controversy.

6
FROM TEXT TO CONTEXT II
Beatus Rhenanus and Secular History

Beatus informed his analysis of the early Church with a sense of the evolution of doctrine and custom which reflected a fundamental historical sensitivity. The breadth of topics he encountered in editing Tertullian's writings required of him equal breadth in uncovering the apposite religious and secular sources to describe the practices of the early Christians, their cultural ambience, and the beliefs of the heretical sects. The growth of the material treating these matters in his annotations further indicates how Beatus related his historical discussions to contemporary religious controversies while never becoming a rigid polemicist. Textual criticism accompanied and helped to spark a serious investigation of several central questions in Christian thought.

As an ecclesiastical historian Beatus found an arena in which he expanded on Erasmus' teachings. Erasmus would have found real but limited value in Beatus' treatment of Church history.[1] We may speculate, however, that he would have been uninterested in, or at least not particularly supportive of, Beatus' cultivation of the early history of the Germans—indeed, secular history in general. As Erasmus grew older, religious questions occupied an ever more central place in his thought at the expense of secular topics. Yet it was as a historian of Germany and the later Roman Empire that Beatus demonstrated his true mastery of textual, philological, and historical details and his ability to rescue the past from error. In his history of Germany Beatus successfully combined textual criticism and history and thereby placed the study of early Germany on a new basis, one that few of his contemporaries could fully appreciate and fewer would follow.

HUMANIST HISTORIOGRAPHY IN GERMANY

Several impediments inhibited the growth of an accurate German Renaissance historiography.[2] The first of these stemmed from the essentially moral and patriotic ideals that dominated early German humanism. History, in proper humanist fashion, was meant to teach men to do good and avoid evil through a variety of *exempla*. It was even better when it taught Germans to act morally and showed that their ancestors had always so acted (unlike their neighbors). Treatment of the past thus became a morally determined activity. A further inhibitor was the continued acceptance of the theory of *translatio imperii*, whereby the authority of the Roman Empire had passed from Rome to the Germans. This idea tied German history to a non-Germanic model and at the same time gave the German people a world-historical importance, but one that underestimated peculiar national elements. It also affected German historiography by focusing on the person and deeds of the German emperors and locating German history in the imperial arena rather than a narrower, more national one.[3] Despite their seeming antithesis, the patriotic and imperial models often combined in the writings of individual humanists. The moral-patriotic-imperial qualities were especially strong in Alsace and in those contemporary historians who would have influenced Beatus. Besides these ideological matters, there were the added limitations of availability and reliability of primary sources. Here the problem was twofold: on the one hand, the sources were full of transcription errors and misattributions; and, on the other, falsifications were commonly accepted. Medieval historiography had taken at face value what was at hand or invented what was felt to be lacking, and this tradition continued into the Renaissance.

All Renaissance German historians maintained that in writing the history of their homeland they were correcting a major deficiency in their countrymen's education and offering a firmer basis for a true picture of the past. They argued that German deeds had always been great, indeed, even more worthy of telling than other people's, in part because they were the inheritors of the authority of the Roman Empire. Further, Germany had lacked the historians capable of relating such outstanding events and of countering the attacks made on German culture by foreigners, above all by Italians and Frenchmen. History could not help but be used as a polemical weapon by the humanists who concurred with this analysis, and through history they found the means to right the balance, at least to their satisfaction and that of their contemporaries.

Given this strong patriotic bias, it is ironic that serious study of late ancient and medieval Germany owed its primary impetus to an Italian.[4] Aeneas Silvius Piccolomini, the future Pius II, was the most prominent Italian humanist to make a temporary home in fifteenth-century Germany.[5] First at the council of Basel and then as a member of the Imperial Chancery, Piccolomini came to know Germany well and had the opportunity to study its geography and history. He used his knowledge of historical sources and his observations of central European geography to write a biography of Emperor Frederick III and a history of Bohemia. Despite his treatment of such topics, it was his short description of Germany, the *Germania,* which had the greatest impact on his contemporaries.

Written while its author was a cardinal, the *Germania* argued that the Germans had prospered under the rule of the Roman pontiffs.[6] In order to establish this, Aeneas cited Tacitus' *Germania* to characterize the early history of the Germans. This brought to the attention of contemporaries the most important source of their ancient past and initiated a series of histories of the early Germans. Aeneas' defense of the Roman papacy was interpreted as an implicit slighting of the cultural integrity of the ancient (and by extension modern) Germans because he assigned to a foreign influence the basis for their greatness. It thereby occasioned several rejoinders. The German responses did not add much that was historically new and were excessively and occasionally belligerently defensive,[7] but they did make clear the need for added discussions founded on more accurate information.

The arch-humanist Conrad Celtis initiated the German study of Tacitus.[8] A vehement patriot, Celtis wished to vindicate the virtues and accomplishments of his ancestors by presenting them as historically and morally superior to those of all other peoples. In this spirit, he wrote historical poems, a treatise in praise of Nuremberg, and gave lectures on Tacitus.[9] The most ambitious of his historical enterprises was a *Germania illustrata* modeled on Flavio Biondo's great *Italia illustrata,*[10] which conceived Germany as a unit and would have provided accurate historical and geographical descriptions of its regions and peoples. In it Celtis sought to propagate a noble version of the German people which would appeal to the deep patriotic feeling of his fellow Germans.

Other humanists offered their own versions of Germany's past. Some were still wedded to essentially medieval interpretations of facts and fables, while others turned to classical and Italian humanist sources but with little critical skill and much animus. In accounting for the traditions that influenced Beatus, it is best to center on the Alsatian school, above all Jacob Wimpfeling, and those humanists who specifically dealt with ancient German history. They established the contours of German history that Beatus knew and revised, and the essential background for his accomplishments.

Wimpfeling was one of the scholarly inspirations to Beatus' generation.[11] He proclaimed a strong patriotism together with a deep respect for the Imperial tradition and a desire for intellectual and religious reforms. He felt duty-bound to defend German honor against Aeneas Silvius. But to do so, he realized the need to find and publish new material on Germany's past. The publication of sources, especially those with an imperial focus, marked an important element in Wimpfeling's historical activity.[12] While he tried his hand at narrating the German past in several treatises, the most important was the *Epitoma rerum Germanicarum usque ad nostra tempora* (1505).[13] Beatus knew this work well and even corrected and published it.[14] Patriotic in inspiration and defensive in intent, the *Epitoma* treated Germany as a national-cultural unit. In Wimpfeling's view the Germans had surpassed all others in their good qualities; hence, any criticism of them was proof of ill will and envy. The Germans, ancient or modern, possessed all the virtues, especially *libertas,* which Tacitus had praised. Germany was clearly an identifiable entity and its people enjoyed a unified culture that bridged the centuries. One of the positive aspects in Wimpfeling's narrative is the praise of artistic and intellectual aspects of

German life rather than the concentration on its military exploits which marked many other such histories. On the negative side, he was not very careful when citing other writers or drawing inferences from his sources. Ultimately, Wimpfeling was involved less in an objective historical investigation than in a patriotic crusade.

Although Wimpfeling did not concentrate exclusively on the ancient Germans—his treatment was comprehensive—he did provide some important programmatic statements.[15] Basing himself primarily on Tacitus, he praised the moral integrity of the German tribes and compared them favorably with the ancient Romans. The deeds of the Germans thus could be positively juxtaposed to those of the other ancient peoples, and, as a consequence, modern Germans need have no feeling of cultural inferiority vis-à-vis the Italians. In addition to Tacitus, Wimpfeling consulted other ancient writers to give breadth to his narrative—Strabo, Plutarch, Caesar, Suetonius, and Flavius Vopiscus (one of the *Scriptores Historiae Augustae,* although the name is dubious), as well as modern historians. While its polemical quality rendered Wimpfeling's work something less than ideal history, the *Epitoma* marked a definite advance over the medieval chronicle and world-historical narratives.

The questions of ancient German history were more fully discussed by other humanists, although not with any greater authority. Among these the most closely associated with Beatus was his old teacher Hieronymus Gebweiler, who, in 1519, issued his *Libertas Germaniae.*[16] Gebweiler's treatment of the German past was replete with legends and strange etymologies, recalling such traditional myths as the Trojan origins of the Germans and Hercules as a German. Among the historical figures he treated, Charlemagne received special care and his Empire was claimed for the Germans, as Beatus would do after him. Among the other Alsatian humanist historians, Franciscus Irenicus (Franz Fritz, 1495–ca. 1550) offers a greater consideration of these matters than Wimpfeling in his *Germaniae Exegeseos volumina duodecim* (1518).[17] In it Irenicus betrayed an intense patriotic zeal, and to a great extent his work can most accurately be described as propaganda. To him all things German surpassed those of other peoples. Despite this chauvinism, his treatise had the merit of including relatively long discussions of early Germanic history, especially the various tribes. The German tribes are seen as noble, and their incursion into the Roman Empire provides proof of their military virtue. Although Irenicus gave an alphabetical listing of the tribes, locating them within Germany, he was often careless in his identifications and did not properly evaluate his large number of sources. A further defect was his lack of appreciation of the changes that had occurred among the tribes and their frequent movements. The poor quality of his work earned Irenicus Beatus' criticism for his lack of both *stilus* and *iudicium*.[18] This was a sharp but accurate assessment from a man who was not inclined to gratuitous harshness; ironically, Irenicus for his part properly had high regard for Beatus.[19]

For all their limits, these historians sincerely searched to uncover material on ancient Germany; others found it preferable to invent what they needed. Myths and fables had always been part of the medieval historical consciousness, but in the Renaissance, with its passion for discovering new sources, there appeared the opportunity to enhance the body of "historical" detail on Germany.[20] The discovery of Tacitus showed that there was much about the German past that was unknown, and that there might exist previously unavailable or unknown ancient sources that would provide valuable information to fill this lacuna. Beatus, for example, duly lamented the loss of a work by Pliny describing the wars between the Romans and the early Germans. As a result of the interest in recent discoveries, there was a certain receptivity to convenient forgeries.

Foreigners as well as natives fabricated sources of the German past. One of the most creative was the Italian Dominican, Johannes Annius of Viterbo (died 1502).[21] Annius published what he claimed to be the lost writings of the ancient historians, including Berosus of Babylon, Manetho, and Metasthenes of Persia. Berosus in particular was portrayed as a chronicle of the Germans. The work was accepted by many Germans as proof of the antiquity and prominence of their ancestors. With such a lineage, they could claim equality with other peoples whose early histories were better documented. Beatus was one who early rejected Annius' fabrications.[22]

Germany did not have to depend on foreigners for such convenient inventions. In the Benedictine monk Johannes Trithemius, she had her equal to Annius. Trithemius[23] was much more than just a forger. He was a learned scholar who made useful contributions to an authentic understanding of the past. His *De scriptoribus ecclesiasticis,* for example, had real historical value. Nevertheless, he agreed with those who lamented the dearth of literary sources depicting the deeds of the early Germans and invented the history of Hunibald to correct this deficiency. He summarized Hunibald in two works on the Franks, the *Compendium de origine regum et gentis Francorum* and the *Compendium de origine gentis Francorum,* both published in 1514 at the request of the Emperor Maximilian. Maximilian had a passion for the mythic origins of his own dynasty and its connection to the Franks, and Trithemius willingly satisfied the Imperial fancy.[24] The citations from Hunibald were used to confirm another favorite theme of the Emperor, the Trojan origins of the German people.

Forgeries such as these greatly clouded the landscape of German history and made it difficult to distinguish the forgeries and fables from authentic ancient sources. The myths were tailor-made to the patriotic prejudices of their readers, and the audience was inclined to take them at face value. Even though some historians rejected such inventions, many more accepted them, so there was a lag between scholarly principle, its implementation, and popular expectations. The circulation of such stories made the task of a serious German historian all the more difficult and required him to spend much time developing arguments for rejecting what should never have been accepted. These inventions, together with so many other myths that had tradition for support, made it difficult to temper Tacitus' idealization of the ancient tribes and arrive at some sound judgment. All this would have been almost an impossible undertaking without a comparative textual critical method.

Somewhat counterbalancing these forgeries was the existence of a growing body of published authentic primary sources on the German Middle Ages, usually in editions by humanists. Conrad Peutinger (1465–1547), for example, published Jordanes' *History of the Goths* and Paul the Deacon's *History of the Lombards.*[25]

Carolingian sources were especially prized. Among the most valuable were Einhard's *Vita Karoli Magni,* first printed in 1505 with many subsequent editions.[26] Also prominent were the *Annales* of Reginus, bishop of Prüm, which covered the years after Charlemagne's death, and the *Annales regni Francorum,* which discussed basically the same years and clearly treated the pope as a subordinate to the divinely appointed emperor.[27] Nearly contemporary with these was Bede's *Historia ecclesiastica gentis Anglorum,* first published in Strasbourg in 1475.[28] Non-Germans also contributed to the circulation of important medieval texts with German themes. The fifth-century bishop Sidonius Apollinaris discussed events in Gaul as the Roman Empire yielded to the Germans; his letters were published in Utrecht in 1473 and his poems in Milan in 1498.[29] Paris was a center of the production of medieval texts, and Beatus' friends in the Lefèvre circle were prominent in this enterprise. Josse Bade issued editions of Gregory of Tours, Pope Leo I, Liudprand of Cremona, the monk Aimonius of Fleury's *De Regum procerumque Francorum origine gestisque clarissimis,* and the *editio princeps* of Paul the Deacon.[30] Lefèvre's group also sponsored Sigibert of Gembloux's *Chronicon* of the eleventh century.[31]

All this activity reflected interest in early medieval German sources, especially the history of the Franks.[32] By the beginning of the third decade of the sixteenth century the audience for historical writings was a large one, and there were several writers who tried to meet the demand. But none of these was very successful when judged on the bases of accuracy and relative dispassion. A reliable history of Germany, especially the confused but vital early history of the tribes, remained to be written, and it was this vacuum that Beatus filled.

BEATUS' CONCEPTION OF HISTORY

Beatus' correspondence documents his growing interest in topics and sources relating to Germany's past. Beginning with a series of letters of 1515 to and from his fellow classmate at Paris, Michael Hummelberg (1487–1527), Beatus discussed a number of historically related topics, including a rumor that

Pliny's books on the German wars had been found, a manuscript of Caesar's commentaries at Paris, alternate versions of ancient names for German areas, and ancient historians.[33] Ancient Roman administrative offices formed the subject of a 1516 letter to Ulrich Zwingli.[34] Beatus received from Peter Gebweiler a copy of *Leodicensium epistola adversus Paschalem papam* by Sigibert of Gembloux discussing events during the Investiture Controversy. Relatedly, Beatus had supplied some verses by Baptista Mantuanus for Gervasius Soupherus' edition of *Carmen de bello saxonico* praising Henry IV, the Emperor of the Investiture Controversy, in 1508.[35] The Italian humanist Francesco Calvo sent him additional historical materials; he promised to send Beatus a copy of Procopius' *De bello Gothorum* and offered to have a manuscript of the historian Agathias corrected against a Roman exemplar.[36] Johannes Huttich, who published the Sachenspiegel together with feudal constitutions of Otto I, reported on historical texts in manuscript.[37] Later, he and Beatus corresponded on medieval documents, especially Carolingian ones, on feudal law, and ancient historians.[38] With Willibald Pirckheimer, Beatus considered the division of the ancient German tribes.[39] Conrad Peutinger supplied Beatus with the manuscripts of Procopius, Jordanes, and the *Tabula Peutingeriana*, and they exchanged information about other medieval historical manuscripts.[40] After the publication of the *Res Germanicae* in 1531, historical topics became even more prominent in Beatus' correspondence. Long letters on historical topics were exchanged with Aegidius Tschudi, Wolfgang Lazius, and Matthias Erb, among others.[41] Beatus also helped Nicolas Brieffer obtain a medieval chronicle that had belonged to Hieronymus Gebweiler.[42]

Beatus' most important historical correspondence was with Johann Turmair, called Aventinus.[43] Aventinus had also attended the University of Paris and studied with Lefèvre. Of all his humanist historian contemporaries, Aventinus was perhaps the closest to Beatus, although his work was not equal to the Alsatian's in overall quality of historical expertise. Still, Aventinus proved his ability in his history of Bavaria, which was a major accomplishment. Beatus discussed a wide variety of historical questions with his friend, and in his first letter to Aventinus in 1525 he praised him for his work *in cognoscenda rerum Germanicarum antiquitate.*[44]

In Aventinus Beatus found a kindred spirit, although the two men never met in person. To his friend Beatus expressed himself eloquently on the qualities he believed necessary to write history.[45] While many of his views on history were humanist commonplaces—the need to learn history to govern the state well, the sad effects of ignorance of the past in making law, the value of history for understanding the future—he also gave expression to elements more in keeping with his own work. *Stilus* and *iudicium* are fundamental to the writing of history, he explained. While these two qualities are not unique to historians, without them there is no true history. Especially important is critical judgment, since without it forgeries and fables pass for truth. But history does have its special elements:

> Peculiar to history is knowledge of the most important matters, to know and to understand much about the mores of regions and peoples, the site, the quality of the earth, the religions, the institutions, the laws, old and new settlers, empires and kingdoms. Moreover, one can neither learn nor inquire into these matters without the careful study of cosmography and mathematics and travel to the point of distaste, and without the wealth and riches of princes. Also new observation is necessary, and old things should be compared to recent ones. . . . Because of changes of things, there is no people in Germany, indeed any in all Europe, Asia and Africa, who retain their old names and ancestral seats: all have changed. To know these things and to pay attention diligently to them is special to history. Further, the old diplomas of the Emperors, kings, popes, the laws, edicts, letters sent back and forth, rescripts are the most true and certain foundations of history: to investigate and study them is a work exceeding private means.[46]

Such exacting standards made a history of Germany a monumental undertaking, which Beatus' own experiences would confirm.

Beatus had come to appreciate the documentary basis for history rather early in his career. He understood the need for exact consultation of written sources, although he admitted his preference for public over private documents. The keen sense of change and the need for comparison between the old and the new had been evident especially in the *Commentariolus* of 1519, but in the letter to Aventinus he extended these observations into a general historical rule. There were other historians who subscribed to similar principles in the Renaissance, including Aventinus, but few were able to carry them out with such skill or with such valuable results as Beatus.

The *Commentariolus,* as noted above,[47] was an impressive accomplishment and surpassed all previous treatments of the *Germania.* In it, however, Beatus had still not resolved many perplexing problems, including the identification of forgeries, the solution of which would make his later treatment of Tacitus so important. Rather, this short work demonstrated that Beatus could use historical information to clarify questionable attributions, marshal support from several sources, and resolve what seemed to be internal inconsistencies. The *Commentariolus* also showed that Beatus needed further study of historical sources and the development of a critical method for employing profitably what he learned from his study of ancient writers.

Another of Beatus' early attempts to write history was biography. While the life of Geiler von Kaylersberg of 1510 was basically a piece of civic *pietas,* it did require him to organize material relevant to his subject.[48] Much more important was the biography of Velleius Paterculus, which was added to the *editio princeps.*[49] What made this biography difficult to write was the lack of definite information about Velleius. Beatus admitted that consequently he had to rely on conjecture for much of his information. Unfortunately, he erred at the outset by giving Velleius the praenomen Publius. This resulted from a misassociation with a P. Velleius mentioned by Tacitus in the *Annales.*[50] Despite this, Beatus was able to extract from references within the text a relatively accurate picture of the writer. All in all Beatus' biography is a careful exposition of the author's life and his period. He gave a positive, perhaps excessively so, judgment on Velleius' worth as a historian and stylist, which no doubt in part indicated his great pride in discovering a previously unknown writer.[51]

There are numerous references to Roman history in the annotations to Pliny, especially to the Emperor Vespasian, to whom Pliny had dedicated the *Naturalis historia.* In general, however, there was little concern for explaining in great detail historical figures or events. This was no doubt due to Beatus' desire to concentrate on explaining and demonstrating his paleographical method, an emphasis that made all else secondary. Still, there could be no mistaking the great knowledge of philology and history that underlay his critical notes and method.

Parallel to Beatus' history of Germany was his edition in 1531 of works of Procopius, Agathias, Jordanes and Sidonius Apollonaris.[52] For it Beatus relied on a manuscript belonging to Conrad Peutinger.[53] This edition allowed Beatus to consider carefully some of the most important descriptions of early medieval history. In his dedicatory letter to Boniface Amerbach, Beatus defended the importance of the study of early German history and identified himself and his German contemporaries with the deeds of the ancient German tribes:

> Forgetful of the Homeric line according to which 'in our house there is good and evil' [Odys. IV, 392], we give too much attention to the histories of other peoples, whereas there are on the other hand remarkable deeds of our own, which in some cases may be considered worthy not only to be known but even to be imitated. For the triumphs of the Goths, the Vandals and the Franks are our triumphs. The states set up by these peoples in the splendid Roman provinces and even in Italy and at Rome itself, once the queen of all cities, are proof of glory for us, even though nowadays there remains only the state founded by the Franks which was always the most fortunate in peace and war. Not that I am an admirer, to speak the truth, of the burning of cities, destruction and the devastation of countrysides, without which victories of this kind are never accomplished, for who indeed has a heart does not hate such madness? But because we know in general that these things are valued so that all nobility is deduced from them.[54]

Certainly Beatus was proud of his ancestors, but there was also a regret for all of the destruction that accompanied their victories. Since there is so little information on these early peoples, Beatus admitted that all writers had to offer their own conjectures. This collection, although according to Beatus issued at the insistence of Herwagen, formed an excellent supplement to Beatus' major work.

THE *RES GERMANICAE*

The *Res Germanicae,* as the first solidly based historical treatment of early Germany,[55] shows the same scholarly thoroughness that is evident in Beatus' editing: his consultation of diverse sources, his openness to new ideas, his care in offering his own opinions and his desire to supply the reader with the necessary material to judge his conjectures and arrive at informed opinions. Part of the importance of the *Res Germanicae* stemmed from its superiority to the standard histories of Germany. To the confused picture of ancient Germany based often on forgeries, which characterized the work of his predecessors, Beatus' great contribution was to bring some order from uncertainty and falsehood. The order he produced was greatly dependent on his textual criticism. The fruit of deep study, the *Res Germanicae*'s three books clarified the complex and confusing relations between the ancient Germans and the Roman Empire.

In his dedicatory letter to King Ferdinand, Beatus detailed the reasons that led him to write the *Res Germanicae.*[56] He first echoed the traditional lament for the ignorance of German history in his day and the confusion surrounding it. While Roman antiquity is diligently studied, "we [Germans] are inactive [in studying] the middle or older [age] which is much more pertinent to us" (*in media aut etiam vetustiori [antiquitate], quae ad nos maxime pertinent, negligenter cessamus*).[57] Beatus admitted that this partly resulted from the problematic nature of the sources. The idea of writing a work explaining German antiquity came to him while attending the Imperial Diet at Augsburg in 1530, when he responded to questions posed by friends concerning the Roman provinces in Germany. The *Res Germanicae* would explain the migrations and changes of locations, which he called *demigrationes,* of the early Germans. He produced this work fully realizing the differences between ancient and modern Germany.

To show what mistakes had arisen from the ignorance of history, Beatus undertook to deal with a major problem in German historiography—the names and locations of the Roman provinces. He was proud of his skill in defining which provinces had belonged to the Roman Empire and which had formed part of ancient Germany, which had remained free of Roman control throughout antiquity. The inability to make such a clear distinction had caused ancient as well as modern writers to err in identifying historical events and the shifting location of several tribes. Such ignorance had led Ermolao Barbaro to confuse the Aenus (Inn) River, which flows through Switzerland and Austria into the Danube, with the Moenus (Main) River in North Central Germany when correcting Pliny (*Naturalis historia* 9, 15) because he did not realize the distinction between Rhetia (Switzerland), which belonged to the Empire, and ancient Germany.[58]

The strongest proof of the value of Beatus' identification of the boundaries of the ancient Empire was his discussion of the defeat of the Roman General Quintilius Varus by the German tribal chieftan Arminius in A.D. 9 at the Teutoburg Forest (in present-day Westphalia, between Paderborn and Osnabrück). No historical event so moved German historians to patriotic ardor as did this military encounter. Renaissance Germans found in this victory proof of their ancestors' greatness and a prefiguring of the struggles between modern Germans and the Roman papacy.[59] German historians following leads from ancient sources believed that the battle had taken place within the borders of the Roman Empire, and thus it was an indication of the ability of the Germans to defeat the Romans on the enemy's home ground and evidence of their refusal to accept the Roman yoke. Beatus broke with his contemporaries in providing a more exact location of the battle.

He errs greatly who does not know how to distinguish the provinces [of the Roman Empire] from ancient Germany. It is assuredly from this ignorance that comes the error of the ancient writers who imagined that Quintilius Varus with his Roman legions had been massacred at Augsburg when he succumbed to the victorious Arminius in the Teutoburg Forest on the other side of the Rhine in ancient Germany. If they had known that *Rhetia prima,* on whose territory Augsburg was situated, was a province belonging to the Romans, no one would have maintained this [thesis]. So in fact, it has been established that Varus had been killed in Germany; but at that period, *Rhetia* was obedient to Rome and had nothing to do with Germany.[60]

Beatus first corrects the belief that Varus had been massacred at Augusburg. Ancient writers did not realize that Varus was in fact killed within the borders of ancient Germany and hence not in Augsburg, which was part of the ancient Roman *Rhetia prima*. Thus, because of this erroneous placement of Varus' defeat at Augsburg (in southern Germany rather than in northwestern Germany where the battle occurred), subsequent German historians had been misled in their interpretations of the event. In this one example Beatus corrected a historical error and worked to mitigate the evil effects of military chauvinism.

Beatus admitted that in his narrative he would discuss the Franks, Alemanni, and Saxons more than other tribes because their histories were so replete with errors and fables and consequently required closer attention. While the ancient Germans were his major concern, he decided that he would not stop with them but would include the later events of these peoples; thus medieval history was to be part of his purview. Perhaps carried away by the high position of the addressee, Beatus provided an unhistorical summary of the origins of the Habsburg family.[61] Despite an occasional willingness to engage in fanciful etymologies, Beatus offered in the three books on Germany abundant proof that he was engaged in a novel and worthwhile historical enterprise.

The first book of the *Res Germanicae* details the deeds of the various tribes both within ancient Germany and in the Empire.[62] To make these clear, Beatus sketched the geographical limits of *vetus Germania* and the surrounding Roman provinces, and distinguished between the movements of the tribes within ancient Germany (*emigrationes*) and outside her borders into Roman territory (*immigrationes*); he divided his narrative accordingly. Beatus tried to avoid the types of problems associated with the location of Arminius' victory—that is, the misattribution of peoples and events both geographically and temporally—by evaluating and comparing various types of information. This section is important for its treatment of name changes, a topic that also occupied Beatus in his 1519 *Commentariolus*. Tribal wanderings are outlined to show what relations they had with each other and how they contributed to the breakup of the Empire. All the major and many of the less important tribes were given consideration and their activities correlated. Beatus also briefly described the Slavs and other non-German peoples who eventually settled on German territory. In many ways this book consists of a series of observations on ancient German history, geography, and language with source criticisms. It established the essential elements for any reliable treatment of the ancient Germans.

The second book is the most focused, since it concentrates on the history of the Franks and has a central theme—that the Franks were indeed Germans. While not a full account of Frankish history, it does offer valuable observations on the key events and customs of their past. Beatus began with the Franks' victory over the Alemanni at the battle of Tolbiac (Zulpich) in 496. The book offers a picture of how the Franks consolidated their power and ruled the tribes they conquered. There is a strong ethnographical quality to this book. The mores, laws, and language of the Franks are described, and primary sources are given extensive citation. For example, he described the Franks' clothing and hair style and the way they marched into battle, on the basis of various poetic and epistolary materials. In keeping with his promise in the dedicatory letter, Beatus advanced his narrative as far as the eleventh century. An understandably major element of this book was Beatus' treatment of Charlemagne and the Carolingian Empire as German. In this book he had moved from a general treatment of the tribes into the Roman Empire to a close consideration of the most successful of these tribes.

The last book is devoted to Rhineland cities and their inhabitants and is rich in textual observations. In many ways it continues topics that were introduced in the first book, but it has the special object of showing the advances of civilization within Germany. Hence there is a concentration on describing urban settings. Beatus understood that the ancient Germans did not live in cities as had the Romans, even though the ancient sources gave conflicting accounts, and that they actually preferred small villages. Nevertheless, modern Germany was a land of cities, which demonstrated her cultural growth. The longest section describes Sélestat. While at first this would seem to be a manifestation of German parochialism, in fact it offers a concise picture

of the development of a medieval city and has more than paren-
thetical interest.

Any history of ancient and medieval Germany requires the
consultation of a wide variety of sources—classical, late ancient,
and early medieval literary, ecclesiastical, legal, diplomatic,
archeological, epigraphic, and numismatic. Beatus understood
this, and it is one of the signs of his historical breadth and
sophistication that he offered his readers abundant citations
from the most famous and many obscure writers, from manuscripts and printed texts, from inscriptions, coins, and archeological remains. A full accounting of the sources used in the *Res
Germanicae* would take us too far afield, and such work has been
done by others.[63] Beatus cited scores of authorities, and a few
observations on them will indicate the care he brought to his
history.

Classical writers constituted the bulk of Beatus' sources. Tacitus, Velleius Paterculus, Pliny, Livy, and the *Panegyrics* he
printed in 1520 all supplied basic material. Caesar, Ammianus
Marcellinus, Florus' *Epitome* of Roman history, Strabo's geography, Flavius Vopiscus and the other writers of the *Scriptores Historiae Augustae*, Pomponius Mela, and Claudius Ptolemey were also
cited with some regularity. One author Beatus exploited and
quoted extensively, especially in the second book, was Sidonius
Apollinaris. Sidonius was one of the last representatives of Gallo-
Roman culture.[64] He had a certain popularity in the Renaissance
among archaistic writers who favored a literary style replete with
archaic vocabulary and convoluted syntax.[65] As a stylist, Beatus
would hardly have considered Sidonius a model; he fully appreciated him as a historical source. In his discussions on the *Species,
cultus et armatura veterum Francorum*,[66] Beatus quoted Sidonius'
description of the weapons and arms of the Franks, Huns, and
Burgundians. Among other works, he relied on Sidonius' panegyrics on Anthemius, Avitus, and Maiorianus, which concern the
mores of the Franks and Huns, and a series of his letters, including those to Domnicius (whom Beatus incorrectly called Domi-
tius, IV, 20) relating a Frankish prince's procession, to Agricola
(I, 2) on the physical appearance of Theodoric, King of the
Ostrogoths (which Beatus had previously published), and to
Syagrius (V, 5) on the Germanic speech of the Burgundians.

Beatus lamented that Sidonius never finished his history of Attila.[67] Sidonius supplied Beatus with colorful anecdotes and a picture of the state of Frankish culture, which helped to give depth to his depiction of that people.

Other materials consulted included the descriptions of administrative and military divisions of the Empire, including the *Tabula Peutingeriana,* the *Itinerarium* of Antonius and the *Notitia Dignitatum.* Of these it is useful to consider more closely Beatus' use of the *Tabula Peutingeriana.*[68] The *Tabula* is a copy of the unique surviving example of Roman cartography. Its date and provenance are uncertain. Indeed, the history of its discovery is not clear. Conrad Celtis first found it in 1507, but it is not certain where. Conrad Peutinger obtained it in 1511 with the intention of publishing it, although it was published only in 1598 by his relative, Marcus Welser. Beatus' first mention of the *Tabula* in the *Res Germanicae* provides a good summary of what is known about it:

> in charta provinciali quam apud Chunradum Peutingerum amicum nostrum Augustae vidimus, sub ultimis Imperatorum depictam et a Celte in quadam bibliotheca repertam, plane veterem.[69]

Michael Hummelberg, Beatus' friend who shared his passion for history, copied it in part; his version is presently in Naples.[70] Beatus obviously prized this manuscript, and considered it authoritative enough to solve a conjectural point.[71] In citing it he was anxious to duplicate the map's form. He, therefore, tried to indicate how it appeared when he described the Suevi in the Silva Marciana:

> Finally this should be repeated, in that marching map which Conrad Peutinger possesses, across the Rhine above Zurzach, Schleitheim, Mufingen, and Rottweil, the grove is depicted with trees and named with capital letters
> S   Y   L   V   A   M   A   R   T   I   A   N   A
> and above these words
> A   L   E   M   A   N   N   I   A
> On the side, parallel with Worms and Brumat, was written above
> S   V   E   V   I   A[72]

Beatus thus gave his readers not only specific geographical information from the *Tabula Peutingeriana* but also an idea of its form and some paleographical information.

In addition to these accounts, Beatus utilized inscriptions and information from ruins. The value of inscriptions in solving problems of medieval German history had been accepted by other humanists, although often in an uncritical manner.[73] Beatus cited inscriptions at several points in the *Res Germanicae:*[74] for example, in his discussion of Dacia he referred to no fewer than four inscriptions,[75] and in his description of his native Sélestat he cited another.[76] He also used inscriptions he found quoted in other printed sources to help him solve disputed questions. In the first book, under the topic *Franci in loca Tencterorum et partim Catthorum usque ad Moeni ripam et Salam fluvium,* in order to prove that the Franks were separated from the Ubii by the Tencteri, two other German tribes, Beatus cited Tacitus and Caesar.[77] He then provided another citation to the *Tabula Peutingeriana* and continued:

> I will introduce in addition another testimony. In the monastery of Deutz near Agrippina [Cologne], commonly called Tuitium but corruptly, when a certain wall was demolished, a stone tablet was found with an inscription which showed that the fortification of Deutz was erected in the land of the Franks by Emperor M. Valerius Constantine for stationing soldiers there in order to guard the provinces of Gaul. . . . Rupert, whom they commonly called Tuitiensis [of Deutz] and who is known to all, tells this story in his commentaries on Sacred Scripture. The old border of the Franks, of which we are now speaking, I have found described nowhere more accurately than in the Chronicles which bear the name of Abbot of Urspurg. In them it is written that the Saxons, when they realized that Charlemagne was away in Spain and they had not been able to move across the Rhine, put to fire and the sword whatever villages and estates lay between Deutz and the Moselle.[78]

The story of the finding of this inscription is also told in Rupert's *De incendio,* which was available to Beatus, as was Johannes Cochlaeus' edition of Rupert's *De divinis officiis* (Cologne, 1526).[79] The *Chronicum* of the Abbot of Ursberg (i.e., the

Premonstratensian Abbot Burchard, who died in 1230) was partly available in a Strasbourg edition of 1472.[80] Similarly, Beatus invoked the ruins of castles, monasteries, and other structures as proof of their former use. There was even a romantic element in his recalling these remains.[81]

Beatus' use of inscriptions and archeological evidence was more than ancillary. He treated them as fundamental resources in determining the antiquity of an area. In his discussion of the reasons for relocations of inhabitants and the destruction of formerly active cities, Beatus discussed the urban areas of his native Alsace.[82] He argued that the ancient Germans hated cities because of the difficulty they had in conquering them; they preferred to live in camps. Consequently, the Roman cities were destroyed and not rebuilt, while new ones developed in open areas. Further, he denied the antiquity of cities when there were no Roman inscriptions or remains of ancient walls that could support such claims.[83] While the antiquity of a city can be established by ancient inscriptions and other remains, it was important to remember, he cautioned, that such artifacts were not distributed equally in all old sites. Former military camps displayed the largest collections of inscriptions and other evidence of Roman presence.[84] In so arguing, Beatus made inscriptions and archaeology into historical sources capable of providing vital information on a people's or a location's past.

A full consideration of the richness of historical detail and argumentation in the *Res Germanicae* would be out of place here. But it is necessary to establish how Beatus used his textual critical talents to deal with his sources and to correct the history of the ancient Germans; in short, to show exactly how his history and textual criticism formed a unit. At one level, the *Res Germanicae* provides a series of new readings of important ancient and early medieval source materials. When it was reprinted in 1551, a list of one hundred and ten places in ancient and early medieval writers whom Beatus emended in one way or another was appended.[85] The authors who received the greatest attention were Ammianus Marcellinus with twenty-two emendations, Pliny with fifteen, and Sidonius Apollinaris with nine. To the ancients who offered information on the German tribes Beatus applied the same critical method that he employed in his classical annotations. Their writings were carefully investigated and scribal errors corrected.[86] A few examples will demonstrate Beatus' procedure and how it influenced his historical writing.

The first instance centers on a seeming reference to German tribes in Cicero's *Epistulae ad Atticum* (XIV, x, 2).[87] Beatus' printed text read *Redeo ad Theobassos, Suevos, Francones*. This passage was used to place the Franks in Gaul well before they had in fact arrived there. Beatus rejected this reading because he had never heard of the Theobassi, and the references in the letter would indicate that the Suevi were in Gaul far from the Rhine, which was not accurate. Fortunately, through his friend Johannes Sichardus,[88] Beatus obtained a manuscript of the letters from the Monastery of Lorsch. This manuscript read *Redeo adtebassos scacuas Frangones,* which Beatus scrutinized carefully with his paleographical skills. He finally decided that the *germana Ciceronis lectio* was *Redeo ad Betasios, Atuas, Vangiones.* Beatus explained that Cicero used these names collectively for all Germans in certain areas. This new reading had nothing to do with the Franks, although it is still far different from the accepted modern version (*Redeo ad Tebassos, Scaevas, Frangones*). Rather than referring to German tribes, the passage gives the names of several of Caesar's veterans who had settled in the area described. The revision of the old reading, on the basis of his conjectural emendation developed from what he found in the Lorsch manuscript, allowed Beatus to dismiss a false attribution. He was correct in his argument that the passage did not refer to the Franks.

In the same letter Beatus offered a further conjectural emendation, which he did *in gratiam studiosorum.*[89] Errors he found in Cicero led him to a broader consideration of the state of that author's works and the reason many such errors remain.

> But the writings of Cicero teem with countless errors, which, nevertheless, because of the divine abundance and richness of that man are not perceived. And the same thing happens with the *Decades* of Livy. Make use of this addition, candid reader.[90]

As he did in his editions, Beatus again expressed his sense of the pervasive corruption of classical literature and the service a scholar performs in helping to remedy this situation.

A second example concerns Julius Caesar's *De bello Gallico,* VI, 25, a section of the work that might well be part of an interpolation. In the discussion of the poorly defined Hercynian Forest (which ancient authors did not locate with any precision, save that it was east of the Rhine, and was often identified with the Hartz mountains),[91] Beatus read: *Oritur ab Helvetiorum, et Nemetum, et Tauracorum finibus, rectaque fluminis Danubii regione pertinet ad fines Dacorum et Anartium* ("[The Hercynian forest] begins in the borders of the Helvetii, the Nemetes, and the Tauraci, and, following the direct line of the river Danube, it extends to the borders of the Daci and the Anartes").[92] Beatus noted that the Nemetes were located around Speyer and not where Caesar placed them. Also, he questioned the name *Tauraci* when he found *Tauriaci* written *in sincerioribus codicibus.* Moreover, it seemed strange to him that Caesar should have ignored the other tribes in the area between the Helvetii and the Nemetes, such as the Rauraci. Obviously the passage was defective in his view (*Crede mihi lector, locus iste mendo non caret apud Caesarem*). He now proposed *Venetum* rather than *Nemetum;* the *Venetes* lived in the appropriate region, as Pliny and Pomponius Mela testified. Further, he emended an inscription that Claudius Ptolemy had transcribed to obtain further support. Beatus noted that the river Taurum or Tauria is presently called Turus, which gives the name Turegum, which was under the *dux Alemanniae,* as he read in a *diploma Ludevvichi regis Francorum.* Beatus' emendation does not concur with the modern reading (*Oritur ab Helvetiorum et Nemetum et Rauricorum finibus rectaque fluminis Danuvi regione pertinet ad finis Dacorum et Anartium*),[93] but he did correctly appreciate a problematic passage.[94]

Especially interesting are the large number of emendations and conjectures Beatus made to Ammianus Marcellinus' *Res gestae.*[95] He had access to a manuscript from the Monastery of Hersfeld, which contained books XXVII–XXXI (books XIV–XXVI were available in print, including a Froben edition of 1518), and Sigismund Gelen used this manuscript for his edition of 1533.[96] In castigating Ammianus, Beatus again called attention to the difficulty of such an endeavor.[97] One of his conjectures has a particularly interesting history. In citing *Res gestae* 18,

2, 15, Beatus questioned the reading, *ubi terminales lapides Romanorum et Burgundionum confinia distinguebant.*[98] He argued that the Romans never controlled the region under discussion and hence *Romanorum* was inappropriate. Instead, Beatus conjectured *Alemannorum.* The Burgundians had fought with the Alemanni but had never been able to defeat them, hence distinct boundaries were enforced between them in order to maintain peace. This conjecture (with *Alemannorum* altered to *Alamannorum*) was taken up by Gelen in his edition. Gelen gave Beatus' conjecture as the proper reading even though his own manuscript clearly had *Romanorum.* From the appearance of Gelen's edition, this conjecture was generally accepted until the nineteenth century. While Beatus' conjecture has been rejected by most (but not all) modern editors, it has had its defenders and a long history. The plausibility of Beatus' conjecture seems to have outweighed manuscript authority for many editors.

Other manuscripts received special attention in the *Res Germanicae.* Among unusual ancient writers Beatus obtained a Greek version of Josephus' *Adversus Appionem* from John a Lasco, which proved to be very useful, since the Latin versions of the treatise were very corrupt.[99] He also had access to several manuscripts of Frankish laws,[100] a collection of Gallic church councils annotated by one Bubulcus, bishop of Windisch near Berne,[101] and decrees of the Council of Lyons.[102] Besides such literary and legal sources, Beatus further consulted some diplomatic documents, even criticizing their Latin style.[103]

In discussing the causes of the corruptions of texts in the *Res Germanicae,* Beatus naturally referred to the poor treatment that ancient texts as well as medieval authorities received from the monks. However, he made his criticisms much stronger than he had in his other works. In discussing the origins of his native town, Beatus complained of fanciful stories and contrasted the greater veracity of antiquity with the medieval tendency to invent stories.

> We properly take refuge in antiquity itself, and we examine and investigate it as much as possible. Now the commentaries of medieval men, most of them monks, are no less silly than the mob itself, from which this for the most part was drawn which was eventually written down in some fashion by newcomers who had been in-

structed by newcomers after such great transformations of events and peoples. These were the Scots and the Irish.[104]

Medieval monks in Beatus' judgment had corrupted everything they touched by their credulity and, in some cases, mendacity.

Beatus expanded on this point in his discussion of the origin of the name *Hellum* or *Helellum,* a village on the Elli river.[105] Beatus believed that the place was of ancient origin because of the presence of inscriptions and other remains that indicated that it had been a Roman military camp. Beatus specifically denied a pious but fraudulent source of the name. This was the story that Saint Maternus, the patron saint of Alsace, had died at Hellum, and that two of his friends petitioned Saint Peter, who brought him back to life even though the man had been dead for a month. Beatus found this story in the Chronicles of the Monastery of Ebersheim, where a monk had misread the Latin *elegia,* which was a transliteration of the Greek for the place where the saint had died and from which the town Hellum received its name. Beatus mocked the "dreams of the monks," whereby they accepted false stories on the basis of tradition.[106] He cited other such contorted etymologies and again contrasted these medieval myths, which are reproduced in Church decorations, manuscripts and printed books, with the need to resort to antiquity.

> I see sometimes there is too little help from the monastic chronicles, in which legendary matters are sewn onto true things, so that what ought to be believed is not at all apparent. Therefore it is preferable to take refuge in antiquity, wherever it is possible. And yet there are those who worship these [legends] almost as oracles.[107]

Monkish inventions corrupted the sources for historical truth just as they did classical manuscripts.

Beatus attacked the monks for the creation of greater fables than that surrounding Hellum. Their acceptance and propagation of the legend of the Trojan origins of the Franks were more significant.[108] The story was one of the most durable fables throughout the Renaissance, and Beatus was instrumental in its rejection.[109] He discussed it when correcting a version of the *Vita Divi Florentii Scoti.* Beatus sarcastically commented that the good father who wrote the life, as ignorant of antiquity as those times were, followed that dream about Troy, conveying the glorious interpretation to us, because he remembered that he had read in historical fables that the Franks took their origin from the Trojans.[110]

Similarly, Beatus rejected the forgeries of Berosus by Annius of Viterbo. When dealing with the origin of the Franks, he commented, "omnium ineptissimus [of Frankish historians] est Annius quidam in Berosum, autoris fabulosi fabulosior interpres." Annius, for example, maintained that the name Ludovicus was to be found among the ancient Celts, when in fact, as Beatus noted, it was unknown in Gaul before the Franks migrated there from Germany.[111]

While Beatus tried to remain as close as possible to his manuscripts, he did on occasion depart from them. There is one interesting example of this, which Prof. Anna Carlotta Dionisotti has analysed in some detail; her conclusions warrant summary here.[112] When describing the Frankish rule in Gaul, Beatus specifically treated the status of the Gauls and other Germans under the Franks.[113] After discussing the governmental administration, Beatus considered a series of Carolingian chartularies as indicators of life under their rule. He quoted several of these laws, which were included in one of his manuscripts. Beatus understood the historical value of laws and legal compilations and cited them as sources in other contexts. In quoting from the Carolingian laws, he did not reproduce them integrally but altered their Latin without indicating the reasons for his changes. Since Beatus usually did not tamper with his sources without specific statements about the problems in the text and justification for his changes, the alterations do raise questions about his treatment of his manuscripts or at least a specific type. As Prof. Dionisotti has noted, the changes are not random. In altering the Latin of the chartularies Beatus made them seem more Roman, reworking them into better Latin with the special quality of legal language. He also made the laws seem less sharp and severe in their treatment of the population.[114] Beatus seems to have wanted to make the reign of the Franks seem more benign. Further, although Beatus could speak about restoring the *sincera lectio* of medieval manuscripts, he felt greater freedom in criticizing their form and in making them concur with proper Latinity and even in changing their sense than he would have when dealing with ancient writers. He maintained different standards in treating classical and medieval authors; the inferior Latinity of the latter did not warrant the same level of fidelity.

The discussion of one particular medieval manuscript will highlight a further dimension of Beatus' historical scholarship. While Latin and Greek were the sources on which Beatus depended, he did make numerous etymological references to the German language (a procedure common among Renaissance historians, although not usually successful). Especially important was his desire to proclaim the unity of the German peoples through their common speech. Beatus had a keen sense of the mobility of language as well as its staying power: "For I think that all languages are somewhat mixed and that none is pure."[115] He even tied language with Empire in discussing the language of ancient Gaul.

> The language that Gaul used for its own, until it was converted into its provincial form by the Romans, is thought to have been thoroughly wiped out, just as the Spanish lost their language. O how obliging the Romans were and how inexpressibly successful. And no one should be amazed that provinces no less Roman than Rome herself can have been snatched from the Romans. For all kingdoms have their allotted spans.[116]

Language, therefore, constituted an identifying element of a people, but there was fluidity to it which the historian must properly assess.

Concern for the language of his own people made Beatus intent on emphasizing the German quality of the Franks. He found support not only in classical authors but also from what was a precious find, a manuscript of the life of Christ in High German from the cathedral library of Freising, which Beatus obtained in 1529.[117] This manuscript was defective, lacking dedicatory epistles and the author's name. Although Beatus did not mention the author, he probably did know from other sources that it was Otfrid, a monk of the Monastery of Weissenburg, who wrote the work probably in the 860s. Beatus discovered the manuscript at the Monastery of Corvey while attending the Diet at Augsburg.[118] He recorded the title as *Liber Evangeliorum in teodiscam linguam versus* and noted that it is in verse and was at least six hundred years old. He provided the colophon, *Vualdo me fieri iussit. Sigefridus presbyter scripsi,* and identified Vualdo as the tenth bishop of Freising (884–906). (His transcription of the colophon was incomplete; it reads *Uualdo episcopus istud evangeliorum fieri iussit. Ego Sigihardus indignus presbyter scripsi.*)[119] He quoted several sections to show the closeness of ancient to modern German and labeled the manuscript *thesaurus antiquitatis.*[120] Beatus so prized it that he used the *Liber* as an authority in a discussion of the various forms of the name Frank.[121]

The value of this manuscript in understanding ancient German led Beatus to relate how the late Emperor Maximilian had been very interested in obtaining ancient works in German.[122] While the state of German as a written language was better than that of Hungarian, which was not even written before that time, Latin had become the dominant written language at the expense of German. Examples of old German, therefore, were valuable for an appreciation of the history of the language. Beatus knew of other examples of old German. One was a codex of the Psalter that belonged to his friend Johannes Huttich. Beatus related an event contemporary with this discussion. The ancient Franks were worthy of praise in Beatus' opinion because they translated the sacred books into the language of the people, but unfortunately such a worthy enterprise was opposed by some theologians in his own day.[123] While no chauvinist, Beatus still cultivated evidence of the German language and its development with great care.

ORGANIZATIONAL PROBLEMS IN THE *RES GERMANICAE*

Beatus developed great sensitivity to the history of the Germans. He understood the nature of their past, that not all Germans had migrated out of Germany, and that some joined other tribes.[124] It was, therefore, necessary to trace carefully a people's movement in order to understand their history and their relationship with other groups. This was true because the ancient Germans were often poorly treated by historians.[125] This realization led Beatus to treat his historical sources extensively in order to extract from them every possible piece of information. He lamented the errors that learned men had introduced into their discussions of the Germans and argued that one must remove these in order to describe ancient Germany properly.[126] In investigating such errors, Beatus depended on his textual critical method. The task went beyond what he had experienced in his editions of classical writers, since he had to take into consideration medieval Latin—diplomatic, religious, and literary, as well as the *historiae mediae aetatis*[127]—and German texts in order to provide a coherent picture of the tribes.

The constant need on Beatus' part to evaluate often unclear and conflicting narratives, to sift through linguistic and geographical quagmires, to emend faulty readings in texts of various ages and styles, and to offer his own opinions on disputed topics make the reading of the *Res Germanicae* a daunting experience. Further, the arrangement of topics that Beatus used resulted in extended arguments concerning one topic or tribe scattered over several places throughout the treatise. One example of this procedure will demonstrate many of the most salient features of the process by which Beatus solved numerous ancillary questions in order to resolve the primary one. This is evident in Beatus' explanation of the proper form for the name "Bohemia." To give an answer Beatus had to deal with the tribes that inhabited the area and their activities and then offer criticism of the ancient versions of the name.

The German tribe that inhabited the area called Bohemia was the Marcomanni, a group especially known for hostile contacts with the Romans and for establishing the first German empire.[128] Beatus treated their activities at several places in the *Res Germanicae* and tried to give a coherent picture of a tribe whose history is still not completely clear. It was in the context of these shifting and separate treatments of the Marcomanni that Beatus turned his attention to the name Bohemia. It was an ancillary matter, but one that required solution and led him to textual criticism. Beatus explained that the Marcomanni had moved into present day Czechoslovakia, and there expelled a

Celtic people called the Boii. This tribe gave the name to the area that the Marcomanni inhabited.[129] He specifically rejected as a fable the opinion that the name was of Slavic origin.[130] Further, he found the name in Strabo's *Geography*, where it was written in his printed text as βουβιάδον (modern reading is βουίαιμον).[131] Beatus did not accept the manuscript reading and appealed to the translation of Guarino of Verona, who had access to a better manuscript and had translated it *Bubiemum*, although he thought that βουϊέμον was also possible. He argued that the problem of the proper form of the name began with Strabo himself: "It is possible that Strabo corrupted the German word, since the Greeks were uninterested in foreigners, even the Latins."[132] Other Greek writers further confused the name. The geographer Ptolemy wrote *Bemos*. This was an abbreviated form and was even common among Germans of his own day. Beatus noted that the Greeks and Romans disliked aspirants in the middle of words; Tacitus, for example, wrote Boiemum and not Boihemum.[133] By the time he came to compose the *Res Germanicae*, Beatus had realized that the ancients were the source of some of the problems later historians had to solve.

In tracing the proper form of the name for Bohemia, Beatus had to provide a series of extended discussions of specific problems. There was not one section devoted specifically to the question; rather, it arose as a consequence of his treatment of the history of the Marcomanni and the other tribes that inhabited that area. This was in general true of all such matters that resulted from his tracing of the tribes' activities. He had to work through a large body of material and try to relate all the information he had at his disposal. In order to incorporate the type of information needed to make a comprehensible presentation, Beatus often had to treat a series of ancillary matters at several different places in his narrative. This permitted him to emphasize his major points—distinguishing between the emigration and immigration of the tribes, describing all the major areas that the Germans inhabited, concentrating on the Franks, highlighting the relationship between Germany's modern and ancient urban areas—and keeping subsidiary matters from overtaking the narrative. However, the organization did not work well for all topics. For example, a full appreciation of the deeds of the Marcomanni, a not particularly significant tribe but one that had been involved in numerous important political and military adventures, requires that the reader move back and forth in the book and obtain various elements of their history and geographical movements scattered throughout the text. Indeed, given the organization he adopted, Beatus was rather successful in bringing together all his information and discussing the appropriate material. Such a procedure made for difficult consultation and must have done much to keep the readership of the *Res Germanicae* limited. Since Beatus was constantly in the process of collating his historical and philological information with his textual critical procedure in order to provide a firm foundation for historical explanation, complexity in his narrative sometimes was inevitable, yet it was always based on a solid methodology.

In a sense the *Res Germanicae* was a preparatory study for a full history of ancient and early medieval Germany. Beatus had laid down certain fundamental principles and had demonstrated how they could be employed, but he could not advance very far beyond them. Time would not permit him to move to the next step of a general narrative. Moreover, Beatus probably would not have been happy undertaking such a task. He was the master of annotation, which gave him the opportunity to bring his philological and historical knowledge to play on specific problems. As a historian he dealt best with small questions within larger ones. Certainly that is what is indicated in his treatment of secular history. This is not to suggest that Beatus was lacking in the traits of a good—indeed, great—historian. Quite the contrary, those very traits would not allow him to wander far from his sources, and they were not in a state that would allow him to write a broad narrative history before he had collected and criticized them as he did in the *Res Germanicae*.

Although his procedure of following the geographical boundaries of *vetus Germania* and the Roman territories required him to divide his narrative of particular tribes, especially in book 1, into several sections, Beatus could be very precise in his explanations and relatively economical. This is evident in his treatment of his native town. The long section devoted to Sélestat combines many of the best features of Beatus' historical writing.[134] It is patriotic in intent and meant to sustain the argument of book 3, which illustrates German civilization, but it is not chauvinistic. Based solidly on literary and epigraphical sources, it provides a narrative of Sélestat's growth and salient elements in its history. Beatus located the city geographically and described its walls and general plan. Because of viticulture Sélestat was an important merchant port.[135] Local lords as well as Frankish and German emperors collected taxes from her, and Beatus sketches the political history of the area under the Carolingian and Saxon Emperors to demonstrate this.

One of the important ecclesiastical structures of the city was the Church of Sainte-Foy, founded by Hildegard of Buren at the end of the eleventh century. Beatus quotes the letter of its foundation as an example of medieval documents.[136] He noted that it proved that earlier there had existed a baptismal church in honor of Sainte-Foy. Sélestat received its walls under Frederick II, and under the Habsburg emperor Rudolph the city was brought into the full jurisdiction of the Empire. He cited a diploma of Rudolph on this matter.[137]

Beatus continued his story to include the later history of the city, and in general what emerges is a short but clear description of the growth of a medieval city, including the civil struggles and violence which marked medieval urban life. Primary sources are cited to give substance to the narrative and to illustrate the status of the city within the Empire. Although Beatus described in summary fashion the citizens and their lifestyles, his interest, in conformity with views we have seen articulated in his letters, lay in the public history of Sélestat.

In composing his picture of ancient and medieval Germany, Beatus lacked any solid modern model and, therefore, had to adapt his narrative to fit the requirement of making his sources' statements explicit and consistent. The *Res Germanicae* in some ways was an extension of Beatus' procedure in his critical editions. They all required the same textual critical method, and the use of it in both his editing and in his history shows how close these were. Textual criticism had to be woven into the narrative, a rather more difficult task when writing history than in providing historical examples in annotations. Beatus was ex-

perimenting with a method that required him to follow different procedures at once. His success is proven by the unique
position the *Res Germanicae* holds in the history of German Renaissance humanism.

FINAL THOUGHTS

Beatus fully realized the tentative nature of the conjectures he
proposed when explaining the complexities of early German
history and in refuting fables. As with a manuscript-based conjecture, he argued from his knowledge of history and collateral
sources, but all such conjectures remained, in his view, open to
improvement or correction. While he felt that he had made his
conjectures free of prejudice, he encouraged readers to judge
for themselves. In discussing the city of Basel, Beatus argued
that Basel was at one time under the administration of the
bishopric of Besançon. He supplied what he considered supporting evidence for this judgment from his volume of Frankish laws, but he maintained that his opinion should not become
the source for new arguments.

> Here we, as in other matters, have presented our opinion frankly,
> we have prejudged nothing. Everyone is free to follow whatever he
> thinks on the matter. For what is more stupid than frivolously to
> engage in a gladitorial contest over those things which depend not
> on definite testimonies but only on conjectures.[138]

Beatus admitted that he did not like to speculate on recent
events (i.e., those of the Middle Ages), but preferred to concentrate on antiquity, where presumably his control of classical
history and philology gave him a better basis for conjecturing.[139] History was for Beatus an activity that required hard
work, intelligence, and a certain willingness to open oneself to
the criticism of others; it was not a matter for acrimonious
debate. Such honesty and integrity were more than simply a
rhetorical device; it was the way Beatus worked, and it characterized him as one of the greatest historians of his day.

The *Res Germanicae* did not mark an end to Beatus' study and
treatment of German history. He continued to revise the his-

tory although he did not succeed in publishing a new edition in his lifetime. However, he was still active in collecting and annotating historical documents. As late as 1543 he was working on a new work, *nugae quaedam Latinogermanicae,* as he called it, which was to be a collection of observations on the foundation charter of the monastery of Murbach, which Beatus emended and explained.[140] One of his last historical exercises was the *Illyrici Provinciarum utrique Imperio cum Romano tum Constantinopolitano servientis descriptio,* which Gelen published in 1552 together with his edition of the *Notitia Dignitatum.*[141]

The breadth and solid learning of Beatus' historical works places him in the front ranks of Renaissance historians. He had few in the way of immediate followers. The political and intellectual statis of contemporary Germany was not hospitable to his type of relatively dispassionate history. Reformation historiography belonged to men like Sleidanus and Flaccius, one a good historian concerned only with modern public events, the other a polemicist but also an indefatigable researcher and publisher of source materials. The editors who followed him, such as Gelen, did not have the historical imagination to attempt what Beatus had done. But throughout the sixteenth century there were German scholars who did continue the historical procedures Beatus had initiated, although without his brilliance.[142]

In many ways the true successors to the historiographical tradition that Beatus' textual-historical work represented were to be found among the French historians of the later half of the sixteenth century.[143] They were the ones who most appreciated his treatment of early German history as well as the philological and textual basis of his work. Beatus had sought to write a national history, but his method and industry coupled with his critical sense made his endeavor of much more than local or even strictly German significance. He had demonstrated the manner in which history should integrate a variety of sources and arrive at conjecturally plausible accounts of peoples and events. Beatus the textual critic was inseparable from Beatus the historian.

CONCLUSION

Although he displayed a tendency toward prolixity in some of his explanations of his textual and historical conjectures, one must admire the attention Beatus gave to so many difficult and complex writers and questions and the clarity with which he articulated his solutions and ideas. While proud of his efforts and confident about his conjectures, he had no illusions about his work being definitive. Rather, he urged other scholars to search out new manuscripts, to consider them carefully, to analyze them paleographically, and not to put their confidence blindly in his or any other scholar's proposals.[1] One's own eyes and experiences with manuscripts should be preferred to those of others. The task of producing a faithful text would continue as long as there were manuscripts that required careful correction. This modesty marked every aspect of his work.

For all his care, there were limitations to Beatus' procedure. After reading through his conjectures, comparing them with the *vulgata* and the modern readings, one is left with the impression that in his desire to propagate his new method and to establish its validity he willingly corrected passages that did not need it and devised overclear solutions. His desire to explain and leave memorable rules and examples could go too far. Certainly paleographical ingenuity could be as dangerous when restoring an author as stylistic and analogical conjectures. Despite these criticisms and for all the tentativeness of his method, the care and wide-ranging expertise Beatus brought to ancient writers justify his place in the front ranks of Renaissance editors, textual critics, and historians.

Beatus was more than simply presenting an alternate method of recovering ancient writings. He was actively educating his audience in the appreciation of the hard work involved in restoring sensible readings and the need for a critical attitude toward all texts and their manipulation. The Renaissance reader no less than the Renaissance editor lacked a consensus on which to base preferences among competing versions of a text or to establish the validity of historical details. In offering a clear demonstration of his method and its application on several fronts, Beatus urged upon his readers the necessity of accurate texts based on his method and their value in correcting knowledge of the past. He wanted them to expect, and to demand, that whatever text they purchased be prepared in accordance with this critical method, for only in that way would they be assured of the relative accuracy of the words they read. Texts so corrected could be held to be authoritative, to be the actual presentation of the words of the author, or so Beatus argued.[2] He was thus in the process of helping to create a critical reading public that would expect accuracy and consistency in both classical and patristic printed books. Beatus was thereby offering a new scholarly model.

The careful application of his method in Beatus' opinion would provide a more or less objective means of arriving at an author's words. He seems to have had no reservations about the validity of his procedure. If his own applications were not always definitive, then a subsequent scholar with new manuscripts would be able to succeed by following his techniques. There was no doubt that the very words of the author had existed in some definitive version and that they were recoverable. This belief was vitiated not only by the problem of what constituted the authoritative text but also by the lack of a sufficiently refined technique of recension that could provide a standard for selecting among competing manuscript readings. Beatus' confidence in his system depended upon his denying any subjective element that accompanied the limited manuscript sources available and the lack of a fully articulated historical attitude toward them.

The humanists' belief in the recoverability of the actual text of an ancient writer did not lead to a form of bibliolatry. The author's text comes to us in a deformed state, even though it had once been an integral product, and this fact provided the humanist textual critic with his justification to alter the faulty version. But this tampering was purposeful because of the existence of the author's original, which was understood to control

any reconstruction. Beatus and other humanists found no problem in this and did not doubt the ultimate value of their reconsti-
tuted products.

Beatus never explained his critical method in such detail as in
the Pliny *Annotationes*. The method described there did, however, remain his basic procedure through the remainder of his
career. He was not alone in his day in understanding the paleographical sources of textual criticism, although he was one of the
best and one of the most persistent in advocating its application.
Still, none of his contemporaries could claim any greater success
in reconstructing the texts of ancient and patristic writers.

All of his hard work on corrupt texts was ultimately meant to
prepare him for his work as a historian. In this he was able to
bridge the gap between classical philology and textual criticism
and history. He understood the problems in writing history,
which resulted from the diffusion of corrupt manuscripts and
printed books. In order to overcome these and write good history, Beatus began with textual criticism. In concentrating on
history, Beatus was also rearranging the balance within the tradition of Erasmian humanism to emphasize textual and historical scholarship over, but not against, the dominant moral and
scriptural emphases of Erasmus' work. The advances in classical
philology and history that occurred in the latter half of the
sixteenth century and are to be found in the work of Carlo
Sigonio, Justus Lipsius, Joseph Scaliger, and the French jurists
followed in a line that had been greatly strengthened by Beatus.
He had been the first to turn Erasmian humanism into classical
philological and historical scholarship. His success was marked
by the popularity of the *Res Germanicae* among the later genera-
tions of Renaissance historians and by his growing distance
from Erasmus.

NOTES

INTRODUCTION

1. A. E. Housman, "The Application of Thought to Textual Criticism," in his *Classical Papers* (Cambridge: Cambridge University Press, 1972), 3: 1058–1069, at p. 1059.

2. For Valla and Poliziano, see below, chapter 1.

3. See the fine study by James Butrica, *The Manuscript Tradition of Propertius* (Toronto: University of Toronto Press, 1984).

4. For an evaluation of the Lachmannian Method from a Renaissance scholar's point of view, see Paul Oskar Kristeller, "The Lachmann Method: Merits and Limitations," *Text: Transactions of the Society for Textual Scholarship* 1 (1981): 11–20.

5. Georg Luck, "Textual Criticism Today," *American Journal of Philology* 102 (1981): 164–194, at pp. 166–167, with reference to Bentley and Markland.

1: TEXTUAL CRITICISM IN THE RENAISSANCE

1. For humanist manuscript searches, see Remigio Sabbadini, *Le scoperte dei codici latini e greci ne' secoli XIV e XV*, 2 vols. (Florence: Sansoni, 1914), and L. D. Reynolds and N. G. Wilson, *Scribes and Scholars: A Guide to the Transmission of Greek and Latin Literature*, 2d ed. (Oxford: Clarendon Press, 1974). For specific texts, see L. D. Reynolds, ed., *Texts and Transmission: A Survey of the Latin Classics* (Oxford: Clarendon Press, 1983).

2. See Phyllis W. G. Gordan, *Two Renaissance Book Hunters: The Letters of Poggius Bracciolini to Nicolaus de Niccolis* (New York: Columbia University Press, 1974); Nicolai Rubenstein, "An Unknown Letter by Jacopo di Poggio Bracciolini on Discoveries of Classical Texts," *IMU* 1 (1958): 383–400; T. Foffano, "Niccoli, Cosimo e le ricerche di Poggio nelle biblioteche francesi," ibid. 2 (1968): 113–128; C. Questa, *Per la storia del testo di Plauto nell'Umanesimo. I: la "recensio" di Poggio*

Bracciolini (Rome, 1968); and Silvia Rizzo, *La tradizione manoscritta della 'Pro Cluentio' di Cicerone* (Genoa: Istituto di filologia classica e medievale, 1979).

3. See Karl Otto Apel, *L'Idea di lingua nella tradizione dell-'umanesimo da Dante a Vico*, trans. Luciano Tosti (Bologna: Mulino, 1975).

4. For the importance of printing, see Lucien Febvre and Henri-Jean Martin, *The Coming of the Book: The Impact of Printing 1450–1800*, trans. David Gerard, ed. Geoffrey Nowell-Smith and David Wootton (London: NLB, 1976); Rudolf Hirsch, *Printing, Selling and Reading 1450–1550*, 2d pr. (Wiesbaden: Harrassowitz, 1974); and Elizabeth Eisenstein, *The Printing Press as an Agent of Change*, 2 vols. (Cambridge: Cambridge University Press, 1979). See also R. H. Rouse, "Background to Print: Aspects of the Manuscript Book in Northern Europe of the Fifteenth Century," *Proceedings of the Patristic, Medieval and Renaissance Conference* 6 (1981): 37–50, and Lotte Hellinga, "Manuscripts in the Hands of Printers," in *Manuscripts in the Fifty Years After the Invention of Printing*, ed. J. B. Trapp (London: Warburg Institute, 1983), pp. 3–11.

5. On medieval textual criticism, see R. J. Gaiepy, "Lupus of Ferrieres: Carolingian Scribe and Text Critic," *Mediaeval Studies* 30 (1968): 90–105, and Vittorio Peri, " 'Correctores immo corruptores': Un saggio di critica testuale nella Rome del XII secolo," *IMU* 20 (1977): 19–125. For the relationship between manuscripts and printed texts with special attention to philosophy, see John F. D'Amico and Paul F. Grendler, "Conditions of Inquiry," to appear in *The Cambridge History of Renaissance Philosophy*, ed. Charles B. Schmitt (Cambridge: Cambridge University Press, 1987). G. Thomas Tanselle, "Classical, Biblical, and Medieval Textual Criticism and Modern Editing," *Studies in Bibliography* 36 (1983): 21–68, provides further discussion and bibliography.

6. Jean Destrez, *La 'Pecia' dans les manuscrits universitaires du XIIIe et du XIVe siècle* (Paris: Vautrain, 1935), and Guy Fink-Errera, "Une institution du monde médiévale: la 'pecia'," *Revue philosophique de Louvain* 60 (1962): 184–243.

7. For what follows, see Remigio Sabbadini, *Il metodo degli umanisti* (Florence: Le Monnier, 1920); Sebastiano Timpanaro, *La genesi del metodo del Lachmann* (Florence: Le Monnier, 1963), chap. 1; Giorgio Pasquali, *Storia della tradizione e critica del testo*, 2d ed., (Florence: Le Monnier, 1971), esp. chap. 4; Sesto Prete, *Observations on the History of Textual Criticism in the Medieval and Renaissance Periods* (Collegeville, Minn.; Saint John's Monastery, 1969); Reynolds and Wilson, *Scribes and*

Scholars; Silvia Rizzo, *Il lessico filologico degli umanisti,* (Rome: Edizioni di storia e letteratura, 1973); E. J. Kenney, *The Classical Text: Aspects of Editing in the Age of the Printed Book* (Berkeley, Los Angeles, London: University of California Press, 1974); J. H. Waszink, "Osservazioni sui fondamenti della critica testuale," *Quaderni urbinati di cultura classica* 19 (1975): 7–21; Anthony Grafton, "Joseph Scaliger's Edition of Catullus (1577) and the Traditions of Textual Criticism in the Renaissance," *JWCI* 38 (1975): 155–181; idem, "On the Scholarship of Politian and its Context," ibid. 40 (1977): 150–188; idem, *Joseph Scaliger: A Study in the History of Classical Scholarship,* vol. 1 (Oxford: Clarendon Press, 1983); Georg Luck, "Textual Criticism Today," *American Journal of Philology* 102 (1981): 164–194; R. J. Schoeck, "The Humanistic Concept of the Text: Text, Context, and Tradition," *Proceedings of the Patristic, Mediaeval and Renaissance Conference* 7 (1982): 13–31; and Letizia Panizza, "Textual Interpretation in Italy, 1350–1450: Seneca's Letter I to Lucilius," *JWCI* 46 (1983): 40–62. Anthony Grafton, "Renaissance Readers and Ancient Texts: Comments on Some Commentaries," *RQ* 38 (1985): 615–649, provides further discussion and bibliography. For general orientation, see Anthony Grafton and Lisa Jardine, *From Humanism to the Humanities: Education and the Liberal Arts in Fifteenth- and Sixteenth-Century Europe* (Cambridge, Mass.: Harvard University Press, 1986).

8. Rizzo, *Il lessico,* pp. 246–249.

9. Ibid., p. 287.

10. Giuseppe Billanovich, "Maestri di retorica e fortuna di Livio," *IMU* 25 (1984): 325–344, at p. 338. Relatedly, see Patricia Easterling, "Before Palaeography: Notes on Early Descriptions and Datings of Greek Manuscripts," in *Studia codicologica,* ed. Kurt Treu (Berlin: Akademie-Verlag, 1977), pp. 179–187.

11. Monika Asztalos and Tore Janson, "Hutten Correctus: An Example of Humanist Editorial Practice," *Eranos* 76 (1978): 65–69, and Clarence H. Miller, "Some Unusual Printer's Copy used for Early Sixteenth Century Editions of Erasmus' *Encomium Moriae,*" *Studies in Bibliography* 25 (1972): 137–143.

12. A detailed discussion of the relationship between printed text and manuscript is given in A. C. de la Mare and L. Hellinga, "The first book printed in Oxford: the *Expositio symboli* of Rufinus," *Transactions of The Cambridge Bibliographical Society* 7 (1978): 184–244. Interesting texts on Renaissance printing practices can be found in James Binns, "STC Latin Books: Evidence for Printing-House Practice," *The Library,* Ser. 5, 32 (1977): 1–27, and idem, "STC Latin Books: Further

Evidence for Printing-House Practice," ibid., Ser. 6, 1 (1979): 347–360. Also of general interest is Jean-François Gilmont, "Printers by the Rules," ibid., Ser. 6, 2 (1980): 129–155.

13. See Waszink, "Osservazioni sui fondamenti," pp. 10–11; Giuseppe Billanovich, "Petrarch and the Textual Tradition of Livy," *JWCI* 14 (1951): 137–208; and idem, "Dal Livio di Raterio (Laur. 63,19) al Livio del Petrarca (B. M., Harl. 2493)," *IMU* 2 (1959): 103–178.

14. The text is quoted in Rizzo, *Il lessico,* pp. 341–344, and discussed in Berthold L. Ullman, *The Humanism of Coluccio Salutati* (Padua: Antenore, 1973), pp. 99–106, and Ronald Witt, *Hercules at the Crossroad: The Life, Works, and Thought of Coluccio Salutati* (Durham, N.C.: University of North Carolina Press, 1983), chap. 9. A. Casacci, "Per la critica del testo nella prima metà del quattrocento," *Rendiconti del reale Istituto Lombardo di scienze e lettere,* Ser. 2, 59 (1926): 91–104, supplies the context.

15. Rita Cappelletto, "Congetture di Niccolò Niccoli al testo delle 'dodici commedie' di Plauto," *Rivista di filologia e di istruzione classica* 105 (1977): 43–56; idem, "Niccolò Niccoli e il codice di Ammiano Vat. Lat. 1873," *Bollettino del Comitato per la preparazione dell'edizione nazionale dei classici greci e latini,* n.s. 26 (1978): 57–84; idem, "Niccolò Niccoli e la tradizione manoscritta di Tertulliano," *Orpheus,* n.s. 2 (1981): 380–396; Lucia Labardi, "Congetture del Niccoli e tradizione estranea all'archetipo sui margini del Laurenziano 39,38 di Valerio Flacco," *IMU* 26 (1983): 189–213; and Philip A. Stadter, "Niccolò Niccoli: Winning Back the Knowledge of the Ancients," in *Vestigia: Studi in onore di Giuseppe Billanovich,* ed. Rino Avesani et al. (Rome: Edizioni di storia e letteratura, 1984), II: 747–764.

16. Cappelletto, "Congetture di Plauto," p. 43.

17. Recent relevant treatments of Valla include Donald R. Kelley, *The Foundations of Modern Scholarship: Language, Law, and History in the French Renaissance* (New York: Columbia University Press, 1970), chap. 1, and S. Camporeale, *Lorenzo Valla: Umanismo e teologia* (Florence: Istituto di Rinascimento, 1972).

18. For the *Elegantiae,* see David Marsh, "Grammar, Method, and Polemic in Lorenzo Valla's *Elegantiae,*" *Rinascimento* 19 (1979): 91–116, and Rizzo, *Il lessico,* esp. pp. 230–233. For the Donation of Constantine, see *De falso credita et ementita Constantini donatione declamatio,* ed. Wolfram Setz (Vienna: Bohlau, 1976).

19. On Valla's *Emendationes,* see R. Valentini, "Le Emendationes in T. Livium di L. Valla," *Studi italiani di filologia classica* 15 (1907): 262–302; G. Billanovich and M. Ferraris, "Le 'Emendationes in T. Livium' del Valla e il codex regius di Livio," *IMU* 1 (1958): 245–264; A.

Borghi, "Il codice Valenziano della terza Deca di Livio e la sua tradizione," *Rendiconti dell'Istituto Lombardo di scienze e lettere, classe di letteratura e scienze morali e storiche* 108 (1974): 803–818; and Mariangela Regoliosi, "Lorenzo Valla, Antonio Panormita, Giacomo Curlo e le emendazioni a Livio," *IMU* 24 (1981): 287–316. Text in Mariangela Regoliosi, ed., *Laurentii Valle Antidotum in Facium*, (Padua: Antenore, 1981). Related is Bartolomeo Facio, *Invective in Laurentium Vallam*, ed. Ennio I. Rao (Naples: Società editrice napoletana, 1978).

20. *Antidotum*, p. 334.

21. Ibid., pp. 336, 344, 365.

22. For these translations, see Giovan Battista Alberti, "Erodoto nella traduzione latina di Lorenzo Valla," *Bollettino del Comitato per la preparazione della edizione nazionale dei classici greci e latini,* n.s. 7 (1959): 65–84; Filippo Ferlauto, *Il testo di Tucidide e la traduzione latina di Lorenzo Valla* (Palermo: Stampatori tipolitografi associati, 1979); Marianne Pade, "The Place of Translation in Valla's Thought," *Classica et mediaevalia* 35 (1984): 285–306; and idem, "Valla's Thucydides: Theory and Practice in a Renaissance Translation," ibid. 36 (1985): 275–301.

23. Valla's *Collatio* and *Annotationes* and his method are analyzed in Jerry H. Bentley, *Humanists and Holy Writ: New Testament Scholarship in the Renaissance* (Princeton, N.J.: Princeton University Press, 1983), chap. 2. Modern edition, *Collatio Novi Testamenti,* ed. Alessandro Perosa (Florence: Sansoni, 1970).

24. For the *Dialectica*, see Kelley, *The Foundations of Historical Scholarship,* pp. 25–366; Linda Gardiner Janik, "Lorenzo Valla: The Primacy of Rhetoric and the De-moralization of History," *History and Theory* 12 (1973): 399–404; Lisa Jardine, "Lorenzo Valla and the Intellectual Origins of Humanist Dialectic," *Journal of the History of Ideas* 15 (1977): 143–164; and Richard Waswo, "The 'Ordinary Language Philosophy' of Lorenzo Valla," *BHR* 41 (1979): 255–271.

25. *Laurentii Valle Gesta Ferdinandi Regis Aragonum*, ed. Ottavio Besomi (Padua: Antenore, 1973).

26. *DBI*, 10: 536–559.

27. Rita Cappelletto, "Origine e fortune di un toponomio di Biondo Flavio (Amm. XVI, 10, 14 e Suet. Dom. 5)," *Quaderni di storia* 17 (1983): 169–183, and idem, *Recuperi ammianei da Biondo Flavio* (Rome: Edizioni di storia e letteratura, 1983). Also A. Mazzocco, "Some Philological Aspects of Biondo Flavio's *Roma Triumphans*," *Humanistica Lovaniensia* 28 (1979): 1–26.

28. Cappelletto, "Origine," p. 173.

29. See E. Casamassima, "Per una storia delle dottrine paleogra-

fiche dall'umanesimo a Jean Mabillion," *Studi medievali*, Ser. III, 5 (1964): 525–578; Rizzo, *Il lessico filologico*, pp. 114–144; and Stefano Zamponi, "Modelli di catalogazione e lessico paleografico nell'inventario di S. Giustina di Padova," *IMU* 27 (1984): 161–174.

30. For humanistic handwriting, see B. L. Ullman, *The Origin and Development of Humanistic Script* (Rome: Edizioni di storia e letteratura, 1955).

31. R. G. G. Mercer, *The Teaching of Gasparino Barzizza with Special Reference to His Place in Paduan Humanism* (London: The Modern Humanities Research Association, 1979), esp. chap. 5. See also Sabbadini, *Il metodo*, p. 58, for the views of Guarino da Verona. See also Grafton and Jardine, *From Humanism to the Humanities*, chap. 1.

32. For Perotti, see Giovanni Mercati, *Per la cronologia della vita e degli scritti di Niccolò Perotti arcivescovo di Siponto: ricerche*, Studi e Testi 44 (Rome: Tipografia Poliglotta Vaticana, 1925), and *Niccolò Perotti's Version of the Enchiridion of Epictetus*, ed. Revilo Pendleton Oliver (Urbana, Ill.: University of Illinois Press, 1954).

33. Giovanni Andrea Bussi, *Prefazioni alle edizioni di Sweynheym e Pannartz*, ed. Massimo Miglio (Milan: Il Polifilo, 1978), and *DBI*, 15: 563–572. Paola Casciano, "Il Ms. Angelicano 1097, fase preparatoria per l'edizione del Plinio di Sweynheym e Pannartz (Hain 13088)," in *Scrittura Biblioteche e Stampa a Roma nel Quattrocento: Aspetti e problemi* (Vatican City: Scuola Vaticana di Paleografia, Diplomatica e Archivistica, 1980), I: 383–394, offers a modern judgment on Bussi's work. For a further example of Sweynheym and Pannartz's work, see Carla Frova and Massimo Miglio, "Dal Ms. Sublacense XLII all'*editio princeps* del 'De Civitate Dei' di Sant'Agostino (Hain 2046)," ibid., pp. 245–273.

34. Sesto Prete, "Problems of Textual Criticism: Niccolò Perotti's Letter to Francesco Guarnieri," in *Acta Conventus Neo-Latini Turonensis*, ed. J.-C. Margolin (Paris: Vrin, 1980), 1: 15–26. Professor John Monfasani has prepared a lengthy treatment of this letter which will appear in *RQ*.

35. Ibid, p. 17.

36. Bussi, *Prefazioni*, pp. 3–11.

37. See the collected articles on Perotti in *Res publica litterarum* 4 (1981) and 5 (1982).

38. Especially important is the work of Anthony Grafton, "On the Scholarship of Politian and Its Context," and *Joseph Scaliger*, chap. 1.

39. On humanist commentaries, see Eva Matthews Sanford, "Renaissance Commentaries on Juvenal," *Transactions of the American Philological Association* 79 (1948): 92–112. For humanist concern for com-

mentary over text, see William S. Anderson, "Valla, Juvenal, and Probus," *Traditio* 21 (1965): 383–424, at pp. 392–393.

40. For Beroaldo, see *DBI*, 9:382–384; Konrad Krautter, *Philologische Methode und humanistische Existenz: Filippo Beroaldo und sein Kommentar zum Goldenen Esel des Apuleius* (Munich: Fink, 1971); and Maria Teresa Casella, "Il metodo dei commentatori umanistici esemplato sul Beroaldo," *Studi medievali*, Ser. 3, 16 (1975): 627–670.

41. For Pio, see Valeriano del Nero, "Note sulla vita di Giovan Battista Pio (con alcune lettere inedite)," *Rinascimento* 21 (1981): 247–263; John F. D'Amico, "The Progress of Renaissance Latin Prose: The Case of Apuleianism," *RQ* 37 (1984): 351–392, at pp. 362–363; and Maria Carmela Tagliente, "G. B. Pio e il testo di Lucrezio," *Res publica litterarum* 6 (1983): 337–345.

42. For Barbaro, see *DBI*, 6: 96–99; and Vittore Branca, "Ermolao Barbaro and Late Quattrocento Venetian Humanism," in *Renaissance Venice*, ed. J. R. Hale (Totowa, N.J.: Rowman and Littlefield, 1973), pp. 218–243.

43. *Castigationes Plinianae et in Pomponium Melam*, Vols. I–IV, ed. G. Pozzi (Padua: Antenore, 1973–1979).

44. See Mario Schiavone, "Dall'*editio princeps* della *Naturalis Historia* ad opera di Giovanni da Spira all'edizione lione 1561," in *Plinio e la Natura* (Como, 1982), pp. 95–108. For background, see Charles G. Nauert, Jr., "C. Plinius Secundus," in *CTC,* 4: 297–422, and idem, "Humanists, Scientists, and Pliny: Changing Approaches to a Classical Author," *American Historical Review* 84 (1979): 72–85.

45. *Castigationes*, I: LXI.

46. Ibid., pp. LXVI–LXVII.

47. Ibid., introduction, chap. 5.

48. For Poliziano as textual critic and philologist, see the edition of his *Miscellaneorum Centuria Secunda,* ed. Vittore Branca and Manlio Pastore Stocchi (Florence: Alinari, 1982); Ida Maïer, *Les manuscrits d'Ange Politien* (Geneva: Droz, 1965); idem, *Ange Politien. La formation d'un poète humaniste (1469–1480)* (Geneva: Droz, 1966); Manlio Pastore Stocchi, "Sulle *curae statianae* del Poliziano," *Atti dell'Istituto veneto di scienze, lettere ed arti, Classe di scienze morali, lettere ed arti,* 124 (1966–1967): 39–74; Lucia Cesarini Martinelli, "Il Poliziano e Svetonio: Osservazioni su un recente contributo alla storia della filologia umanistica," *Rinascimento,* Ser. 2, 16 (1976): 111–131; Julia Haig Gaisser, "Catullus and His First Interpreters: Antonius Parthenius and Angelo Poliziano," *Transactions of the American Philological Association* 112 (1982): 83–106; Vittore Branca, *Poliziano e l'umanesimo della parola,*

(Turin: Einaudi, 1983), esp. pp. 157–167; Anthony Grafton, "On the Scholarship of Politian and Its Context"; idem, *Joseph Scaliger,* Vol. I, chaps. 1 and 2; and Jill Kraye, "Cicero, Stoicism and Textual Criticism: Poliziano on *KATOPΘΩMA,*" *Rinascimento* 23 (1983): 79–110.

49. See especially Branca, *Poliziano e l'umanesimo,* chap. 10.

50. In his *Miscellaneorum centuria secunda,* pp. 10–11, Poliziano attacked Domizio Calderini and gave a clear exposition of the principles just described. For Calderini, see *DBI,* 16: 596–605, and D. Coppini, "Il commento a Properzio di Domizio Calderini," *Annali della Scuola Normale Superiore di Pisa, Classe di lettere e filosofia,* Ser. 3, 9 (1979): 1119–1173.

51. Gianna Gardenal, *Il Poliziano e Svetonio: Contributo alla storia della filologia umanistica* (Florence: Olschki, 1975), p. 49.

52. Riccardo Ribuoli, *La collazione polizianea del codice bembino di Terenzio* (Rome: Edizioni di storia e letteratura, 1981), chap. 2. Also Lucia Cesarini Martinelli, "Uno sconosciuto incunabolo di Terenzio postillato dal Poliziano," *Rinascimento* 25 (1985): 239–246.

53. See *Miscellaneorum centuria secunda,* pp. 26, 27, 30, 36.

54. Ibid, pp. 38, 42, 50.

55. Ibid, pp. 49–50.

56. Gardenal, pp. 45–46.

57. Ibid., p. 46: "Nam cum ipsa quoque mendosissima plerisque sunt locis vestigia tamen adhuc servant haud obscura verae indagandae lectionis, quae de novis codicibus ab improbis librariis obliterantur."

58. Ibid., p. 48: "Sed quoniam locus esse [Suetonius, *Vita Augusti,* 83, 2] coniecturae solet ubi nil lectio suppeditat variaque a diversis afferunt, non ab re videor mihi facturus si ceterorum coniecturis ego quoque aliud velut affixero. Neque autem in re dubia perplexaque refellam quod alii dixerint, sed ipse afferam simpliciter, non dixerim quid sentiam, sed quid suspicer."

59. Ribuoli, *La collazione,* p. 64, and the citation from Poliziano's collation of Terence, Florence, Bibl. Naz., B. R. 97, fol. 66v. See also colophons Poliziano added to his manuscripts in Maïer, *Les manuscrits,* pp. 331–362.

60. *Miscellaneorum centuria secunda,* pp. 27–28.

61. Ibid., p. 27.

62. Ibid., p. 28.

63. Gardenal, *Il Poliziano,* p. 49.

64. See Laura Perotto Sali, "L'opuscolo inedito di Giorgio Merula contro i *Miscellanea* di Angelo Poliziano," *Interpres* 1 (1978): 146–183.

65. See E. Bolisani, "Vergilius o Virgilius? L'opinione d'un dotto umanista," *Atti dell'Istituto Veneto di Scienze, Lettere, ed Arti, Classe di*

scienze morali e lettere 117 (1958–1959): 131–141. For Poliziano's position, see *Opera omnia,* ed. Ida Maïer (Turin: Bottega d'Erasmo, 1971; reprint of Basel 1553 edition of the *Miscellanea*), 2: 286–287.

66. See *De honesta disciplina,* ed. Carlo Angeleri (Rome: Fratelli Bocca, 1955), and Renata Fabbri, "Pietro Crinito e il Virgilio aldino del 1501," *Materiali e discussioni per l'analisi dei testi classici* 17 (1986): 151–160.

67. Ibid., pp. 115, 342, 361.

68. See Sesto Prete, *Il codice Bembino di Terenzio* (Vatican City; Biblioteca Apostolica Vaticana, 1950), Studi e Testi 153, and Anthony Grafton, "Pietro Bembo and the 'Scholia Bembina'," *IMU* 24 (1981): 405–407.

69. Grafton, *Joseph Scaliger,* chap. 2; Antonietta Porro, "Pier Vettori editore di testi greci: la 'Poetica' di Aristotele," *IMU* 26 (1983): 307–358; and Lucia Cesarini Martinelli, "Pier Vettori e gli umanisti tedeschi," in *Firenze e la Toscana dei Medici nell'Europa del '500 II: Musica e spettacolo. Scienze dell'uomo e della natura* (Florence: Olschki, 1983), pp. 707–726. A related aspect of Vettori's work is discussed in Marco Pratesi, "Gli 'Argumenta in Euripidis et Sophoclis Tragoedias' di Pier Vettori," *Rinascimento* 25 (1985): 139–156. Robert C. Melzi, "Giuntini's Correspondence with 'Il Dubbioso Accademico' and Observations on Editorial Principles of the Renaissance in Italy and France," *Library Chronicle* 45 (1981): 30–43, discusses vernacular textual criticism in the same period.

70. For humanistic scholarship in Northern Europe, see Rudolf Pfeiffer, *History of Classical Scholarship from 1300 to 1850* (Oxford: Clarendon Press, 1976). For Germany in particular, see the dated but useful Conrad Bursian, *Geschichte der classischen Philologie in Deutschland von den Anfängen bis zur Gegenwart,* pt. I (Munich, 1883), pp. 91–219. For background, see Lewis W. Spitz, "The Course of German Humanism," *Itinerarium italicum,* eds. Heiko A. Oberman and Thomas A. Brady, Jr. (Leiden: Brill, 1975), pp. 371–436, and Winfried Trillitzsch, "Das Antikeverhältnis namhafter deutscher Renaissancehumanisten," *Klio* 64 (1982): 485–512.

71. James H. Overfield, *Humanism and Scholasticism in Late Medieval Germany* (Princeton, N.J.: Princeton University Press, 1985), provides the most recent discussion.

72. See E. P. Goldschmidt, *Medieval Texts and Their First Appearance in Print* (London: Bibliographical Society, 1943); Friedrich Luchsinger, *Der basler Buchdruck als Vermittler italienischen Geistes 1470–1529* (Basel: Helbing & Lichtenhahn, 1953); Miriam Usher Chrisman, *Lay Culture, Learned Culture: Books and Social Change in Strasbourg, 1480–*

1599 (New Haven, Conn.: Yale University Press, 1983); Rudolf Hirsch, "Printing and the Spread of Humanism in Germany: The Example of Albrecht von Eyb," in his *The Printed Word: Its Impact and Diffusion* (London: Variorum, 1978), chap. 3; and Richard Crofts, "Books, Reform and the Reformation," *ARG* 71 (1980): 21–35.

73. See Kurt Adel, "Die Arbeitsmethoden des Konrad Celtis," *Codices manuscripti* 3 (1977): 1–13.

74. See Lewis Spitz, *The Religious Renaissance of the German Humanists* (Cambridge, Mass.: Harvard University Press, 1963).

75. Kelley, *Foundations of Modern Historical Scholarship*, chap. 3; a general discussion of Budé that does not center on his textual work is David O. McNeil, *Guillaume Budé and Humanism in the Reign of Francis I* (Geneva: Droz, 1975). Also *Contemporaries*, 1: 212–217.

76. For Lefèvre, see August Renaudet, *Préréforme et humanisme à Paris pendant les premières guerres d'Italie (1494–1517)*, 2d ed. (Paris: Librairie d'Argences, 1953); V. Carriere, "Lefèvre d'Etaples à l'Université de Paris (1475–1520)," in *Etudes historiques dediées à la mémoire de M. Roger Rodière* (Arras, 1947), pp. 109–120; Eugene F. Rice, "The Humanist Idea of Christian Antiquity: Lefèvre d'Etaples and His Circle," *Studies in the Renaissance* 9 (1962): 126–160; idem, "Jacques Lefèvre d'Etaples and the Medieval Christian Mystics," in *Florilegium Historiale. Renaissance Studies in Honor of Wallace K. Ferguson* (Toronto: University of Toronto Press, 1970); idem, "Humanist Aristotelianism in France: Jacques Lefèvre d'Etaples and His Circle," *Humanism in France*, ed. A. H. T. Levi (Manchester: Manchester University Press, 1970), pp. 132–149; Philip Edgcumbe Hughes, *Lefèvre* (Grand Rapids, Mich.: Erdmann, 1984); and *Contemporaries*, 2: 315–318.

77. See *The Prefatory Epistles of Jacques Lefèvre d'Etaples and Related Texts*, ed. Eugene F. Rice, Jr. (New York: Columbia University Press, 1972); A. E. Tyler, "Jacques Lefèvre d'Etaples and Henry Estienne the Elder, 1502–20," in *The French Mind: Studies in Honour of Gustave Rudler*, ed. Will Moore, Rhoda Sutherland, Enid Starkie (Oxford: Clarendon Press, 1952), pp. 17–33; and R. Wiriath, O.P., "Les rapports de Josse Bade Ascensius avec Erasme et Lefebvre d'Etaples," *BHR* 11 (1949): 66–71.

78. Rice, "The Humanist Idea of Christian Antiquity."

79. *Prefatory Epistles*, p. 88.

80. Ibid., index under "exemplum."

81. Tyler, "Jacques Lefèvre d'Etaples," p. 21.

82. See Guy Bedouelle, *Le Quincuplex Psalterium de Lefèvre d'Etaples: Un guide de lecture* (Geneva: Droz, 1979).

83. See John B. Payne, "Erasmus and Lefèvre d'Etaples as Interpreters of Paul," *ARG* 65 (1974): 54–82.

84. See Payne, "Toward the Hermeneutics of Erasmus," in *Scrinium erasmianum,* ed. J. Coppens (Leiden: Brill, 1969), 2: 13–49.

85. For Marsi, see John W. O'Malley, *Praise and Blame in Renaissance Rome* (Durham, N.C.: Duke University Press, 1978), index.

86. *Correspondence* 2, 152 (1975): 30–31.

87. For Erasmus as a textual critic, see Pierre Petitmengin, "Comment étudier l'activité d'Erasme éditeur de textes antiques?" in *Colloquia Erasmiana Turonensia* (Toronto: University of Toronto Press, 1972), 1: 217–222, and Jean Hadot, "La critique textuelle dans l'édition du Nouveau Testament d'Erasme," in ibid., 2: 749–760. I have not been able to consult A. E. Cruz, "Erasmo, editor critico de la patrologia latina," *Boletin de la Biblioteca de Menendez Pelayo,* vol. 44, pp. 103–120, but have relied on the summary in *Neuf années de Bibliographie érasmienne,* ed. J.-Cl. Margolin (Paris: Vrin, 1977), pp. 292–293. Also Georges Chantraine, S.J., "Erasme et saint Basile," *Irenikon* 52/4 (1979): 451–490.

88. See Bentley, *Humanists and Holy Writ. Annotationes* are available in *Desiderii Erasmi Roterodami Opera Omnia,* Vol. VI (rpt. of 1705 Leiden ed.; London: Gregg, 1962), and in a fascimile reproduction (London, 1986).

89. See Jacques Chomarat, "Les *Annotationes* de Valla, celles d'Erasme et la grammaire," in *Histoire de l'exégèse au XVIe siècle* (Geneva: Droz, 1978), pp. 203–228.

90. Bentley, *Humanists and Holy Writ,* pp. 125–134.

91. See Georges Chantraine, S. J., "Le mustérion paulinien selon les Annotations d'Erasme," *Recherches de science religieuse* 58 (1970): 351–382; Jerry H. Bentley, "Erasmus' *Annotationes in Novum Testamentum* and the Textual Criticism of the Gospels," *ARG* 67 (1976): 33–53; and Erika Rummel, *Erasmus' Annotationes on the New Testament: From Philologist to Theologian* (Toronto/Buffalo: University of Toronto Press, 1986). See also the forthcoming article by Erika Rummel, "God and Solecism: Erasmus as a Literary Critic of the Bible," in *Erasmus Yearbook.*

92. See Bentley, *Humanists and Holy Writ,* pp. 144–161, for examples of Erasmus' conjectures.

93. Jerry H. Bentley, "Erasmus, Jean Le Clerc, and the Principle of the Harder Reading," *RQ* 31 (1978): 309–321.

94. See *Desiderii Erasmi Roterdami Apologia respondens ad ea quae Iacobus Lopis Stunica taxauerat in Prima duntaxat Noui Testamenti Aeditione,* ed. and intro. H. J. de Jonge (Amsterdam: North Holland Publishing

Company, 1983), and Henk Jan de Jonge, " 'Novum Testamentum a Nobis versum.' The Essence of Erasmus' Edition of the New Testament," *The Journal of Theological Studies,* n.s. 35, pp. 394–413.

95. Winfried Trillitzsch, "Erasmus und Seneca," *Philologus* 109 (1965): 270–293, and L. D. Reynolds, *The Medieval Tradition of Seneca's Letters* (Oxford: University Press, 1965), introduction.

96. *Correspondence,* 3, 325 (1976): 65, 67.

97. Ibid., 5, 648 (1979): 648.

98. For Erasmus and Jerome, see F. Husner, "Die Handschrift der Scholien des Erasmus von Rotterdam zu den Hieronymusbriefen," in *Festschrift für G. Binz* (Basel: Schwabe, 1935), pp. 132–146; Denys Gorce, "La patristique dans la réforme d'Erasme," in *Festgabe Josef Lortz* (Baden-Baden: Grimm, 1968), I: 233–276; and Eugene F. Rice, Jr., *Saint Jerome in the Renaissance* (Baltimore, Md.: Johns Hopkins University Press, 1985). For earlier editions of Jerome, see Herve Savon, "Le *de Vera Circumcisione* du Prêtre Eutrope et les premières éditions imprimées des *Lettres* de Saint Jérôme," *Revue d'histoire des textes* 10 (1980): 165–197.

99. *Correspondence,* 3, no. 395: 252–266.

100. Ibid., pp. 260–261.

101. See *Omnium Operum Divi Eusebii Hieronymi Stridonensis Tomus Primus* (Basel, 1516), ff. 53v, 61v, 70r, 99r, 106v, 110v, for examples.

102. See Silvana Seidel-Menchi, "Un'opera misconosciuta di Erasmo? Il trattato pseudo-cyprianeo 'De duplici martyrio.' " *Rivista storica italiana* 90 (1978): 709–743.

103. Letter in *Correspondence,* 6, no. 975 (1982): 385–386.

104. Ibid., no. 984, p. 983.

105. *Briefwechsel,* no. 105.

106. *EE,* 4, no. 1000: 23–29, especially introduction.

107. See Seidel-Menchi, "Un opera. . . ."

108. Bentley, *Humanists and Holy Writ,* pp. 127–128.

109. Waszink, "Osservazioni," pp. 11–12; the introductions to Erasmus' translations of Greek texts in *Opera Omnia Desiderii Erasmi Roterodami,* Vol. I-1 (Amsterdam: North-Holland Publishing Company, 1969); and Erika Rummel, *Erasmus as a Translator of the Classics* (Toronto: University of Toronto Press, 1985).

110. Jan Hendrik Waszink's introduction to *Galeni tractatus tres,* in *Opera Omnia,* p. 633. At least in translating theological works from the Greek, Erasmus was capable of changing the meaning of a writer to fit his own theological views; see Irena Backus, "Deux traductions latines du *De Spiritu sancto* de saint Basile. L'inédit de Georges de Trebizonde

(1442–1467?) comparé à la version d'Erasme (1532)," *Revue des études augustiniennes* 31 (1985): 258–269.

111. Max Schär, *Das Nachleben des Origenes im Zeitalter des Humanismus* (Basel/Stuttgart: Helbing & Lichtenhahn, 1979), index.

112. See below, chapter 5.

113. See James D. Tracy, "Erasmus becomes a German," *RQ* 21 (1968): 281–288.

114. For example, Paul Lehmann, *Iohannes Sichardus und die von ihm benutzten Bibliotheken und Handschriften* (Munich: Beck, 1911), and Niklas Holzberg, *Willibald Pirckheimer* (Munich: Fink, 1981).

2: THE NOVICE CRITIC

1. Paul Joachimsen, *Geschichtsauffassung und Geschichtsschreibung in Deutschland unter dem Einfluss des Humanismus* (Leipzig/Berlin: Teubner, 1910), p. 126.

2. See Paul Joachimsen, "Humanism and the Development of the German Mind," in *Pre-Reformation Germany*, ed. Gerald Strauss (New York: Harper & Row, 1972), pp. 162–224, and Lewis W. Spitz, *The Religious Renaissance of the German Humanists* (Cambridge, Mass.: Harvard University Press, 1963).

3. Still useful are Charles Schmidt, *Histoire littéraire de l'Alsace à la fin du XVe et au commencement du XVIe siècle*, 2 vols. (Paris, 1879); *L'humanisme en Alsace* (Paris: Société d'Edition 'Les Belles-Lettres', 1939); *Les lettres en Alsace* (Strasbourg: Istra, 1962); and Paul Adam, *L'humanisme à Sélestat: L'école, les humanistes, la bibliothèque*, 1st and 4th eds. (Sélestat: Alsatia, 1962/1978). See also Francis Rapp, "Die elsässischen Humanisten und die geistliche Gesellschaft," in *Die Humanisten in ihrer politischen und sozialen Umwelt*, ed. O. Herding and R. Stupperich (Boppard: Boldt, 1980), pp. 87–108.

4. For Beatus' biography and printing career, see Jacob Mahly, *Beatus Rhenanus von Schlettstadt* (Mulhausen, 1857); the articles by Adalbert Horawitz, "Beatus Rhenanus: Ein biographischer Versuch," *Sitzungsberichte der kaiserlichen Akademie der Wissenschaften: Philosophisch-historische Classe* 70 (1872): 189–244; "Des Beatus Rhenanus literarische Thätigkeit in den Jahren 1508–1531," ibid. 71 (1872): 643–690; "Des Beatus Rhenanus literarische Thätigkeit in den Jahren 1531–1547," ibid. 72 (1872): 323–376; "Die Bibliothek und Correspondenz des Beatus Rhenanus zu Schlettstadt: Ein Bericht," ibid. 73 (1874); 313–340; *Briefwechsel* and the review of this edition by Gustav

Knod in *Zentralblatt für Bibliothekswesen* 4 (1887): 305–315; Gustav Knod, *Aus der Bibliothek Beatus Rhenanus: Ein Beitrag zur Geschichte des Humanismus* (Leipzig, 1889); Hans Kaiser, "Aus den letzten Jahren des Beatus Rhenanus," *Zeitschrift für die Geschichte des Oberrheins*, n.f. 31 (1916): 30–32. For more recent treatments, see Paul Adam, *L'Humanisme à Sélestat*, pp. 51–67; H. Meyer, "Beatus Rhenanus (de Sélestat) et sa bibliothèque," *Librarium* 19 (1976): 21–31; Sigrid von der Gonna, "Beatus Rhenanus und Otfrid von Weissenburg: Zur Otfrid-Überlieferung im 16. Jahrhundert," *Zeitschrift für deutsches Altertum und deutsche Literatur* 107 (1978): 248–257; Paul Adam, "Beatus Rhenanus (1485–1547), l'humaniste de Sélestat," in *Grandes figures de l'humanisme alsacien: courants, milieux, destin* (Strasbourg: Istra, 1978), pp. 42–47; Robert Walker, "Un texte de Beatus Rhenanus: l'appel aux habitants de Sélestat pour les exhorter à la paix civile et religieuse (1523?)," ibid, pp. 49–56; John F. D'Amico, "Beatus Rhenanus and Italian Humanism," *Journal of Medieval and Renaissance Studies* 9 (1979): 237–260; idem, "Beatus Rhenanus, Tertullian and the Reformation: A Humanist's Critique of Scholasticism," *ARG* 71 (1980): 37–63; idem, "Ulrich von Hutten and Beatus Rhenanus: Medieval History as Religious Propaganda in the Early Reformation," to be published in *Studies in Medievalism;* James Michael Weiss, "The Technique of Faint Praise: Johannes Sturm's 'Life of Beatus Rhenanus'," *BHR* 43 (1981): 289–302; Robert Walker, "Beatus Rhenanus (1485–1547) entre l'Eglise traditionelle et la Réformation," in *Les Dissidents du XVIe siècle entre l'Humanisme et le Catholicisme,* ed. Marc Lienhard (Baden-Baden: Koerner, 1983), pp. 97–109; idem, "Beatus Rhenanus et Sebastien Brant: l'affaire des Pénitentes de Sainte Marie-Madeleine," *Revue d'Alsace* 107 (1981): 61–70; and the short notice in *Contemporaries*, 1: 104–109. The entire issue of *ASABHS* 35 (1985) is devoted to the papers of a conference in honor of Beatus' 500th birthday. Of biographical interest are the following: a French translation of the first biography of Beatus by Johannes Sturm, pp. 7–18 (original Latin in *Briefwechsel*, pp. 1–11); Niklas Holzberg, "Beatus Rhenanus (1485–1547): Eine biographisch-forschungsgeschichtliche Bestandsaufnahme zum 500. Geburtstag des Humanisten," pp. 19–32; Maurice Kubler, "Beatus Rhenanus Selestadiensis: A la recherche de l'identité de l'humaniste à travers archives et épitaphes," pp. 33–48; and Robert Walker, "Beatus Rhenanus et Sélestat," pp. 261–268. Also see Frank Hieronymus, "Beatus Rhenanus und das Buch," *ASABHS* 36 (1986): 63–114.

   5. For the humanist school at Sélestat, see Ch. Fr. Walter, *Histoire*

de la Réformation et de l'école littéraire à Sélestat (Strasbourg, 1834); Timotheus Wilhelm Rohrich, "Die Schule zu Schlettstadt, im 15ten Jahrhundert," *Mittheilungen aus der Geschichte der evangelischen Kirche des Elsässes* 1 (1855): 78–108; A. Dorlan, "Nouvelles études historiques sur l'Ecole et la Société littéraires de Schlestadt aux 15e et 16e siècles," in *Revue d'Alsace* 6 (1855): 308–322, 337–349, 387–402; Wilhelm Struver, *Die Schule zu Schlettstadt von 1450–1560: Ein Beitrag zur Culturgeschichte des Mittelalters* (Leipzig, 1880); Gustav Knod, *Aus der Bibliothek des Beatus Rhenanus: Ein Beitrag zur Geschichte des Humanismus* (Leipzig, 1889), pt. I, chap. 1; J. Geny, "Das Schulwesen Schlettstadts bis zum Jahre 1789," *Mitteilungen der Gesellschaft für deutsche Erziehungs- und Schulgeschichte* 11 (1901): 315–351; Paul Adam, "L'école humaniste de Sélestat," in *Les lettres en Alsace,* pp. 93–107; Adam, *L'humanisme à Sélestat,* pp. 9–36; George M. Durance, "From Brethren to Humanists: A Study of the Sélestat Latin School, 1441–1525" (Master's thesis, University of Calgary, 1978); Francis Rapp, "L'école humaniste de Sélestat," in *Sélestat. 12 siècles d'histoire* (Strasbourg: Istra, 1975), pp. 66–76; idem, "Die Lateinschule von Schlettstadt: eine grosse für eine Kleinstadt," in *Studien zum stadtischen Bildungswesen des späten Mittelalters und der frühen Neuzeit,* ed. Bernd Moeller, Hans Patze, and Karl Stackmann (Göttingen: Vandenhoeck & Rupprecht, 1983), pp. 215–234; and Frederick Hartweg, "Das 'Bildungsangebot' in Schlettstadt in der zweiten Hälfte des XV. und im ersten Viertel des XVI. Jahrhunderts," in *Literatur und Laienbildung im Spätmittelalter und in der Reformationszeit,* ed. Ludger Grenmann and Karl Stackmann (Stuttgart: J. B. Metzler, c. 1984), pp. 24–38.

6. In addition to the above citations, see Paul Adam, "Il y a cinq siècles, en 1477, mourut a Sélestat. . . . Louis Dringenberg, père de l'humanisme alsacien," *ASABHS* 27 (1977): 11–18.

7. See Paul Adam, "Craton Hoffman (1450–1501), maître d'école (1477–1501) et notaire impérial," *ASABHS* 28 (1978): 9–16.

8. *Briefwechsel,* no. 163, p. 222.

9. Knod, *Aus der Bibliothek,* pp. 16–17, and *Contemporaries,* 2: 81–82.

10. E. H. Alton, D. E. W. Wormell, and E. Courtney, "A Catalogue of the Manuscripts of Ovid's *Fasti,*" *Bulletin of the Institute of Classical Studies* 24 (1977): 37–63, at p. 59. The manuscript is Sélestat Ms. 50.

11. See *T. Livii Patavini Latinae Historiae Principis Decades. . . .* (Basel, 1535), p. 20.

12. Knod, *Aus der Bibliothek,* analyses of Beatus' notebooks and library. Also see below, note 51.

13. For the University of Paris at the time of Beatus' residence, see A. Renaudet, *Préréforme et humanisme à Paris pendant les premières guerres d'Italie (1494–1517)*, 2ᵈ ed. (Paris: Librairie d'Argences, 1953).

14. For these men, see ibid., index, and Carlo Vecce, "Il giovane Beato Renano e gli umanisti a Parigi all'inizio del XVI secolo," *ASABHS* 35 (1985): 134–140. For Andrelini, see Index, nos. 6 and 8. Also Gustav Knod, "Zur Bibliographie und Bibliothek des Beatus Rhenanus," *Centralblatt für Bibliothekswesen* 2 (1885): 253–276, which lists Beatus' editions to 1522.

15. For Lefèvre, see above, chapter 1. For Beatus and Lefèvre, see Stanislas Musial, "Beatus Rhenanus étudiant de philosophie à Paris (1503–1507)," *ASABHS* 35 (1985): 271–279. For Lefèvre's circle, in addition to Renaudet, *Préréforme*, see *The Prefatory Epistles of Jacques Lefèvre d'Etaples and Related Texts*, ed. Eugene F. Rice, Jr. (New York: Columbia University Press, 1972).

16. A. E. Tyler, "Jacques Lefèvre d'Etaples and Henry Estienne the Elder, 1502–1520," in *The French Mind*, ed. W. Moore, R. Sutherland, and E. Starkie (Oxford: Clarendon Press, 1952), pp. 17–33.

17. See Jean-Pierre Massaut, *Josse Clichtove: l'humanisme et la réforme du clergé*, 2 vols. (Paris: Les Belles Lettres, 1968); *Prefatory Epistles*, no. 31; *Briefwechsel*, p. 627; and *Contemporaries*, 1: 317–320.

18. *Prefatory Epistles*, nos. 49 and 53, and *Briefwechsel*, pp. 628–629.

19. Ibid., no. 45, and *Briefwechsel*, p. 627.

20. See Ph. Renouard, *Bibliographie des impressions et des oeuvres de Josse Badius Ascensius imprimeur et humaniste 1462–1535*, 3 vols. (Paris, 1908), indices; R. Wiriath, "Les rapports de Josse Bade Ascensius avec Erasme et Lefèvre d'Etaples," *BHR* 11 (1949): 66–71; idem, "Josse Bade, éditeur et préfacier (1462–1535)," *Renaissance and Reformation/ Renaissance et Réforme*, n.s. 5 (1981): 63–71; Adolphe Koch, "L'exemplaire personnel de Beatus Rhenanus de la 'Nef des folles' de Josse Bade," *ASABHS* 30 (1980): 43–50; and *Contemporaries*, 1: 79–81.

21. *Rerum Germanicarum libri tres* (Basel, 1531), pp. 182–185.

22. *Briefwechsel*, no. 3.

23. See Joseph Lefftz, *Die gelehrten und literarischen Gesellschaften im Elsäss vor 1870* (Colmar: Alsatia, 1931), chap. 1.

24. For Gruninger, see *Contemporaries*, 2: 140.

25. See François Ritter, *Histoire de l'imprimerie alsacienne aux XVe et XVIe siècle*, (Strasbourg: Le Roux, 1955), pp. 160–170; idem, "Les imprimeurs de Sélestat aux XVe e XVIe siècles," *ASABHS* 9 (1959): 49–58, at pp. 51–53; Miriam Usher Chrisman, "Matthias Schuerer, humaniste imprimeur," in *Grandes figures*, pp. 159–172, and *Contemporaries*, 3: 233.

26. Index, nos. 5 and 6.

27. *Prefatory Epistles*, no. 67, and *Briefwechsel*, pp. 21, 35.

28. *Prefatory Epistles*, no. 87.

29. See Friedrich Luchsinger, *Der basler Buchdruck als Vermittler italienischer Geistes, 1470–1529* (Basel: Helbing & Lichtenhahn, 1952), and Peter G. Bietenholz, *Der italienische Humanismus und die Blütezeit des Buchdrucks in Basel* (Basel: Helbing & Lichtenhahn, 1958).

30. For Basel at this time, see Rudolf Wackernagel, *Humanismus und Reformation in Basel* (Basel: Helbing & Lichtenhahn, 1924), chap. 6; Ernest Staehelin, "Bâle et l'Alsace," in *L'Humanisme en Alsace* (Paris: Les Belles Lettres, 1939), pp. 30–41; and Hans R. Guggisberg, *Basel in the Sixteenth Century: Aspects of the City Republic before, during, and after the Reformation* (St. Louis, Mo.: Center for Reformation Research, 1982).

31. Beatus' printed correspondence of 159 letters in Horawitz's edition is exclusively in Latin save for one in Greek. For the uniqueness of this, see Joel Lefèvre, "Le latin et l'allemand dans la correspondance humaniste," in *Acta Conventus Neo-Latini Turonensis*, ed. J.-C. Margolin (Paris: Vrin, 1980), pp. 501–511. Beatus did on occasion write letters in German; see Karl Stenzel, "Beatus Rhenanus und Johann von Botzheim," *Zeitschrift für Geschichte des Oberrheins* 68 (1914): 120–129. Robert Walter has published a selection of Beatus' letters including some previously unedited ones with extensive comments and French translations, together with extensive remarks on Beatus' Latinity, *Beatus Rhenanus Citoyen de Sélestat, Ami d'Erasme. Anthologie de sa Correspondance* (Strasbourg: Oberlin, 1986). There is also to appear N. Holzberg, P. Petitmengin, F. Rott, and R. Walter, "Un première supplément à la correspondance de B. Rhenanus," in a forthcoming issue of *ASABHS*.

32. See Martin Sicherl, "Die griechischen Handschriften des Beatus Rhenanus," *ASABHS* 29 (1979): 59–78, at pp. 60–61; see also *Contemporaries*, 2: 185–186, for Hermonymus.

33. *Briefwechsel*, p. 39.

34. For Cuno, see H. D. Saffrey, "Un humaniste dominicain, Jean Cuno de Nuremberg, précurseur d'Erasme en Bâle," *BHR* 33 (1971): 19–62; Martin Sicherl, *Johannes Cuno: Ein Wegbereiter des Griechischen in Deutschland: Eine biographisch-kodikologische Studie* (Heidelberg: Winter, 1978); idem, "Neue Handschriften Johannes Cunos und seiner Schüler," *ASABHS* 35 (1985): 141–148; and *Contemporaries*, 1: 333–334.

35. In addition to Saffrey and Sicherl, see also Deno John Geanakoplos, *Byzantium and the Renaissance: Greek Scholars in Venice*, 2^d ed.

(Hamden, Conn.: Archon, 1973), chap. 5, and *Contemporaries*, 2: 472–473, for Musurus, and ibid., 2: 44–45, for Fortiguerra.

36. Saffrey, "Un humaniste," p. 31

37. Martin Lowry, *The World of Aldus Manutius: Business and Scholarship in Renaissance Venice* (Oxford: Blackwell, 1979), index. For Aldus, see also *Contemporaries*, 1: 376–380.

38. *Briefwechsel*, pp. 45–50; *Prefatory Epistles*, pp. 261–267; text and French translation in Walter, *Beatus Rhenanus*, pp. 109–131. See also Helen Brown Wicher, "Gregorius Nyssenus," in *CTC*, 5: 79–80; *Briefwechsel*, nos. 25 and 27; and Rice, "The Humanist Idea of Christian Antiquity," p. 137. Beatus also issued in 1513 his translation of Basil the Great's *Sermo de differentia Usiae et Hypostasis*, see Index, no. 25.

39. Article on Gregory of Nazianzus, *CTC*, 2: 114–115.

40. *Briefwechsel*, no. 24, pp. 41–45; no. 25 for Cuno's dedication to Beatus.

41. Saffrey, "Un humaniste," pp. 45–52.

42. See Sichel, *Johannes Cuno*, pp. 169–195, and idem, "Die griechischen Handschriften des Beatus Rhenanus," for further information.

43. See Earle Hilgart, "John Froben and the Basle University Scholars, 1513–1523," *Library Quarterly* 41 (1971): 141–169; Luchsinger, *Der basler Buchdruck;* and Peter G. Bietenholz, *Basel and France in the Sixteenth Century: The Basle Humanists and Printers in Their Contacts with Francophone Culture.* (Toronto/Geneva: University of Toronto Press, 1971). Much information can be obtained from *Die Amerbachkorrespondenz*, ed. Alfred Hartmann (Basel: Verlag der Universitätsbibliothek, 1943), Vol. I. On this collection, see Beat Rudolf Jenny, "Die Amerbachkorrespondenz von der humanistischen Epistolographie zur bürgerlichen Briefstellerei," in *Der Brief in der Zeit der Renaissance* (Boppard: Boldt, 1983), pp. 204–225. See also *Contemporaries*, 2: 60–63, for Froben. On the general matter of humanists and editing in Germany, see Peter Amelung, "Humanisten als Mitarbeiter der Drucker am Beispiel des Ulmer Frühdrucks," in *Das Verhältnis der Humanisten zum Buch*, ed. Fritz Krafft and Dieter Wuttke (Boppard: Boldt, 1977), pp. 129–144.

44. See J. de Ghellinck, S.J., "La première édition imprimée des 'Opera Omnia S. Augustini'," in *Miscellanea J. Gessler* (Deurne-Anvers, 1948), pp. 530–547; idem, "Les éditions des 'Opera Omnia S. Augustini' avant les mauristes," in his *Patristique et Moyen Age: Etudes d'histoire littéraire et doctrinale* (Gembloux: Duculot, 1948), 3: 366–411; and Victor Scholderer, "The First Collected Edition of Saint Augustine," in

his *50 Essays in 15th and 16th Century Bibliography* (Amsterdam: Hertzberger, 1966), pp. 275–278.

45. See the letters in the *Amerbachkorrespondenz*, vol. 1.

46. See Max Hossfeld, "Johannes Heynlin aus Stein. Ein Kapitel aus der Frühzeit des deutschen Humanismus," *Basler Zeitschrift für Geschichte und Altertumskunde* 6 (1907): 308–356, 7 (1908): 79–431, esp. 283–303; and the letters in *Die Amerbachkorrespondenz*, vol. 1, nos. 17 and 31.

47. James W. Halporn, "The Editing of Patristic Texts: The Case of Cassiodorus," *Revue des études augustiniennes* 30 (1984): 107–126, at pp. 113–114.

48. Jean-Claude Margolin, "Beatus Rhenanus et Boniface Amerbach: une amitié de trente ans," *ASABHS* 35 (1985): 157–175. For the Amerbach sons, see *Contemporaries*, 1: 42–46.

49. See *Amerbachkorrespondenz*, vol. 2, nos. 609 and 611.

50. Discussion and documentation in D'Amico, "Beatus Rhenanus and Italian Humanism."

51. Knod, *Aus der Bibliothek des Beatus Rhenanus*, and Adam, *L'Humanisme à Sélestat*, pp. 85–91. For the later elements of Beatus' library, see Miriam Usher Chrisman, *Lay Culture, Learned Culture: Books and Social Change in Strasbourg, 1480–1599* (New Haven, Conn.: Yale University Press, 1982), pp. 62–64. For a list of many of Beatus' volumes now in Sélestat, see Ville de Sélestat, *Catalogue général de la Bibliothèque municipale. Première série: Les livres imprimés, Troisième partie: Incunables et XVIème siècle*, ed. Joseph Walter (Colmar: Alsatia, 1929). See also Hubert Meyer, "Propos sur la bibliothèque de Beatus Rhenanus," *ASABHS* 35 (1985): 85–96, and Hubert Meyer and Pierre Petitmengin, "Ex libris Beati Rhenani: Les imprimés qui ont quitté la Bibliothèque de Sélestat depuis le milieu du XVIIIème siècle," ibid., pp. 123–133. For a particular example, see Koch, "L'exemplaire personnel de Beatus Rhenanus de la *Nef des Folles* de Josse Bade." I have not seen Michel de Bellefroid, "La bibliothèque humaniste de Sélestat," *Le livre et l'estampe* 21 (1985): 126–153.

52. See P. S. Allen, "Erasmus' Relations with his Printers," *Transactions of the Bibliographical Society* 13 (1913–1915): 297–321; Victor Scholderer, "Some Notes on Erasmus and His Printers," *Gutenberg Jarhbuch*, 1962, pp. 195–197; Eileen Bloch, "Erasmus and the Froben Press: The Making of an Editor," *The Library Quarterly* 35 (1965): 109–120; and S. Diane Shaw, "A Study of the Collaboration between Erasmus of Rotterdam and His Printer Johann Froben at Basel during the Years 1514 to 1527," *Erasmus of Rotterdam Yearbook* 6 (1986): 31–124. Also *Briefwechsel*, no. 40.

53. See *Correspondence,* vol. 3, no. 327, and vol. 6, nos. 976 and 1206.

54. Ibid., vol. 3, nos. 575 and 581. For Lachner, see *Contemporaries,* 2: 279–280.

55. Ibid., vol. 5, nos. 594 and 628. Also Shaw, "A Study of the Collaboration," pp. 63–64.

56. For Beatus' biography of Erasmus, see the English translation in *Christian Humanism and the Reformation,* ed. John C. Olin (New York: Harper and Row, 1965); Bruce Mansfield, *Phoenix of His Age: Interpretations of Erasmus (c. 1500–1750)* (Toronto: University of Toronto Press, 1979), pp. 17–21; and Robert Walter, "Une amitié humaniste: Erasmus et Beatus Rhenanus," *ASABHS* 36 (1986): 13–23.

57. See John B. Payne, "Erasmus and Lefèvre d'Etaples as Interpreters of Paul," *ARG* 65 (1974): 54–82. Erasmus and Lefèvre also clashed over the historicity of Pseudo-Dionysius the Aereopagite; see Jean-Pierre Massaut, *Critique et tradition à la veille de la Réformation en France* (Paris: Vrin, 1974), pp. 179–229, and *Contemporaries,* 2: 315–318.

58. See D'Amico, "Beatus Rhenanus and Italian Humanism," and Peter Bietenholz, *Basle and France,* pt. 2, chap. 3.

59. See above, chapter 1.

60. See chapter 1, note 73.

61. *Correspondence,* vol. 3, no. 328.

62. Ibid., p. 80.

63. Ibid., vol. 3, no. 330, p. 82.

64. Ibid., pp. 329 and 82; *Contemporaries,* 3: 12–14.

65. Ibid., no. 325, pp. 65–66.

66. Horawitz, "Des Beatus Rhenanus literarische Thätigkeit 1508–1531," pp. 648–651, 654–656; Remigio Sabbadini, "Il testo interpolato del *Ludus* di Seneca," *Rivista di filologia e di istruzione classica* 47 (1919): 338–347; François Spaltenstein and Pierre Petitmengin, "Beatus Rhenanus éditeur de l'*Apocoloquintose* et le *Codex Wissenburgensis,*" *Revue d'histoire des textes* 9 (1979): 315–327, at pp. 315–316; and *Texts and Transmission,* pp. 361–362. See, for the context, *Calvin's Commentary on Seneca's De Clementia,* intro. and ed. Ford Lewis Battles and André Malan Hugo (Leiden: Brill, 1969), p. 73*; Marcia L. Colish, "Seneca's *Apocolocyntosis* as a Possible Source for Erasmus' *Julius Exclusus,*" *RQ* 29 (1976): 361–368; Index, no. 30; and *Briefwechsel,* nos. 44 and 45.

67. I cite from *In hoc opere contenta Ludus L. Annaei Senecae, De morte Claudii Caesaris. . . .* (Basel, 1515), f. b 4v: "*Non potest esse.*] Graeca hic restituere nequivimus. Exemplar enim ne notas quidem aliquas habuit, quae ansam coniecturae praestitissent. . . .*"

68. *Vellei Paterculi historiae Romanae duo volumina* (Basel, 1520 [1521]), p. 70.

69. *Amerbachkorrespondenz,* vol. 2, no. 545.

70. *Briefwechsel,* no. 105.

71. See below, chapter 5.

72. See *Correspondence,* vol. 5, no. 704; vol 4, no. 586; and vol. 5, no. 648 for these.

73. See *Die Strassburger Chronik des elsässischen Humanisten Hieronymus Gebweiler,* ed. and intro. Karl Stenzel (Berlin/Leipzig: de Gruyter, 1926).

74. See below, chapter 6.

75. See Jakob Wimpfeling/Beatus Rhenanus, *Das Leben des Johannes Geiler von Kaysersberg,* ed. Otto Herding (Munich: Fink, 1970).

76. The text was *Carmen de bello saxonico,* which dealt with the Emperor Henry IV; he was also involved in the edition of Otto of Freising's *Gesta Friderici I.* See D'Amico, "Ulrich von Hutten and Beatus Rhenanus. . . ."

77. *Briefwechsel,* no. 13.

78. Walter, *Beatus Rhenanus,* no. 4.

79. See Joachimsen, *Geschichtsauffassung und Geschichtsschreibung,* pp. 60–79, and Ada Hentschke and Ulrich Muhlack, *Einführung in die Geschichte der klassischen Philologie* (Darmstadt: Wissenschaftliche Buchgesellschaft, 1972), chap. 2.

80. On the *Commentariolus,* see Joachimsen, *Geschichtsauffassung,* pp. 127–128; Hentschke and Muhlack, *Einführung,* pp. 34–35; and Jacques Rude, *L'Image du Germain dans la pensée et la littérature allemandes de la redécouverte de Tacite à la fin du XVIème siècle* (Lille: Université de Lille, 1977), 1: 332–333.

81. See Hentschke and Muhlack, *Einführung,* pp. 34–39.

82. See below, chapter 4, for full details.

83. I cite from the May 1519 Basel edition, *P. Cornelii Taciti De moribus et populis Germaniae libellus. Cum commentariolo vetera Germaniae populorum vocabula paucis explicante,* and the reprint in *Schardius Redivivus sive Rerum Germanicarum Scriptores Varii,* pp. 45–46 (Giessen, 1673), 1: 69: "Nam dici non potest, quantis mutationibus, et regna et populi mutati sint. Igitur, amice lector, sive veterum sive recentiorum evolvas monumenta, non statim, ut ante diximus, ad vivum [sic] rem exigas, sed etiam atque etiam circumspice, quo tempore scriptum fuerit, quod legis, a quo et de quibus, deinde confer nova cum veteribus, aut e converso, mutationum semper memor. Hanc monitionem nostram si secutus fueris, magnopere te senties in Historiis adiutum."

84. Beatus also offered a series of annotations for Tacitus' *Historiae*

together with the *Commentariolus*. In the *Commentariolus*, at p. 75/1: 75, Beatus described his procedure of correcting scribal errors.

85. For Alciati, see *DBI*, 2: 69–77; *Contemporaries*, 1: 23–26; and Kenneth C. Schellhase, *Tacitus in Renaissance Political Thought* (Chicago, Ill.: University of Chicago Press, 1976), index.

86. For Berosus, see *Commentariolus*, p. 58/1: 72.

87. For Velleius, see e.g. ibid., p. 52/1: 71 and p. 68/1: 74.

88. See ibid., p. 59/1: 72, for the *Hercynia sylva*.

89. *Commentariolus*, p. 73/1: 75.

90. For Beatus and medieval history, see Peter Shaeffer, "The Emergence of the Concept of 'Medieval' in Central European Humanism," *The Sixteenth Century Journal* 7 (1976): 21–30.

91. See below, chapter 4.

92. *P. Vellei Paterculi historiae Romanae duo volumina;* see Index, no. 49. Also see Daniel Albert Feuter, *Die Amerbachische Abschrift des Vellejus Paterculus und ihr Verhältniss zum Murbacher Codex und zur Editio Princeps: Eine Untersuchung* (Basel, 1844); Horawitz, "Des Beatus Rhenanus literarische Thätigkeit 1508–1531," pp. 675–678; Remigio Sabbadini, "Il testo interpolato del *Ludus* di Seneca," pp. 346–347; Gerd von der Gönna, "Beatus Rhenanus und die Editio Princeps des Velleius Paterculus," *Würzburger Jahrbücher für die Altertumswissenschaft*, n.f. 3 (1977): 231–242; J. Hellegouarc'h, "Lire et comprendre. Quelques remarques sur le texte de l'"Histoire romaine' de Velleius Paterculus," *Revue des études latines* 54 (1976): 239–256; and *Velleius Paterculus: The Tiberian Narrative (2. 94–131)*, ed., intro., and comm. by A. J. Woodman (Cambridge: Cambridge University Press, 1977), introduction.

93. On Velleius, see G. V. Sumner, "The Truth about Velleius Paterculus: Prolegomena," *Harvard Studies in Classical Philology* 74 (1970): 257–297; A. J. Woodman, "Velleius Paterculus," in *Empire and Aftermath: Silver Latin II*, ed. T. A. Dorey (London/Boston: Routledge and Kegan Paul, 1975), pp. 1–25; R. J. Starr, "The Scope and Genre of Velleius' History," *Classical Quarterly* 31 (1981): 162–174; and J. Hellegouarc'h, "Etat présent des travaux sur l'"Histoire Romaine' de Velleius Paterculus," in *Aufstieg und Niedergang der Römischen Welt: II Principat* (Berlin: de Gruyter, 1984), 32.1: 401–436.

94. *Briefwechsel*, p. 258.

95. *P. Vellei Paterculi*, f. A 3r.

96. Ibid., p. 1.

97. Ibid., p. 1.

98. *Briefwechsel*, p. 225; Woodman, *Velleius Paterculus;* and Velleius

Paterculus, *Histoire Romaine,* Vol. I, ed. Joseph Hellegouarc'h (Paris: Les Belles Lettres, 1982), introduction.

99. For Burer, see *Briefwechsel,* no. 197 and index.

100. Burer's letter is in *P. Vellei Paterculi,* fol. G 1r; the emendations are at ff. G 1r–G 5v and are entitled *Emendationes velleianae ex codice vetusto.*

101. Ibid., f. G 4v, and ibid., f. G 2v.

102. Ibid., f. G 1v: "Qui aliquando veterum exemplaria evolverunt, saepicule imo ferme semper et ubique *t* pro *d,* et rursus *d* pro *t* positum legerunt: ut *haut* pro *haud; aput* pro *apud,* et *at* pro *ad;* multaque huiusmodi. Noverunt item pleraque veterum exemplaria sine maiusculis literis, sine punctis, demum etiam sine omni sententiarum discrimine scripta." Full passage quoted in J. C. M. Laurent, "Über die Murbacher Handschrift des Vellejus," *Serapeum* 8: 188–192, at pp. 189–190.

103. Ibid., pp. 24, 39. See also *Vellei Paterculi ad M. Vinicium libri duo,* ed R. Ellis (Oxford, 1898), p. xx.

104. *P., Vellei Paterculi,* p. 57: "Nam hic in exemplari lacunulam omissae dictionis offendimus."

105. Ibid., p. 68: "Post Caesaris deest forma, vel simile, quae dictio oscitantia librarii in tertium versum translata est, ut videtur, ubi plane superest."

106. *Briefwechsel,* pp. 254–256.

107. Beatus' friend Boniface Amerbach made a copy of the Velleius manuscript; see Fechter, *Die Amerbachische Abschrift.* Occasionally Beatus discussed historical points in his sidenotes; see, for example, p. 20. For all the defects evident in the Velleius Paterculus edition, Beatus' skill at conjecture still commands modern attention; see Sven Blomgren, "Ad Velleium Paterculum adnotationes," *Eranos* 81 (1983): 35–45, at p. 37.

108. *Velleius Paterculus: The Caesarian and Augustan Narrative (2.41–93),* ed. and comm. A. J. Woodman (Cambridge: Cambridge University Press, 1983), pp. 150–153.

109. Ibid., p. 151.

110. Ibid., pp. 238–240.

111. *Veterum aliquot de arte rhetorica traditiones, de tropis in primis et schematis verborum et sententiarum. . . . opuscula,* see Index, no. 51. At p. 4, Froben notes in his introductory letter, "[Beatus] hunc codicem ex Spirensi bibliotheca obliteratum alioqui, velut ab inferis in vitam reduxit." See also the introduction of Carl Halm to *Rhetores latini minores* (Leipzig, 1863), pp. vi–vii, and Paul Lehmann, "Die mittelalterliche

Dombibliothek zu Speyer," in his *Erforschung des Mittelalters* (Stuttgart: Hiersemann, 1959), 2: 205. For background, see Giuseppe Billanovich, "Il Petrarca e i retori latini minori," *IMU* 5 (1962): 103–164.

112. Index, no. 48, and Horawitz, "Des Beatus Rhenanus literarische Thätigkeit, 1508–1531," pp. 660–661. For the panegyrical form, see Sabine MacCormack, "Latin Prose Panegyrics," in *Empire and Aftermath*, pp. 143–205.

113. *Contemporaries*, 1: 99, and *Briefwechsel*, no. 187.

114. *Panegyrici*, pp. 234, 268, 285.

115. *Briefwechsel*, no. 197, p. 270.

116. For the Tertullian edition, see Horawitz, "Des Beatus Rhenanus literarische Thätigkeit, 1508–1531," pp. 662–674; Pierre Fraenkel, "Beatus Rhenanus, Oecolampadius, Theodore de Bèze et quelques-unes de leur sources anciennes," *BHR* 41 (1979): 63–81; idem, "Melanchthon, Beatus Rhenanus et Tertullien," ibid. 44 (1982): 357–360; D'Amico, "Beatus Rhenanus, Tertullian and the Reformation"; and Jean-Claude Fredouille, "Beatus Rhenanus, commentateur de Tertullien," *ASABHS* 35 (1985): 287–295.

117. For Renaissance patrology, see August Buck, "Der Rückgriff des Renaissance-Humanismus auf die Patristik," in *Festschrift Walther von Wartburg*, ed. K. Baldinger (Tübingen: Niemeyer, 1968), 1: 153–175. Also of interest is R. W. Hunt, "The Need for a Guide to the Editors of Patristic Texts in the 16th Century," *Studia patristica* 16/1 (1982): 365–371.

118. See Alfred Hornbogen, "Die Baseler Ausgabe der Werke des Tertullians (Froben 1521): Ein Beitrag zur Geschichte des frühen illustrierten Buches," *Kunstmuseen der Deutschen Demokratischen Republik* 2 (1959): 52–60; Paul-Emile Schatzmann, "Passage du manuscrit à la première édition imprimée de 'La patience de Tertullien'," *Gutenberg-Jahrbuch* 39 (1964): 151–154; Werner Becker, "Die Frobensche Tertullianausgabe von 1521: Zu den Bildgeschichten von Ambrosius und Hans Holbein d.J.," *Marginalien* 52 (1973): 25–32.

119. See Paul Lehmann, "Tertullian im Mittelalter," in his *Erforschung des Mittelalters* (Stuttgart: Hiersemann, 1962), 5: 184–199.

120. For orientation, see Robert D. Sider, "Approaches to Tertullian: A Study of Recent Scholarship," *The Second Century* 2 (1982): 228–259. Ignorance of Tertullian had consequences even in the Reformation. Jaroslav Pelikan, in *The Vindication of Tradition* (New Haven: Yale University Press, 1984), p. 9, writes: "Drawing a sharp distinction between *gospel* and *tradition* had been a major plank in the platform of the Protestant Reformation. Luther, for example, had the impression,

mistaken though it was, that Tertullian, at the end of the second and the beginning of the third century, was the earliest of the ancient Christian writers after the apostles, so that it was possible to make the distinction between Scripture and tradition also, though not only, on chronological grounds."

121. See Johannes Quasten, *Patrology* (Westminster, Md.: The Newman Press, 1964), 2: 251–253.

122. *Briefwechsel*, no. 207, pp. 282–288. For Turzo, see José Ruysschaert, "Johann Hess et Valentine Crautwald rédacteurs en 1514–1515 du manuscrit Vat. Lat. 524 pour l'évêque de Breslau Johann Turzo," *Quellen und Forschungen aus italienischen Archiven und Bibliotheken* 64 (1984): 397–401; and *Contemporaries*, 3: 324–325. Beatus praised Turzo in his annotations to Pliny; see *Beati Rhenani Selezestadiensis in C. Plinium Annotationes* (Basel, 1526), p. 27 and (Cologne, 1615), p. 8.

123. In his introduction, Kroymann, *Tertulliani Opera* (see below, note 126), p. viii, lists the contents of the Payerne manuscript; also idem, "Kritische Vorarbeiten für den II. und III. Band der neuen Tertullianausgabe," *Sitzungsberichte der kaiserlichen Akademie der Wissenschaften, Philologisch-historische Classe* 143 (1900): 1–39; but compare Adam, *L'Humanisme à Sélestat*, no. 88, p. 99, and Albert Bruckner, "A propos du problème d'un *scriptorium* de Payerne," in *L'Abbatiale de Payerne* (Lausanne: Association pour la Restauration de l'Abbatiale, 1966), pp. 207–219, at pp. 208–212. See also Paul-Emile Schazmann, "Le manuscrit de Tertullien 'sur la patience' dit de Payerne à la Bibliothèque de Sélestat et sa publication par Beatus Rhenanus, humaniste rhénan," *Publication du Centre d'études burgundo-medianes* 5 (1964): 100–104. Adam reproduces a page from the Payerne manuscript, *L'Humanisme*, plate v; another page is reproduced in Meyer, "Beatus Rhenanus (de Sélestat) et sa bibliothèque," p. 28. The manuscripts are also discussed in the various editions of Tertullian's works in the *Sources Chrétiennes* series: *Contre les Valentiniens*, vol. I (Paris: Cerf, 1980); *De la Patience*, no. 310 (1984); *Exhortation a la Chasteté*, no. 319 (1985). On the manuscript's cover in Beatus' hand is the note "A domino Iacobo Timmerman Decano Colmariensi."

124. *Briefwechsel.*, p. 284.

125. Ibid., pp. 287–288.

126. Ibid., p. 288. For these manuscripts, see Emil Kroymann's introduction to *Quinti Florentis Tertulliani Opera*, pars III (Corpus Scriptorum Ecclesiasticorum Latinorum, XXXXVI, par. 3) (Vienna: Tempsky, 1906), pp. v–xxxv, and J. P. Waltzing, *Le Codex Fuldensis de*

Tertullian (Liège/Paris: Vaillant-Carmanne, 1914–1917). See also Pierre Petitmengin, "Le Tertullien de Fulvio Orsini," *Eranos* 59 (1961): 116–135.

127. Beatus published the following works of Tertullian: *De patientia, De carne domini, De carnis resurrectione, Adversus Praxeam, Adversus Valentinianos, Adversus Iudeos, Adversus omnes haereses, De praescriptione haereticorum, Adversus Hermogenem, De corona militis, Ad martyres, De poenitentia, De virginibus velandis, De habitu muliebri, De cultu foeminarum, Ad uxorem suam, De fuga in persecutione, Ad Scapulam, De exhortatione castitatis, De monogamia, De pallio, Adversus Marcionem, Apologeticus.* An English translation of Beatus' introduction (*argumentum*) to *Ad uxorem suam* was published with a translation of the text in 1550. This was also done in the case of Beatus' introductory letter to the edition of Marsilius of Padua's *Defensor pacis,* see above, note 149.

128. Pierre Petitmengin, "Comment on imprimait à Bâle au début du seizième siècle. A propos du 'Tertullien' de Beatus Rhenanus (1521)," *ASABHS* 30 (1980): 93–106.

129. Kroymann's introduction to *Opera,* pp. xvi–xix.

130. *Opera Tertulliani* (Basel, 1521), pp. 2, 133, and 347. *De praescriptione haereticorum,* pp. 94–95, at the words *Omne genus ad originem suam censeatur* in the margin: "Ex Hirsaugiense codice non minus mendoso quam erat Paternacensis, coniicio sic legi. . . ."

131. Ibid., p. 126.

132. Ibid, p. 5, *De patientia,* at the words, *Per haec impatientiae tunc infantis quodammodo incunabula,* Beatus writes: "Hirsaugiense exemplar sic habet. . . . Ego malim legere. . . ."

133. Ibid., pp. 77 and 138, and below, note 137.

134. Ibid., p. 337, at *argumentum* to *Adversus Hermogenem,* p. 497; p. 497 at *argumentum* to *Ad Scapulam,* and p. 528 at the *argumentum* to *De pallio.*

135. Ibid., p. 490, in *De fuga in persecutione:* "Si debito passione.] *Debito* pro *devito, b* pro *v.* Qui scribendi modus frequens est in hoc opere, nec semper animadversus aut iudicatus."

136. *Opera Tertulliani* (1521), pp. 408–414 and 427, respectively.

137. Ibid., p. 414: "In autore tam mire corrupto quid agas nisi divinans, si vacet." This annotation includes a reference to Poliziano's *Miscellanea.*

138. Ibid., p. 414; "Inscitia librarii verba haec partim depravavit, partim confudit."

139. Ibid., p. 408, in the *argumentum* to the book: "Porro quoniam in hoc libro ceremoniarum quarundam meminit, quibus maiores

nostri sub Apostolorum tempora sunt usi, libet hic annotationes praemittere quo studiosis antiquitatis Christianae gratificer, adiectis etiam quae cum apud alios scriptores, tum apud hunc nostrum de iisdem rebus comperi. Quae res etiam occasionem mihi dedit explicandi loca aliquot obscuriora."

140. Ibid., p. 408.

141. Ibid., p. 411.

142. For example, ibid., p. 413; see also p. 153.

143. Ibid., pp. 593–614, and p. 615, respectively.

144. For Pellikan and Beatus, see Francis Rapp, "Rhenanus et Pellikan, une passion commune, des destinées divergentes," *ASABHS* 35 (1985): 211–220. Several scholars like Pellikan produced indices or other ancillary materials for important texts Froben published.

145. Pierre Petitmengin, "Beatus Rhenanus et les manuscrits latins," *ASABHS* 35 (1985): 235–246, at p. 237.

146. For Beatus and the Reformation, see W. Teichmann, "Die kirchliche Haltung des Beatus Rhenanus," *Zeitschrift für Kirchengeschichte* 26 (1905): 363–381; Henri Meylan, "Beatus Rhenanus et la propagande des écrits lutheriens en 1519," in his *D'Erasme à Theodore Bèze* (Geneva: Droz, 1976); D'Amico, "Beatus Rhenanus, Tertullian and the Reformation," and Walker, "Beatus Rhenanus (1485–1547) entre l'Eglise traditionelle et la Réformation."

147. *Briefwechsel,* nos. 75, 79, 81, 90, 95, 97, 99, 101, 113, 118; Walter, *Beatus Rhenanus,* nos. IX–XIII, and Jean Rott, "Beatus Rhenanus et Martin Bucer: l'humaniste chrétien et le réformateur," *ASABHS* 35 (1985): 62–72. See also the letters in *Correspondance de Martin Bucer,* vol. 1, ed. Jean Rott (Leiden: Brill, 1979). For Bucer, see also *Contemporaries,* 1: 209–212.

148. Meylan, "Beatus Rhenanus et la propagande."

149. See D'Amico, "Beatus Rhenanus, Tertullian, and the Reformation," for details.

150. Ibid., pp. 49–50.

151. Ibid., pp. 55–56.

152. See below, chapter 5.

153. *Index,* no. 53. For Beatus' contribution to the *editio princeps* of the *Defensor,* see Gregorio Piaia, "Beato Renano e il *Defensor Pacis* agli inizi della Riforma," *Studia patavina* 21 (1974): 28–79; idem, *Marsilio da Padova nella Riforma e nella Controriforma: Fortuna ed interpretazione,* (Padua: Antenore, 1977); and John F. D'Amico, "Ulrich von Hutten and Beatus Rhenanus as Medieval Historians" to appear in *Studies in Medievalism.*

154. See Giovanni Mercati, "Scritti ecclesiastici greci copiati da Giovanni Fabri nella Vaticana," in his *Opere minori*, vol. 4, Studi e Testi no. 79 (Vatican: Biblioteca Apostolica Vaticana, 1937), pp. 110–130.

155. Index, no. 54; Horawitz, "Des Beatus Rhenanus literarische Thätigkeit, 1508–1531," pp. 678–682; and Walter Jacob, *Die handschriftliche Überlieferung der sogenannten Historia Tripartita des Epiphanius-Cassiodor* (Berlin: Akademie Verlag, 1954), pp. 164–169.

156. *Briefwechsel*, pp. 322–325.

157. For modern judgments on Rufinus, see J. E. L. Oulton, "Rufinus's Translation of the Church History of Eusebius," *The Journal of Theological Studies* 30 (1929): 150–174, and Monica M. Wagner, *Rufinus, the Translator* (Washington, D.C.: Catholic University of America, 1945). In 1516 Beatus published Xystus Pythagoricus' *Sententiae* in a translation by Rufinus; Index, no. 31.

158. *Autores Historiae Ecclesiasticae* (Basel, 1523), pp. 123, 124, 221, 301, 463.

159. Ibid., p. 175. Beatus also discussed various historical questions; see pp. 113, 124, 175.

160. Jacob, *Überlieferung*, pp. 168–169.

161. *In C. Plinium* (Basel, 1526), pp. 26–27, and (Cologne, 1615), p. 8.

3: A NEW TEXTUAL CRITICAL METHOD

1. See Robert Walker, "Beatus Rhenanus (1485–1547) entre l'Eglise traditionelle et la Réformation," in *Les Dissidents du XVIe siècle entre l'Humanisme et le Catholicisme*, ed. Marc Lienhard (Baden-Baden: Koerner, 1983), pp. 97–109; idem, "Un texte de Beatus Rhenanus: l'appel aux habitants de Sélestat pour les exhorter à la paix civile et religieuse (1523?)," in *Grandes figures de l'humanisme alsacien*, pp. 42–47; and idem, "Un manuscrit de Beatus Rhenanus perdu et retrouvé," *ASABHS* 31 (1981): 29–35. Of a broader scope are Paul Adam, *Histoire religieuse de Sélestat* (Sélestat: Alsatia, 1967), 1: 179–200, and *Histoire de l'Alsace*, ed. Philippe Dollinger (Toulouse: Privat, 1970), pp. 201–217.

2. This is discussed in Peter G. Bietenholz, *Basle and France in the Sixteenth Century: The Basle Humanists and Printers in Their Contacts with Francophone Culture* (Toronto/Genève: University of Toronto/Droz, 1971), p. 28, fn. 1. As Bietenholz points out, Beatus was not particularly generous to his employees. When Burer, who had served Beatus well in scholarly and business matters, asked Beatus for a loan to

continue his studies, Beatus simply advised him to find a job. One letter, dated 29 November 1526, contains Beatus' advice for Froben on acquiring a Greek font; see *Briefwechsel*, no. 261, and *Amerbachkorrespondenz*, vol. 3, no. 1162.

3. See Index, no. 55, for full title; Charles Nauert, Jr., in *CTC*, pp. 367–369; and Horawitz, "Des Beatus Rhenanus literarische Thätigkeit, 1508–1531," pp. 682–690. Beatus also edited Pliny the Younger's letters; see Index, no.26.

4. For the *Naturalis historia*, see *Pauly-Wissowa*, vol. 21/1, cols. 299–430, and Marjorie Chibnall, "Pliny's *Natural History* and the Middle Ages," in *Empire and Aftermath: Silver Latin II*, ed. T. A. Dorey (London/Boston: Routledge and Kegan Paul, 1975), pp. 57–78.

5. For the history of the text, see Nauert, *CTC*, pp. 367–369; idem, "Humanists, Scientists, and Pliny: Changing Approaches to a Classical Author," *American History Review* 84 (1979): 72–85; and *Texts and Transmission*, pp. 307–317. For Beatus and Collenuccio, see Index, no. 17.

6. See the introduction to the Italian edition of the *Castigationes*.

7. For Sabellico, see *DBI*, 26: 510–515, and Nauert in *CTC*, pp. 344–350. Beatus also edited Sabellico's *Exemplorum libri decem;* see Index, no. 9.

8. For Bérault, see Marie-Madeleine de la Garanderie, *Christianisme et lettres profanes 1515–1535. Essai sur les mentalités des milieux intellectuels parisiens et sur la pensée de Guillaume Budé* (Lille/Paris: Université de Lille, 1976), pp. 56–65, and *Contemporaries*, 1: 126–128.

9. For Budé, see *Contemporaries*, 1: 212–217; for Longueil, see Th. Simar, *Christophe de Longueil, humaniste 1488–1522* (Louvain: Peeters, 1911); R. Aulotte, "Une rivalité d'humanistes: Erasme et Longueil, traducteurs de Plutarque," *BHR* 30 (1968): 549–573; and *Contemporaries*, 2: 342–345.

10. For Erasmus and Pliny, see *EE*, 6, no. 1544 (1926); 16–21.

11. Ibid., pp. 19–20.

12. Ibid., p. 20.

13. I cite first from *Beatus Rhenanus Selezestadiensis in C. Plinium* (Basel, 1526), p. 7, and then the reprint of the annotations in *C. Plinii Secundi Historiae Mundi libri XXXVII* (Cologne, 1615), p. 4. For Pliny's *Praefatio*, see Giovanni Pascucci, "La lettera prefatoria di Plinio alla *Naturalis historia*," in *Plinio il Vecchio sotto il profilo storico* (Como, 1982), pp. 171–197, and N. Ph. Howe, "In Defense of the Encyclopedic Mode: on Pliny's *Preface* to the *Natural History*," *Latomus* 44 (1985): 561–576.

14. Ibid., pp. 22–23/p. 7.

15. See ibid., pp. 12, 26, 33, 36, 44, 46, 73, 86, 88, 89/pp. 5, 8, 10, 12, 13, 18, 21, 22.

16. Ibid., p. 26/p. 8.

17. Ibid., p. 73/p. 18: "Et hic cogor dissentire ab Hermolao Barbaro, non quod is diversam a mente Plinii lectionem hic tradat, sed quod aliam longe quam Plinius scripserit. Est autem aliquid non modo sensum autoris, sed etiam ipsa verba quibus ille sit usus restituere."

18. Ibid., p. 34/p. 10: "Aperiemus rem exemplo [of one who ignores manuscripts]. Christophorus Longolius, eruditissimus iuvenis, et ad eloquentiam natus, ad quam se elegantissime exercebat, profecto dignus longiore vita multis de causis, in Plinio non pauca restituere conatus est; verum quantum ego e quibusdam locis obiter deprehendere potui, cum Parisiensem aeditionem evolverem, coniecturis plerumque propriis, vel ratione stili, vel quod aliter hoc alibi lectum sit. Fallax est hic modus." See also p. 45/p.12. Beatus did admit when he thought Longueil conjectured correctly; see p. 12/p.42. See also p. 92/p. 18.

19. For the correspondence between Erasmus and Budé, see *La Correspondance d'Erasme et de Guillaume Budé*, trans. Marie-Madeleine de la Garanderie (Paris: Vrin, 1967). At p. 29, M. de la Garanderie quotes a passage from Erasmus' *Annotationes* to the Gospel of Saint Luke, in which he mentions Beatus' calling his attention to a text of Budé.

20. *In C. Plinium*, p. 34/p. 10: "Mihi magis placet institutum Guilielmi Budaei, viri laudatissimi, qui seculum nostrum cum primis illustrat, posteros etiam scriptis suis adiuturus. Dii boni, quam multa loca nobis ille restituit in Pliniana historia subsidio plerunque vetusti voluminis, quibus Assem suum non inepte locupletavit. Nam exemplaria vestusta nusquam consulere dedignatur. Utinam id opus diligentius inspexissem ob quendam locum, priusquam ipse castigationem eius aggrederer. Ademisset mihi certe multum laboris." Also p. 101/p. 24, and *Briefwechsel*, no. 72, p. 103.

21. Ibid., p. 103/p. 25.

22. *Briefwechsel*, no. 252, pp. 355–358. For Lasco, see J.-Cl. Margolin, "Laski, lecteur et annotateur du 'Nouveau Testament' d'Erasme," in *Scrinium erasmianum*, ed. J. Coppens (Leiden: Brill, 1969), 1: 93–128, and *Contemporaries*, 2: 297–301. Beatus seem to have communicated with Lasco on manuscripts; *In C. Plinium*, p. 12/p. 5.

23. *Briefwechsel*, pp. 356–357.

24. Paul Lehmann, *Iohannes Sichardus und die von ihm benutzten Bibliotheken und Handschriften* (Munich: Beck, 1911), pp. 164–165. Beatus

mentioned other manuscripts in passing in his work. In *In. C. Plinium,* p. 57/p. 15, Beatus referred to a manuscript of Fulda of Quintilian.

25. *Briefwechsel,* p. 356: "Et profecto sic est, ad manuscriptos codices et eos vetustos confugere oportet eum, qui in autorum monumentis restitutendis cum laude versari velit. Nam hic certissimus sincerae lectionis indagandae modus e mendis, inquam, et ruinis veterum exemplarium germanam scripturam eruere, hoc est, aurum e stercore colligere. Alioqui fallaces plerumque sunt coniecturae ex ingenio potius quam e vestigiis libris desumptae."

26. Ibid., p. 357.

27. Discussion and examples in Walter Allen, Jr., "Beatus Rhenanus editor of Tacitus and Livy," *Speculum* 12 (1937): 382–385.

28. *In C. Plinium* p. 66/p. 17: "Nam aliquid vetus lectio cum vulgata consentit."

29. See Rizzo, *Il lessico filologico,* pp. 211–212. However, Beatus found Barbaro's use of the term *vetus lectio* confusing. See *In C. Plinium,* p. 73/p. 18 and p. 86/p. 21.

30. Ibid., p. 67/p. 17: "Enimvero video quid in vulgatis aeditionibus legatur, video etiam quid manuscriptus codex contineat. Non discedo libenter a lectione exemplaris vetusti, quantum fieri potest, quod clarum sit qualiter eruditorum temeritas Plinium nobis interpolarit: imo vulgatam lectionem adhibito iudicio potius castigandam censeo, si res patiatur, ad eam quae nobis vetus appellatur, quam e diverso veterem ad recentiorem."

31. Ibid., p. 49/ p. 13, all in one annotation: "Hic est germanus Plinii sensus. . . . Nam recentior [lectio] hoc indicat. . . . Vetus lectio mutila est . . . vetus hic exemplar inspexissem, synceram me Plinii lectionem de qua invenienda spem omnem antea abieceram, tandem deprehendisse, quam non caelabo."

32. *In C. Plinium,* pp. 35–36/p. 10: "Vide quam sacra res sit castigare libros, et quam religiose circumspecteque tractanda. Alibi fortassis laudem mereatur festinantia, at in hoc negotio nihil magis obest. Candidos viros in his et similibus locis deceret ingenue testari, vel vitiatam esse sententiam, vel intelligentiam non liquere. Verum tales sumus, ut omnia scire videri velimus, et nihil ignorare. Interim imponimus crassis lectoribus et stultis auditoribus, hoc uno freti, quod mundus iudicio caret, et maiore studio nonnunquam indocta amplectitur."

33. Ibid., p. 11/p. 5: "Vide quam oporteat esse curiosum mi lector." pp.13–14/p. 5: "Verum cum hunc locum curiosius excuterem."

34. Ibid., p. 13/p. 5, "Opus est coniectura, quando nullum aliunde subsidium." Beatus then goes on to a discussion of the *elementa dictionis.*

35. Ibid., pp. 33–34/p. 10.

36. Ibid., p. 72/p. 18, for example: "Sic in vulgatis aeditionibus legitur. Libet more nostro veteris quoque voluminis lectionem apponere: non quod multo sit rectior, sed ut appareat quanto ipse labore sententiam, quam postremo subiungam, e mendis ineptiisque librariorum exculpserim." Also pp. 86/21: "Verum conemur bonis avibus, ex ruinis istis, germanam Plinii sententiam eruere."

37. Ibid., p. 46/p. 13.

38. Ibid., p. 37/p. 11 and p. 32/p. 10.

39. Ibid., p. 71/p. 18: "In antiquis libris *a* literam saepe sic depictam reperias, ut α Graecanici speciem referat superne hians, quare in *u* vocalem saepe perperam demutatum a librariis invenitur."

40. Ibid., p. 44/p. 12: "Porro cum nullum eorum quae veniebant in mentem magnopere arrideret, singulis elementis atque ipsorum elementorum figuris etiam diligenter excussis, in eam adductus sum opinionem, ut sic scriptum fuisse putem, interstitibus spaciosiusculis intervallis, qualia adhuc in vetustissimis libris, qui sint ab indoctis descripti. . . ."

41. Ibid., p. 36/p. 10: "Haec res non minus depravavit nobis Plinium, quam librariorum veterum inscitia. Interpolata enim nimium multis locis huius autoris volumina habemus, nec syncera, per sinistram eruditorum quorundam diligentiam."

42. Ibid., p. 9/p. 4: See above, chapter 2 for an earlier version of harder reading theory.

43. Ibid., p. 78/p. 19: "Non satis est autem Plinii aut alterius cuiuscunque autoris sensum alicunde habuisse, nisi ipsa elementa veterum codicum apicesque ipsos et horum singulos propemodum ductus diligentissime etiam atque etiam inspicias: praesertim si germanam eius autoris, quem castigandum susceperis, lectionem et qualis ab ipso prodita est restituere coneris." Also p. 21/p. 7.

44. Ibid., p. 50/p. 14, p. 54/p. 14, and pp. 65–66/p. 17.

45. Ibid., p. 63/ p. 16: "Nam in Murbacensi codice nescio quis *c* elementum supra *a* ascripserat: quae res in varias ac vanas coniecturas diu me distraxit."

46. Ibid., p. 93/p. 21: "Quanto vero tutior via est autores restituendi, quam nos indicamus, nempe per veterum exemplariorum collationem." For "collatio," see Rizzo, *Il lessico filologico,* index.

47. For examples, see ibid., pp. 7, 13, 48, 84, 86/pp. 4, 5, 13, 21.

48. Ibid., p. 13/p. 5, *Praefatio 9,* "*Cum apud Catonem illum ambitus hostem, et repulsis tanquam honoribus ineptis gaudentem.*] ". . . Itaque cum hunc locum etiam atque etiam inspicerem, et elementa huius dictionis

ineptis verterem, atque reverterem, tandem propitio Apolline venit in mentem, id quod non dubito verum esse, scriptum videlicet fuisse *meritis*, librarium autem indoctum pro *m* litera *i n* legisse, ut fieret *ineritis*, idque cum non placeret, quippe quod auribus illius alienius esset, pro *ineritis* statim scripsisse *ineptis*. Ausim autem affirmare legendum hic *meritis*, sicque Plinium scripsisse." *Inemptis* is the modern reading. See also pp. 64–65/p. 17, Book VIII. 210, at the words *quibus usitata*.

49. Ibid., p. 8/p. 4, *Praefatio*, 3: "*AV eraniolis suis et Fabullis.*] In codice veteri legitur, *a veraniolis tuis et famulis*. Quorum postremum hoc aperte mendosum est a sciolo quopiam depravatum, qui *fauullis, u* pro *b* usurpato, veterum more, statim in *fanulis* commutarint, *u* priorem literam *n* esse putans, cui sane non multum est absimilis, sed cuius loco *m* foret scribendum, ut ipsi videbatur."

50. Ibid., pp. 17–18/p. 6, *Praefatio* 19: "*Quod dum ista, ut ait M. Varro, mussitamus.*] Sic hactenus ab omnibus lectum est. At manuscriptum volumen hic *musinamur* habet, indubio argumento *muginamur* esse legendum. Est autem *muginari*, autore Festo, nugari, et quasi tarde conari. Adducit Nonius Marcellus Lucilium testem, qui eo verbo sit usus pro murmurare. Potest igitur fieri, ut *mussitamus* glossa fuerit per quam *muginamur* verbum aliquis exposuerit. Ea cum esset notior quam vocabulum quod exponebatur, recepta est in contextum, et verbum e thesauro antiquitatis depromptum per librarii socordiam negligenter omissum, imo e sua possessione eiectum." The modern reading is ". . . *quod, dum ista (ut ait M. Varro) muginamur.*"

51. Ibid., p. 86/p. 21.

52. Ibid., p. 14/p. 5.

53. Ibid., p. 87/p. 21: "Quod vero *Ante lucem* manuscriptus codex habet [instead of Beatus' proposed *Ante ducem*], inde accidit, quod monacho [word missing in 1615 reprint] librario cum haec describeret Psalmographi venit in mentem quodam loco inquientis: Vanum est vobis ante lucem surgere. Erat autem illi notior Psalmorum liber, quam phrasis Pliniana." Also p. 48/p. 13.

54. *Ibid.,* p. 7/p. 4: "Mihi simplicius videtur, nec quicquam de hoc ambigo. . . ." P. 85/ p. 21: "Tametsi non prorsus displicet ut *ibi* hoc loco legatur, quod potuerit etiam in *sive* mutatum esse, sed simplicius est quod nos indicavimus." P. 93/p. 23: "Alius simpliciter legit *candidam.*"

55. Ibid., p. 11/p. 5.

56. See S. E. Stout, "The Mind of the Scribe," *The Classical Journal* 22 (1927): 405–417; Ernest C. Colwell, "Method in Evaluating Scribal Habits," in his *Studies in Methodology in Textual Criticism of the New*

Testament (Grand Rapids: Eerdmans, 1969), pp. 106–122; and R. M. Ogilvie, "Monastic Corruption," *Greece and Rome* 18 (1971): 32–34. See also *In C. Plinium,* p. 8/p. 4.

57. *In C. Plinium,* p. 9/p. 4: "Atque hic eruditorum iudicium appello: nam semidoctus sufficere putabit, quod nihil inveniat aperte cum grammaticorum regulis pugnans."

58. Ibid., p. 8/p. 4.

59. Ibid., p. 45/p. 13: "Deinde cum renascentibus studiis ab hinc annos ferme centum Plinius legi coepisset, doctus aliquis videns nihil sensum esse, statim substituit. . . ." and p. 85/p. 21, "Doctus quispiam circa tempus illud quo Plinius renascentibus in Italia primum studiis in manibus eruditorum haberi coepit. . . ."

60. Ibid., p. 17/p. 6, p. 35/p. 10, and p. 36/p. 10: "Proinde facile apparet, haec duo verba, *ita reprobent,* ab aliquo docto fuisse adiecta, qui voluerit imperfectam Plinii sententiam hoc pacto supplere et adiuvare. Sic autem irrepunt in scripta veterum mendae. Doctus aliquis annotat in margine libri sui coniecturam, quae forte venit in mentem, non quod approbet, sed quia sic videtur legi posse. Deinde studiosus quispiam, praeceptoris sui vel eius quem alias sectatur inspecto libro, statim veluti oraculum arripit quod illi levis coniectura suggesserat. Et iactans veluti rem magnam ac plane triumphans, Sic, inquit, legit Beroaldus, sic Sabellicus, et proculdubio non aliter legendum est. Statimque eradit veterem lectionem; et novam istam infulcit. Nec vero nisi charissimis sodalibus et vix his quidem huiusmodi mysteria communicat. Haec res non minus depravavit nobis Plinium quam librariorum veterum inscitia."

61. Ibid., p. 65/p. 17: "Huiusmodi indiligens eruditorum diligentia plurimum Plinii scriptis nocuit, qui interpolatum illius divinum opus nobis dare studuerunt magis quam castigatum." The long passage that follows reiterates Beatus' general points about the value of his method.

62. Ibid., p. 35/p. 10: "Dii deaeque, in quos anfractus, imo in quae praecipitia aberrarunt hic docti viri, dum exemplaria vetusta consulere negligunt, nec quisquam e ruinis corruptae lectionis synceram restituit? Quae hic somnia hactenus secuti sumus? Quam egregie se ulciscitur contempta antiquitas?" See also p. 85/p. 21 and p. 97/p. 23.

63. Ibid., p. 50/p. 14; "Sic depravantur autores. At nescias plus ne nocuerit supina librariorum indoctorum incuria, quemadmodum iam saepe diximus, an eruditorum diligentia parum attenta. Porro ut in inquirendi labore persisterem, in causa fuit quod hic vocabulum additum invenissem, quod non esset in antiquo codice, nempe *rabiem.* Expende nunc tecum quid his debeatur, qui hanc autores castigandi

molestiam pro communi studiosorum utilitate subeunt. Ubi pro inventis quidem ac restitutis locis fortassis lector paulo humanior gratiam habet: at pro illis in quibus, quantumlibet ingenii nervos intenderis, conatus non successit, nemo quicquam emendatori se debere agnoscit. Qualia necesse est multa incidere in opere, praesertim longo. Ipse scio quandiu hic ante laborarim, et nihil tamen effecerim, quod nullus sciturus erat. Postea resumpto labore, praeter spem, ni fallor, divinatio successit."

64. Ibid., p. 93/p. 23: "Multis autem locis coniecturarum diversitas vitiandis invertendisque Plinii scriptis praebuit occasionem, dum omnium coniecturae sedulo, sed absque iudicio converruntur in contextum. Enimvero sic primum autores sunt castigati, hoc est depravati. Nemo voluit laborare, et turpe erat diu haerere. Quicquid ergo in buccam venit, statim libris illitum est."

65. See above, note 30.

66. Ibid., p. 42/p. 12: "Vel hic videas quantum bonis autoribus periculi sit etiam a doctis. Quae res non minus Plinium perdidit, quam librariorum incuria. Porro non satis mirari possum quorundam facilitatem, qui statim infulciunt quod docti casu nonnunquam annotarunt in libris suis. Religiosissime tractanda sunt autorum scripta." Also see p. 50/p. 14.

67. Ibid., p. 12/p. 5: "Meam tamen coniecturam, qualis qualis est, nolui caelare studiosos, cum hunc laborem susceperim, ut Plinianae lectioni deditos iuvem et doctos admoneam." And see following note. Also p. 15/p. 5, p. 16/p. 6, and p. 41/p. 12.

68. Ibid., p. 19/p. 6: "Nec vero haec citavi in medium ut interpretes rideam, qui sedulos illorum conatus probo. Alioqui si is mihi fuisset animus, potuissem fortassis nimium multis locis illorum sive inscitiam, sive incuriam potius arguere. Sed in hoc mihi sumptus est praesens castigationis labor, ut pro virili studiosos adiuvem et doctos admoneam."

69. Ibid., p. 37/p. 11: "Oedipo coniectore opus sit." P. 69/p. 18, "Hic certe Oepido rursum opus est. . . ."

70. Ibid., p. 9/p. 4: "O certissimam bonorum autorum pestem, librarios, sciolos et indoctos. Utinam autem hodie etiam in typographos quosdam idem dici non possit." Also p. 8/p. 4: "Hinc autem erroris occasio nata est, quod librarius eruditionis expers, quales apud nos hodie typographorum sunt operae. . . ."

71. Ibid., p. 93/p. 23: "Cur ergo non asterisci notam hic apposuerunt?"

72. Ibid., p. 38/p. 11; "Quae lectio, cum melior non occurreret, et nemo quaereret amplius, aut dubitaret propterea quod magni in li-

teris viri sic legerent, in omnia exemplaria deinde transfusa est, idque per artem istam typographicam, qua celerrime libri propagantur, non minus mendosi quam castigati."

73. Ibid., p. 37/p. 11: "Id quod [confusion of letters] stanneis typographorum formis accidere minime potest."

74. Ibid., pp. 15–16/p. 6, *Praefatio* 11: "*Verum et diis lacte rustici multaeque gentes supplicant, et mola tantum salsa litant, qui non habent thura.*] Vetus codex non habet, *verum et diis,* sed tantum, *verum diis.* Praeterea nec *supplicant* in eo legitur, nec *litant.* Mirum est omissum utrunque esse. Vix hoc casu fieri potuit. Nec tamen reprehendo, quod in libro meo non est. Eos tantum candide moneo, qui vetustos Plinii codices vel habent, vel ubi serventur sciunt, ut hunc locum inspiciant. Nam meus librarius diversam lectionem invehere voluit, quasi sic iudicarit legendum, *multaeque gentes e more tantum salsa* (intellige aqua, quemadmodum etiam frigidam aut calidam usurpant autores) *qui non habent thura.* Sed recepta melius placet. Annotavi tantum hoc, ut magis extimulem studiosos ad inspiciendum exemplaria vetera." Modern reading is *Verum dis lacte rustici multaque gentes et mola tantum salsa litant qui non habent tura. . . .*

75. Ibid., p. 15/p. 6: ". . . ut ex probabili coniectura talis fuit antiqua lectio . . ."

76. For one example of a correct conjecture, see ibid. At p. 8/p. 4, *Praefatio* 1, Beatus correctly conjectured on the phrase *Ut obiter molliam Catullum.*

77. See *In C. Plinium, Praefatio* 24, pp. 21–22/pp. 18–19, "*Iam iam Musae*"; cf. Barbaro, *Castigationes Plinianae,* pp. 18–19.

78. I have consulted the Teubner edition of Pliny, ed. L. Ian and C. Mayhoff (rpt.: Stuttgart, 1967), I: 8, and Pliny, *Natural History* trans. H. Rackham (rpt.: Cambridge, Mass.: Harvard University Press, 1979), I: 16, *Praefatio* 26. See *In C. Plinium,* pp. 28–30/p. 9: "*Et ne in totum videar Graecos insectari, ex illis nos velim intelligi, pingique conditoribus.*] Id primo sciendum est, in vetere libro non *ex illis nos velim,* sed *ex illis mox velim intelligi pingique conditoribus.* Quae postrema verba nondum est repertus qui perite explicarit. Quid enim sibi hoc vult, *pingique conditoribus?* Torsit hic nodus multos, receptam istam lectionem mutare etiam ausos. Nam quidam *pingendi conditoribus* legunt pro *pingique conditoribus.* Quidam pro *conditoribus* substituunt *coloribus.* Mihi neutra lectio probatur, nec placet antiqua quam mendosam esse liquet. In manuscripto codice quippiam aliud fuisse scriptum video. Nam extat rasura post *pingi* (quod tamen aliud fuit quam *pingi*) elementorumque expunctorum loco *que* particula supraposita est in summo. Quare prima mea coniectura erat, scriptum fuisse *pictoribus*

tantum, distantibus inter se literis et syllabis, ut fit hoc pacto fortassis *p i c toribus,* idque ab aliquo sciolo suppletis lacunis istis in *pingique conditoribus* mutatum, propter Apellem qui sequitur, quod *pictoribus* debebat esse. Deinde cum cogitarem quam exacte loquantur autores, et viderem etiam Polycleti mentionem fieri, qui pictor non fuisset, sed statuarius, nullo modo mihi satisfaciebat quod inveneram. Coepi itaque diligentius laceras veteris lectionis ruinas inspicere, et post longum incredibilemque laborem, tandem e vestigiis hoc erui, ut a Plinio scriptum existimem *iconon,* sive potius εικονων *autoribus.* Cum autem ω simile sit *co* latinae syllabae, facile [word missing in 1615 reprint] factum est ut ων *autoribus* mutaretur in *conditoribus,* et ειχον quod supererat, primum in *pingo,* mox in *pingique.* Enimvero possunt cum pictores tum caelatores aptissime dici autores. . . . An vero recte pictorem appellemus conditorem nescio. Hoc satis constat, etiam si pingens aliquid condere diceretur, hanc tamen lectionem ineptam esse ut *pingendi conditoribus* scribatur. Haec et alia huiusmodi monere debebant interpretes, et non satis putare, si dixissent *conditoribus,* id est, *compositoribus,* ut legum conditoribus dicuntur."

79. I have followed the translation in *Natural History,* trans. H. Rackham, p. 17, Preface 24. Equally valuable would be the examples in the annotation *Omnique haec reipub. et nobis quidem qualis in castrensi contubernio*], at pp. 10–11/pp. 4–5.

80. See *Hermolai Barbari Castigationes Plinianae et in Pomponium Melam,* I: 19–21.

81. Ibid., pp. 19–20.

82. For the poet M. Furius Bibaculus, see *Pauly-Wissowa,* 7/1: 321–322, and K. J. McKay, "Furius Bibaculus fr. 1 Baehrens (17 Morel)," *Latomus* 42 (1983): 395–396.

83. Ibid., p. 22/p. 7.

84. *In C. Plinium,* p. 22/p, 7: "Luctatus est cum hoc loco Hermolaus ille Barbarus non Venetiae modo, verum Italiae totius, imo Christiani orbis eximium in literis decus. De quo viro quoties cogito, videor mihi videre M. illum Varronem, qui inter Romanos olim doctissimi elogio ornatus est, terris postliminio redditum. Tanta est eruditio, tanta facundia priscae illius aemula, tantus in aeditis monumentis insumptus labor."

85. Beatus cited Barbaro's *Corollarium* on Dioscorides and his translation of Themistius. See *In C. Plinium,* pp. 22–23/p. 7. For the *Corollarium* or *Commentary,* see John Marion Riddle, "Dioscorides" in *CTC,* 4: 1–143, at pp. 46–48, and Giovanni Pozzi, "Appunti sul 'Corollarium' del Barbaro," in *Tra latino e volgare per Carlo Dionisotti,* ed. Gabriella Bernardoni Trezzini, et al. (Padua: Antenore, 1974), 2:

46   *Notes to Pages 87–88*

619–640. Interestingly, in his article, at p. 621, Pozzi notes that the 1516 edition of the *Corollarium* by Battista Egnazio was partly directed against the translation of Dioscorides by the French humanist Jean Ruel. One reason for Egnazio's claims for Barbaro's superiority is that the Italian's Greek text was based on a better manuscript than Ruel's. Barbaro's translation of Themistius in the Venice, 1499, edition has been reprinted (Minerva GmbH, 1978).

86. See John F. D'Amico, "The Progress of Renaissance Latin Prose: The Case of Apuleianism," *Renaissance Quarterly* 37 (1984): 351–392, at p. 364, fn. 42.

87. Ibid., pp. 23–24/p. 7.

88. Ibid., p. 24/p. 7: "Vetus exemplar Murbacensis bibliothecae sic habet, *Nostri grossioris antiquitatum exemplorum artiumque facetissimi lucubrationem puto quia ut Baculus erat et vocabatur paulominus. Asserit Varro in satyri sui sustulit et flexiabula.* Quis hanc lectionem non aeque monstrificam vocet? Eant [erant in 1603 ed.] nunc quidem, et dicant nullam mereri laudem, qui e codicibus vetustis aliquid reponant, tam bene habentibus scilicet, et tam pulchre castigatis. Quam gloriosum sit nescio, laboriosissimum esse expertus sum ex depravatis exemplaribus veterem et germanam lectionem addivinare. Exprobrare beneficium meum studiosis viderer, si enumerarem hic quoties mihi inspectus sit codex manuscriptus, quoties in manum sumptus et depositus, quamdiu etiam aliud agenti vetus ea scriptura obversata sit in animo."

89. Ibid., p. 24/pp. 7–8.

90. Ibid., pp. 24–25/p. 8: "Ut sit Plinii sensus, *Nostri,* hoc est, Latini, crassiores, subaudi sunt, quam Graeci. Inter hos qui facetissimi fuerunt, paulo festiviores titulos excogitarunt, videlicet *Antiquitatum, Exemplorum,* et *Artium,* de quibus tractabant. Lucubrationis titulum, nisi fallor, P. Valerius is qui Antii oppidi civis fuit, et ab eo cognomen habuit, dictus Antias, primus asserit. Varro in satyris suis sustulit et Flexibula. Habes sententiae Plinianae paraphrasim. Quod vero Hermolaus *Sexculyxem* legit pro *sustulit,* non prorsus displicet propter *et* coniungentem particulam, alioqui ipse ex coniectura ad quam me sane tenuia vetusti codicis vestigia ducunt, *astruit* legere mallem quam *sustulit.* Sic autem dictum est hoc a Plinio, Lucubrationem puto, qui Antii civis erat et vocabatur, P. Valerius, primus asserit, ac si quis hodie diceret, *Antibarbaros* (nam exemplo res est explicanda quo clarior evadat) puto, qui Roterodami civis est et vocatur, D. Erasmus, primus asserit. Aut, *Miscellanea,* puto qui Politiani civis erat et vocabatur, Angelus, primus asserit. Est vero Roterodamum, oppidum Hollandiae, sicut Politianum Hetruriae, quod cognomen et vitam dedit Angelo Politiano." For Valerius, see K. W. Nitzsch, *Die römische Annal-*

istik von ihren ersten Anfängen bis auf Valerius Antias (Berlin, 1873), pp. 346–350; Albert A. Howard, "Valerius Antias and Livy," *Harvard Studies in Classical Philology* 17 (1906): 161–180; R. A. Laroche, "Valerius Antias and his Numerical Totals: A Reappraisal," *Historia* 26 (1977): 358–368; and idem, "Valerius Antias as Livy's Source for the Number of Military Standards captured in battle in Books I–X," *Classica et mediaevalia* 35 (1984): 93–104.

91. *In C. Plinium,* p. 25/p. 8: "Nunc indicemus, quantum assequi divinando licet, quid librarios seduxerit, ut hunc locum tam foede depravarent; ne quis somnium putet esse nostram castigationem, sed videat quid me moverit, ut sic potius legerem quam aliter. Primum, cohaerentibus syllabis scriptum erat *QuiantIi,* id indoctior adhuc librarius mutavit in *Quia Vt,* et pro *I* maiuscula litera, cum altera minore, *b* pinxit, cui si parum attente observes in scriptura non ita sunt multum absimiles. Haec quae nunc dico melius demonstrari possent in literis ductu calami protractis, quam in iis quas excursorii typi exprimunt. Sufficit tamen aliquid tenuisse. Deinde *civis* sic erat casu scriptum ut prius lineamentum *u* literae, elementi *l* speciem praeberet, et *i* cum altero lineamento, nempe posteriori videretur *u* esse. Loco vero primarum literarum eius dictionis *c* et *i* quod inferne forent coniunctae, et *c* curvitate sua in superiori parte careret, *u* rursus suppositum est, ut tandem fieret *ulus.* Iam *Ii* duae literae speciem elementi *b* praeferentes solae stabant. Nec placebat *ulus,* quod nihil significabat. Quid factum est? Librarius statuit omnino componere ex his literis et syllabis aliquam dictionem. Nec erat melius consilium, quam si ex *b* et *ulo* additis duabus tantum literis *a* et *c,* faceret baculum. Itaque pulchre procedente depravatione quod debebat esse, *Qui Antii Civis,* iam legebatur *Quia ut baculus.*"

92. Ibid., p. 25/p. 8.

93. Ibid., pp. 25–26/p. 8, "Porro quod *Bibaculus* legitur in excusis exemplaribus, et fortassis etiam in nonnullis manuscriptis, doctis quibusdam debemus, qui cum viderent, *Qui aut baculus erat, et vocabatur paulominus,* nihil esse, seorsim fortassis coniecturam suam annotarunt, *baculum* in *Bibaculum* mutantes, hoc est, lignum sensu carens in dicacissimum poetam, et *aut* in *ait* vertentes, ac *paulominus* in *pantomimum* [sic]. Qua lectione recepta, necesse fuit *Erat et vocabatur* tertiae personae verba in primam commutare. Enumeravimus iam multos depravationis gradus."

94. Ibid., p. 26/p. 8: "Nec dubito quin multi meam hanc diligentiam quasi superstitiosam quandam anxietatem sint irrisuri, quod in literarum minutiis expendendis religiose verser. Sed quid facias? Video hoc negocium esse tale, ut qui id rite exequi velit, omnino

repuerascere ad tempus cogatur? Nec aliud in causa fuit, quantum ego iudico, quo minus feliciter quaedam Hermolaus restituerit, quam quod ad indices autorum aliquando recurrere maluit, quam in vestigiis veterum codicum diutius laborare. In hunc modem ex Aristotele, Aeliano, Theophrasto similibusque autoribus sensum nonnunquam verius restituit quam verba; tametsi mihi sensus non satis restitui videtur, nisi verbis recte castigatis. Equidem, meo iudicio, nuda emendatio, sed quae felix sit, multo plus prodest, quam prolixa dissertatio innumeris communita testimoniis, verum ad rem parum pertinens. Atque haec est Magia mea, qua tot egregia loca restitui in hoc autore. . . . Paulo copiosius autem nonnunquam coniecturas meas explicui, non ostentationis causa, sed ut alios ad idem agendum instruam animemque."

95. Ibid., pp. 39–40/p. 11, at the conclusion of the annotations to the *Praefatio:* "Vidisti hactenus, clarissime Lasce, quanta diligentia Plinianam Praefationem excusserimus, et quam fortassis non luserimus operam, tot locis restitutis, quae ante nos nemo quidem intelligebat; docti vero ita dissimulabant, ut vulgo nihil facilius existimaretur, quam hunc prologum enarrare, haesitare autem uspiam plusquam puerile. Nos rem secus habere docuimus. Nunc pro candore nostro loca quaedam in ipsis Naturalis historiae libris passim a nobis animadversa, proferre in medium libet, ut hoc quasi auctario Lascum nostrum ac studiosos omneis demereamur, et doctis viam indicemus quo pacto nobilissimus autor restitui possit. Id quod certe non est unius hominis opus, non tam ob voluminum immensitatem, quam quod Apollo non semper favet, immo plerunque quod quamlibet cogitando invenire non queas, alteri citra laborem etiam in mentem venit. Quemadmodum autem in libris Plinianis vaga lectione versati sumus, ita non continuas castigationes, sed intercisas et saltuatim annotatas proferemus."

96. *Amerbachkorrespondenz*, 3: 326–329.

97. Ibid., p. 326.

98. Ibid., p. 327 and n. 19. The passage discussed is quoted above in note 76.

99. See Nauert, *CTC*, p. 367. Beatus' letter is in *Briefwechsel*, no. 274.

100. I cite from *Naturalis Historia*, ed. L. Ian and C. Mayhoff, II: 153; for the translation I have followed Pliny, *Natural History*, trans. H. Rackham (Cambridge, Mass.: Harvard University Press, 1962), pp. 144–145.

101. *In C. Plinium*, pp. 67–68/pp. 17–18: "*Quanquam onerato capite vastis cornibus gladiorumque vaginis, in haec se librant, ut tormento aliquo*

rotati, in petris potissimam e monte aliquo in alium transilire cupientes, atque recursu pernici quo libuerit exultant.] Difficilis est hic locus, et dubio procul a nemine intellectus. Exemplar manuscriptum huiusmodi lectionem continet: *Quanquam onerato capite vastis cornibus gladiorumque vaginis in haec se librat ut tormento aliquo rotatus in petras potissimum et monte aliquo in alium transli* [*sic*] *quaerens atque recursu su pernicius quo libuit exultat.* Nodus vero omnis in his duobus vocabulis est *gladiorumque vaginis,* quidnam haec sibi velint. Nam alioqui vetus lectio cum vulgata consentit, nisi quod doctus quispiam in plurativum numerum mutavit quae illic in singulari ponuntur, nihilo melius quam *petras* in *petris,* et *recussu* in *recursu.* Christophorus Longolius huic loco manum admolitus, *in his se librant* legendum putavit, ut referatur ad vaginas gladiorum, quod esse debet, *in haec se librat,* quemadmodum vetus exemplar testatur; hoc est, germanam Plinii lectionem mutavit in adulterinam. Id quod necesse est illis accidere, qui duntaxat ex ingenio suo non inspectis antiquis voluminibus autores restituere conantur. Quibus si vel centies tentent, non semel res succedet. Tam fallax est quod absque veterum codicum praesidio tentatur, ceu iam saepenumero diximus. Quod si etiam *in iis se librant,* non *in haec se librat* legamus, id quod tamen faciendum non est, quid tum? An bene propterea habebit sententia? Minime sane. Quis interim docet quid sibi velint *gladiorum vaginae?* Mirabile vero animal quod gladiorum vaginis oneratum caput habet. Num in vaginis conditi sunt gladii, an vacuae vaginae sunt? Vastis certe cornibus, et alia quaedam animantia praedita reperiuntur: at monstro similis est, imo monstrum potius, belua gladiorum vaginas in capite circumferens. Enimvero video quid in vulgatis aeditionibus legatur, video etiam quid manuscriptus codex contineat. Non discedo libenter a lectione exemplaris vetusti, quantum fieri potest, quod clarum sit qualiter eruditorum temeritas Plinium nobis interpolarit: imo vulgatam lectionem adhibito iudicio potius castigandam censeo, si res patiatur, ad eam quae nobis vetus appellatur, quam e diverso veterem ad recentiorem. Itaque cum reliqua satis recte habeant, video nondum omnem, ut ante dixi, in his duabus dictionibus *gladiorumque vaginis* consistere, quarum utranque mendosissimam reor, qui putem a Plinio scriptum fuisse *lateque vagis,* quod vocabulum cum distantioribus syllabis exaratum esset, hoc forte pacto *la te que va gi s,* librarius aliquid deesse existimans, expletis per sinistram suam diligentiam lacunis, hoc est *g* litera addita, et *t* in *d* mutata (nam *glate* non placebat) et *orum* genitivi plurativi terminatione annexa, ac postremo *ni* syllaba introserta, in hunc tandem modum tam foede depravarit. Enimvero dum hunc locum curiosissime excuterem, cum quo, crede mihi, diutissime sum luctatus, visum est mihi legendum esse, *lateque vagis. Ibix in haec se rotat*. Nam coniicio *ibix* in *ivix*, primum eo quod *u* pro *b* usurpent librarii, mox in *ivis*, et postremo in *inis* facile mutari potuisse. Quae vox ad *vagis* addita, *vaginis* indubie constituit, quanquam etiam si non exprimatur ibix, subintelligitur tamen in hac oratione, *in haec se librat*, additum vero, sensum illustriorem reddit. Imo plane vaginas gladii consecuti sunt. Nam cum hoc erratum admissum esset, ut *vaginis* pro *vagis ibix* scriberetur, iam non quadrabat praecedens dictio *lateque*. Male enim sonabat in auribus librarii quamlibet crassis haec oratio, *lateque vaginis*. Quare cum vaginae fiant, ut in iis gladii condantur, vocabulum *lateque* mutavit in *gladiorumque*, pulchro futuro sensu, *gladiorumque vaginis*, ut stipiti illi videbatur. . . . Leges itaque, et distingues totum Plinii locum hoc modo: *Sunt ibices pernicitatis mirandae, quanquam onerato capite vastis cornibus lateque vagis. Ibix in haec se librat, ut tormento aliquo rotatus in petras, potissimum e monte aliquo in alium transilire quaerens atque recussu pernicius quo libuit exultat*. Sententia nunc est clarissima, quae hactenus obscurissima fuit. Restituimus praeterea e codice manuscripto *petras* ubi perperam in vulgatis aeditionibus *petris* legebatur, et *quaerens*, quod doctus quispiam in *cupientes* mutarat, non putans satis latine dici, *quaerens transilire*. Item *recussu pernicius quo libuit exultat* quod prius scriptum erat, *recursu pernici quo libuerit exultat*."

102. *In Omnes C. Plinii* (Paris, 1530), p. cxx.

103. *Briefwechsel*, p. 389.

104. Ibid., pp. 390–391.

105. Ibid., p. 391.

106. I cite from *Beati Rhenani Selestadiensis Rerum Germanicarum libri tres* (Basel, 1531, and Basel, 1551) pp. 27/25, 111/116, 112/117. At p. 111/116 Beatus corrected a passage from book XV, chap. 25 and commented, "Porro contuli in hoc capite vulgatam aeditionem cum manu descripto codice, mihique visus sum hanc e quibuscunque vestigiis et mendis eruisse lectionem."

107. Ibid., pp. 113–116/pp. 119–123, entitled *C. Plinii Secundi caput XIIII. Ex libro quarti repurgatum a mendis atque explicatum*. p. 114;120: "Hinc apparet illorum foeda hallucinatio Vandalos nobis ex Vvindis, hoc est Germanos ex Scalvinis Scythis facientium. Ita quibusdam non labor, non animus deest, sed iudicium."

108. Ibid., pp. 114–115/pp. 120–121.

109. Ibid., p. 116/p. 123. "Porro videre facile est, quantus labor sit emendare Plinium, et quam res necessaria, ut pessime de literis mereantur, qui hoc agenteis non solum rident, sed et conviciis proscindunt."

110. Index, no. 65.

111. *Briefwechsel*, nos. 444–445. Beatus offered a further annota-

tion to Pliny in his edition of Tertullian. For example, see *Adversus Marcionem*, I, 13, 5, at the words *Una tetraonis penula Opera Tertulliani*, p. 162/p. 92.

112. See below, chapter 4, for examples.

113. See Kenney, *The Classical Text*, pp. 26–27.

114. *In C. Plinium*, pp. 46–47/p. 13.

115. *In C. Plinium*, p. 51/p. 14: "Ego profero lectionem unius exemplaris Germanici, proferat alius lectionem Italici codicis, vel Hispanici, alius Gallici, alius Britannici, et polliceor futurum ut intra breve tempus Plinius in pristinam faciem restituatur. Nam nudis coniecturis hic nihil agitur quantumlibet ingeniosus sis, exemplaribus antiquis opus est. Excutiantur itaque bibliothecae. . . ."

116. Ibid., p. 86/p. 21: "Et solent manuscripta volumina, quemadmodum alibi quoque monui, non magnopere discrepare, erroribus depravati cuiuspiam forte fortuna codicis per descriptos libros veluti propagines quasdam ad nos usque traductis." Also pp. 73–74/p. 19.

117. See Petitmengin, "Beatus Rhenanus et les manuscrits latins," p. 242.

118. *Opera*, ed. I. Maier, pp. 253, 265, 271, 278.

119. *Miscellanea centuria prima*, pp. 23–24, 30, 36, 38, 50, 51, 65–73.

120. *Opera*, p. 271.

121. The passage from Beatus' *Annotationes* is quoted above in note 50. Barbaro did not annotate this reading.

122. *Sexti Pompei Festi De verborum significatu quae supersunt cum Pauli Epitome*, ed. Wallace M. Lindsay (Leipzig: Teubner, 1913), p. 131.

123. *Noni Marcelli Compendiosa doctrina*, ed. Lucian Mueller (Leipzig: Teubner, 1903), I: 202.

124. For Robortello, see *Francisci Robortelli Utinensis De arte sive ratione corrigendi antiquorum libros disputatio*, ed. and intro. G. Pompella (Naples: Loffredo, 1985), introduction, and Marsh McCall, "Robortello's 'Conjecture' at Aeschylus. *Supplices 337*," *The Classical Quarterly* 32 (1982): 228–230.

125. For Sigonio, see William McCuaig, "Sigonio and Grouchy: Roman Studies in the Sixteenth Century," *Athenaeum*, n.s. 64 (1986): 147–183.

126. Text available in Latin with Italian translation in Pompella edition, in note 124; it is summarized in Kenney, *The Classical Text*, pp. 29–36.

127. *De arte*, p. 40.

128. Ibid., p. 41.

129. Ibid., p. 43.

130. Ibid., p. 44.

131. Kenney, *The Classical Text,* p. 35.

132. See ibid., pp. 45–53, for examples.

133. Ibid., p. 53. Relatedly, see Luigia Ceretii, "Critica testuale a Terenzio in una lettera del Faerno a Paolo Manuzio," *Aevum* 28 (1954): 522–551.

134. For these men, see *Contemporaries,* 2: 105–108, and 1: 274–278.

135. *De arte,* p. 53. In the annotations that Robortello wrote to follow his text, he mentioned Beatus' collaborator, Sigismund Gelen. See *Lampas, sive Fax Artium Liberalium,* ed. J. Gruter (Frankfurt, 1604), 2: 118; the Latin text of the *De arte* is also included in the *Lampas.*

136. Ibid., pp. 16–17.

137. For Petit, see *Contemporaries,* 3: 71–72.

138. *In C. Plinium,* p. 51/p. 14.

139. For full title of the *Opera Tertulliani,* see Index, no. 52b. A new element in this edition was the *Loca quaedam ex utroque Testamento sparsim a Tertulliano diligentius accuratiusque excussa,* placed after the Index, at pp. b 4v–b 5v.

140. The dedicatory letter is *Briefwechsel,* no. 266, pp. 374–376.

141. *Briefwechsel,* p. 375.

142. *Opera Tertulliani* (1528), *Adversus Hermogenem,* prologue to the *Annotationes,* pp. 355–356.

143. See below, note 146. For Beatus' later use of the *De spectaculis,* see Pierre Fraenkel, "Une lettre oubliée de Beatus Rhenanus; Sa preface à la liturgie de S. Jean Chrysostome dediée à Johannes Hoffmeister 24 janvier 1540," *BHR* 48 (1986): 387–404, at p. 394. For Fabritius, see *Briefwechsel,* no. 202, p. 275, and *Contemporaries,* 2: 8–9. In the Pliny *Annotationes,* at p. 47/p. 13, Beatus mentioned other of Fabritius' manuscripts.

144. See Lehmann, *Iohannes Sichardus,* p. 151.

145. For Erasmus' edition of Irenaeus, see José Ruysschaert, "Le manuscript 'Romae descriptum' de l'édition érasmienne d'Irenée de Lyon," in *Scrinium erasmianum,* 1: 263–276.

146. *Opera Tertulliani* (1528), p. 403, *Adversus Valentinianos,* prologue to *Annotationes* (this was deleted in 1539 edition).

147. See *Opera Tertulliani* (1528), p. 545, *De fuga in persecutione,* for *ipsissima Tertulliani lectio.*

148. *Tertulliani Opera, Corpus Christianorum* (Turnholt: Brepols, 1954), pt. II, p. 1040.

149. *Opera Tertulliani* (1521), p. 415.

150. *Opera Tertulliani* (1528), pp. 450–451, in *De corona militis;* "Nec

dubito quosdam scripturas emigrare.] Mirum est quid sibi velit scripturas emigrare. Putavi legendum aliquando, *iuxta scripturas.* Deinde quum ea lectio non admodum arrideret, *scripturas* in *hypocritas* censui mutandum. Nunc video scarptas [sic] quoque legi posse. Videlicet ut eo in contemptores Paracleti Montanici et martyriorum quodammodo recusatores, ob ignaviam et timiditatem hoc convitium iaculetur, mulieres eos vocando. Nam scarptas [sic] ex autoritate Verrii docet Festus mulieres esse nugatorias ac despiciendas, ab iis quae screa iidem appellabant, id est, quae quis excreare solet, quatenus id faciendo se purgaret. Allegatur Titinnius. Verum codex Festi tam mendosus est, ut non libuerit ea verba ascribere. Nec ad rem multum pertinet. Eius vocabuli meminit et Marcellus Plautum in Aulularia citans. Porro virilis res est occumbere pro Christi religione, et cruciatus quos libet ferre. Semper fugere, timiditatem arguit. Adiuvat coniecturam nostram quod mox subiungit, *Novi,* inquit, *et pastores eorum in pace leones, in praelio cervos* [this is a sentence that follows in Tertullian's text]. Si quid divinare licet, notat Romanos qui novam prophetiam paracleti Montanici constantissime respuebant. Tametsi in libro contra Praxean parum abfuisse scribit, *quin Episcopus Romanus illam agnoverit.* Verum in hac re deceptus est hic bonus vir. Nomine pastorum intelligit Pontifices. Porro cogitare debemus Tertullianum omne genus veterum autorum excussisse, qui ipsius aetate extabant adhuc. Nunc quid nobis superest, nisi quod ex fragmentis Festi et Nonii Marcelli videre licet quantum amiserimus. Facile vero fieri potuit, ut scarptas [sic] vocabulum incognitum librarius mutaret in *scripturas.* Ego sane legere malim, ut ingenue fatear, *hypocritas* propter sensum: quod nesciam an scarptas [sic] etiam communi genere enunciarint veteres. Sed mirum est, *hypocritas,* vocem non ita raram (si modo ita legendum est) in scripturas a librario versam fuisse. Exemplar Hirsaugiense scripturas habet. Nec mutatus est in contextu locus, ut liberum lectori sit quidvis adhuc substituere, vel, quod consultius erit, in margine codicis ascribere. Quod utinam fuisset etiam in aliis autoribus observatum, in quibus multa perperam a doctis mutata sunt, quae tamen difficile est hodie deprehendere, quod inserta sint libris, non seorsim ascripta." This annotation is not in the 1539 edition, whose text, p. 518, reads, *Nec dubito quosdam scripturas emigrare,* without a sidenote. Perhaps the Gorze manuscript had this reading and Beatus accepted its authority as final.

151. *Sexti Pompei Festi De verborum significatu quae supersunt cum Pauli Epitome,* p. 448, and *Noni Marcelli Comendiosa doctrina,* p. 249. Beatus' copy of these texts (Sélestat 1038b), which is the Venice 1492 edition (Hain 11906), at p. xviii gives the correct spelling *scraptas* in

Nonnius, but Festus does not include it. Festus does have the following (fol. 21r): "Sartae nugatoriae ac despiciendae mulieres." It was
perhaps this reading that led Beatus to note the poor state of Festus.
In any case, Beatus must have had access to another manuscript copy
of Festus, and may have found *scraptas* there.

152. Continuing from note 150: "Caeterum, mi lector, quantus
labor est, imo quanta crux est autores depravatos restituere? Certe
praemio digni sunt qui in hanc rem insumunt operam, indigni vero
qui rideantur. Vides quomodo me torserim dum huic mendoso loco
succurrere nitor, nunc, *hypocritas,* legendum putans: nunc ex usu
priscorum petitum vocabulum substituens. Haec omnia frustra fuere.
Legendum enim est, id quod nunc postremo venit in mentem, *Nec
dubito quosdam in cryptas emigrare.* Loquitur autem de cryptis quae
Romae etiamnum visuntur, in quas persecutionis tempore Christiani
secedere solebant, taxans, ut ante dixi, Romanos, qui magis fugerent,
iuxta monitionem illam evangelicam Matthaei .X. quam intrepido
animo mortem pro Christi gloria subirent. Sane dicavit huic rei libellum, cui titulus, *De fuga in persecutione.* Scimus autem non con-
venisse Tertulliano cum ecclesia Romana propter Montani doctrinam,
ut supra quoque subindicavimus. κρύπτας Graeci vocant cameras et
testitudines subterraneas. Latini vero hoc vocabulum usu suum propemodum fecerunt, sicut et ὑπόγειον in eadem ferme significatione.
Quod autem addit de quaestionibus confessionum, intellige de profes-
sione nominis Christiani. Iam vide lector quam periculosum sit
mutare etiam mendosam lectionem. Si statim *scripturas* convertissem
in *hypocritas,* quae spes amplius fuisset deprehendendi *cryptas* esse legendum? Longe minor certe, propter prioris syllabae variationem."

153. Eduard Norden, *Die antike Kunstprosa vom VI. Jahrhundert v.
Chr. bis in die Zeit der Renaissance* (Leipzig, 1898), p. 615. See also Gosta
Saflund, *De Pallio und die stilistische Entwicklung Tertullians* (Lund:
Gleerup, 1955); Antonio V. Nazzaro, *Il 'De Pallio' di Tertulliano* (Naples: Editrice Intercontinentalia, 1972) and Dante Tringli, *O 'De
Pallio' de Tertuliano* (Sao Paulo: Universidade de Sao Paulo, 1980). In
his copy of the *editio princeps* Beatus had written in under the *vita* of
Tertullian: "Tertullianus est varius in phrasi. In disputationibus
dilucidior est ac simplicior. In locis communibus velut de pallio, de
cultu mulierum est durior et affectior." This was printed in the *vita* in
1528, p. BB4v.

154. *Opera Tertulliani* (1521), p. 528, *argumentum* to *De pallio,* "Hic
liber tam est corruptus, ut nulla propemodum sententia citra offen-
sam legi queat. Nec quisquam credet hic aliquid a nobis restitutum,
nisi qui Hirsaugiensem codicem inspexerit. Ineptum autem censui-

mus, marginem chartarum coniecturis opplere, in quibus plerumque
nihil est certitudinis. Consulantur antiqua exemplaria, quae scimus
extare Romae, Fuldae et Gorziae, prope Mentensem urbem. Mal-
uissem illorum sequi consilium, qui suam lectionem seorsim annotant,
sed non vacabat."

155. *Opera Tertulliani* (1528), *argumentum* to *De pallio*, replacing section quoted in note 154: ". . . Hic liber valde corruptus est propter
phrasim affectatam. Apposuimus nos lectionem alteram per coniecturas alicubi mutatam, in hoc maxime quo doctos extimularemus ad
subveniendum huic opusculo. Manebit interim vetus ille contextus,
qui, tametsi depravatus, non est tamen abiiciendus propter ansam
quam coniecturis praebet. Nec displicet hoc consilium in autoribus
mendosis, ut sic seorsim lectio mutata apponatur. Arbitror autem nos
tantum effecisse, ut quanquam non adamussim omnia restituerimus,
possit tamen nunc intelligi, quid hoc libro Tertullianus agere voluerit.
Tantum momenti nonnunquam habet commoda distinctio."

156. In the 1528 edition of the *Opera Tertulliani*, Beatus supplied
only one annotation to this passage, p. 605: "*De ovilibus dico Milesiis et
Seligicis.*] Selga Pisidarum urbs est, qui Lyciae Ciciliaeque contermini
sunt. Aliqui libenter legissem Belgicis."

157. For the modern versions I have used *Tertulliani Opera*, pt. II,
p. 740. English translation from *The Ante-Nicene Fathers* (rpt.: Grand
Rapids, Mich.: Eerdmans, 1982), 4: 8. *Opera Tertulliani* (1521), p. 532;
(1528), p. 614; (1539), p. 684.

158. See the edition and commentary by Alois Gerlo of *De pallio*
(Wetteren: De Meester, 1940), p. 10, and Kroymann, *Opera*, p. XVIII,
fn. 2.

159. *Briefwechsel*, p. 288.

160. *Opera Tertulliani* (1528) pp. AA 2–AA 6r. This section reads:
"Subiunximus hic Annotationes in librum de patientia quem paulo
festinantius transcurreramus, et in caeteros item libros sed breviores
et intercisas, neque enim commentarium scribere noluimus."

161. Ibid., p. AA 4r.

162. See D'Amico, "The Progress of Renaissance Latin Prose: The
Case of Apuleianism."

163. *Opera Tertulliani* (1528), p. AA 5v.

164. Ibid., p. AA 4r.

165. See below, chapter 4.

166. *Opera Tertulliani* (1528), fol. AA 5v: ". . . Indicavimus nos in
scholiis nostris coniecturam fortassis nimium coactam. Sed tamen
noluimus caelare studiosos quid nobis legendum videretur. Coniectura nostra eiusmodi fuit, legi videlicet posse. . . ." Cf. ibid., p. 408.

167. Occasionally Beatus discussed contemporary matters in these notes. For example, at ibid., p. AA 4v, he complained of a grocer-preacher and Anabaptists in the area around Strasbourg and urged the civil authorities to maintain order.

4: THE MATURE CRITIC

1. See the excellent article by James M. Weiss, "The Technique of Faint Praise: Johann Sturm's 'Life of Beatus Rhenanus,'" *BHR* 43 (1981): 290–302; see also Hans Kaiser, "Aus den letzten Jahren des Beatus Rhenanus," *Zeitschrift für die Geschichte des Oberrheins*, N.F. 31 (1916): 30–52, and Beat von Scarpatetti, "Beatus Rhenanus, historien de la paix," *ASABHS* 35 (1985): 253–260.

2. See Adolphe Koch, "Les lettres de noblesse et les armoiries de Beatus Rhenanus," *ASABHS* 35 (1985): 73–84.

3. See Index, no. 62, for Origen, and Max Schär, *Das Nachleben des Origenes im Zeitalter des Humanismus* (Basel/Stuttgart: Helbing & Lichtenhahn, 1979), pp. 295–296. Beatus also supervised editions of John Chrysostom's *Missa;* see Index no. 6, and Andre Jacob, "L'édition 'érasmienne' de la liturgie de Saint Jean Chrysostome et ses sources," *IMU* 19 (1796): 291–324. Among Beatus' enterprises were the editions of *Catalogus Erasmi*, Index, no. 64, and *Opera Erasmi*, Index, no. 67. See Albert Hyma, *The Youth of Erasmus* (Ann Arbor: University of Michigan Press, 1930), pp. 239–331, for Beatus' edition of the *Antibarbari.*

4. *Opera L. Annaei Senecae* (Basel 1529); see Index, no. 30, for details. I am especially dependent on François Spaltenstein and Pierre Petitmengin, "Beatus Rhenanus éditeur de l'*Apocoloquintose* et le *Codex Wissenburgensis*," *Revue d'histoire des textes*, 9 (1979): 315–327.

5. *Opera Senecae*, p. 677. Erasmus also did this in issuing a new edition of Seneca's *Opera* in 1529; see *EE*, vol. 8, no. 2091, introduction.

6. Ibid., p. 677 and p. 684.

7. Ibid., pp. 678, 679, and 683.

8. Ibid., p. 679: "*Eius princeps non tulisset.*]" See also Remigio Sabbadini, "Il testo interpolato del *Ludus* di Seneca," *Rivista di filologia e di istruzione classica* 47 (1919): 338–347, at p. 345.

9. Spaltenstein and Petitmengin, "Beatus Rhenanus éditeur," p. 317.

10. Index, no. 58, and Horawitz, "Des Beatus Rhenanus literarische Thätigkeit in den Jahren 1530–1547," pp. 323–325.

11. *Briefwechsel,* no. 282, p. 404. For Herwagen, see *Contemporaries,* 2: 186–187.

12. See below, chapter 6.

13. Index, no. 60. See also Peter Shaeffer, "Beatus Rhenanus als Tacitus-Rezipient," *ASABHS* 35 (1985): 149–156. Beatus dedicated the edition to Cardinal Bernhard of Cles; see Luigi Bressan, "Beatus Rhenanus et le cardinal Bernardo Clesio," *ASABHS* 85 (1985): 51–61. Robert Walter has announced an article, "Rhenanus et Tacite," to appear in the *Revue des études latines* for 1986.

14. See, in general, Paul Joachimsen, "Tacitus im deutschen Humanismus," in his *Gesammelte Aufsätze* (Aalen: Scientia Verl., 1970), pp. 275–295; Clarence W. Mendell, *Tacitus: The Man and his Work* (New Haven, Conn.: Yale University Press, 1957), pt. II; Kenneth C. Schellhase, *Tacitus in Renaissance Political Thought* (Chicago, Ill.: University of Chicago Press, 1976); and Jacques Ridé, *L'Image du Germain dans la pensée et la littérature allemandes de la redécouverte de Tacite à la fin du XVIème siècle,* 3 vols. (Lille: Université de Lille, 1977), Vol. I.

15. See Revilo P. Oliver, "The First Medicean MS of Tacitus and the Titulature of Ancient Books," *Transactions of the American Philological Association* 82 (1951): 232–261, and *Texts and Transmission,* pp. 406–411.

16. I cite from *P. Cornelii Taciti Equitis Romani Annalium ab excessu Augusti sicut ipse vocat, sive Historiae Augustae.* . . . (Basel, 1533) p. 125 and (Basel 1544), p. 125 (in most cases the paginations in both editions are identical; only when they differ will two numbers be provided in these notes).

17. See Revilo P. Oliver, "The Second Medicean Ms. and the Text of Tacitus," *Illinois Classical Studies* I (1976): 190–225.

18. For the minor works, see Francesco della Corte, "La scoperta del Tacito minore," in *La fortuna di Tacito dal sec. XV ad oggi,* ed. Franco Gori and Cesare Questa, *Studi urbinati di storia, filosofia e letteratura* 53 (1979): 13–45. Beatus owned a copy of the 1497 Venice version of Puteolanus' edition (Hain *15222); see Walter, *Catalogue général,* p. 163.

19. Beroaldo's letter is quoted in *P. Cornelii Taciti Annalium,* pp. 5v–6r.

20. Alciati's *annotationes* are in ibid., pp. 492–[504].

21. Rodney Potter Robinson, *The Germania of Tacitus: A Critical Edition* (Middletown, Conn.: American Philological Association, 1935), p. 330. For the history of the *Germania,* see Ludwig Krapf, *Germanenmythus und Reichsideologie: Frühhumanistische Rezeptionsweisen der taciteischen Germania* (Tubingen: Niemeyer, 1979).

22. *Schardius Redivivus sive Rerum Germanicarum Scriptores Varii* (Giessen, 1673), I: 70–76: "Commentariolus doctissimi viri Henrici Glareani in P. Cornelii Taciti, *De moribus et populis Germaniae libellum* . . ." Glareanus worked for Froben during Beatus' tenure, see *Contemporaries*, 2: 105–108.

23. Ier. Ioc. Oberlinus, "Praefatio" in *Cornelii Taciti Opera* (Leipzig, 1801), 1: xiii–xx; Walter Allen, Jr., "The Yale Manuscript of Tacitus (Codex Budensis Rhenani). Its History and Affiliations" (Ph.D. Thesis, Yale University, 1936); idem, "The Yale Manuscript of Tacitus (Codex Budensis Rhenani)," *The Yale University Library Gazette* 2 (1937), 2: 81–86, where the title page is reproduced; idem, "Beatus Rhenanus editor of Tacitus and Livy," *Speculum* 22 (1937): 382–385; idem, "Tacitus, Histories IV, 46–53," *Yale Classical Studies* 6 (1939): 31–38; C. W. Mendell, "Manuscripts of Tacitus XI–XXI," ibid., pp. 39–70, at pp. 68–69; Else Lilly Etter, *Tacitus in der Geistesgeschichte des 16. und 17. Jahrhunderts* (Basel/Stuttgart: 1966), pp. 28–30; *Bibliotheca Corviniana. The Library of King Matthias Corvinus of Hungary*, intro. and comm. Csaba Csapodi and Klara Csapodi-Gardonyi (New York: Praeger, 1969), p. 61, and pl. XLIX, where the first page of the manuscript is reproduced; and *Catalogue of Medieval and Renaissance Manuscripts in the Beinecke Rare Book and Manuscript Library. Yale University*, vol. 1, ed. Barbara A. Shailor (Binghamton, N.Y.: Medieval and Renaissance Texts and Studies, 1984), Ms. no. 145, pp. 194–196. Relatedly, see José Ruysschaert, *Juste Lipse et les Annales de Tacite: Une méthode de critique textuelle au XVIe siècle* (Louvain: Bibliothèque de l'Université, 1949), index. I cite from *Cornelius Tacitus exacta cura recognitus, et emendatus,* Venice 1534, and from the Basel 1544 reedition.

24. The first page of the manuscript has the following notes: "Ex dono Iacobi Spiegelli Iureconsulti. An. Salut. M. D. XVIII." and "Hic liber sumptus est ex bibliotheca Budensi, iussu inpensaque Matthiae Corvini Hungariae Boehmiaeque regis scriptus." See reproduction in Allen, "The Yale Manuscript" (1937). In the *Castigationes,* p. 129, Beatus also described the manuscript. See also Hans Ankwicz-Kleehoven, *Der Wiener Humanist Johannes Cuspinian* (Graz/Cologne: Bohlau, 1959), pp. 114–115, fn. 17.

25. Thomas Burger, *Jacob Spiegel: Ein humanistischer Jurist des 16. Jahrhunderts* (Augsburg: Werner Blasaditsch, 1973); Peter Schäffer, "Zur Menschlichkeit der Humanisten: Das Buch *De Immanitate* Joviano Pontanos mit den Scholien Jakob Spiegels," *ASABHS* 28 (1978): 17–24; Karl Heinz Burmeister, "Die Bibliothek des Jakob Spiegel," in *Das Verhältnis der Humanisten zum Buch,* ed. Fritz Krafft and Dieter Wuttke (Boppard: Boldt, 1977); and Steven Rowan and Gerhild

Scholz Williams, "Jacob Spiegel on Gianfrancesco Pico and Reuchlin: Poetry, Scholarship and Politics in Germany in 1512," *BHR* 44 (1982): 291–295.

26. For the library of Matthias Corvinus see *Bibliotheca Corviniana,* introductory essay.

27. Allen, "The Yale Manuscript" (1936), chap. II; for *Budensis 9,* see *Bibliotheca Corvinana,* p. 41, and Ilona Berkovits, *Illuminated Manuscripts from the Library of Matthias Corvinus* (Budapest: Corvina, 1964), pp. 38–40.

28. Allen, "The Yale Manuscript" (1936), p. 21, discusses the evidence that the manuscript was travelling by 1534.

29. Ibid., chap. III, discusses the manuscript's affiliations.

30. *Briefwechsel,* no. 288, pp. 411–414. See also Luigi Bressan, "Beatus Rhenanus et le cardinal Bernard Clesio," *ASABHS* 35 (1985): 51–61, and *Contemporaries,* 1: 313–315.

31. *Briefwechsel,* no. 288, p. 414.

32. Letter in *P. Cornelii Taciti. . . . Annalium* pp. 129–130.

33. Ibid., p. 129: "In hoc tamen fortunatior videtur, quod primum in manus certe eruditissimorum hominum venit, qui magna religione aeditionem castigare et adiuvare conati sunt. Post quorum laborem quid nos huic autori contulerimis, indicabunt sequentia. Caeterum communis est haec veterum scriptorum omnium infelicitas, quod errata nemo facile sentit, nisi qui confert, aut exactius singula rimatur."

34. Ibid., p. 129. For Livy, see below, note 48. The Ciceronian example is from *De senectute,* 20, *Proveniebant oratores, novi, stulti adulescentuli,* which Beatus changed to *proveniebantur ad res, novi, stulti, adulescentuli,* arguing that the reference was to those unable to aid the *res publica.* Modern reading is *proveniebant oratores, novi, stulti adulescentuli.*

35. Ibid., p. 130: "Porro nemo putet me tam mutandi avidum, ut quicquam citra autoritatem manuscripti codicis vel addiderim vel dempserim. Nec quoties occurret, sic scripsi, castigavi, reposui, suspicetur quisquam id ex meo tantum factum ingenio. Nam quum meum secutus iudicium aliquid muto, quod tamen, nisi in manifestis erratis, non feci, lectorem ea de re in castigationibus admoneo."

36. See Oliver, "The First Medicean MS," and B. Baldwin, "Herodotus and Tacitus: Two Notes on Ancient Book Titles," *Quaderni urbanisti di cultura classica* 16 (1984): 31–34.

37. *P. Cornelii Taciti . . . Annalium,* pp. aa 3v–aa 4v; section is entitled "Annalium inscriptionis reddita ratio."

38. See ibid., p. 4r.

39. Ibid., p. aa 4v. See also B. Baldwin, "Herodotus and Tacitus:

Two Names on Ancient Book Titles," *Quaderni urbinati di cultura classica* 16 (1984): 31–34.

40. Ibid., p. aa 4v.

41. Ibid., p. aa 4v. See below, chapter 6, for Beatus' negative view of monks.

42. Ruysschaert, *Juste Lipse*, index.

43. *Briefwechsel*, p. 414.

44. *P. Cornelii, Taciti . . . Annalium*, pp. 421, 422, 424, 426, 430, 439. Robinson, *The Germania*, p. 331, identifies this edition with the 1473 edition from Nuremberg.

45. For Artolf, see *Briefwechsel*, p. 213, n. 4, and *Contemporaries*, Vol. I, pp. 73–74.

46. *Annotatiunculae* are mentioned at pp. 426 and 427.

47. *P. Cornelii Taciti . . . Annalium*, pp. aa 5r–ff 4v.

48. See the changes Beatus made to the *Thesaurus locutionum*, pp. dd 4r–5v, at the words *More gentico, pro more gentili*, when in 1533 he wrote of the word *genticus:* "Quam vocem [gentilis] sciolus aliquis emendare volens vertit in *gentico*. Hoc vocabulum corruptum quum adhuc in memoria haberet librarius, ausus est libro quinto pro *more gentis* supponere *more gentico*. Atque haec est mea coniectura. Nam hic loquendi modus magis Sidonium ac Fulgentium, linguae latinae corruptores, decuerit meo iudicio quam Tacitum. Et erat olim monachis creber in manibus Sidonius, cum quia Christianus, tum quia rithmicae compositionis optimus magister. Idem sentimus de *sonore*. Quippe librariis olim mira licentia fuit sive potius libido priscas nonnunquam voces infulciendi, quale potest esse *apisci* pro *adipisci*. Sane ego reor Tacitum *adipisci* scripsisse. Neque enim historico remota ab usu vocabula conveniunt. Et adhuc satis purum fuit Taciti seculum. Livius libro octavo Dec. quartus. *A pueris ii more quodam gentis* etc." In his own copy of the 1533 edition (Sélestat 1130), Beatus wrote in the margin (p. dd 5v) "Sonor est vocabulum Lucretianum," and on pp. cc 3v–4r, he produced a whole note on *Sonore pro sano* based on Lucretius, which, however, is not in the 1544 edition. Instead, in 1544 (p. dd 4v), Beatus produced a new note that he first wrote in part in the margin of the 1533 edition. This new note supplies further examples of the use of the word by Tacitus and a reference to the word in Ammianus Marcellinus and concludes: "Porro suspicor *genticum* pro *gentili* militaris esse vulgi vocabulum." Obviously, as Beatus came to appreciate the development of the Latin language in late antiquity, he had to revise his view of scribal errors and the "purity" of Tacitus' and other writers' language. For the appreciation of vulgar and archaic Latin

writers in the Renaissance, see D'Amico, "The Progress of Renaissance Latin Prose."

49. Ibid., p. 147, *Annales* 12, 18: "*Romanorum nemo eius autoritatis aderat.*] Miror quid ei venerit in mentem, qui in aeditione Romana aut Basiliensi locum hunc adulteravit, pro *id autoritatis* scribere *eius autoritatis.*" Modern reading: *Romanorum nemo id auctoritatis aderat.* Also pp. 260–261.

50. Ibid., p. 130: "Sane multum debemus Bernardino Lanterio Mediolanensi, atque Francisco Puteolano, et aliis, quibus ante illos hunc autorem pro virili restituere studio fuit." On pp. 127–128 Beatus published Puteolanus' letter to Jacobus Antiquarius.

51. Ibid., pp. 147, 148, 173, 263, 371.

52. Ibid., pp. 371, 372.

53. Ibid., p. 297: "... quum mea sit inventio. Mutet, qui velit."

54. Ibid., p. 125: "Haec non in hoc proferimus, ut quisquam libro suo statim illinat; quum sit mera coniectura e vestigiis depravatae scripturae sumpta, sed ne quis putet me quaerendi laborem subterfugisse."

55. Ruysschaert, *Juste Lipse,* p. 21, and Pierre Petitmengin, "Beatus Rhenanus et les manuscrits latines," *ASABHS* 35 (1985): 235–246, at pp. 242–245.

56. Cf. Kenney, *The Classical Text,* pp. 26–27.

57. See C. O. Brink, "Justus Lipsius and the Text of Tacitus," *Journal of Roman Studies* 41 (1951): 32–51; *P. Cornelii Taciti ... Annalium* p. 6; there is no annotation to this passage.

58. Ibid., pp. 172, 302, 303, 375.

59. Ibid., pp. 194, 219.

60. Ibid., p. 296.

61. Ibid., pp. 218, 219, 222, 265, 338.

62. Ibid., pp. 194, 218, 296, 341, 372, 373.

63. For example, ibid. p. 236. See above, note 48.

64. Ibid., p. 173.

65. Ibid., pp. 130, 265.

66. See Ruysschaert, *Juste Lipse,* p. 21, n. 3, and C. O. Brink, "Justus Lipsius and the Text of Tacitus," p. 35. Also *C. Cornelii Taciti Opera....* (Paris, 1599), pp. 156, 410, 431–432, 434, 446, 461–462, 463, 481, 483, 495, 514, 517, 523, 525, 532.

67. *Taciti Opera,* Oberlin edition (1801), I: xlvi.

68. See *The Annales of Tacitus,* ed. F. R. D. Goodyear (Cambridge: Cambridge University Press, 1981), pp. 164 and 260, for evaluations of two emendations.

69. *The Annales of Tacitus: Books 1–6*, ed. and comm. F. R. D. Goodyear (Cambridge: University Press, 1972), 1: 6–7.

70. Ibid., p. 469.

71. *P. Cornelii Taciti . . . Annalium* pp. 445–446.

72. See *P. Cornelii Taciti . . . Annalium*, p. 421.

73. See *Commentariolus*, pp. 54 and 55, 70, 72, for Alciati.

74. Rodney Potter Robinson, *The Germania of Tacitus: A Critical Edition* (Middletown, Conn.: American Philological Association, 1935), p. 331.

75. *P. Corneli Taciti . . . Annalium*, p. 428.

76. Ibid., p. 431.

77. Ibid., p. 194, at *Annales*, nos. 13, 14.

78. Ibid., p. 428.

79. Ibid., pp. 428–429.

80. Ibid., p. 424: "Ac videmus Italos, Hispanos, ac etiam hodie Gallos in alienis terris commode habere, nostrateis contra ad omnem plerunque externi coeli affatum languescere."

81. Ibid., p. 426; passage translated in Schellhase, *Tacitus*, p. 63. It seems that Beatus continued to make some changes to the text. At 29.3, *Eos qui decumates agros exercent*, the annotation in the 1544 edition (pp. 428–429) differs from the 1533 edition and the version that accompanies the 1610 edition of the *Rerum Germanicarum libri tres*, p. 396.

82. See Ruysschaert, *Juste Lipse*, and Brinck, "Justus Lipsius."

83. *T. Livii Patavini Latinae Historiae Principis Decades tres cum dimidia*, see Index, no. 6. I cite from the 1535 edition with the text of Livy published by Froben. The *Annotationes* were also issued separately by Froben in 1537. For Livy, see above, note 48.

84. For background, see A. H. McDonald, "Livius, Titus," in *CTC* 2 (1971): 331–348, and B. Doer, "Livy and the Germans" in *Livy*, ed. T. A. Dorey (London: Routledge and Kegan Paul, 1971), pp. 97–176. For the early history of Livy among the humanists, see Giuseppe Billanovich, *La tradizione del testo di Livio e le origini dell'umanesimo*, vol. 1 (Padua: Antenore, 1981), and the other articles by Billanovich cited below; Albinia de la Mare, "Florentine Manuscripts of Livy in the Fifteenth Century," in *Livy*, pp. 17–199; and *Texts and Transmission*, pp. 205–214. See G. Billanovich, "Petrarch and the Textual Tradition of Livy," *JWCI* 14 (1951): 137–208.

85. See above, chapter 1.

86. See Bussi, *Prefazioni*, pp. 29–34.

87. See introductory letter in *T. Livii Patavini Historiarum*, ed. Arnold Drakenborch (rpt.: Stuttgart, 1828), 14: 493–494.

88. *CTC*, p. 378, and Drakenborch, pp. 494–495.

89. Drakenborch, p. 494.

90. Ibid., pp. 496–502.

91. Ibid., pp. 512–516. For Carbach, see *Contemporaries*, 1: 266.

92. Drakenborch, p. 516.

93. Ibid., pp. 503–513.

94. Ibid., pp. 517–518; see *Contemporaries*, 3: 262–263.

95. Drakenborch, pp. 518–519; see *Contemporaries*, 1: 290.

96. Drakenborch., p. 520.

97. Ibid., pp. 523–524, and *CTC*, p. 337. For Grynaeus, see *Contemporaries*, 2: 142–146.

98. *EE* 9, no. 2435, 143–145.

99. See Horawitz, "Des Beatus Rhenanus literarische Thätigkeit," pp. 268–269, and *Tite-Live Histoire Romaine*, ed. J. Bayet (Paris: Les Belles Lettres, 1967), I: lxxxviii–xc.

100. *T. Livii Patavini*, pp. 6 and 28. See also the letter to Westerman, in *Briefwechsel*, no. 268, pp. 377–378.

101. *T. Livii Patavini*, p. 33: "In fragmenta libri sexti Tertiae Decades Annotationes. Quod nos nacti fuimus a Spira Livianum exemplar, ex fragmentis vetustissimorum codicum saltuatim descriptum videbatur, praesertim in hoc libro sexto tertiae Decadis. Nam initium voluminis fecerat librarius a particula, quam nos vix tandem in medio libro reperimus, abruptis verbis. Cum ea cohaerebat aliquot paginis intermediis omissis, libri finis. Deinde quum septimum librum conferre coepissemus, iterum particulam invenimus quae ad sextum librum pertinebat. Vide miram confusionem. Nos in hiis annotationibus excusorum codicum ordinem sequimus." See also S. K. Johnson, "A Text of the Spirensian Sources of Livy's Text to Books XXVI–XXX," *Classical Philology* 37 (1933): 195–199, and *Titi Livi Ab Urbe Condita*, Vol. IV, Libri XXVI–XXX, ed. R. S. Conway and S. K. Johnson (Oxford: Clarendon, 1934), pp. xix–xx; G. Billanovich, "Petrarch and the Textual Tradition of Livy," *JWCI* 14 (1951): 137–208, at pp. 180–184; idem, "Dal Livio di Raterio (Laur. 63, 19) al Livio del Petrarca (B.M., Harl. 2493)," *IMU* 2 (1959): 103–178, at pp. 169–174.

102. See Wilhelm Weissenborn, "De ratione, qua Sigismundus Gelenius quartam T. Livii decadem emendaverit," in *Commentationes philologae in honorem Theodori Mommseni* (Berlin, 1877), pp. 302–20; August Luchs, *De Sigismundi Gelenii codice Liviano Spirensi commentatio* (Erlang, 1890); A. Souter, "The Gelenian Codices of Livy," *Classical Review* 38 (1923): 115; Alois Schmanns "Sigismundus Gelenius und sein Lexikon Symphonum, 1537," in *Festschrift für Max Vasmer* (Wiesbaden: Harrassowitz, 1956), pp. 434–443; Pasquali, *Storia della tradi-*

zione, index; Nauert in *CTC,* 4: 386–390; Renato Uglione, "A proposito dell'edizione geliana del 'De Monogamia' di Tertulliano," *Giornale italiano di filologia,* n.s. 11 (1980): 83–94, and *Contemporaries,* 2: 84–85.

103. *T. Livii Patavini. . . ,* pp. 53–54.

104. Ibid., p. 60.

105. Ibid., p. 53.

106. Ibid., p. 63, XL, 39, 9: "*Cum vim dedistis venisset admonens.*] In archetypo est, *cum bis deditis rem esse admonens.* Id qui legere non potuit, ob characterum formas ut opinor nostro seculo ignorantes, male divinando sensum vitiavit, atque idem fere ex eadem causa in caeteris accidit, quae deinceps usque ad finem libri indicabuntur." Modern reading is *cum bis deditis rem esse admonens.*

107. See below, chapter 6.

108. *Briefwechsel,* p. 445. See also *EE,* vol. 6, introduction to letter no. 1544, p. 17.

109. *T. Livii Patavini,* p. 5. See also Drakenborch, XV: 525–526, at p. 525.

110. *T. Livii Patavini,* p. 5, and Drakenborch, pp. 525–526. See also *ibid.,* p. 68,

111. Paul Lehmann, "Die mittelalterliche Dombibliothek zu Speyer," in his *Erforschung des Mittelalters* (Stuttgart: Hiersemann, 1959), 2: 186–228, at pp. 193–194, 205, 206.

112. For these editions, see McDonald in *CTC.* Also see *T. Livii Patavini,* p. 37: "Demiror Venetos et Colonienses non dignatos inspicere aeditionem Romanam. . . ." See also the discussion in *T. Livi Ab Urbe Condita libri a vicesimo sexto ad tricesimum,* ed. August Luchs (Berlin, 1879), pp. viii–xi, where Beatus' use of his manuscript is analyzed.

113. Ibid., p. 43, at 28. 17. 12.

114. Allen, "Beatus Rhenanus, Editor of Tacitus and Livy," discusses this.

115. *T. Livii Patavini,* p. 28. See also *Titi Livi Ab urbe condita,* ed. C. F. Walters and R. S. Conway (Oxford, Clarendon, 1919), II: xii–xv.

116. Ibid., p. 22, IV. 15. 6.

117. Ibid., p. 18: "Hunc locum sciolus quispiam pro libidine sua tractavit."

118. Ibid., p. 27: "Conjecturas quibus adducor ut librarium hallucinatum putem, dum maiusculas literas vetustissimorum exemplarium partim non agnoscit, partim agnitas perperam connectit, referre piget."

119. Ibid., pp. 16 and 18.

120. Ibid., p. 41.

121. Ibid., p. 39: "Id postea castigator non consyderans, sed alio properans ac nimium fidens ingenio suo, vertit in sententiis. Sic accrescunt in monumentis autorum mendae. Facilius autem sit ex primis librariorum erratis sinceram lectionem reperire, quam ex posterioribus nonnunquam eruditorum castigationibus." See also p. 21, for Beatus linking scribes' and learned men's errors.

122. Ibid., pp. 1, 9, and 43.

123. Ibid., p. 12, at II, 23, 4: "*Ad hoc prolixa barba.*] O factum flagris dignum. . . . amusus aliquis erasa dictione *promissa,* supposuit *prolixa.*" Modern reading is *ad hoc promissa barba.*

124. Ibid., p. 42, at XXVIII, 1, 1: "*Quum transitu Hasdrubalis quantum in Italia declinaverat belli.*]. . . . Cupiam hic audire professores hunc locum exponentes. Mihi libet cogitare in verbo *declinaverat,* ingens esse mendum. Habet et vetus volumen depravatam lectionem, nempe, *inclaverat* sive *indaverat,* adeo sunt ambiguae literae. Ego vero scribendum arbitror, *inundaverat,* quod verbum hic mire quadrat. Franciscus Petrarcha aut Victorinus Feltrensis pro illo *indaverat,* fortassis primum substituit, *declinaverat.* Id postea Laurentium quoque Vallam virum in literis prorsus incomparabilem fallere potuit. Nam aiunt hunc in restituendo Livio multum operae sumpsisse. Porro libet hoc erratum propemodum alicui monacho tribuere, qui pro *indaverat* supposuerit hic *declinaverat,* quod *transitum* acciperet pro *interitu.* Nam Christiana pietas transitum divorum vocat, mortem intelligens. Huic mendoso loco mederi conatus est doctus aliquis in aeditione Eucharii Cervicorni scribens, *quantum in Italiam declinaverat belli.*" Beatus made another negative statement about Petrarch and other Italian commentators at book XXVIII, 2, 16, pp. 42–43; Beatus' emendation has not been accepted.

125. For Beroaldo the Elder, see above, chapter 1.

126. *T. Livii Patavini,* p. 12: "Demiror quomodo se hinc explicent professores, qui in publicis auditoriis Livium enarrant. Et vix est autor in scholis tritior. Quid hic afferebat ille professorum Achilles Philippus Beroaldus, qui toties privatim et publice Livianas Decades Bononiae praelegit?"

127. Ibid., p. 43: "Sed nemo vult laborare. Quicquid in mentem primum venit, id infulcimus. Deinde nisi manifestus sit soloecismus huiusmodi lectionem omnes sequuntur. Sic legit Beroaldus, inquiunt, sic Sabellicus, sic Baptista Pius. Et quis amplius dubitat? Equidem fuerunt viri celebres et literati, sed qui mallent omnia interpretari quam intelligere. Fidebant ingenio suo, fidebant eruditioni. Nec putabant opus esse scripta consulere exemplaria. Id quod rarenter admodum faciebant. Quin erant contenti autoritate et opinione nomi-

nis, quam apud omnes sibi pepererant, ut iam propemodum sufficeret illud αὐτὸς ἔφα. At alia res est castigare veterum autorum libros. Eget enim non solum eruditione, sed et pertinaci studio, labore et diligentia, ac cum primis acri iudicio."

128. Ibid., p. 18.

129. Ibid., p. 44, XXVIII, 8, 11: "*Ipse ab Oenotriis praeter terram Atticam super sinum navigans inter medias prope hostium classes Chalcidem pervenit.*] Quomodo in Italia subito Philippus ex Corintho? Nam Oenotria est [in] Italia. Videtur mihi plane quispiam lectores ludere voluisse. Sed mirum est hactenus hoc a nemine perceptum. Oportet hic ingenue dicere quod verissimum est, nimia securitate fidunt studiosi quibusdam typographicis officinis, ut in Italia Asulanicae, quasi vero castigatissima sint omnia quae ex illis prodeunt. Quibus hactenus credendum erat, ut rem iudicio prius et collatione exploraremus. Interim studiosi meritas suae credulitatis poenas saepe luunt. . . ." Modern reading is *ipse ab Cencheis praeter terram Atticam super Sunium navigans inter medias prope hostium classes.*

130. Ibid., p. 47: "Fide mihi lector hic non te decipiam." And p. 11: "Tu tamen meum sequutus consilium, scribe. . . ."; and p. 57.

131. Ibid., p. 6: ". . . recentior manus scripserat in codice Vormaciensi. . . "

132. Ibid., p. 12, p. 22: ". . . satis indicat marginaria adnotatiuncula in codice Borbetomagensi," and p. 25: "Istam lectionem in margine annotatam reperio."

133. Ibid., p. 23: "Verum extremae duae literae in erasae scripturae locum suppositae videntur."

134. Ibid., p. 36: "Hic unam paginam transilire coacti fuimus ob defectum qui erat in exemplari manu scripto, quod ex Spirensi bibliotheca nacti fueramus."

135. Ibid., pp. 39 and 40.

136. Ibid., p. 13, at II, 30, 5: "*Ut imperium suo vehemens mansueto permitteretur ingenio.*] Hic nodus est superiore intricatior. Mirum est cur huiusmodi loca non notentur astericis. Nam verba ista nullo sensu dicuntur. Et nescio an seculo nostro quisquam hanc Livianam sententiam intellexerit. O securitatem lectorum, o nimiam securitatem enarrantium!" Modern reading is *ut imperium sua vi vehemens, mansueto permitteretur ingenio.*

137. Ibid., pp. 26, 27, 28, 29, 49, and passim.

138. Ibid., pp. 6, 10, and 40.

139. Ibid., p. 49: "Verum quando me vestigia scripturae veteris huc duxerunt, non studium novitatis, ut putarem aliter legendum, nolui id lectorem latere."

140. Ibid., pp. 7, 9–10 at I, 55, 7: "*Itaque Pontinae manubiae.*] Tametsi vetustum volumen continet *Pomptinae*: censeo tamen legendum, *Pometinae manubiae.* Nam exemplaria antiqua abhinc annos mille fere maiusculis fuere literis perscripta, modo *E* maiusculum non est ita dissimile *P.* Facile ergo *POMETINAE* versum est in *POMPTINAE.*" Modern reading is *Itaque Pometinae manubiae.*

141. Ibid., p. 41: "Gaudet autem antiquis interdum uti vocabulis Livius. . . ."

142. Ibid., p. 39, XXVII, 28, 4: "*Ne cui dolus necteretur.*] Legendum, *nequi dolus.* Sic enim in libro veteri legitur. Porro Livius usurpat *qui* pro *quis.* Id quod et Cicero saepe facit. Ut *pro Cecinna, si qui familiam meam de fundo meo deicerit. Si qui mihi praesto fuerit cum armatis.* Idem peculiare est Septimio Tertulliano, quemadmodum indicavimus in nostris annotationibus quas in illum scripsimus. Porro res haec non animadversa corrumpendis autorum locis infinitis ansam dedit. Venit nunc in mentem unius loci, qui depravate apud Ciceronem legitur, in libello cui titulus est *De senectute sive Cato maior* [21]. Habent enim sic exemplaria typis excusa quae vidimus hactenus: *Omnia quae curant, meminerunt, vadimonia constituta, qui sibi, quibus ipsi debeant.* Quum indubie Cicero scripserit, *qui sibi, cui ipsi debeant,* pro *quis sibi.* Nam eam germanam lectionem continet exemplar Ciceronis manu scriptum, quod nos S[e]letstadii invenimus apud divum Ioannem. Sed de hiis alias." The modern Livian reading is *ne qui dolus necteretur.* The modern reading of Cicero is *quis sibi, cui ipsi debeant.*

143. Ibid., p. 7: *Hunc lumen quondam.* There Beatus offers *contra receptam et Vormaciensis codicis et vulgatarum editionum lectionem* the reading *Hunc columen quondam rebus nostris dubiis futurum* on the basis of an analysis of the events. The modern reading is *Hunc lumen quondam.*

144. Ibid., p. 56, at XXX, 3, 7.

145. Ibid., p. 38: "Porro non dubito quin eruditi albo, quod aiunt, calculo meum sint probaturi iudicium. Nolui tamen lectionem receptam eradere, ne quis me temeritatis argueret. Sufficit hic doctos esse admonitos."

146. Ibid., p. 14: "Id mendum e manu scriptis exemplaribus in excusos typis codices postea transfusum est, nec quisquam observavit. Debent hanc mihi gratiam studiosi. . . ."

147. Ibid., p. 12: "Et ego meliorum admonenti, non solum in hiis Livianis, sed et in Plinianis ac aliorum autorum castigationibus libenter cedam. Quin gratias insuper sum habiturus. Nam cupio subveniri rei literariae."

148. Ibid., p. 35, at XXVII, 3, 3: "*Stramento intecta, omnibus velut de industria alimentis ignis.*] Hic locus cum mihi displiceret propter abla-

tivum *omnibus,* inspexi vetus exemplar, et reperi illic scriptum non *omnibus* sed *omne.* . . ." Modern reading is *stramento intexta, omne velut de industria alimentum ignis.*"

149. *T. Livii Patavini,* p. 39, at XXVII, 25, 3: "*Aliis sententiis notantibus praefectum.*] Mendae postquam semel fuerint in libros receptae, sic germanae lectioni immixtae latent, ut etiam a doctis vix sentiantur. Quis putaret in istis verbis aliquid esse vitii? Et tamen est hic erratum prodigiosum. Quum hunc locum legerem primum, non placebat vocabulum *sententiis,* quod tamen septimo casu dictum videri poterat, pro *per sententias.* Sed quid opus erat voce plurativa? Inspexi Spirense exemplar, et reperi scriptum, *aliis socii notantibus.* Videbam et hoc mendosum esse, sed sperabam ex aperto mendo germanam lectionem me facilius addivinaturum." This passage is also discussed in the letter *ad lectorem,* p. 129. Modern reading is *aliis senatus consulto notantibus praefectum quod eius socodia Tarentum proditum hosti essent.*" See below, note 152.

150. *In C. Plinium,* p. 103/p. 25: "Hic locus . . . inter primos est, quos restituere sum aggressus." Passage is book IV, 5, 49.

151. *T. Livii Patavini,* p. 8: "Proinde, quemadmodum indicat volumen Vormaciense, eius exemplar quod olim a Dextro Flaviano Nicomacho et Victoriano VV.CC., emendatum est. . . ." See also J. E. G. Zetzel, "The Subscriptions in the Manuscripts of Livy and Fronto and the Meaning of *Emendatio,*" *Classical Philology* 75 (1980): 38–59.

152. Ibid., p. 14: "Ibi in Vormaciensi codice e margine mehercule elegantem annotatiunculam, quae Clementianum, sive huius filium Flavianum Nicomachum Dextrum, sive Victorianum, certe veterem aliquem authorem arguit, in medium contextum retulit scriba."

153. See Billanovich, "Petrarch and the Textual Tradition of Livy," p. 180. Beatus also discussed Sabellicus in the 1533 *Castigationes; P. Cornelii Taciti . . . Annalium,* p. cc 1r.

154. *T. Livii Patavini,* p. 9: "Vide mi lector quam necessaria res sit authores ad exemplaria antiqua conferre. Haec non sunt imputanda Laurentio Vallae, sed Pogio, Aurispae, Aleriensi, Victorino, et Petrarchae, qui doctissimi quidem fuere, verum non usquequaque Latine callebant."

155. See above, chapter 1, for Valla.

156. C. Flamstead Walters, "Codex Agenensis (Brit. Mus., Harl. 2493), and Laurentius Valla," *Classical Quarterly* 11 (1917): 154–158, at pp. 155–156.

157. See Index, no. 52c.

158. See prefatory letter, "Beatus Rhenanus theologis et piis omnibus," *Opera Tertulliani* (1539), p. a*2r: ". . . iterum damus vobis [Tert-

ullianum], sed emendatiorem quam antehac. Cuius rei causa, quod collationem eius codicis, qui Gorziae in Mediomatricibus asservatur, diligentia ac dexteritate Huberti Custinei viri quum pietate tum eruditione excellentis, adiuvante Domenico Florentino sodali peractam, cura clarissimi iurisconsulti D. Claudii Cantiunculae Ferdinandi Caesaris a consilio, tandem nacti sumus." See also *Quinti Septimi Florentis Tertulliani . . . Opera Omnia*, Vol. I (Patrologia Latina, 1) (Turnholt: Brepolis, s.d.), col. 58. See for Chansonette, Guido Kisch, *Claudius Cantiuncula: Ein Baseler Jurist und Humanist des 16. Jahrhunderts* (Basel: Helbing & Lichtenhahn, 1970), pp. 140–141, and *Contemporaries*, 1: pp. 259–261.

159. Use of others to collate was hardly unusual, and it has continued into recent times. See Georg Luck, "Textual Criticism Today," *American Journal of Philology* 102 (1981): 166.

160. See *Opera Tertulliani* (1539 ed.), p. a*2r.

161. See ibid., pp. a*2v–a*3v, entitled "Proverbia aut proverbii speciem referentia, quibus passim in scriptis suis utitur Septimus Tertullianus, a vulgo maximam partem desumpta." Beatus' copy of the 1539 edition (Sélestat 1039) includes additions by Beatus on p. a*3r. These *Proverbia* are excerpted in *PL* edition, vol. 1, cols. 209–250. See also *Opera*, p. 420/p. 66.

162. For convenience, I shall cite from the 1539 edition first and the 1609 reprint in *Q. Septimi Florentis Tertulliani, Carthagiensis Presbyteri, Opera Omnia. Ex editione Iacobi Pameli Brugensis*, p. 432/p. 68, at the phrase, "*Dum ita rerum habet.*" See Heinrich Hoppe, *Sintassi e stile di Tertulliano*, trans. Giuseppina Allegri (Brescia: Paideia, 1985), p. 259, n. 5.

163. *Opera Tertulliani* (1539), p. 424/p. 69. Hoppe, *Sintassi e stile . . .*, pp. 92–93.

164. For the place of "African" Latinity in the Renaissance, see John F. D'Amico, "The Progress of Renaissance Latin Prose: The Case of Apuleianism," *RQ* 37 (1984): 351–392.

165. *Opera Tertulliani* (1539) p. 3r/p. 23, p. 421/p. 67, pp. 422–423/pp. 68–69, p. 414/p. 82, p. 12/p. 84, p. 41/p. 88, p. 42/p. 89, p. 218/p. 97.

166. Ibid., pp. 100–101/p. 53: "*Necesse est itaque tot ac tantae, etc.*]. . . . Eleganter autem a *tessera* novator vocabulorum Tertullianus verbum finxit *contesserare*, unde *contesseratio*. Id significat coniunctionem familiariorem quae per signum fiat. Nam *tessera* signum erat apud veteres hospitale, cuius ostensione si quem redisse contigisset, statim agnoscebatur."

167. *Ibid.*, p. 383/p. 58.

168. For example, ibid., p. 131/p. 9: "Restituimus ex Gorziensibus adnotamentis. . . ." Also see p. 161/p. 91; p. 659/p. 115; "Restituimus locum ex indice ad nos missae collationis. . . ."

169. For a listing of the contents of the various manuscripts, see *Corpus Christianorum,* vol. 1, tabula II. The *editio princeps* includes twenty-three treatises, as does the 1528 edition, but the third edition has only twenty-two. This is because Beatus (again perhaps on the basis of the Gorze manuscript) no longer considered the *De praescriptionibus haereticorum* and the *De haeresibus* (or the *Adversus omnes haereses*) as separate books. Even in 1521 (and again in 1528), Beatus doubted the integrity of the two works. See *Opera Tertulliani* (1521), p. 106, and (1528), p. 114. In the Codex Paterniacensis, Beatus had marked at fol. 116v the end of the *De praescriptionibus* but had not signaled the beginning of a new text.

170. Kroymann, "Kritische Vorarbeiten," pp. 7–8, 10–11. For example, *Opera Tertulliani* (1539) p. 104/p. 56; *Adversus omnes haereses,* VIII, 2; p. 13; p. 84; *De carne Christi,* III, 3; p. 465/p. 109. *Ad Praxeam.*

171. For examples, see ibid., p. 381/p. 27; p. 609/p. 34; p. 411/p. 61; p. 414/p. 63; p. 419/p. 66: "Sententia depravata et confusa in omnibus exemplaribus, censeo legendum . . ."; p. 419/p. 72.

172. See ibid., p. 439/p. 78, *Adversus Valentinianos,* XXXI. 1, "*Comparcinus ille Soter, sponsus.*] Scio religiose versandum esse in monimentis veterum autorum, nec temere aut statim mutandum quod non intelligas, et hic meus est mos. Tamen non potui mihi temperare quin hic pro *comparcinus* scriberem, *compactitius ille Soter. . . .*" *Corpus Christianorum,* p. 775, reads "*compacticius ille Soter, sponsus scilicet.*"

173. *Opera Tertulliani* (1539) p. 656/p. 113, *De monogamia,* III, 10: "*Quod et abstulisse docuisset.*] Mutavimus posterius verbum, et pro eo scripsimus *decuisset.* Confirmat castigationem nostram Gorz. collatio." Also p. 333/p. 105, *Adversus Marcionem,* V, 10, 1, "*Viderit institutio ista, Calendae si forte Februariae respondebunt.* Hunc locum ex sola divinatione pridem restitueram adiecta in margine libri adnotatiuncula. Nunc quoniam consentit codex Gorgiensis. . . ."

174. Ibid., *Ad uxorem,* II, 2, 4, p. 609/p. 34: "*Christus cecinit.*] Suspicor quod abbreviate scriptum erat, *Apostolus,* oscitantia librarii putantis esse *Christus,* locum hic *Christo* dedisse. Proinde scripsi, meum secutus iudicium, *Apostolus cecinit.* Hoc est, Non obscure, sed clare est locutus, Apertis nimirum tibiis, iuxta proverbium." See below, note 177.

175. Ibid., p. 2v/p. 22; p. 104/p. 55, p. 415/ p. 63, p. 419/p. 66, p. 434/ p. 76, pp. 442–445/pp. 81–82.

176. Ibid., p. 645/p. 112: "*Nunc virginitate, nunc viduitate periurant.*"

177. *Ibid.*, p. 609/p. 34, quotation in note 174, which continues: "*Ille igitur Christus sanctus*]. Eundem errorem et hic commissum apparet.*" The note in the *Corpus Christianorum*, 1: 386, reads: "significari hic apostolum Paulum recte cognovit Rhenanus; sed idem apostolus verbis *ille sanctus* satis dilucide designatur."

178. Ibid., p. 741 (1539). The annotations are pp. 741–753; they are not included in the 1609 reprint.

179. See Kroymann, "Vorarbeiten," pp. 10–11.

180. *Opera Tertulliani* (1539) pp. 411–445/pp. 60–83: *Adversus Valentinianos.*

181. Ibid., p. 445/pp. 82–83. The *Nomina Aeonum et Deorum Valentinianorum, imo criminum potius quam numinum, ut inquit Tertullianus*" is located on (1528) p. 386, and (1539) p. 445/p. 83. Figure in 1539 only, p. 446.

182. Ibid., p. 443/p. 81. *Corpus Christianorum*, 2: pp. 777–778, reads, "Accipe alia ingenia, circui iam anima, insignioris apud eos magistri. . . ."

183.*Corpus Christianorum*, p. 765.

184. *Opera Tertulliani* (1528), pp. 409–410: "*Quia nullum catuli laureolum fuerit exercitata.*] Opinor sic a Tertulliano fuisse scriptum, *quia millum catuli aureolum fuerit exercitata.* Iocus est in Achamotham quasi tenellam et delicatulam, quae nullis laboribus adsueta, sed tantum in delitiis versans, nullarum etiam virium, instar catuli melitaei, cuius collum aureo millo, non coriaceo et ex capitatis clavis constante collari, circumdatur. Unde diminuitivis usus est. Huiusmodi catuli in altum salire non possunt. Nec Achamoth poterat supervolare crucem. Significat millus collare canum venaticorum factum ex corio, confixumque clavis ferreis eminentibus adversus impetum luporum, autore Festo Pompeio, qui citat haec verba ex oratione quadam Scipionis Aphricani dicta ad populum, *Nobis* [*Vobis* in modern version], inquit, *reique publicae praesidio eritis* [*erit is* in modern version], quasi millus cani. Porro dixit exercitata millum, Graeco loquendi modo quo frequenter utitur. Quemadmodum et illud Graece enunciavit, *Nec habens* pro *non valens.* Nam ἔχω pro *possum* usurpant Graeci. Habes coniecturam meam, expende nunc an absurda non sit, sed huic loco conveniens. Mihi sane non arridet, ut ingenue fatear, quod attuli in medium, propter genitivum catuli. Proinde malim legere, *quia millum catulilla urceolum fuerit exercitata.* Ut fortassis alludat ad morem quo catulos ad saltum quidam assuefaciunt, urceo aqua pleno in medio posito."

185. *Sexti Pompei Festi De verborum significatu quae supersunt cum Pauli Epitome*, ed. Wallace M. Lindsay (Leipzig: Teubner, 1913), p. 13. See also Hoppe, *Sintassi e stile*, pp. 47–48.

186. *Opera Tertulliani* (1539), p. 454. The text reads *quia nullum Catulli Laureloum fuerit exercitata. Opera*, pp. 424–425/p. 69: "*Quia nullum Catulli Laureolum fuerit exercitata.*] Nevius poeta Laureolum fabulam et Leontem in carcere scripsisse fertur. Post hunc Catullus Mimographus, qualis Laberius quoque fuit, duos mimos composuit, quorum uni *Phasmati* nomen fuit, alteri *Laureolo.* [Beatus cites the appropriate ancient sources at some length, and concludes the annotation with the following words.] Porro Tertulliani qui omnis antiquitatis peritissimus fuit, sensus hic est, Enthymesin non fuisse exercitatam in scena, in agenda fabula illa quam Catullus Mimographus *Laureolum* inscripsit, in qua iudex in crucem agebatur. Alioqui si illam scenicorum histrionum in repraesentanda in crucem acti praesidis fabula dexteritatem habuisset, fortassis crucem supervolasset, id est Horon."

187. See John G. Griffith, "Juvenal and Stage-struck Patricians," *Mnemosyne* 15 (1962): 256–261.

188. See below, chapter 5.

189. See for example the changes in the *argumentum* to the *De praescriptionibus haereticorum* (*Opera Tertulliani* [1521], p. 86, [1528], p. 92), where at first Beatus had criticized the Roman Papacy and tried to show its oppression of Germany in his day, but later (ibid. [1539], p. 99) he praised the peace-keeping qualities of the papacy and noted the support given it by the German Emperors from Charlemagne. (See D'Amico, "Beatus Rhenanus, Tertullian and the Reformation," for details.) Similarly, he concluded his introductory letter addressed "theologis et piis omnibus" (ibid., [1539], p. a*2r) with the following sentiments: "Vestrum est nunc optimi viri nostrum hunc laborem boni consulere, et Tertullianum ardentem totum amore Christi, cuius religionem adversum veteres haereticos tam enixe propugnat, tametsi ipse quoque non perstitit, sed secessit, quod est prorsum inexcusabile, vel ob hoc inquam diligenter evolvere, quo videatis quanti faciat ecclesiam Romanam, cui summam tribuit autoritatem, cuius etiam et omnium recte sentientium iudicio hasce annotationum mearum quisquilias subiicio."

190. *Briefwechsel*, no. 359, p. 485, and Pierre Petitmengin, "Beatus Rhenanus et les manuscrits latins," *ASABHS* 35 (185): 238. M. Petitmengin has announced two studies that will deal with this manuscript in whole or in part: "John Leland, Beatus Rhenanus et le Tertullien de Malmesbury," to appear in the *Ninth International Conference on Patristic Studies*, and the forthcoming *La transmission et l'étude de*

Tertullien. On this manuscript, see also R. W. Hunt, "The Need for a Guide to the Editors of Patristic Texts in the 16th Century," *Studia patristica* 17/1 (1982): 365–371, at pp. 366–367. For Gois, see *Contemporaries,* 2: 113–117. The 1539 edition also had a new index that included references to Tertullian's texts and Beatus' annotations by Johannes Gast.

191. Beatus' own copy of the 1539 edition (Sélestat 1039) shows him adding corrections and annotations, perhaps in preparation for a new edition. See for example, p. 656, the additions to the annotation "*Iam carni fibulam imponere,*" where Beatus solved the problem of Tertullian's reference.

5: FROM TEXT TO CONTEXT I

1. For the *Germania illustrata,* see below, chapter 2.
2. *EE,* vol. 6, letter no. 1635.
3. Ibid., letter no. 1674.
4. *Contemporaries,* 1: 107.
5. See above, chapter 1.
6. See William Harrison Woodward, *Desiderius Erasmus Concerning the Aim and Method of Education* (rpt.: New York: Columbia University Teachers' College Press, 1964), and John F. D'Amico, "The Progress of Renaissance Latin Prose: The Case of Apuleianism," *RQ* 37 (1984); 351–392.
7. For the *Ciceronianus,* see the Latin edition with Italian translation by Angelo Gambaro (Brescia: La Scuola, 1965). There are English translations by Izora Scott (New York: Columbia University Teachers' College, 1910) and in the *Collected Works of Erasmus,* vol. 28 (Toronto: University of Toronto Press, 1986). See also F. Férère, "Erasme et le Ciceronianisme au XVIe siècle," *Revue de l'Agenais et des anciennes provinces du Sud-Ouest* 3, 4, 5 (1924): 176–182, 283–294, 342–357; Julian Gerard Michel, *Etude sur le Ciceronianus d'Erasme avec une édition critique* (Thèse: Université de Paris, 1951); Pierre Mesnard, "L'année érasmienne," *Etudes* 328 (February 1968); 236–255; idem, "La religion d'Erasme dans le 'Ciceronianus'," *Revue thomiste* 78 (1968): 268–272; G. W. Pigman, III, "Imitation and the Renaissance Sense of the Past: The Reception of Erasmus' *Ciceronianus*," *Journal of Medieval and Renaissance Studies* 9/2 (1979): 155–177; and John F. D'Amico, *Renaissance Humanism in Papal Rome: Humanists and Churchmen on the Eve of the Reformation* 2d printing (Baltimore. Md.: Johns Hopkins University Press, 1985), chap. 5. In general, see also D. F. S.

Thomson, "The Latinity of Erasmus," in *Erasmus,* ed T. A. Dorey (Albuquerque, N.M.: University of New Mexico Press, 1970), pp. 115–137.

8. Gambaro's important introduction to his edition and translation stresses this point.

9. See Myron P. Gilmore, *"Fides et Eruditio:* Erasmus and the Study of History," in his *Humanists and Jurists: Six Studies in the Renaissance* (Cambridge, Mass.: Harvard University Press, 1963), pp. 87–114; Peter G. Bietenholz, *History and Biography in the Works of Erasmus of Rotterdam* (Geneva: Droz, 1966); J. Ijsewijn and C. Matheeussen, "Erasme et l'historiographie," in *The Late Middle Ages and the Dawn of Humanism Outside Italy,* ed. G. Verbeke and J. Ijsewijn (Louvain: University Press, 1972), pp. 31–43; Brad Inwood, "Erasmus' Use of Historical Exempla," *Erasmus in English* 12 (1983): 10–13; F. De Michelis Pintacula, "Erasmo e le origini della storiografia moderna," in *La storia della filosofia come sapere critico: Studi offerti a Mario Dal Pra* (Milan, 1984), pp. 659–683; and Silvano Cavazzo, "Erasmo e l'uso della storia," in *Renaissance Studies in Honor of Craig Hugh Smyth,* ed. Andrew Morrogh, et al. (Florence: Giunti Barbera, 1985), 1: 53–63.

10. For Erasmus' biography of Jerome, see Eugene F. Rice, Jr., *St. Jerome in the Renaissance* (Baltimore, Md.: Johns Hopkins University Press, 1985), chap. 5.

11. Billanovich, "The Textual Tradition of Livy," p. 182.

12. See John P. Dolan, "Liturgical Reform among the Irenicists," in *Sixteenth Century Essays and Studies* (St. Louis, Mo.: Foundation for Reformation Research, 1970), 2: 72–94.

13. See below.

14. André Godin, "Erasme, l'hérésie et les hérétiques," in *Les dissidents du XVIe siècle entre l'Humanisme et le Catholicisme,* ed. Marc Lienhard (Baden-Baden: Valentin Koerner, 1983), pp. 43–60, at pp. 43–45.

15. See Eric Cochrane, *Historians and Historiography in the Italian Renaissance* (Chicago, Ill.: University of Chicago Press, 1981), for background.

16. Ibid., chap. 2; Massimo Miglio, *Storiografia pontificia del Quattrocento* (Bologna: Patron, 1975); and John F. D'Amico, "Papal History and Curial Reform in the Renaissance: Raffaele Maffei's *Breuis Historia* of Julius II and Leo X," *Archivum Historiae Pontificiae* 18 (1980): 157–210.

17. For Platina, see introduction by G. Gaida to Platina's *Liber de Vita Christi et Omnium Pontificum, Rerum Italicarum Scriptores,* vol. 3/1

(Città di Castello: Lapi, 1913), and, most recently, Outi Merisalo, "Platina et le Liber pontificalis," *Arctos* 16 (1982): 73–97.

18. See Richard J. Palermino, "Platina's History of the Popes" (Master's thesis, University of Edinburgh, 1973).

19. For patristics in the Renaissance, see above, chapter 2.

20. See the listing in Hughes Oliphant Old, *The Patristic Roots of Reformed Worship* (Zurich: Theologischer Verlag, 1975), pp. 156–180.

21. *Opera Tertulliani* (1521), f. abv; (1528), p. 680; (1539), p. 754/p. 119. The Latin is in D'Amico, "Beatus Rhenanus, Tertullian and the Reformation," pp. 43–44, fn. 21.

22. See Jerome, *De viris inlustribus,* ed. G. W. Herdin (Leipzig, 1870), chap. 9.

23. See *Opera Tertulliani* (1539), pp. 500, 507, 542/pp. 38, 42, 10. In the *Admonitio,* p. 763/p. 125, Beatus writes about provincial synods: "Haec dicta sunt velut a praefante in volumen tribus distinctum libris, quorum primus ea continebat quae sunt de poenitentia et poenitentibus, criminibus atque iudiciis . . . . Testatur in calce se non tantum Oecumenica concilia secutum, sed quaedam ex provincialium synodorum constitutionibus accepisse, in quibus praesidere solet Metropolitanus episcopus, quo libentius legere velim modo dictos libros. Nam constitutiones provincialis synodi, quam iussu Ludovici Pii Caesaris Magonciaci habuit Rabanus Archiepiscopus cum coepiscopis suis, Samuele, Gozbaldo, Hebone, Gozbratho, Hemmone, Vualdgario, Ans[e]gario, Otgario, Lantone, Salomone et Gebaharto, cum reliquis collegis, coepiscopis, abbatibus, monachis, presbyteris, et caeteris ecclesiasticis ordinibus, dici vix potest quam mihi placuerint, cum nuper in meas manus casu venissent." This section was in both 1521 (ff. b 6v–b 7n) and 1528 (p. 689) editions.

24. See Marjorie O'Rourke Boyle, "For Peasants, Psalms: Erasmus' *Editio Princeps* of Haymo (1533)," *Mediaeval Studies,* 44 (1982): 444–469, and Daniel J. Sheerin, "A Carolingian Cure Recovered: Erasmus' Citation of Hucbald of St. Armand's *Ecloga de Calvis,*" *BHR* 42 (1980): 167–171.

25. See also Eugenio Garin, "Alle origini rinascimentali del concetto di filosofia scolastica," in his *La cultura filosofica del Rinascimento italiano* (Florence: Sansoni, 1961), pp. 466–479.

26. D'Amico, "Beatus Rhenanus, Tertullian and the Reformation," p. 43; Beatus did not identify the manuscript he mentioned.

27. Ibid., p. 43.

28. See above, chapter 2. See also the introductory letter to them in *Briefwechsel,* no. 209. For Bathodius, see *Contemporaries,* 2: 99.

29. See *Briefwechsel,* p. 290.

30. Ibid., pp. 290–291.

31. *Christian Humanism and the Reformation,* ed. J. C. Olin (New York: Harper and Row, 1965), p. 49.

32. See Gabriella D'Anna, "Abelardo e Cicerone," *Studi medievali* 10 (1969): 333–419, and Tullio Gregory, "Abelard et Platon," ibid. 13 (1972): 539–562.

33. Index, no. 18, and Charles Munier, "Beatus Rhenanus et le Decret de Gratien," *ASABHS* 35 (1985): 227–234.

34. See Barbara Halporn, "Sebastian Brant as an Editor of Juristic Texts," *Gutenberg-Jahrbuch* 59 (1984): 36–51, idem., "Sebastian Brant's Editions of Classical Authors," *Publishing History* 16 (1984): 33–41; Robert Walter, "Beatus Rhenanus et Sebastian Brant: L'affaire des pénitentes de Sainte Marie-Madeleine," *Revue d'Alsace* 107 (1981): 61–70; and Adolphe Koch, "L'exemplaire personnel de Josse Bade," *ASABHS* 30 (1980): 43–50. For Beatus' interest in legal texts, see *Briefwechsel,* no. 365, and *Amerbachkorrespondenz,* 3, pp. 327–8, and 5: 433–434. In his copy of the 1539 edition (p. 752), Beatus added a marginal note referring to the Roman law on manumission.

35. *Opera, De corona militis,* p. 507/p. 42: "De quibus Bonifacius martyr et episcopus interrogatus si liceret in vasculis ligneis sacramenta conficere, respondit, *Quondam sacerdotes aurei ligneis calicibus utebantur, nunc e contrario lignei sacerdotes aureis utuntur calicibus.* Sic enim in Decretis Burchardi Vuormatiensis episcopi legitur quem secutus est Gratianus. Cuius excusum typis volumen, Dii boni, quam mendosum reperietur si quis cum manuscriptis antiquarum sanctionum libris conferat! Opinor autem in gratiam sacerdotum elegantissimam istam verissimamque divi Bonifacii sententiam Antitheti schema referentem, ab aliquo castigatore fuisse truncatam. O ligneum emendatorem et vere ligneis gratificantem." And p. 509/p. 44; ". . . Porro non me fugit idem caput a Gratiano repetitum esse Dist. XI. Verum quia mendosissime legitur in vulgatis Decretorum codicibus indubie studio depravatum ac mutatum, volui synceram lectionem hic proponere. Itaque per Christum te rogo lector ut cum excusis libris conferas. Videbis quam corrupte multa apud Gratianum legantur. Quasi enim parum fuisset praeter innumeras clausulas vitiatas, pro *attentaveris* scribere *attenderimus,* pro *multifariam, trifariam,* pro *accommodantia, commendantia,* ausus est tandem depravator, quicunque ille fuit. . . ." Neither section is in the 1521 or 1528 edition.

36. Text of Burchardus, in *PL,* vol. 140, col. 698, and of Gratian, ibid., vol. 187, cols. 58–59. For Basil the Great's view of tradition, see E. Amand de Mendieta, *The 'Unwritten' and 'Secret' Apostolic Traditions*

in the Theological Thought of St. Basil the Great of Caesarea (Edinburgh: Oliver and Boyd, 1965).

37. For Gregory's letter, "Ad Leonardum Episcopum Hispalensem," see *PL,* vol. 77, cols. 496–498. For Rabanus' letter, "Ad Regimbaldum Chorepiscopum Moguntinum," see ibid., vol. 112, cols. 1507–1510.

38. The specific ceremony discussed is baptism; however, Beatus did not have access to Tertullian's treatise on baptism.

39. In general, see Hans Von Campenhausen, *Ecclesiastical Authority and Spiritual Power in the Church of the First Three Centuries,* trans. J. A. Baker (Stanford, Calif.: Stanford University Press, 1969), chaps. 8 and 9. For Tertullian's views on penance, see Oscar D. Watkins, *A History of Penance* (London: Longman, Green and Co., 1920), 1: 113–129; Johannes Quasten, *Patrology* (Westminster, Md.: Newman Press, 1953), 2: 332–335, and W. P. Le Saint, "*Traditio* and *Exomologesis* in Tertullian," in *Studia patristica* (Berlin: Akademie Verlag, 1966), 8: 414–419.

40. *Opera Tertulliani,* p. 425/p. 70.

41. *Admonitio* is in ibid. (1521), ff. a 6v–b 8v.

42. See *Dictionnaire de théologie catholique* for penitence, vol. 21/1, cols. 722–1070, for the period up to the Council of Trent; the Carolingian period is covered in cols. 862–891.

43. *PL,* vol. 39, cols. 1533–1549.

44. On Oecolompadius' text, see Ernst Stahelin, *Das theologische Lebenswerk Johannes Oekolampad* (Leipzig: Heinsius, 1939), pp. 121–134, also Fraenkel, "Beatus Rhenanus, Oecoplampade . . . ," pp. 66–69.

45. *Opera Tertulliani* (1521), f. b 8r, quoted in D'Amico, "Beatus Rhenanus, Tertullian and the Reformation," p. 50, n. 44. Despite Beatus' attempt to make this discussion more acceptable in the later editions, it was condemned by the Spanish Inquisition; p. 127 in the 1609 edition of Tertullian reproduces the Inquisition's condemnation. Specifically on the material under consideration, it states, "Argumentum libri de Poenitentia totum expungatur. Nam commode repurgari non potest."

46. *Ibid.* (1521) pp. 432–434; (1528) pp. 476–478; (1539) pp. 541–545/pp. 10–11 for *argumentum* to *De poenitentia,*

47. *Opera Tertulliani* (1521), p. 432; (1528), p. 476; (1539), pp. 542–543/p. 10.

48. *Opera Tertulliani* (1539), p. 543/p. 10.

49. *Ibid.* (1521), p. 133; (1528), p. 477; (1539), p. 543/p. 11.

50. For Beatus' biography of Geiler, see Jacob Wimpfeling/Beatus

Rhenanus, *Das Leben des Johannes Geiler von Kayslersberg*, ed. Otto Herding (Munich: Fink, 1970), pp. 88–96; also *Briefwechsel*, pp. 31–35. For Geiler, see also Jane Dempsey Douglass, *Justification in Late Medieval Preaching: A Study of John Geiler von Kayslersberg* (Leiden: Brill, 1966).

51. See, in general, Thomas N. Tentler, *Sin and Confession on the Eve of the Reformation* (Princeton, N.J.: Princeton University Press, 1977). *Opera*, p. 545/p. 12, not in 1521 or 1528; quoted in D'Amico, "Beatus Rhenanus, Tertullian and the Reformation," pp. 51–52, fn. 48.

52. *Opera Tertulliani* (1539), p. 545/p. 12; "Caeterum sciat lector librum hunc visum Erasmo nostro Roterodamo bonae memoriae non esse Tertulliani propter phrasim diversam."

53. The text is in *Desiderii Erasmi Roterodami Opera Omnia*, ed. J. Leclerc (Leiden, 1704), vol. 5, cols. 145–170. See also Thomas N. Tentler, "Forgiveness and Consolation in the Religious Thought of Erasmus," *Studies in the Renaissance* 12 (1965): 110–113. On the differences between Erasmus and Beatus, see Fraenkel, "Beatus Rhenanus, Oecolampade. . . ," pp. 75–77. See also *EE* no. 2136, pp. 214–220, for Erasmus' acceptance of private confession. *Opera Tertulliani* (1539), p. 545/p. 12; see discussion in D'Amico, "Beatus Rhenanus, Tertullian and the Reformation," pp. 53–54.

54. See Tentler, "Forgiveness and Consolation," pp. 117–118, and Payne, *Erasmus: His Theology of the Sacraments* (Richmond, 1970), pp. 193–194, 199–209.

55. *Opera Tertulliani* (1539), p. 550/p. 15; see also D'Amico, "Beatus Rhenanus, Tertullian and the Reformation," pp. 52, 55–56.

56. See Quasten, *Patrology*, pp. 332–337, and article on Tertullian in *Dictionnaire de théologie catholique*, vol. 15, cols. 130–171, at cols. 156–161.

57. *Opera Tertulliani* (1539), p. 498/p. 36.

58. Ibid., p. 411/p. 60, not in 1521 or 1528 editions: "*Et disciplina non terretur*]"; quoted in D'Amico, "Beatus Rhenanus, Tertullian and the Reformation," p. 60, fn. 77. See also above, chapter 4, note 191.

59. *Opera Tertulliani* (1539), p. 500/p. 38; "*Aquam adituri.*] Baptizandi ritum ostendit qui in usu veterum fuit, de quo consuetudo quaedam mutavit. Nam tum adulti fere regenerationis lavacro tingebantur, cottidie externis e paganismo ad nostram religionem confluentibus. Siquidem id temporis ubique reperire erat ethnicos Christianis admixtos. Postea statis temporibus nempe bis in anno celebrari baptismus coeptus, eius enim rei nullam hic facit mentionem, alioqui non omissurus. Qui mos antiquus etiam per tempora Charoli Magni et Ludovici Augusti servatus est. Indicant hoc leges ab illis sanctae,

quibus cavetur ne quenquam sacerdotes baptizent, excepto mortis articulo, praeterquam in Pascha et Pentecoste. Eas sanctiones complectitur volumen Legum Pipini, Charoli Magni, Ludovici Pii, et Lotharii, quas Ansegisus abbas collegit, et extant adhuc in multis bibliothecis, Seletstadii sane habetur apud Fidei, et Argentorati in libraria templi maioris." Sections in 1521 (p. 408) and 1528 (p. 451) editions differ from 1539 edition in length.

60. Ibid., p. 500/p. 38; "Hoc sic accipiendum ut sciamus infantes post Pascha natos ad baptismum Pentecostes reservatos, et natos post Pentecostem ad Paschalem festum diem baptismo offerri solitos, excepta, ceu dixi, necessitate, unacum adultis catechumenis qui de externis nationibus Danorum, Nortmannorum, Sclavinorum, et similium populorum, Christianae religioni initiabantur. Ex hiis enim gentibus propter continua Germanorum bella nunquam non in has regiones mancipia afferebantur. Quin ipsi maiores nostri propter Hunnorum, Avarum, Ugrorum assiduas et exitiabiles devastationes suis interdum sacris privabantur ad tempus." This section was in neither the 1521 nor the 1528 edition.

61. Ibid., p. 500/p. 38: "Sane quod de infantibus dixi, libri rituales, [quos] Agendas vulgo vocant, aperte testantur, dum indicant quo ordine puellorum et puellarum baiuli unacum susceptoribus suis stare debeant." Section not in 1521 or 1528 edition.

62. Ibid., p. 501/p. 38; "Et suas consuetudines habuit Oriens quemadmodum liquet ex Dionysio Graeco autore quem Ariopagitam vocant, suas habuit et occidens. Nam ceremoniae secundum ecclesiarum et regionum diversitatem variant." Section only in 1539 edition. Beatus mentioned Dionysius always with some qualifying term, indicating that he followed Erasmus in rejecting the attribution to Dionysius, against his old teacher Lefèvre.

63. Ibid., p. 501/p. 38: "Sufficiat autoritas Ecclesiae, nec novationem ullam aut hic aut alibi quaeramus, quae dissidii mater solet esse." Only in 1539.

64. Ibid., pp. 501–502/p. 39.

65. See Old, *The Patristic Roots of Reformed Worship*, chap. 1.

66. *Opera Tertulliani* (1539), p. 504/p. 40. This is part of a long annotation on the words *Eucharista sacramentum* which Beatus expanded in the last edition; see ibid. (1521), pp. 410–411; (1528), pp. 453–455; (1539), pp. 503–506/pp. 40–41.

67. Ibid., p. 505/p. 41.

68. Ibid. (1521), p. 411; (1528), p. 454; (1539), p. 505/p. 41: "Vides igitur aliquid legi solitum, vel ex veteri instrumento, vel ex novo, videlicet Evangeliis et epistolis Apostolorum. O sanctum conventum!

Utinam redeat ad nos ista consuetudo, Christi praecepta frequenter
mentibus hominum inculcandi. Idem ostendit Christianos super coe-
nam communem cantillasse vel de piorum felicitate, vel de impiorum
cruciatibus. . . ."

69. Ibid. (1521), p. 411; (1528), p. 454; (1539), p. 505/p. 41: "Porro
non possum caelare studiosos antiquitatis Christianae, laicos olim
canna solitos haurire dominicum sanguinem e calice: quod pridem
mihi indicavit Paulus Volzius Abbas Hugoniani coenobii, quod vulgus
Hugonis curiam, et lingua vernacula Hugeshoffium appellat in valle
Albertina, vir pius et literatus, erutum ex libro signorum, qui frequens
extat apud Benedictinos." See *Contemporaries*, 3: 417–418.

70. Ibid. (1521), p. 411; (1528), p. 455; (1539), pp. 505–506/p. 41;
"Idem nuper reperit in primis Cartusiorum constitutionibus Chonra-
dus Pellicanus homo mirae sanctitatis ac eruditionis, ubi prohibetur
ne quicquam preciosorum vasorum possideant, praeter calicem ar-
genteum et fistulam qua laici dominicum exorbeant sanguinem." See
Contemporaries, 3: 65–66.

71. Ibid. (1528), pp. 454–455; (1539), p. 506/p. 41, not in 1521
edition. The 1539 edition continues "Siquidem etiamnum Romanus
Pontifex quoties publice sacrificat, aureo calamo sugit sanguinem
domini e calice cum diacono et subdiacono." All three versions contain
the following: "Sed de his iam plus satis, quanquam meo iudicio
pulchrum est in Christianismo pie et prudenter curiosum esse, cum
alios videamus in ethnicorum rebus ad unguem investigandis tam
praepostere diligentes, ut de Christo vix illis semel per omnem vitam
cogitare vacet."

72. Ibid. (1521), pp. 411–412; (1528), p. 455; (1539), p. 506/p. 42;
quoted in D'Amico, "Beatus Rhenanus, Tertullian and the Reformation," p. 57, n. 67.

73. Ibid. (1539), pp. 506–507/pp. 42–43.

74. See above, note 35.

75. Only in *Opera Tertulliani* (1539), p. 507/p. 43; quoted in
D'Amico, "Beatus Rhenanus, Tertullian and the Reformation," pp.
56–57, n. 67.

76. See Index, no. 66, and André Jacob, "L'édition 'érasmienne' de
la liturgie de Saint Jean Chrysostome et ses sources," *IMU* 19 (1976):
291–324; Pierre Fraenkel, "Beatus Rhenanus, historien de la liturgie," *ASABHS* 35 (1985): 247–260; idem, "Une lettre oubliée de
Beatus Rhenanus: sa preface à la liturgie de S. Jean Chrysostome
dediée à Johannes Hoffmeister, 24 janvier 1540," *BHR* 48 (1986):
387–404.

77. Fraenkel, "Une lettre," p. 395.

78. Ibid., pp. 399–400.
79. Ibid., p. 399, n. 65.
80. See especially Fraenkel, "Beatus Rhenanus, historian de la liturgie."
81. See Oliver K. Olson, *The 'Missa Illyrica' and the Liturgical Thought of Flacius Illyricus* (Hamburg, 1966), p. 105.
82. In addition to the articles by Fraenkel, see also John P. Dolan, "Liturgical Reform Among the Irenicists," *Sixteenth Century Essays and Studies*, ed. Carl S. Meyer (St. Louis, Mo.: Foundation for Reformation Research, 1971), 2: 72–94.
83. D'Amico, "Beatus Rhenanus, Tertullian and the Reformation."
84. Ibid., pp. 57–61.
85. For the *Adversus Valentinianos*, see Jean-Claude Fredouille, "Beatus Rhenanus, commentateur de Tertullien," *ASABHS* 35 (1985): 287–295. For the *Adversus Marcionem*, see *Tertulliani adversus Marcionem*, ed. C. Moreschini (Milan: Istituto editoriale cisalpino, 1971); Tertullian, *Adversus Marcionem* (bks. I–III), ed. and intro. Ernest Evans (Oxford: Clarendon, 1972). See also David L. Balas, "Marcion Revisited: A Post-Harnack Perspective," in *Texts and Testament: Critical Essays on the Bible and Early Church Fathers*, ed. W. Eugene March (San Antonio, Tex.: Trinity University Press, 1980), pp. 95–108, and Réné Brown, "Tertullien et le Montanisme: église institutionelle et église spirituelle," *Rivista di storia e letteratura religiosa* 21 (1985): 244–257.
86. *Opera Tertulliani* (1539), p. 415/p. 63.
87. See the introduction to the *Sources Chrétiennes* edition, nos. 280, 281, by Jean-Claude Fredouille, *Contre les Valentiniens*, 2 vols. (Paris: Cerf, 1980/1981), Vol. I.
88. See *Opera Tertulliani* (1539), p. 444/p. 82: *Adversus Valentianos* XXXVIII, 1, "*Tantum quod desultricem et defectricem illam virtutem.*] Desultricem intelligit inconstantem ac instabilem, pro quo habes apud Irenaeum, discedentem etiam, et deinde descendentem, ubi discedentem etiam legendum arbitror. Nam indubie Tertullianus Irenaeum in hoc libro praecipue sequitur, ubique eum fere de verbo ad verbum exprimens." Also p. 410/p. 60.
89. "Nomina Aeonum et Deorum Valentinianorum," ibid., p. 445/pp. 82–83.
90. In *argumentum* to *Adversus valentinianos*, ibid., p. 410/p. 81.
91. Ibid., pp. 444–445/p. 82. See Ferdouille, "Beatus Rhenanus," pp. 293–294. Beatus was familiar with the Fugger collection. See K. Bursian, "Die Antikensammlung Raimund Fuggers," *Sitzungsberichte der k. b. Akademie der Wissenschaften* (Munich), Philosophisch-philoogische Classe 4 (1874): 133–160, at pp. 134–135. For Luscinius, see

Yvonne Rokseth, "Othmar Nachtgall, dit Luscinius," in *L'humanisme en Alsace* (Paris: Les Belles Lettres, 1939), pp. 192–204.

92. *Opera Tertulliani* (1539), p. 413/p. 62, annotation at the words *Deduxit et Heracleon inde tramites quosdam, et Secundus, et Magus Marcus]*. Not in 1528 edition.

93. Ibid., p. 416/p. 64: "*Bythios et Mixis.*] In exemplaribus manu descriptis post *Mixis* statim sequitur, *Et Hedone,* ut certum sit trium Aeonum nomina per librarii incuriam omissa esse. Hunc defectum nescio unde melius sit sarcire quam ex Irenaeo apud quem ista decuria Aeonum sic infertur.

Bythius et Mixis   Ageratos et Henonis
Autophyes et Hedone   Acinetos et Syncrasis

Sic malo scribere quam αὐτοφυὴ nam semper mas cum foemina copulatur. Item pro Agne et Hosiosyncrasis magis libuit scribere Acinetos et Syncrasis [another correct conjecture]. Ergo in contextu reponenda haec tria nomina, Ageratos, Henonis, Autophyes."

94. *Corpus Christianorum,* p. 759. Several of Beatus' annotations are printed in the *PL* edition of the works of Tertullian.

95. *Opera Tertulliani* (1539), p. 423/pp. 68–69: "*Dum ita rerum habet.*] Hellenismus est. . . . Caeterum nemo mirari debet Graecum loquendi consuetudinem Tertullianum imitari subinde. Nam id temporis nihil extabat apud Latinos in sacris praeter utrumque testamentum: tantum Victor tertiusdecimus Romanae urbis episcopus opuscula quaedam scripserat, et Apollonius, autore Hieronymo. Legebat ergo Tertullianus fervens in studio sacrarum literarum Ignatium Antiochenum, Polycarpum, Papiam, Quadratum, Aristidem, Agrippam, Egesippum, Iustinum philosophum et martyrem, Melitonem Asianum, Theophilum Antiochenum, Apollinarium, Dionysium Corinthium, Pinytum Cretensem, Tacianum, Philippum Cretensem, Musanum, Modestum, Bardesanen, Irenaeum, Pantaenum, Rhodonem, Clementem Pantaeni discipulum, Militiadem, Apollonium, Serapionem, Theophilum Caesariensem, Bacchylum Corinthium, Polycartem Ephesinum, Heraclitum, Maximum, Candidum, Apionem, Sextum, Brabianum, et similes scriptores alios Graecos. Non mirum igitur si ex istorum assidua lectione adeo Graecas loquendi formulas imbibit, ut etiam latine scribens illarum interoblivisci nequiret. Non quod negem autorum quos recensui monumenta latine fuisse versa, si non omnia certe aliqua. Sed ipse maluit ex fontibus bibere quam ex lacunis. Et quae tralata erant, nimia religione et simplicitate erant conversa, quales sunt quinque illi libri Irenaei quos apud Celtas, id est Lugduni, quidem scripsit vir sanctissimus Rhodanensium mulierum faciens mentionem quas Valentiniani deceperint, sed proculdubio Graece, nam inter

Graecos scriptores Irenaeum annumerat Hieronymus, alioqui Tertullianum quartum facturus Latinorum, non tertium. Taleis inter Pontifices illos primos Romanae urbis non paucos fuisse crediderim, qui melius Graece noverint quam Latine. Verum habebant adhaerentes sibi interpretes. Sic Divus Bernhardus ille Burgundio in templo Spirensi per interpretem Germanice concionatus est coram Chuonrado Augusto et principibus Imperii Romani sive Germanici, quum adornaretur expeditio illa memorabilis ad recuperandam Palaestinam e manibus Sarracenorum. Idem multi sancti olim viri factitarunt, ut instaurantes olim collapsam religionem in hac superiori Germania Anglosaxones illi, Vunnefridus qui et Bonifacius Romano nomine, Quilianus, Burchardus, Arbegastus, Gallus, Fridolinus, Pirminus, et apud Prussios Italus Bruno." See also Fredouille, "Beatus Rhenanus," p. 292.

96. See Jerome, *De viris inlustribus*, chap. LIII, for Tertullian: "... primus post Victorem et Apollinum Latinorum ponitur. . ."; for Victor, see chap. XXXIV, and for Apollonius, see chap. XL.

97. For the Montanists, see *Dictionnaire de théologie catholique*, vol. 10, cols. 2355–2370, and Pierre de Labriolle, *La crise montaniste* (Paris: Leroux, 1913).

98. See *Opera Tertulliani* (1539), p. 430/p. 72, and p. 436/p. 76.

99. Ibid. p. 655/p. 113; *De monogamia*, I, 1, p. 464/p. 109. *Adversus Praxeam*, I. 6,

100. Ibid., p. 464/p. 109.

101. See annotation to *De pallio, Opera* p. 678/p. 5; "*Praesentis Imperii triplex virtus, deo tot Augustis in unum favente.*]" See also Nazzaro, *21 'De pallio,'* pp. 33–47.

102. For Spartianus, see *Scriptores Historiae Augustae*, vol. 3 (Cambridge, Mass.: Harvard University Press, 1922).

103. See Quasten, *Patrology*, p. 316.

104. *Autores historiae ecclesiasticae* (1523), p. 211.

105. Ibid., p. 113.

106. For the *Notitia Dignitatum*, see Guido Clemente, *La 'Notitia Dignitatum'* (Cagliari: Fossataro, 1968).

107. See, for the manuscript, the introduction of E. A. Thompson, *A Roman Reformer and Inventor* (Oxford: Clarendon Press, 1952), and I. G. Maier, "The Giessen, Parma and Piacenza codices of the 'Notitia Dignitatum' with some related Texts," *Latomus* 27 (1968): 96–141.

108. *Autores historiae ecclesiasticae*, p. 175: "Scotus in libro de insignibus magistratuum ad Theodosium Augustum, quem nuper ex Spirensi biblioteca accepimus. . . ." And in *De fuga in persecutione, Opera Tertulliani* (1539), p. 622/p. 118: "Liber, cui titulus Notitia Orientis et Occidentis indicat . . ." Also *Adversus Valentinianos*, ibid., p. 417/p.

64: "Notitia dignitatum militarium Orientis et Occidentis"; and p. 437/p. 77 and p. 622/p. 118.

109. *Opera Tertulliani* (1539), pp. 428–429/p. 72: "*Hac autoritate trium scilicet liberorum.*] De iure trium liberorum multa sunt passim in constitutionibus veterum imperatorum. Vetus interpres, hoc est expositor codicis Theodosiani, qui mutilus extat . . ." Manuscripts and printed versions of the *Codex* are described in *Theodosiani libri XVI cum Constitutionibus Sirmondianis*, ed. Th. Mommsen and P. M. Meyer (Berlin: Weidmann, 1905).

110. *Opera Tertulliani* (1539), p. 611/p. 35; *De uxorem II, "Ut exerta eminent.*]"

111. Ibid., p. 678/p. 5: "*Chamaeleontem.*] Theodoricus Ostrogotus Romanorum rex ad Habundantium praepositum scribens de quodam Frontoso decoctore et debita maligne solvente, *Merito Chamaeleonti bestiae conferendus, quae parvorum serpentum formae consimilis, aureo tantum capite, et reliquis membris subalbentis prasini colore distinguitur.*" The letter quoted is in *Magni Aurelii Cassiodori Senatoris Variarum libri duodecim*, V. 34; see edition of Th. Mommsen, *Cassiodori Senatoris Variae* (Monumenta Germanicae Historica: Scriptores, Vol. XII) (Berlin, 1894), pp. 161–162. See Horawitz, "Des Beatus Rhenanus literarische Thätigkeit, 1530–1547," p. 342, and letter to Beatus in *Konrad Peutingers Briefwechsel*, ed. Erich König (Munich: Beck, 1923), no. 292, pp. 476–477.

112. Ibid., pp. 636–637/p. 8; *Ad Scapulam*: "*In Germanica expeditione.*]"

113. Ibid. (1521), p. 67v; (1528), pp. 690–691; (1528), pp. 764–765/p. 126 *Admonitio*. Beatus attacked Aeneas Silvius Piccolomini and Raffaele Maffei in the *Admonitio* (1521), p. b 2v (1528), p. 683, and (1139), p. 757/p. 121, on the penitential practices of the church of Halberstadt.

114. *Corpus Christianorum*, p. 378.

115. In *Opera Tertulliani* (1521), p. 475, Beatus had written as a sidenote: "Alius gallicos mulos. Adhuc baiulos agunt germani, hodie Pontificii corporis gestatores." Later he wrote the following. Ibid. (1528), p. 527: "*Non Gallicos vultus, nec Germanicos baiulos.*] Si dicam quamdiu laborarim, dum vocabulum ex mendosae dictionis vestigiis quaero quod pro *vultus* substituam, vix credetur. Non placebat in aeditione priori indicata coniectura, si videlicet, *non gallicos vultus*, sed *Gallicos mulos* legeremus. Tametsi in animo obversaretur locus ille qui est in secundo libro, dum inquit, *Unde nisi a diabolo maritum petant, bonum exhibendae sellae, et mulabus itinerariis peregrinae proceritatis?* Sic enim nos castigavimus. Videbam ibi mularum fieri mentionem. Sed

tamen quia sequebatur, *Germanicos baiulos,* volebam habere officii sive ministerii vocabulum. Et cogitabam raram aliquam vocem fuisse quam sic librarius indoctus depravasset, non facturus hoc in mulis. Itaque si quis locus coniecturae datur, divino scriptum fuisse, *Non Gallicos acoluthos, nec Germanicos baiulos.* Sunt autem ἀκόλουθοι Graecis ministri qui nos sequuntur, ab particula quae hic ὀπίσω significat, et ἐλεύθω. Taleis Latini pedissequos appellant. Inter Imperialis aulae officia posteaquam Imperii sedes Byzantium translata est per Constantinum Magnum, reperio sub huius successoribus acoluthum dictum fuisse qui Caesarem sequeretur quocunque iret, sicut scuterium qui praecederet, a scuto nominatum quod praeferebat. Quemadmodum autem ex Graecis et Romanis erat aula mixta, sic et officiorum vocabula partim Graeca partim Latina fuere, partim ex utrisque conflata."

116. Ibid., pp. 527–528: "Porro quod ait, *Nec germanicos baiulos,* sciat lector hunc fuisse morem apud priscos, ut matronae divites non temere in publicum prodirent, ut hodie fit, ab omnibus conspiciendae, sed in lecticis ac sellis undique tectis gestarentur, omnia videntes, a nemine tamen visae. Nam in libro *de pallio* [IV. 9] taxat mulieres Tertullianus, quod non solum tegmenta vestium abiecerint, sed et lecticis ac sellis uti in publico desierint, hiis quidem verbis, *At nunc,* inquit, *in semetipsas lenocinando, quo planius adeantur, et stolam, et supparum, et crepidulam, et calliandrum, ipsas quoque iam lecticas ac sellas quis in publico quoque domestice ac secrete vehebantur, eieravere.* Nam sic nos eam sententiam castigavimus, non paucioribus quam decem insignibus mendis sublatis. Caeterum in illis lecticis ac sellis vehebantur domestice, hoc est, ut non minus clausae essent, ac erant domi suae. Serviebant ad hoc ministerium Germani."

117. Ibid., p. 528: "Vides autem et olim fecisse Gallos et Germanos, quod proximis seculis Romae fecerunt, ad omne serviendi genus promptissimi, nisi quod nuperrime in illo lamentabili casu Urbis, ex magna parte domum redire compulsi sunt."

118. Ibid. (1539), pp. 660–661/p. 32, "*Non Gallicos vultus.*] Propter candorem, praesertim si cum Graecis, Syris, Hispanis, aut etiam Italis hodie comparentur. Divus Hieronymus ad Furiam. . . ."

119. Ibid. pp. 600–601/p. 32: "*Nec Germanicos baiulos.*] Hoc est, lecticarios servos, qui in lectica aut sella gestent. Ad hanc operam ob staturae proceritatem Germanis utebantur, olim etiam Syris; unde Iuvenalis.
Nec quae longorum vehitur cervice Syrorum.
Aiunt antiquitatis periti lecticam istiusmodi gestatoriam non absimilem sandapilae fuisse qua mortui hodie efferuntur, sed obductilem

velis, si ita res postulasset, affixis etiam inferne sustentaculis, quae nunc suspendi, nunc dimitti possent, si quando baiulos interquiescere necessitas coegisset, denos plerunque vel duodenos, quibus etiam recentes succedebant vicarii. Nam non per urbem modo, verum etiam per agros magna itinera huiusmodi gestatione conficiebantur."

120. Ibid., p. 601/p. 32: "Porro Romanus pontifex usum lecticae ex antiquitate retinuit, ut alia multa, faventibus et concedentibus hoc Imperatoribus Flavio Constantino Magno et caeteris qui hunc insecuti sunt. Nam de vehiculo sive sella curruli clarum testimonium habemus ex Ammiano Marcellino. Denique Romae baiulos agunt hodieque Germani, pontificii corporis gestatores, ex cohorte illa stipatorum Palatina, quam a multis iam annis Romani pontifices alunt."

6: FROM TEXT TO CONTEXT II

1. Erasmus' edition of Hilary contains themes that seem to have benefited from Beatus' historical treatment in the Tertullian edition; see John C. Olin, "Erasmus and His Edition of St. Hilary," *Erasmus in English* 9 (1978): 8–11, and the translation of the introductory letter in idem, *Six Essays on Erasmus* (New York: Fordham University Press, 1979), pp. 93–120, with notes.

2. See Richard Buschmann, *Das Bewusstwerden der deutschen Geschichte bei den deutschen Humanisten* (Göttingen: Göttinger Handelsdruckerei, 1930); Ulrich Paul, *Studien zur Geschichte des deutschen Nationalbewusstseins im Zeitalter des Humanismus und der Reformation* (Berlin: Ebering, 1936); Paul Joachimsen, *Geschichtsauffassung und Geschichtsschreibung in Deutschland unter dem Einfluss des Humanismus* (Leipzig/Berlin: Teubner, 1910); Ada Hentschke and Ulrich Muhlack, *Einführung in die Geschichte der klassischen Philologie* (Darmstadt: Wissenschaftliche Buchgesellschaft, 1972), chap. 1; and Ulrich Muhlack, "Beatus Rhenanus, Jacob Wimpfeling und die humanistische Geschichtsschreibung in Deutschland," *ASABHS* 35 (1985): 193–208.

3. See Frank L. Borchardt, *German Antiquity in Renaissance Myth* (Baltimore, Md.: Johns Hopkins Press, 1971).

4. See Jacques Ridé, *L'image du Germain dans la pensée et la littérature allemande de la redécouverte de Tacite à la fin du XVIème siècle*, 2 vols. (Lille/Paris: Université de Lille, 1977), in general, and John F. D'Amico, "Ulrich von Hutten and Beatus Rhenanus as Medieval Historians."

5. For Aeneas Silvius and German humanism, see Gianni Zippel, "E. S. Piccolomini e il mondo germanico: Impegno cristiano e civile dell'umanesimo," *La Cultura* 19 (1981): 267–350; Richard Clark

Dales, "Aeneas Sylvius Piccolomini: His Historical Works and His Influence on German Historiography" (Master's Thesis, University of Colorado, 1952); Nicola Casella, "Pio II tra geografia e storia: la *Cosmographia*," *Archivio della Società romana di Storia patria* 95 (19/2): 35–112; and Jacques Ridé, *L'Image du Germain*, 1: 165–182.

6. For the *Germania*, see the modern edition by Adolf Schmidt (Cologne: Bohlau, 1962); Giacchino Paparelli, "La Germania di Enea Silvio Piccoliomini," *Italica* 25 (1948): 203–216; and Ridé, *L'image*.

7. Ridé, *L'image*, pp. 178–179.

8. For Celtis, see Lewis Spitz, *Conrad Celtis: the German Arch-Humanist* (Cambridge, Mass.: Harvard University Press, 1957); Ridé, *L'Image*, chap. 4; and Lawrence V. Ryan, "Conrad Celtis' *Carmen Saeculare:* Ode for a New German Age," in *Acta Conventus Neo-Latini Bononiensis*, ed. R. J. Schoeck (Binghamton, N.Y.: Medieval and Renaissance Texts and Studies, 1985), pp. 592–606.

9. For these, see Albert Werminghoff, *Conrad Celtis und sein Buch über Nurnberg* (Freiburg i. B.: Boltze, 1921), for text, and Giulio Mazzuoli Porru, "L'umanista tedesco Konrad Celtis e le prime lezioni universitarie sulla *Germania* di Tacito," in *Filologia e critica. Studi in onore di Vittorio Santoli,* ed. Paolo Chiarini et al. (Rome: Bulzoni, 1976), I: 195–214.

10. See Jacques Ridé, "Un grand projet patriotique: *Germania illustrata*," in *L'humanisme allemand (1480–1540)* (Munich: Fink, 1979), pp. 97–111. For Biondo, see *DBI*, 10 (1968); 536–559, and Paolo Viti, "Umanesimo letterario e primato regionale nell' 'Italia illustrata' di F. Biondo," in *Studi filologici, letterari e storici in memoria di Guido Favati* (Padua: Antenore, 1977), 2: 711–732.

11. Charles Schmidt, *Histoire littéraire de l'Alsace à la fin du XVe et au commencement du XVIe siècle,* vol. 1 (Paris, 1879); Emil v. Borries, *Wimpfeling und Murner im Kampf um die ältere Geschichte des Elsässes: Ein Beitrag zur Characteristik des deutschen Frühhumanismus* (Heidelberg: Carl Winter, 1926); Ridé, *L'image,* I: 303–326; Muhlack, "Beatus Rhenanus, Jacob Wimpfeling," and excerpts in *L'Alsace au siècle de la Réforme 1482–1621. Texts et Documents,* ed. Jean Lebeau and Jean-Marie Valentin (Nancy: Presses Universitaires de Nancy, 1985), pp. 230–244. For Alsace generally, see Joseph Knepper, *Nationaler Gedanke und Kaiseridee bei den elsässichen Humanisten* (Freiburg im Breisgau, 1898).

12. Ridé, *L'image,* I: 387.

13. For *Epitoma,* see edition in *Witichindi Saxonis rerum ab Henrico et Ottone I Impp. Gestarum libri III* (Basel, 1532), pp. 315–380.

14. Mulhack, "Beatus Rhenanus, Jacob Wimpfeling," pp. 203–204.

15. Ridé, *L'image*, I:315–316.

16. Borchardt, *German Antiquity*, pp, 154–155.

17. For Irenicus, see Gunter Cordes, *Die Quellen der Exegesis Germaniae des Franciscus Irenicus und sein Germanenbegriff* (Marburg: Georg Nolte, 1966), and *Contemporaries*, 2: 225–226.

18. *Briefwechsel*, no. 243, p. 340.

19. Irenicus' praise for Beatus can be found in the 1518 Basel edition, f. XLIIIIr.

20. See Borchhardt, *German Antiquity*, in general; for a specific example, see Ian Short, "A Study in Carolingian Legend and Its Persistence in Latin Historiography," *Mittellateinisches Jahrbuch* 7 (1972): 127–152.

21. Paul, *Studien zur Geschichte des deutschen Nationalbewussteins*, pp. 121–128; E. N. Tigerstedt, "Ioannes Annius and *Graecia mendax*," in *Classical, Mediaeval and Renaissance Studies in Honor of Berthold Ullman*, ed. Charles Henderson, Jr. (Rome: Edizioni di storia e letteratura, 1964), 2: 293–310; Robert Weiss, "Traccia per una biografia di Annio da Viterbo," *IMU* 5 (1962): 425–441; Borchhardt, *German Antiquity*, index; Roland Crahay, "Reflexions sur le faux historique: le cas d'Annius de Viterbe," *Académie royale de Belgique. Bulletin de la classe des lettres et des sciences morales et politiques*, Ser. 5, 69 (1983): 241–267; Edoardo Fumagalli, "Un falso tardo-quattrocentesco: lo Pseudo-Catone di Annio da Viterbo," in *Vestigia: Studi in onore di Giuseppe Billanovich*, ed. Rina Avesani et al. (Rome: Edizioni di storia e letteratura, 1984), 1: 337–363; and *Contemporaries*, 1: 60–61.

22. Tigerstedt, "Ioannes Annius," p. 296. *Rerum Germanicarum libri tres* (Basel, 1531), p. 179.

23. See Noel L. Brann, *The Abbot Trithemius (1462–1516): The Renaissance of Monastic Humanism* (Leiden: Brill, 1981).

24. See Gerd Althoff, "Studien zur habsburgischen Merowingersage," *Mitteilungen des Instituts für Österreichische Geschichtsforschung* 85 (1979): 71–100.

25. For Jordanes, see *Iordanis Romana et Getica*, ed. Th. Mommsen (Berlin, 1882), pp. liv, lxx; for Paul the Deacon, see *Pauli Historia Langobardorum* (Hannover, 1878), p. 47. For Peutinger, see *Contemporaries*, 3: 74–76.

26. For Einhard, see O. Egger, "Zur Überlieferung von Einhards Vita Caroli Magni," *Neues Archiv der Gesellschaft für altere deutsche Geschichtskunde* 37 (1911): 395–414.

27. See Wolf-Rudiger Schleidgen, *Die Überlieferungsgeschichte der Chronik des Regino von Prum* (Mainz: Selbstverlag der Gesellschaft für Mittelrheinische Kirchengeschichte, 1977).

28. For Bede, see *Historia ecclesiastica gentis Anglorum,* 2 vols. (Cambridge, Mass.: Harvard University Press, 1962–1963). Bede is also mentioned in *Opera Tertulliani* (1539), p. 415/p. 63, *Adversus Valentinianos.*

29. For Sidonius, see Giovanni Battista Pio's edition, *Sidonii Apollinaris poema aureum eiusdemque epistolae* (Milan, 1498) (L. Hain, *Repertorium bibliographicum* [Stuttgart/Paris, 1821–1838], no. 1287). See also edition *Sidoine Apollinaire,* ed. Andre Loyen (Paris: Les Belles Lettres, 1960), 1: xli.

30. See Jean-Pierre Massaut, *Josse Clichtove, l'humanisme et la réforme du clergé* (Paris: Les Belles Lettres, 1968), 1: 400–401.

31. Rice, *The Prefatory Epistles of Jacques Lefèvre d'Etaples,* p. 81.

32. See Rosamond McKitterick, "The Study of Frankish History in France and Germany in the Sixteenth and Seventeenth Centuries," *Francia* 8 (1980): 556–572. For French attitudes, see also Philippe Desan, "Nationalism and History in France during the Renaissance," *Rinascimento* 24 (1984): 261–288.

33. *Briefwechsel,* nos. 52, 230, 233, 257, 262. For Hummelberg, see Adalbert Horawitz, *Michael Hummelberger: Eine biographische Skizze* (Berlin, 1875) and *Contemporaries,* 2: 213–214. Also Walter, *Beatus Rhenanus,* no. XV. In 1532 Beatus issued Hummelberg's *Epitome Grammaticae Graecae,* Index, no. 59, and *Briefwechsel,* no. 283.

34. *Briefwechsel,* no. 59. For other letters, previously unpublished, to Zwingli, see Walter, *Beatus Rhenanus,* nos. IX–XIII.

35. Ibid., no. 93. See also D'Amico, "Ulrich von Hutten and Beatus Rhenanus." Beatus also contributed to the printing of Otto of Freising's *Gesta Friderici I;* see above, chapter 2, note 71.

36. Ibid., no. 120. For Calvo, see *Contemporaries,* 1: pp. 245–247.

37. Ibid., no. 264. For Huttich, see also *Contemporaries,* 2: 220–221.

38. *Briefwechsel,* nos. 305, 351, 376.

39. Ibid., no. 271. For Pirckheimer, see *Contemporaries,* 3: 90–94.

40. Ibid., no. 269, and *Konrad Peutingers Briefwechsel,* nos. 123, 212, 213.

41. See *Briefwechsel,* nos. 306, 368, 401, 423, 540.

42. See Christian Wilsdorf, "Beatus Rhenanus et le manuscrit du Chroniqueur dominicain de Colmar: une lettre inédite du grand humaniste," *Annuaire de la Société historique et littéraire de Colmar* 11 (1961): 37–41.

43. For the relationship between Beatus and Aventinus, see Max Lenz, "Beatus Rhenanus und Aventin," in his *Geschichtsschreibung und Geschichtsauffassung im Elsäss zur Zeit der Réformation* (Halle, 1895), pp. 18–32, and Gerald Strauss, *Historian in an Age of Crisis: The Life and*

Works of Johannes Aventinus 1477–1534 (Cambridge, Mass.: Harvard University Press, 1963), index. See also *Contemporaries*, 1: 76–77.

44. See *Briefwechsel*, no. 243.

45. Ibid., no. 246.

46. Ibid., p. 345: "Proprium historiae est maximarum rerum cognitio, nimirum agnoscere atque scire regionum gentiumque mores, situm, qualitatem telluris, religiones, instituta, leges, novos veteresque colonos, imperia, regna. Haec autem absque cosmographiae mathematicaeque diligenti studio ac peregrinatione usque ad fastidium, etiam sine ope principum ac sumptibus nec disci nec inquiri possunt. Nova quoque observatione opus est, ac vetera cum recentioribus comparanda sunt. . . Ob commutationes rerum nulla gens in Germania est, adde etiam, si libet, in universa Europa, Asia, Aphrica, quae aut vetera cognomina aut avitas sedes retineat: ita omnia commutata sunt. Istaec scire et diligenter animadvertere proprium historiae est: praeterea diplomata vetera imperatorum, regum, principum, pontificum, leges, edicta, epistolae ultro citroque missae, rescripta verissima certissimaque historiae sunt fundamenta: illa indagere ac evolvere opus est maius privatis opibus."

47. See above, chapter 2.

48. For Geiler's biography, see Jakob Wimpfeling/Beatus Rhenanus, *Das Leben des Johannes Geiler von Kaylersberg*, ed. Otto Herding (Munich: Fink, 1970).

49. *P. Vellei Paterculi Historiae Romanae* (Basel, 1521), ff. A 3r–v.

50. Ibid., f. A 3r.

51. Ibid., f. A 3v.

52. See above, chapter 2; Index, no. 58, and Horawitz, "Des Beatus Rhenanus literarische Thätigkeit in den Jahren 1530–1547," pp. 323–325.

53. *Briefwechsel*, no. 282, p. 404.

54. Ibid., p. 402; I have followed the translation in Santo Mazzarino, *The End of the Ancient World*, trans. George Holmes (New York: Knopf, 1966), pp. 87–88.

55. See Index, no. 57; Horawitz, "Des Beatus Rhenanus," pp. 325–362; Joachimsen, *Geschichtsauffassung*, pp. 126–150; Brigitte Ristow-Stieghahn, "Zur Geschichtsschreibung des Beatus Rhenanus," in *Festschrift für Ingeborg Schrobler, Beiträge zur Geschichte der deutschen Sprache und Literatur* 25 (1973): 362–380; Ridé, *L'image*, 1: 329–344; and Mulhack, "Beatus Rhenanus, Jacob Wimpfeling." Brigitte Ristow-Stieghahn, "Zur Geschichtsschreiburg," p. 363, fn. 2, has announced a modern edition of the *Res Germanicae*, although to the best of my knowledge it has not yet appeared.

56. *Briefwechsel,* no. 273, pp. 384–387; for French translation, see Walter, *Beatus Rhenanus,* no. XVI.

57. *Briefwechsel,* p. 385.

58. Ibid., pp. 385–386.

59. See Ridé, *L'image,* vol. 1, chap. 7; for Beatus, pp. 549–550.

60. *Briefwechsel,* p. 386, and Walter, *Beatus Rhenanus,* p. 257: "Plurimum enim erret necesse est qui Provincias a veteri Germania discernere nesciat. Equidem hinc ille veterum error manavit putantium Varum Quintilium cum legionibus Romanis apud Augustam esse caesum, qui in Teutoburgiensi saltu trans Rhenum in veteri Germania, vincente Arminio, occubuit. Quod si scissent Rhetiam primam, in cuius fine sita est Augusta, Romanorum fuisse provinciam, nemo hoc dicturus fuerat. Siquidem constat Varum in Germania trucidatum; at Rhetia ad Germaniam id temporis minime pertinebat, Romanis obediens."

61. Walter, *Beatus Rhenanus,* p. 264, n. 38.

62. Horawitz, "Des Beatus Rhenanus literarische Thätigkeit, 1531–1547," pp. 328–334, provides a book-by-book analysis. Selected sections of the *Res Germanicae* are translated in *Der deutsche Renaissance-Humanismus,* ed. Winfried Trillitzsch (Leipzig: Reclam, 1981), pp. 421–431.

63. Horawitz, "Des Beatus Rhenanus literarische Thätigkeit 1531–1547," pp. 335–340.

64. For Sidonius, see C. E. Stevens, *Sidonius Apollinaris and His Age* (Oxford: Clarendon Press, 1933).

65. D'Amico, "The Progress of Renaissance Latin Prose," p. 363.

66. I cite from *Beati Rhenani Selestadiensis Rerum Germanicarum libri tres* (Basel, 1531), pp. 100–109, and (Basel, 1551), pp. 104–112.

67. Ibid., p. 61/p. 62.

68. See Luciano Bosio, *La tabula peutingeriana: Una descrizione pittorica del mondo antico* (Rimini: Maggioli, 1983).

69. *Res Germanicae,* p. 36/p. 35.

70. Bosio, *La tabula peutingeriana,* p. 173. For Hummelberg, see *Contemporaries,* 2: 213–214.

71. *Res Germanicae,* p. 175/p. 187: "*Gessoriacum.* De hoc variae sunt coniecturae. Sed tollit omnem nobis ambiguitatem charta militaris quam apud Chunradum Peutingerum nostrum Augustae vidimus. In qua sic scriptum, *Gessoriaco,* quod nunc Bononia [i.e., Boulogne]."

72. Ibid., p. 51/p. 52: "Hoc postremo referendum, in charta itineraria illa quae est apud Chunradum Peutingerum, trans Rhenum supra Tenedonem, Iuliomagum, Brigobannem, et Aras Flavias, nemus esse depictum cum arboribus et ascriptum maiusculis literis,

S   Y   L   V   A   M   A   R   T   I   A   N   A
                    Et supra haec verba
A   L   E   M   A   N   N   I   A
      In latere vero e regione Bobetomagi et Brocomagi, supradditum
S   V   E   V   I   A."

73. See Christian Hülsen, "Eine Sammlung römischer Renaissance-Inschriften aus den Augsburger Kollektaneen Konrad Peutingers," *Sitzungsberichte der bayerischen Akademie der Wissenschaften:* Philosophisch-philologische und historische Klasse, 1920, Abhandlung 15, and Paul Hans Stemmermann, *Die Anfänge der deutschen Vorgeschichtsforschung Deutschlands. Bodenaltertümer in der Anschauung des 16. und 17. Jahrhunderts* (Quakenbruck i. Hann.: Trute, 1934).

74. Horawitz, "Des Beatus Rhenanus literarische Thätigkeit, 1531–1547," p. 338, provides a catalogue of them.

75. See *Res Germanicae,* pp. 69–70/pp. 70–71.

76. Ibid., p. 154/p. 164, and Robert Will, "Répertoire des inscriptions romanes de l'Alsace," *Revue d'Alsace* 98 (1959): 49–84, at p. 73.

77. *Res Germanicae,* pp. 29–40.

78. Ibid., p. 36/pp. 35–36: "Afferam adhuc aliud testimonium. In coenobio Diuitensi contra Agrippinam, vulgus Tuitium vocat corrupte, quum murus quidam dirueretur, reperta est tabula lapidea cum inscriptione, quae docebat Diuitense munimentum in terra Francorum ab Imperatore Caesare M. Val. Constantino pro militibus illic in tutelam Galliarum collocandis esse erectum. [. . . .] Hanc rem narrat Rupertus, quem vulgo Tuitiensem appellant, aeditis in sacras literas commentariis nemini ignotus. Veteres istos Francorum terminos de quibus nunc loquimur, nusquam exactius descriptos reperi quam in Chronicis quae titulum Abbatis Urspergensis habent. In iis scriptum est Saxones quum Carolum Magnum in Hispania abesse cognovissent, et transire Rhenum non potuissent, quicquid a Tuitio civitate usque ad fluvium Mosellam vicorum villarumque fuit, ferro et igni populatos esse."

79. See Herbert Grundmann, "Der Brand von Deutz 1128 in der Darstellung Abt Ruperts von Deutz: Interpretation und Text-Ausgabe," *Deutsches Archiv für Erforschung des Mittelalters* 22 (1966): 385–371, at p. 399, n. 26, and p. 449 for text. For Cochlaeus, see *Contemporaries,* 1: 321–322.

80. Hain, no. 8718, and *Res Germanicae,* p. 88. For Burchard, see Carol L. Neel, "The Historical Work of Burchard of Ursberg, V: The Historian, The Emperor and the Pope," *Analecta Praemonstratensia* 50 (1984): 224–255.

81. Ibid., p. 135/p. 143. Discussing aqueducts: "Venit mihi ruinas

illas contemplanti in mentem aliquando Romanorum Aquaeductuum, de quibus Procopius . . . inquit. . . ." Relatedly, Beatus was knowledgeable about ancient art and architecture, especially Vitruvius, whom he occasionally cited; see Maurice Kubler, "Souvenirs et curiosités du vieux Sélestat. Les médaillons des empereurs Neron et Nerva," *ASABHS* 28 (1978): 65–75, at pp. 70–73.

82. Ibid., pp. 149–151/pp. 158–161, entitled *Unde mutatae locorum appellationes, et eversionis causa.*

83. Ibid., p. 150/p. 160.

84. Ibid., pp. 150–151/p. 160.

85. *Rerum Germanicarum libri tres* (Basel, 1551), f. D 4v, lists the following: Abbas Urspergensis, Agathias, Ammianus Marcellinus, *Itinerarium Antonianum*, Berosus, Julius Capitolinus, Cicero, Claudianus, Decreta, Eumenius, Eutropius, Florus, Herodotus, Jerome, Isidore, Caesar, *Liber de magistratuum Romanorum insignibus*, Martianus Capella, Nazanius Panegyricus, Orosius, Paulus Diaconus, Pliny, Procopius, Ptolemy, Sextus Rufus, Sidonius Apollinaris, Stephanus, Strabo, Virgil, and Flavius Vospiscus.

86. For example, ibid., p. 165/p. 176: "In causa fuit foedus librarii error, qui Cl. Ptolemaei codicem describens in Germaniae superioris annotatione Argentorati vocabulum quod inter Tribonorum oppida statim post Brocomagum sive Breucomagum, ut Ptolemaeus nominat, subdere debebat, ipse similitudine vocis deceptus inter Vangionum oppida post Borbetomagum addidit, Argentoratum Vormaciae propinquam faciens, quam integre quondam Borbetomagum appellatam, corrupte vero Vormaciam hodie dici constat, B litera in V mutata, quasi dicas Vormagium, ceu supra monuimus."

87. *Res Germanicae*, pp. 98–99/pp. 103–104: "*Francorum nomen apud Ciceronem non extare, depravatumque esse foede locum.* Apud M. Ciceronem epistolarum libro xiiii, quas ad Pomponium Atticum scripsit abstrusis sensi[bu]s et aenigmatis plenas, in aeditione vulgata sic legitur: *Redeo ad Theobassos, Suevos, Francones.* Est autem eius epistolae initium *Pridie Iduum Fundis accepi tuas literas coenans.* Quare plerique eruditorum hoc loco freti tradunt Francones a Cicerone nominatos. Equidem mihi perpensis Tullii verbis quum viderem eum de Germanis agere qui in Galliam ante Iulii Caesaris adventum transiissent, suspitio nasci coepit, totum locum esse depravatum. Quis enim Theobassorum nomen unquam aut audivit aut legit? Et quid Suevi in Gallia faciunt adeo procul a Rheno dissiti? Itaque volumen manu scriptum require quod ex Laurisheimensi bibliotheca Ioannes Sichardus noster nuperrime attulerat. In eo mera portenta verborum scripta reperi, in hunc modum, *Redeo adtebassos scacuas*

Frangones. Coepi deinde literarum ductus scrupulosius rimari, deprehendique germanam Ciceronis lectionem hanc esse: *Redeo ad Betasios, Atuas, Vangiones.* Quid seduxerit scribam non pigeret me referre, nisi lectori molestum id futurum putarem, nec respondent veteribus notulis formulae typographorum. Iam ut melius Ciceronis mens intelligatur, operaeprecium est ascribere verba quae praecedunt. [The text of the letter follows.] Sunt autem Betasii populi Germaniae secundae non procul ab amne Mosa habitantes. . . . Caeterum Atuae sunt, quos Caesar Advaticos appellat, Cimbrorum Teutonorumque soboles. . . . Vangiones vero notiores sunt quam ut indicari debeant, quorum caput est Borbetomagus, quod Germani Vuormaciam nominant, quasi dicas Bormagum sive Vormagiam. Accipit autem Cicero Vangiones pro omnibus Germanis qui ripas Rheni incolebant, sicut Betasios et Atuas pro nationibus ulterioribus. . . . Igitur Francorum non factam Ciceroni mentionem sed Vangionum, et pro Theobassis et Suevis Betasios ac Atuas reponendum, satis nunc puto liquere ex hiis quae diximus." See also Horawitz, "Des Beatus Rhenanus literarische Thätigkeit 1531–1547," p. 351.

88. Lehmann, *Iohannes Sichardus,* does not mention this manuscript.

89. *Res Germanicae,* p. 100/p. 104.

90. Ibid., p. 100/p. 105: "Sed innumeris erratis scatent Ciceronis scripta, quae tamen propter divinam illius copiam ac ubertatem non sentiuntur. Id quod et in Livianis Decadibus accidit. Hoc velut auctario lector candide fruitor."

91. See above, chap. 2, note 88.

92. *Res Germanicae,* p. 119/pp. 125–126: "*Expositus et emendatus apud Caesarem locus de ortu sylvae Herciniae,* [sic] *ubi vulgo legitur, oriri id nemus a Nementum et Tauracorum finibus.* C. Iulius Caesar Commentariorum libro sexto de Hercynia sylva loquens, *Oritur,* inquit, *ab Hervetiorum, et Nemetum, et Tauracorum finibus, rectaque fluminis Danubii regione pertinet ad fines Dacorum, et Anartium.* Sed quid hic Nemetes faciunt, quos hodie pro Spirensis dioeceseos cultoribus omnes accipiunt, et quidem recte. Qui vero sunt isti Tauraci, sive ut in sincerioribus codicibus legitur, *Tauriaci?* Cur autem ab Helvetiis statim ad Nemetas transilit Caesar, populos intermedios omittens, Rauracos, Sequanos, Tribocos sive Mediomatricos, qui potius era[n]t nominandi? An memoria lapsum dicere volumus? Crede mihi lector, locus iste mendo non caret apud Caesarem. Ego scribo pro *Nemetum, Venetum.* Sunt autem Venetes Rhetiae populi sui parte ad inferiorem lacum pertinentes, a quibus Venetus dictus est. Pomponius Mela: *Rhenus ab Alpibus decidens, prope a capite duos lacus efficit, Venetum et Acromum.* Istos Venetes [venetos in 1551] arbitror apud Plinium dici Vennotes et Venonetes, ubi recen-

sentur in inscriptione illa Trophaei Alpium, apud Claudium Ptolemaeum in descriptione Rhetiae Vennontes. Unicae vero literae inversio nobis istum errorem peperit. Ex Nenetum enim doctus aliquis fecit Nemetum. Porro nomine Tauriacorum accipio, Turgavos. Siquidem suspicor Taurum sive Tauriam fluvium illum fuisse dictum, quem haec aetas Turum vocat, a quo Turgaviae vocabulum quam video tam late protensam olim ut Turegum etiam complecteretur, ab amne quoque Turo sive Turgavia nominatum, nimirum quod Tauriaci tractus velut angulus et extremitas esset, ut primo libro docuimus. Turegum autem in Turgavensi pago situm sub administratione Duci Alemanniae, docet diploma Ludevvichi regis Francorum. Nam ab Alemannis Tauriacus tractus totus occupatus est cum vicinis regionibus, ut supra tradidimus."

93. See *C. Iulii Caesaris Commentariorum Libri,* ed. Renatus du Pontet (Oxford: Clarendon Press, 1937).

94. Horawitz, "Des Beatus Rhenanus literarische Thätigkeit, 1531–1547," pp. 253–254, especially note 1.

95. This was not edited by Erasmus, as the title page indicates; see *EE,* vol. 10, p. 61, n. 14.

96. On the *Codex Hersfeldensis,* see R. P. Robinson, "The Hersfeldensis and the Fuldensis of Ammianus Marcellinus," *The University of Missouri Studies* 11/3 (1936): pp. 118–140.

97. See *Res Germanicae,* p. 162/p. 173: "Vide quantus labor sit ex tam depravatis autorum locis antiquitatem eruere, et quanto facilius sit haec ridere quam praestare."

98. See Eduard Norden, *Alt-Germanien: Völker- und Namensgeschichte Untersuchungen* (rpt. 1934 ed, Darmstadt: Wissenschaftliche Buchgesellschaft, 1962), pp. 9–14. *Res Germanicae,* p. 52/pp. 52–53: "Caeterum ignoraturi eramus quem nam Alemanniae tractum invasissent Burgundiones, nisi Marcellinus hanc rem explicuisset. Is de Iuliano Caesare scribens qui reges quosdam Alemannorum castigaturus nolentes Romanum imperium agnoscere, primum navigiis deinde ponte prope Magunciacum constructo, milites trans Rhenum miserit. *Quum ventum,* inquit, *fuisset ad regionem cui Capellatii vel Palas nomen est, ubi terminales lapides Romanorum et Burgundionum confinia distinguebant, castra sunt posita.* Quid hic faciunt lapides Romanorum, quum Alemannia provincia non fuerit, nisi quod Probus Caesar partem quae cis Nicrum fluvium est aliquot annis obsequentem habuit. Lego, *ubi terminales lapides Alemannorum et Burgundionum confinia distinguebant.* Nam verisimile fit, Alemannos quum advenas Burgundiones vi repellere non possent, quod tamen tentatum est, tandem, ubi inter eos convenisset, in sua regione sedes ponere

permisisse, sed limitibus distinctas, quae res ad pacem populorum pertinebat."

99. *Res Germanicae,* p. 79/p. 81.

100. Ibid., p. 91/p. 95: "Volumen legum Francicarum in vetustis bibliothecis extat, ex quo nos unam aut alteram adhuc apponemus."

101. Ibid., p. 92/pp. 96–97: "Extat in volumine legum Francicarum, caput Meldensis synodi. . . . Sane repperi [reperi in 1557] in quodam vetusto codice qui de conciliis antiquis Galliarum tractat, inter subscribentes, sic annotatum: Bubulcus episcopus Vindonissensis."

102. Ibid., p. 131/p. 139: "Nam in vetusto quodam codice post decreta Lugdunensis synodi in catalogo subscribentium antistitum sic legitur. . . ." In the same place Beatus mentions, "In libro provinciarum Gallicarum. . . ."

103. Ibid., pp. 96–97 pp. 101–102.

104. Ibid., p. 160/p. 170: "Nos sane confugimus ad ipsam antiquitatem, atque illam scrutamur ac excutimus quantum possibile est. Nam commentarii mediae antiquitatis hominum plerumque monachorum non minus ineptiunt quam vulgus ipsum, a quo magna ex parte haustum est quod adventitii ab adventitiis edocti post tantas rerum ac populorum mutationes in literas utcumque retulerunt. Hi fuerunt Scoti et Hyberni."

105. Ibid., pp. 160–162/pp. 170–172.

106. Ibid., p. 161/p. 171. The word *elegia* does not appear in the *Chronicon Ebersheimense,* ed. L. Weiland (Leipzig: Hiersemann, 1925) (*Monumenta Germaniae Historica, Scriptores,* Vol. XXIII), but is found in *Alberici Monachi Triumfontium Chronicon a Monacho Novi Monasterii Hoiensis interpolata,* ed. P. Scheffer-Boichorst, ibid., p. 680, which reads, ". . . apud *Elegiam* vicum grandem Gallie Argentinensis dyocesis beatus Maternus obiit."

107. Ibid., pp. 161–162/p. 172: "Et tamen haec historia, si ita vocare libet, non solum picta est in templis ac scripta sed etiam typis excusa. Video nonnunquam parum praesidii esse a chronicis coenobiorum, in quibus ita veris fabulosa assuuntur, ut vix appareat quid sit credendum. Quare magis libet ad antiquitatem confugere, sicubi datur. Et tamen sunt qui illa tantum non pro oraculis adorent."

108. Ibid., p. 29/p. 27.

109. George Huppert, "The Trojan Franks and Their Critics," *Studies in the Renaissance* 12 (1965): 227–241, at pp. 232–234.

110. *Res Germanicae,* pp. 162–163/p. 173: "Nam in vita divi Florentii Scoti, qui VII Argentoratensium episcopus fuit, sic legitur: *Eo quoque tempore rex Dagobertus apud municipium tunc Troniam quasi Troiam novam, nunc Kircheim dictum, sibi domicilium fixerat.* Ego Troniam

nihil aliud esse puto quam vocabulum vernaculi sermonis, quo vulgus a maioribus suis accepto Tribonos per abbreviationem exprimeret. Bonus vero pater ille qui vitam conscripsit, ignarus vetustatis ut tunc fuere secula, somnium illud secutus est de Troia pulchram nobis interpretationem allaturus, quod Francos a Troianis originem ducere in fabulosis historiis se legere meminisset." The text can be found in *Acta Sanctorum Novembris,* tom. III (Brussels: Bollandius, 1910), pp. 400–403, at p. 400. At p. 29/p. 27, when referring to those who associated the Franks with Troy, Beatus wrote: "Nec mirum si rudibus illis seculis olim ausi sunt talia configere haud dubie monachi; nam praeter hos tum nemo norat literas."

111. *Res Germanicae,* pp. 40/39 and 179/191.

112. Anna Carlotta Dionisotti, "Beatus Rhenanus and Barbaric Latin," *ASABHS* 35 (1985): 183–192.

113. *Res Germanicae,* pp. 90–91/pp. 93–95, section entitled *Status Galliarum et Germaniarum sub Francis regibus et Imperatoribus.*

114. Dionisotti, "Beatus Rhenanus and Barbaric Latin," p. 186.

115. *Res Germanicae,* p. 110/p. 116: "Nam puto hodie linguas omneis nonnihil esse mixtas, et puram nullam."

116. Ibid., p. 111/p. 117: "Sermo quo peculiariter Gallia fuit usa priusquam in Provinciae formam redigeretur a Romanis, prorsum putatur abolitus; non secus suum amisere et Hispaniae. O miram Romanorum dexteritatem et indicibilem felicitatem. Et non miretur quis eripi potuisse [a] Romanis provinicias quae non minus Romanae erant quam ipsa Roma. Sed habent regna suas periodos."

117. See Sigrid von der Gonna, "Beatus Rhenanus und Otfrid von Weissenberg. Zur Otfrid-überlieferung im 16. Jahrhundert," *Zeitschrift für deutsches Altertum und deutsche Literatur* 107 (1978): 248–256. Section translated in *Der deutsche Renaissance-Humanismus,* pp. 428–431.

118. *Res Germanicae,* pp. 106–107/pp. 112–113. See Johann Kelle, *Otfrids von Weissenburg Evangelienbuch* (Regensburg, 1856), Vol. I, Leitung, pp. 99–100, and Wolfgang Kleiber, *Otfrid von Weissenburg. Untersuchungen zur handschriftlichen Überlieferung und Studien zur Ausgabe des Evanglienbuches* (Berlin/Munich: Franck, 1971), pl. xxii. p. 89.

119. The colophon is reproduced in Friedrich Maurer, *Die religiösen Dichtungen des 11. und 12. Jahrhunderts,* vol. 1 (Tübingen: Niemeyer, 1964), pl. 1.

120. Kelle, *Otfrids von Weissenburg Evangelienbuch,* pp. 99–100, reproduces the texts Beatus cites. These texts are: I, 113, 114; 121–124; 59–60; 64.

121. *Res Germanicae,* p. 100/p. 104.

122. *Res Germanicae,* pp. 107–108/p. 113: "Solebat olim Maximilianus Caesar proposita mercede suos provocare ad quaerenda vel diplomata quae ante quingentos essent annos conscripta. Nam tantum Latini sermonis usus apud Germanos in conficiendis tabulis receptus fuit. Id quod cum caeteris nationibus commune habuimus. Ab annis tamen centum et quinquaginta secus apud nos factum videmus. Sic ungaricus sermo nostra aetate primum scribi coepit. Itaque si quis monstrasset duntaxat talem codicem, non indonatus abisset. Nam princeps fuit liberalissimus. Huius generis Psalterium vidimus apud Ioannem Huttichium nostrum Argentorati."

123. For Huttich, see *Briefwechsel,* index, and *Contemporaries,* 2: 220–221. Huttich was active in publishing works dealing with antiquities; see his *Collectanea antiquitatum in urbe, atque agro Moguntino repertarum* (Mainz, 1520). Beatus' remarks on contemporary opposition to translation into German is in *Res Germanicae,* p. 108/p. 113. "Perpetua vero laus Francorum veterum qui sacros libros in suam, hoc est, Germanicam linguam vertendos curarint, quod nuper a theologis quibusdam improbatum scimus."

124. Ibid., p. 28/p. 26: "Quotiescunque enim aliquis populus emigrarat, non emigrabat totus, et multi se ex vicinis nationibus adiungebant."

125. Ibid., p. 29/p. 28: "Fuere autem apud Germanos multae nationes, quae tamen quod celebres minime essent, a scriptoribus non sunt commemoratae. . . ."

126. Ibid., p. 56/p. 57: "Dii boni si docti viri in hanc partem incumberent, quantum lucis afferri posset rebus antiquis? Hoc vere esset illustrare Germaniam."

127. See ibid., p. 77/p. 79, for phrase *historiae mediae aetatis.*

128. For the Marcomanni and their contacts with the Romans, see *Pauly-Wissowa,* 14/2, cols. 1600–1637; Th. Mommsen, *The Provinces of the Roman Empire: The European Provinces,* ed. T. Robert S. Broughton (Chicago, Ill.: University of Chicago Press, 1968), index; Josef Dobias, "Wo lagen die Wohnsitze der Markomanner?" *Historica* 2 (1960): 37–75; Josef Dobias, "King Marobobuus as a Politician," *Klio* 38 (1960): 155–156; and Ronald Syme, "The End of the Marcomanni," in his *Historia Augusta Papers* (Oxford: Clarendon Press, 1983), pp. 146–155. See also Ristow-Stieghahn, "Zur Geschichtsschreibung des Beatus Rhenanus," pp. 364–373.

129. Ibid., p. 68/pp. 69–70.

130. Ibid., p. 125/p. 132.

131. Ibid., p. 126/p. 133. I cite from *The Geography of Strabo,* trans.

Horace Leonard Jones (Cambridge, Mass.: Harvard University Press, 1967), III: 155–157.

132. *Res Germanicae*, p. 126/p. 133. "Porro depravatus est, nec hic tantum. Asulanicus codex Graecus in quo βονιάσμον legitur. Emendatius exemplar habuit Guarinus Veronensis Strabonis interpres, qui Bubiemum vertit. Quanquam fortassis βονιέμον legendum fuerat. Sed fieri potest ut ipse Strabo Germanicam dictionem sic corruperit, ut sunt in peregrinis etiam in Latinis incuriosiores Graeci." For Guarino, see Aubrey Diller, *The Textual Tradition of Strabo's Geography* (Amsterdam: Hakkert, 1975), index.

133. *Res Germanicae*, p. 126/pp. 133–134. "Nec vero Graeci in mediis dictionibus nisi per illas suas duplices, vocalibus aspirant. Latinis etiam spiritum subinde respuentibus, unde Tacitus Boiemum nominavit, non Boihemum."

134. Ibid., pp. 151–160/pp. 161–170.

135. Ibid., p. 151/p. 161.

136. Ibid., pp. 152–153/p. 162.

137. Ibid., pp. 153–154/p. 163.

138. *Res Germanicae*, p. 142/p. 151. "Nos hic, ut in caeteris, ingenue nostram opinionem aperuimus, in nullis certe praeiudicium. Liberum esto cuique sentire quod libet. Quid enim stultius quam de iis rebus frivole digladiari, quae non certis testimoniis, sed solis coniecturis nituntur." The *Res Germanicae* received critical comment by later historians. Especially significant is J. Daniel Shoepflin, who in his *Alsatia illustrata Celtica Romana Francica*, 2 vols. (Colmar, 1751), at several points criticized and praised Beatus; for example, vol. 1, pp. 2, 34, 40, 41, 60–61, 94, 137, 145, 188–190, 197, 204, 208, 220, 224, 228, 230, 233, 236, 297, 309, 332, 333, 349, 401, 417, 492, 527, 610, 638, 640, 642, 647, 684, 702, 802. The last edition of the Res Germanicae was Ulm, 1693, with notes by Jacob Otto, *Beati Rhenani Selestadiensis libri tres Institutionum Rerum Germanicarum Nov-Antiquarum Historico-Geographicarum*. This consists of the original text together with extensive commentary by Otto. While this latter corrects some of Beatus' errors, it is longer than the original.

139. Ibid., p. 142/p. 151: "Verum nos ad Rauricos nostros revertamur, quandoquidem magis nobis animus est antiquitatem excutere quam nova stilo persequi."

140. See *Amerbachkorrespondez*, vol. 5, no. 2539, p. 422. Jean-Luc Eichenlaub and Christian Wilsdorf are preparing a study of this manuscript, "Beatus Rhenanus précurseur dans l'étude de l'ancien droit allemand: les lucubrationes in fundationem Muorbacensem et confir-

mationem Luceriensem, un opuscule inédit," which will appear in a future number of the *ASABHS*.

141. *Notitia utraque cum Orientis tum Occidentis ultra Arcadii Honoriique Caesarum tempora, illustre vetustatis monumentum, imo thesaurus prorsum incomparabilis* (Basel, 1552), at pp. *3r–*5r.

142. Ridé, *L'image,* provides detail on many German historians.

143. See Huppert, "The Trojan Franks," and Donald R. Kelley, *Foundations of Modern Historical Scholarship: Language, Law and History in the French Renaissance* (New York: Columbia University Press, 1970), index.

CONCLUSION

1. See *In C. Plinium,* p. 46/13.

2. See M. D. Feld, "The Early Evolution of the Authoritative Text," *The Harvard Library Bulletin* 26 (1978): 81–111.

Index

Designer: U.C. Press Staff
Compositor: Huron Valley Graphics, Inc.
Text: 11/13 Baskerville
Display: Baskerville
Printer: Braun-Brumfield, Inc.
Binder: Braun-Brumfield, Inc.